Nazi Empire-Building and the Holocaust in Ukraine

The University of
North Carolina Press
Chapel Hill
Published in association
with the
United States
Holocaust Memorial
Museum

WENDY LOWER

Nazi Empire-Building and the

Holocaust in Ukraine

Published in association with the United States Holocaust Memorial
Museum. The assertions, arguments, and conclusions contained
herein are those of the author. They do not necessarily reflect the
opinions of the United States Holocaust Memorial Museum.

Set in Gill and Quadraat types by Tseng Information Systems, Inc.
Manufactured in the United States of America
The paper in this book meets the guidelines for permanence and
durability of the Committee on Production Guidelines for Book
Longevity of the Council on Library Resources.

Portions of the text have been previously published: Wendy Lower, "A
New Ordering of Space and Race: Nazi Colonial Dreams in Zhytomyr,
Ukraine, 1941–1944," *German Studies Review* 25, no. 2 (2002): 228–54;
used by permission of *German Studies Review*. Wendy Lower, "'Anticipa-
tory Obedience' and the Nazi Implementation of the Holocaust in the
Ukraine: A Case Study of Central and Peripheral Forces in the
Generalbezirk Zhytomyr, 1941–1944," *Holocaust and Genocide Studies* 16,
no. 1 (2002): 1–22; used by permission of Oxford University Press.

Library of Congress Cataloging-in-Publication Data
Lower, Wendy.
Nazi empire-building and the Holocaust in Ukraine / Wendy Lower.
     p. cm.
"Published in association with the United States Holocaust Memorial
Museum."
Includes bibliographical references and index.
ISBN 0-8078-2960-9 (alk. paper)
1. Ukraine—Zìhytomyrs'ka oblast'—History—German occupation, 1941–1944.
2. Germany—Politics and government—1933–1945. 3. Holocaust, Jewish
(1939–1945)—Ukraine—Zìhytomyrs'ka oblast'. 4. World War, 1939–1945—
Ukraine—Zìhytomyrs'ka oblast'. 5. Germany—Colonies—Ukraine—
Zìhytomyrs'ka oblast'—History—20th century. I. Title.
DK508.833.L69 2005
940.53'4778—dc22   2005001620

09 08 07 06 05   5 4 3 2 1

For the mothers and daughters of the Czilug family:
Gitia Malik (born in Liubar, 1909), Rakhilia Stepanskii
(born in Liubar, 1901; killed at Babi Yar, 29 September 1941),
Liuba Stepanskii (born in Sarapul, 1926; killed at Babi Yar,
29 September 1941), and Klavdia Malik (born in Novohrad-
Volyns'kyi, 1937)

Contents

Illustrations and Maps

Acknowledgments

Little did I know when I started the research for this book that my interest in Ukraine and Holocaust history would end up demanding so much time and energy from family, friends, mentors, and colleagues in Ukraine, Germany, and the United States. Many people who helped me trusted that I would do justice to the material that they generously shared with me. I am responsible for any flaws in the book, but I cannot take full credit for its merits. During my research trips to Zhytomyr, Ukraine, I stayed with the Starovoitov family, without whom I could not have completed this study. I am forever grateful to Klavdia (Malik) Starovoitov, my host "mother." She introduced me to Zhytomyr's Holocaust survivor community; she helped me translate handwritten sources in Russian and Ukrainian; and she opened up her home and dacha to me. She and her son Felix negotiated on my behalf with the local archives; as a "Westerner" with admittedly little sense of how to "work the Soviet system" of *blat* (personal favors, barter) and the like, I would have certainly been denied research opportunities without their involvement and know-how.

At the Zhytomyr State Archives, Tat'iana Nikolaevna Franz and Hrihorii Denisenko answered my many inquiries about the holdings, brought new material to my attention, and helped arrange interviews with former partisans and forced laborers. Mary Poltorak, Aleksei Pavlov, and Sergei Gonzar assisted me with additional translations and served as interpreters. Zhytomyr scholars Efim Melamed and the late professor Boris Kruglak shared their invaluable insight into the region's history. Kira Burova at the local Office of Jewish Affairs and Emigration provided me with recorded interviews of Holocaust survivors and invited me to conduct additional interviews with her. I am also grateful to Zhytomyr's veterans association led by Ivan Shinal'skii. The newly revived synagogue in Zhytomyr opened its doors to me as well, allowing me to view its newspaper collections and use its copy machine.

In Germany, reference staff at the Zentrale Stelle der Landesjustizverwaltungen (Ludwigsburg) provided me with very useful materials. I am especially grateful to Dr. Dieter Pohl at the Institute for Contemporary History in Munich who helped me a great deal by commenting on my manuscript. Dr. Karel Berkhoff at the Center for Holocaust and Genocide Studies in the Netherlands also offered a constructive critique.

In the United States, thanks go to my Ukrainian language instructors, Natalie Shostak and Natalie Gawdiak (at the Library of Congress). At the National Archives, archivist and historian Timothy Mulligan saved me countless hours of research by guiding me through the labyrinth of captured German records. Just as I was preparing to return to the Zhytomyr archives for a second time in the spring of 1993, the United States Holocaust Memorial Museum opened. Thanks to the museum's specialist on former Soviet archival collections, Carl Modig, I learned of additional files in Zhytomyr. In the museum's Center for Advanced Holocaust Studies, fellows and scholars including Hans Mommsen, Susannah Heschel, Berel Lang, Aron Rodrigue, Götz Aly, Peter Longerich, Gerhard Weinberg, Jean Ancel, Dennis Deletant, Konrad Kwiet, Rebecca Boehling, Henry Friedlander, Hans Safrian, Christian Gerlach, Rebecca Golbert, Viorel Achim, Kate Brown, Alexander Prusin, Katrin Reichelt, Misha Tyaglyy, Tim Cole, David Furber, Dirk Moses, Robert Bernheim, and especially the center's staff historians Peter Black, Jürgen Matthäus, Geoff Megargee, Martin Dean, Vadim Altskan, Radu Iaonid, and Michael Gelb engaged me in scholarly discussions of my research and gave me pertinent materials. Alexander Rossino and Peter Black reviewed all or parts of the book manuscript. Museum staff in the archives and library, including Henry Mayer, Mark Ziomek, Michlean Amir, Anatol Steck, Aleksandra Borecka, Bill Connelly, Steve Kanaley, Sharon Muller, and Sara Sirman guided my use of the collections. The director of the Center for Advanced Holocaust Studies, Paul Shapiro, supported this work as a valued mentor and tireless advocate of Holocaust scholarship. Thanks also to my CAHS colleagues Robert Ehrenreich, Tracy Brown, and Lisa Zaid for sustaining me with their savvy computer skills and good humor. This work also benefited from continued exchange with former 1999 Summer Research Workshop participants Ray Brandon and Edward Westermann. On countless occasions I turned to the center's director of publications, Benton Arnovitz, for his counsel. I have enjoyed and appreciated working with the center's editorial coordinator, Dr. Aleisa Fishman, who conscientiously carried my work through the center's review process. Thanks to the distinguished scholars of the Publications Subcommittee for taking valuable time away from their full schedules to read and comment on this work. The transformation of this work from a dissertation to a book could not have been accomplished without the commitment and hard work of many people at the University of North Carolina Press, above all Senior Editor Chuck Grench, Editor Paul Betz, and Assistant Editor Amanda McMillan. I am especially grateful to Doris Bergen at the University of Notre Dame and Tim Snyder at Yale University, who devoted many hours to critiquing the manuscript. Dr. Vladimir Melamed helped with the Ukrainian transliterations.

For my research and writing, I received fellowships and grants from American University, the German Historical Institute, and the Center for Advanced Holocaust Studies. The Harvard Ukrainian Research Institute also contributed funding toward my Ukrainian language studies. My dissertation committee members—Richard Breitman, James Malloy, and Martha Bohachevsky-Chomiak—nurtured this work in its infancy. Richard Breitman, the committee chair, read through several drafts of each chapter, shared many documents with me, and commented on every aspect of this work with the utmost care and erudition. For the past fourteen years, he has inspired me as a model researcher, teacher, and mentor. I cannot thank him enough.

Last, but certainly not least, I owe my biggest thanks to my family. My parents instilled in me an appreciation of history. Their boundless generosity and optimism sustained me throughout. My husband and fellow scholar, Christof Mauch, has been a constant source of inspiration, wisdom, and comfort. Regrettably these past years I gave up valuable time with our young sons, Ian and Alexander, to complete this book, whose subject matter remains a mystery to them. My hope is that someday they too will develop an appreciation of history, and perhaps an understanding of the tragic events in the pages that follow.

Glossary

Many of the abbreviations given here are used in the notes, although some appear in the text as well. Abbreviations for archival sources appear at the start of the notes.

AOK: Armeeoberkommando, German Army Field Command/Headquarters.

BdS: Befehlshaber der Sipo-SD, commander of the Sipo-SD.

DG: Durchgangsstrasse, highway or autobahn.

DVL: Deutsche Volksliste, German People's List. The Nazi registration and classification system for ethnic Germans that divided them into one of four categories based on their Aryan characteristics and willingness to be Germanized.

EG: Einsatzgruppe, "Task Force." Einsatzgruppen were special mobile killing units composed mainly of Security Police (Sipo) and Security Service (SD) personnel that were assigned to Poland and the Soviet Union to apprehend and execute so-called racial and political enemies of the Reich, primarily Jews. They arrived just behind or sometimes with the advancing Wehrmacht troops.

General Government: Nazi-occupied Poland, consisting of five districts: Cracow, Warsaw, Radom, Lublin, and eastern Galicia.

GFP: Geheime Feldpolizei, Army Secret Field Police. Wehrmacht security units attached to the Abwehr. In 1942 they were taken over by the SD.

HSSPF: Höherer SS- und Polizeiführer, higher SS and police leader. Established in 1937, this office was the highest regional authority overseeing the actions of all SS and police forces in a given district (Wehrkreis) in the Reich. The office was later established in the occupied territories of Poland, the Czech lands, Norway, the Netherlands, and the Soviet Union. The higher SS and police leaders reported directly to Reichsführer SS and Police Heinrich Himmler and were regarded as "Little Himmlers" in the field. During Operation Barbarossa, three higher SS and police leaders (Russia North, Central, and South) planned and implemented the mass shootings of Jews in collaboration with the most senior officials in the field—Wehrmacht field commanders, Einsatzgruppen leaders, Waffen-SS commanders, and Order Police chiefs.

For Ukraine, Himmler appointed Friedrich Jeckeln and his successor Hans-Adolf Prützmann to the position of HSSPF Russia South.

NKVD: Narodnyi Komissariat Vnutrennikh Del, People's Commissariat for Interior Affairs. The Soviet political police established in 1934, successor to the GPU and predecessor to the MGB and KGB.

NSV: Nationalsozialistische Volkswohlfahrt, National Socialist People's Welfare Agency. An organization established by Hitler to coordinate Nazi Party relief and charity work for Party members and their families, especially for mothers and children. The organization was also active in welfare programs for ethnic Germans in the East.

Oblast: A Russian term for an administrative district or province within the Soviet Union, in size bigger than a county but not as large as a state.

OKH: Oberkommando des Heeres, Army High Command.

OKW: Oberkommando der Wehrmacht, Armed Forces High Command.

Orpo: Ordnungspolizei, Order Police. Consisted of regular uniformed police and rural gendarmes.

OT: Organisation Todt, Organization Todt. A semi-military organization responsible for military construction projects, such as installations and fortifications, as well as the autobahn. Its leader, Fritz Todt, also served as Reich minister for armaments and munitions.

OUN: Orhanizatsiia Ukrains'kykh Natsionalistiv, Organization of Ukrainian Nationalists. The leading interwar and wartime Ukrainian nationalist (mostly émigré) movement that split into two factions, one under Andrii Mel'nyk (OUN-M) and the other under Stepan Bandera (OUN-B).

RKFDV: Reichskommissariat für die Festigung des Deutschen Volkstums, Reich Commission for the Strengthening of Germandom. This Himmler agency led the Germanization and resettlement programs for ethnic Germans in the East.

RKU: Reichskommissariat Ukraine, Reich Commissariat Ukraine. The Nazi-occupied civilian administration for Ukraine (excluding eastern Galicia, which was attached to the General Government, Nazi-occupied Poland). The Commissariat Ukraine was joined with the Reich Commissariat Ostland (Belorussia and the Baltic States) under the Reich Ministry for the Eastern Occupied Territories. The Commissariat Ukraine was headed by Erich Koch, and its capital was Rivne.

RMfdbO: Reichsministerium für die besetzten Ostgebiete, Reich Ministry for the Occupied Eastern Territories. The Nazi government agency for administering the civilian occupied zones of the East, which were divided into commissariats. It was led by Alfred Rosenberg.

RSD: Reich Sicherheitsdienst, Reich Security Service. This elite force developed from a special protection service for the Führer, known as the Führerschutzkommando. Personally selected by Himmler and Hitler, officers of the RSD were charged with securing and guarding the Führer's field headquarters and also served as Hitler's bodyguards.

RSHA: Reichssicherheitshauptamt, Reich Security Main Office. Created in September 1939, the RSHA combined in one agency the German state's political and criminal police detective forces (Gestapo, Kriminalpolizei) and the Nazi Party's Security Service (SD), the top political intelligence service of the Reich. Among its key functions were managing and coordinating the murder of the European Jews as well as other perceived enemies of the Reich, monitoring millions of foreign forced laborers, and conducting domestic and foreign intelligence operations. In addition to the central office in Berlin, led by Reinhard Heydrich (and his successor Ernst Kaltenbrunner), the RSHA had regional offices and mobile units called Einsatzgruppen.

RuSHA: Rasse und Siedlungs-Hauptamt, Race and Settlement Office. Established in 1931 as the central SS office tasked with establishing Nazi "standards" for determining membership in the German "race" and membership in the SS, as well as evaluating prospective brides of SS men. During the war, its jurisdiction expanded to include assessments of the "Germanizability" of ethnic Germans and non-Germans, assessments that affected decisions on resettlement expropriation and were often matters of life and death. RuSHA's staff of "race experts" helped plan the expulsion of non-Germans from the eastern territories and facilitated the resettlement of ethnic Germans in occupied Europe.

SD: Sicherheitsdienst, Security Service. The intelligence service of the SS. The SD was created in 1931 with the main task of exposing and observing enemies of the Nazi Party. Its powers expanded in the Third Reich to intelligence-gathering and counter-intelligence operations against state enemies. Under Reinhard Heydrich's command, SD personnel managed the planning and implementation of the "Final Solution," in particular, as members of the Einsatzgruppen and in Adolf Eichmann's SD office of Jewish Affairs.

Sipo: Sicherheitspolizei, Security Police. A Nazi government agency that joined criminal and secret police forces (the Kripo and the Gestapo). It was combined with SS agencies in the Reich Security Main Office.

SK: Sonderkommando, Special Detachment. A subunit of an Einsatzgruppe sent out to find and kill "enemies" of the Reich in the newly conquered areas of the East. The unit was generally composed of no more than 100 men from the SS and the police; often the squadrons were divided into smaller reconnaissance units, or Vorkommandos, that advanced into the conquered areas with the military's armored divisions.

SS: Schutzstaffel, "Protection Squadron." Originally formed in 1925 to serve as Adolf Hitler's bodyguards, this elite police unit was taken over by Heinrich Himmler, who expanded it into an enormous organization of secret police, concentration camp personnel, and paramilitary units.

SSPF: SS- und Polizeiführer, SS and police leader. A title for regional commanders of the SS and police. The SSPF in Zhytomyr reported to the higher SS and police leader for Ukraine who was directly subordinate to Himmler. As chief of Security Police and SD for his region, the SSPF was responsible for maintaining security, an activity that involved the investigation and eradication of real and perceived political, criminal, and racial threats to German rule. The combined SS and police functions in this position reflected at the regional level the merger of the SS (a Nazi Party organization) and the police (an agency of the German state) under Himmler's direct command.

UPA: Ukraïns'ka Povstan's'ka Armiia, Ukrainian Insurgent Army. This term first appeared in February–March 1943, describing the Ukrainian partisans in Polissia and Volhynia. It was the combined military force of Ukrainian nationalists formed to liberate Ukrainians from both the Nazis and the Soviets.

VoMi: Volksdeutsche Mittelstelle, Ethnic German Liaison Office. This 1930s agency for the welfare and repatriation of ethnic (non-Reich) Germans was absorbed by the SS when Himmler was appointed Reich commissioner for the strengthening of Germandom (1939). Its chief was SS Lieutenant General Werner Lorenz.

Nazi Empire-Building and the Holocaust in Ukraine

Introduction

People arriving from Kiev say that the Germans have placed a
cordon of troops around the huge grave in Babi Yar where the
bodies of 50,000 Jews slaughtered in Kiev at the end of September 1941 are buried. They are feverishly digging up corpses and
burning them. Are they so mad as to hope thus to hide their
evil traces that have been branded forever by the tears and the
blood of Ukraine, branded so that it will burn brightly on the
darkest night?
—Vasilii Grossman, *Red Star*, October 1943

With moral outrage, Soviet wartime correspondent Vasilii
Grossman scorned the Germans' hasty attempt to destroy the physical evidence
of their horrific crimes. The atrocities were too enormous to be concealed and,
for this Jewish writer, too personally searing to be forgotten. Grossman (who
lost his own mother to the Holocaust in Berdychiv, Ukraine) struggled to document and publicize the distinct history of the Jews during World War II, despite
Soviet censorship and banning of his work. Drawing from newly available archival collections from the former Soviet Union and the pioneering work of
Grossman as well as Holocaust scholars Shmuel Spector, Philip Friedman, and
Raul Hilberg, this book examines the history of the Shoah in Ukraine within
the context of Nazi occupation aims and practices in the East, and specifically
the devastation that occurred in the Zhytomyr region, where Grossman came
of age. The study seeks to deepen our understanding of how individuals empowered by government and private agencies come to accept and then perpe-
trate campaigns of destruction and mass murder, and often do so in the name
of progress.

During World War II, the most powerful military forces ever amassed
clashed over Ukrainian territory while Nazi occupiers initiated their criminal
schemes against the population. Nearly 4.1 million civilians in Ukraine died
under Nazi rule. The Germans and their collaborators murdered at least 1.2 million Jews. Of the 2.8 million laborers forcibly deported from the former Soviet
territories to Hitler's Germany, an estimated 2.3 million were from Ukraine.
More than 700 cities and towns and about 28,000 villages were completely or
partially destroyed.[1] The figures alone, however, do not describe, let alone ex-

plain, the significance of this horrendous history. Ukraine suffered destruction to an extent that other regions of Nazi-occupied Europe did not, and all of this devastation came in the wake of the worst years of Stalinism. In Ukraine's history of man-made disasters, mostly imposed from the outside, the Nazi occupation stands out as the worst episode.

Until recently, Ukraine (which gained its independence in 1991) was a territory inhabited by generations of Russian rulers, Polish landlords, ethnic German settlers, Jewish traders, and Ukrainian peasants, who comprised the overwhelming majority within its porous borders. For centuries the Great Powers of Europe viewed Ukraine as the continent's "breadbasket," valued for its natural resources more than its diverse population of Ukrainians, Jews, Russians, Poles, Belorussians, Bulgarians, Romanians, Hungarians, Crimean Tatars, Roma, and ethnic Germans. The perception that this "space" and its people could be exploited and radically transformed was most extreme in the 1930s and 1940s when Soviet and then Nazi empire-builders unleashed their utopian schemes in Ukraine. In about two decades, the area was transformed, as historian Kathryn Brown aptly described it, from an "ethnic borderland to a Soviet heartland."[2]

This study sheds light on how the Nazis conceptualized, conquered, and governed Ukraine in a manner that was historically familiar, as well as distinctive and even unprecedented. It explores new questions about the ideological roots and manifestations of Nazi colonialist thinking toward Ukraine, the interaction of the center and periphery in Hitler's Europe, the implementation and interrelation of Nazi policies toward Jews, ethnic Germans and Ukrainians, and the impact of Nazi rule on Zhytomyr, a central region in Ukraine. It elucidates how Nazi-style militarism, colonialism, and genocidal population policies came together in one particular place and how the indigenous population there coped and, in inconceivably large numbers, tragically died under German rule.

With its fertile plains and northern valleys safely nestled west of the Dnepr, the Zhytomyr region was envisioned by Nazi leaders as a future Aryan stronghold consisting of German agricultural colonies, SS-estates, and defense fortifications.[3] In mapping this space, Nazi empire-builders pieced together the former Soviet administrative districts (oblasts) of Vinnytsia and Zhytomyr, western sections of Kiev Oblast, and a northern patch of marshland from Belorussia to create the Zhytomyr General District. The district (Bezirk) was 25,000 square miles (roughly the area of the combined U.S. states of Connecticut, Vermont, and Massachusetts) with close to 3 million inhabitants, therefore sparsely populated in most parts. On German administrative maps it looked indistinguishable from the other five regional districts that comprised the *Reichskommissariat Ukraine* (RKU). Yet during the war it became the hub of elite activity in Ukraine and a laboratory for Reichsführer of the SS and Police Heinrich Himmler's resettlement activists. Adolf Hitler, Hermann Göring, and Himmler all placed their elaborate headquarters and retreats around Vinnytsia and Zhytomyr. Here both pillars of Hitler's racist, revolutionary ideology—the elimination of the Jews and German colonization of the East—transformed the landscape and devastated the population to an extent that was not experienced in other parts of Nazi-occupied Europe besides Poland.

Often scholars have quoted Hitler's musings about Ukraine's being a German "India" as evidence of his delusions of grandeur. However, little has been written about how Europe's history of imperialism, and Germany's history of migration to Eastern Europe and *völkisch* utopian fantasies, shaped the policies and behavior of Nazi leaders and their functionaries who tried to colonize Ukraine during World War II.[4] The Third Reich's population planners, technocrats, Nazi Party "missionaries," and other white-collar professionals who furthered Reichsführer Himmler's resettlement schemes placed themselves within a longer tradition of a Germanic "drive to the East."[5] As Hitler asserted in *Mein Kampf*: "We National Socialists consciously draw a line beneath the foreign policy of our pre-War period. We take up where we broke off six hundred years ago. We stop the endless German movement to the south and west, and turn our gaze to the east. At long last we break off the colonial, commercial policy of the pre-War period and shift to the soil policy of the future."[6] Hitler's "soil policy of the future" derived from various strands of thought that had become especially popular as of the late nineteenth century and gained wider currency among the frustrated, right-wing German nationalists who felt cheated by their World War I defeat and the "humiliating" Versailles Treaty. Determined to give Germany its "natural" place on the world stage as an empire, German geopolitical theorists, Nazi ideologues, and Hitler's officials governing Ukraine promoted their expansionist aims relative to other European models of imperialism, often comparing themselves to the pioneers of North America or to the high-brow British overseers in India. They likened the indigenous peoples of Eastern Europe to the "inferior" and "disappearing races" of Indians, "Negroes," and Africans. In addition to distributing colonial literature to regional functionaries in Ukraine and Poland, Nazi leaders encouraged subordinates to fashion themselves literally as imperial rulers. They were obsessed with enforcing the proper Nazi salute and militaristic dress codes, down to every insignia and medal. Like the Nazi flag that was dutifully raised each day by functionaries in the most remote outposts, the salute and uniform

Nazi-Dominated Europe in 1942 and Plans for a Greater Germanic Empire

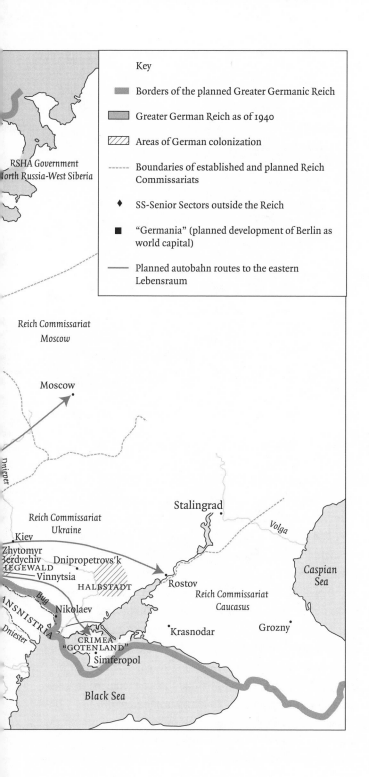

Key

Borders of the planned Greater Germanic Reich

Greater German Reich as of 1940

Areas of German colonization

Boundaries of established and planned Reich Commissariats

SS-Senior Sectors outside the Reich

"Germania" (planned development of Berlin as world capital)

Planned autobahn routes to the eastern Lebensraum

RSHA Government
North Russia-West Siberia

Reich Commissariat
Moscow

Moscow

Dnieper

Reich Commissariat
Ukraine

Stalingrad

Volga

Kiev

Zhytomyr
Berdychiv
HEGEWALD
Vinnytsia
HALBSTADT
Dnipropetrovs'k

Rostov

Caspian
Sea

Reich Commissariat
Caucasus

Bug

Nikolaev

TRANSNISTRIA

Dniester

CRIMEA
"GOTENLAND"
Simferopol

Krasnodar

Grozny

Black Sea

The Reich Commissariat Ukraine, 1 May 1942. The five general districts of the Commissariat shown on the map are the General District Volhynia, General District Zhytomyr, General District Kiev, General District Nikolaev, and General District Dnipropetrovs'k. To the east of the commissariat is the much larger area occupied by the military. The map was issued by the Reichsführer SS and Chief of Police, Department S II B2. Source: Central State Archive, Minsk, courtesy of U.S. Holocaust Memorial Museum, RG 53.002M, reel 4, 393-1-1.

were assertions of German power and "Aryan" solidarity.[7] The caste of Nazi adventurers who ran Ukraine from 1941 to 1944—most of them were SA "old fighters" who had grown up with the Party in the 1920s—perceived their actions as legitimately linked to Europe's history of conquest and rule; they also prided themselves on being revolutionaries with a new, utopian vision of an Aryan-dominated Europe.

Ultimately, the exigencies of the war effort and mounting partisan warfare behind the lines prevented Nazi leaders from fully developing and realizing their colonial aims in Ukraine. The experiments that the Nazis were able to test out around their Zhytomyr headquarters failed. Aside from demonstrating the sad fact that it is easier to destroy than create, especially in the context of a major war, the inability of German leaders to realize their colonial aspirations sheds light on the history of Nazi policy-making and implementation as it occurred at the periphery of Hitler's empire, which is another theme of this study.

The essence of Reich policies in Ukraine originated with Hitler's prophecies and offhand remarks that were then realized by his subordinates, an ensemble

Key:
- – – Boundaries of the General District
- ——— Boundaries of the counties
- ----- Boundaries of the raions
- ⊙ District capitals
- ○ Raion centers

Administrative Map of the General District of Zhytomyr. Source: Zhytomyr State Archive, P1151-1-51.

of ignoble characters who vied for ever-increasing power. Often Martin Bormann (chief of the Nazi Party bureaucracy), Heinrich Himmler (chief of the SS-police), Alfred Rosenberg (head of the Reich Ministry for the Occupied Eastern Territories), and Erich Koch (Reich commissar for Ukraine) would, fresh from a visit with the Führer in his Ukrainian headquarters at Vinnytsia, formulate a policy based on Hitler's casual, sinister observations of the local people.[8] This style of "on the spot" decision-making characterized the political culture of Nazism; it was secretive, corrupt, and valued action.

Speaking from his Hegewald compound near Zhytomyr, Himmler urged his subordinates to "make decisions in the field!" Then he described his own "model" approach to the attentive SS-policemen at the conference: "I do not make decisions in Berlin, rather I drive to Lublin, Lemberg, Reval, etc., and at these places in the evening, then, eight, ten, twelve major decisions are made on the spot."[9] In fact, only two months earlier when he arrived at his Hegewald field headquarters, Himmler rushed to Hitler's Werwolf compound nearby. They lunched there on 25 July 1942, and discussed among other things plans for ethnic Germans, the Waffen-SS, and antipartisan warfare. Later that evening and during the day that followed, Himmler held a series of meetings with Ukraine's SS-police commanders at his Zhytomyr headquarters. He told his men that the earlier order to kill all the Jews must be carried out immediately and entirely. According to the postwar testimony of one SS-policeman who was present, Himmler demanded that they "clean the territory of Ukraine for the future settlement of Germans." In addition to the immediate destruction of all Jewish communities, Himmler insisted that the Ukrainian civilian population be brought to a "minimum." Four months later all of Ukraine's shtetls and ghettos lay in ruins; tens of thousands of Jewish men, women, and children were brutally murdered by stationary and mobile SS-police units and indigenous auxiliaries. Meanwhile, Ukrainians in Kiev were reliving the nightmare of an artificial famine—this time at the hands of the Nazis, who blocked food shipments to the city in an effort to deurbanize Ukraine by depopulating the cities of non-Germans.[10]

In the Nazi system, major policy decisions were often made "on the spot" or in the field, as Himmler revealed to his men. This style of policy-making and decision-making has puzzled historians of the Third Reich, who have tried to piece together the inner workings of the state and party system with sparse documentation about the origins of new policies or shifts in policies, but ample source material about the bureaucratic machinery of the Reich. Nazi rule in Ukraine was a combination of this rather arbitrary form of Hitler-centered goal setting and the dynamic, frequently contradictory actions of his subordinates

Reichsführer SS and Police Heinrich Himmler (left) speaking with Felix Steiner,
commander of Waffen-SS Armoured Division Viking, Ukraine 1941
(U.S. Holocaust Memorial Museum, courtesy of James Blevins, #60400)

who "worked toward the Führer," pursued their own self-interests, and held
mixed views about the future of the Reich.[11] Regional leaders adapted the most
radical policies to local conditions, demonstrating an uneven, albeit powerful
combination of zealous initiative, sycophantic obedience, and uneasy compli-
ance. Yet there was order in this chaos. In the case of policies with clear aims
and strong support, the Nazi system functioned very systematically and thoroughly. The history of the Holocaust offers the most glaring example of how
a National Socialist consensus developed on certain issues that overrode personal, professional, and political rivalries.

Nazi leaders relished their mobility because it allowed them to participate
in the historic events that they set in motion. Hitler, Göring, and Himmler
commissioned planes and elaborate trains so that they could see firsthand how
their goals and visions were taking shape in the field. The chief of the Reich's
Secret Police and Security Service, Reinhard Heydrich, who wanted to show
off his toughness, patriotism, and prowess, flew with the Luftwaffe during the
first six weeks of Operation Barbarossa. After his plane was shot down near
Zhytomyr, he was rescued by some of his men who were active in a mobile killing unit, an *Einsatzgruppe*. According to the postwar testimony of an Einsatz-

gruppe member, Heydrich met with his mobile killing units at this time, and thereafter in early August 1941 the units began killing Jewish women and children in massive numbers.[12] The elite's trains, airstrips, and secret headquarters marked the landscape of Ukraine and other parts of Eastern Europe. The direct influence of these leaders on the periphery of the Third Reich has not been fully explored by historians, and the Zhytomyr region's wartime history offers a powerful demonstration of the center's impact on local events.

This regional case study, however, is not strictly about the dynamics of German policy implementation in Zhytomyr. The region's population suffered tremendously at the hands of the Nazis, and the fate of some groups and the actions of others illuminate significant aspects of Ukraine's history. When the Germans arrived in the region in 1941, they confronted a population that was much more politically demoralized and economically destitute than they had expected. Ukrainians who were still haunted by the terror of 1930s Stalinism did not uniformly embrace the Nazis as "liberators." While all Ukrainians viewed Germans as outsiders or foreigners, as individuals they experienced the occupation differently depending on where they lived, the character of the local German rulers, the type of work they obtained, whether they were male or female, old or young, and whether they could speak or read German. Historian Karel Berkhoff's exceptional study of daily life in Ukraine, *Harvest of Despair*, has deepened understanding of these varied responses and experiences. By defining the colonial setting of Nazi rule, my study of Zhytomyr builds on Berkhoff's social history because it provides an ideological framework for understanding German aims and behavior in Ukraine. It also focuses on the history of the Shoah, which was in its scope and methods the most extreme genocidal policy of the Reich and indeed the defining feature of Nazi empire-building.

I chose to organize the book chronologically and thematically into nine chapters. The first chapter explores the ideological roots of Nazi colonialist thinking in Ukraine. Besides the historical German fascination with the East, in what ways did Europe's history of imperialism and colonialism influence Hitler's projections of Ukraine and Nazi policy aims there? The second chapter examines the military invasion and occupation of the Zhytomyr region. It introduces the first of two governing systems that ravaged the region—the German army's occupation administration of *Kommandanturen* and mobile SS-police units; and the subsequent civilian administration of *Kommissare* and stationary gendarme and SS units. The third chapter investigates how the Wehrmacht ruled over Zhytomyr between mid-July 1941 and November 1941. In this initial stage of the occupation, Ukrainians and ethnic Germans willingly served the Germans as mayors, district leaders, village elders, and auxiliary police-men. Did these collaborators wield any power, or were they simply German puppets? What were their relations with German officials and, moreover, with their neighbors? What were the Wehrmacht's main policies for governing the newly conquered areas as compared to the subsequent policies of the civilian government?

The fourth chapter is the first of two on the Holocaust. In Zhytomyr, Ger-mans and non-Germans from all walks of life participated in the murder of the entire population of Jewish men, women, and children, as many as 180,000 per-sons. Most regional leaders fully exploited anti-Jewish measures to meet local needs, their superiors' expectations, and their own self-interests. While many left their individual mark on the persecutory apparatus, the killing campaigns down to the most remote villages were not totally disconnected from a central chain of command.

The fifth chapter—on the Zhytomyr Commissariat—explores how the Ger-mans tried to establish their colonial-style occupation system and pursued con-flicting, ad hoc Ukrainian policies. Regional Nazi administrators in Ukraine, known as general and district commissars, functioned within the hierarchy of Alfred Rosenberg's Reich Ministry for the Occupied Eastern Territories. On paper they were the leading civil authority; however, in reality they had to share power with Himmler's SS and police forces. To what extent did the commissars control Nazi policies at the local level? What were the interrelations among the different German and non-German agencies present in the region?

In chapter seven, the study moves chronologically into a more focused look at the fall of 1942, when Hitler and Himmler created the *Volksdeutsche* settlement called Hegewald. This first experimental colony contained roughly 10,000 of the region's Volhynian Germans who were concentrated into protected farm-ing communities. Although German leaders celebrated the inaugural colony, most of their subordinates doubted the success of such initiatives. What do conflicts over the Volksdeutsche programs reveal about the lower-level com-mitment to Hitler's utopian vision of a German *Lebensraum* in Ukraine?

The last chapter analyzes the unraveling of Nazi rule from late fall 1942 until early 1944. It traces the impact of the partisan movement on the local popula-tion and German administration. In Zhytomyr there were at least four under-ground movements with varying political agendas. Although seemingly at odds with one another, Ukrainian resistance and Ukrainian collaboration actually overlapped. Many resistance fighters worked undercover in the administration. Moreover, Ukrainian police collaborators and administrators who were central agents of the Nazi terror and Holocaust in 1941–42 later deserted their posts and joined the partisans in 1943–44. In other words, many Ukrainians and ethnic Germans changed sides during the war, often blurring the categorical distinctions of victim, perpetrator, and bystander.

Ukraine on the Eve of the Nazi Occupation, 1939–1941

In the interwar era and especially in the years leading up to the Nazi conquest of Ukraine, the territory's borders were redrawn at least three times, and Ukrainians found themselves divided among Soviet, Polish, Romanian, Hungarian, and German rulers. By 1939, the vast majority (over 20 million or 80 percent) resided within the borders of the Soviet Republic of Ukraine, while 7 million more lived in Polish-held Galicia and Volhynia. Ukrainians also fell under Romanian rule in Bukovina and Bessarabia, and after March 1939 Hungary governed the Ukrainian majority in the newly annexed Subcarpathian Rus'. Then Hitler and Stalin carved up Poland under the terms of the Molotov-Ribbentrop pact, sparking the outbreak of World War II in September 1939. Over 3 million Ukrainians who had been living in interwar Poland were suddenly swept up in Stalin's sovietization of eastern Galicia, western Volhynia, and western Polissia, the hallmark of which was the rapid collectivization of agriculture. In addition, Stalin's secret police (NKVD) initiated mass arrests and deportations of the leading noncommunist Ukrainians and nearly the entire Polish upper classes and intelligentsia. They were crammed into freight cars and shipped to central Asia and Siberia. According to historian Timothy Snyder's work on Volhynia, Soviet occupiers and their local collaborators deported as many as 70,000 or 20 percent of the entire Polish population between 1939 and 1941.[13]

Meanwhile, over 3,000 Ukrainians (including the émigré nationalists who fled the Soviets) remained in Cracow and other formerly Polish territory seized by the Germans in 1939. Consistent with the Nazi divide-and-rule strategy, the Germans granted this Ukrainian minority leading positions in the occupation administration of Poland. Ukrainian nationalist leaders and the Nazis had a few things in common. They both wished to see the demise of Poland and Soviet Russia. They both assumed that the Jewish minority in Eastern Europe would be rendered powerless in the New Order. Anti-Semitism was a significant force in both movements, but it was more central to the Nazi Weltanschauung. In this era when ethnic cleansing did not have a bad name, Ukrainian leaders sought an independent Ukraine for Ukrainians only, not a multiethnic society with its perceived political instability, "racial" impurity, and vulnerable borders. They mistakenly assumed that Ukrainian autonomy would be acceptable to Hitler, who had much larger ambitions of European (and later global) domination, and certainly little sympathy for the plight of Ukrainians, who were in his mind inferior Slavs.

Within two years of Poland's defeat, France and the other continental powers of Europe were at Hitler's knees, and he turned his attention to his main enemy, the Soviet Union. On 22 June 1941 Hitler and his allies launched Operation Barbarossa and quickly conquered most of Ukraine west of the Dnepr. Ukrainian nationalist leaders and their supporters ended up in concentration camps or in the mass graves that were fast becoming a major feature of Ukraine's landscape. As Hitler described it to his coterie on 16 July 1941, the ultimate aim of this *Vernichtungskrieg* (war of destruction) against the Soviet Union was to make a "Garden of Eden" out of the newly won territories in the East. One of the areas being eyed by Nazi leaders as a future Aryan paradise was Right Bank Ukraine around Zhytomyr.

The Zhytomyr Region and Its People

"Zhytomyr," a compound word meaning "rye-peace" or "wheat-universe," is a little-known place on the map of Eastern Europe. For centuries the population of this region, situated about ninety miles west of Kiev, subsisted on crops grown on the fertile black soil of Ukraine's southern forest steppe that begins below the Teterev River (a tributary of the Dnepr) and extends southward to the Podolian town of Vinnytsia. In the 1930s it was the sugar beet capital and major agricultural center of the Soviet Union, with 500,000 acres of sugar beet crops and over 5 million acres of wheat. Other than some local crafts and trade, the region's industries were tied to local farming and animal husbandry: for example, textile mills, sugar refineries, distilleries, slaughterhouses, and tanneries.[14]

While most of the Zhytomyr region, as it was defined by German occupiers, lay in the Volyn-Podolia upland, the northern border with Belorussia was historically part of the Polish *kresy* also known as Polissia. This borderland territory, which was heavily populated by Poles in districts such as Markhlevsk (Dovbysh) as well as by Belorussians, was one of the poorest "backwaters" of Europe. Its swamps, the Pripiat' marshes, and dense forests were not appealing to farmers and traders but inviting to outlaws and persecuted groups, who sought refuge there.[15]

Before and after World War II, Ukrainians made up the majority of the population of the Zhytomyr region. They dominated the countryside and formed most of the peasantry. In the 1930s, however, many Ukrainians moved to the region's centers at Zhytomyr, Vinnytsia, Berdychiv, and Ovruch. Zhytomyr was the largest of these with 95,000 inhabitants in 1939. Vinnytsia, also an oblast capital, contained 92,000 inhabitants, and Berdychiv had 70,000 dwellers, more than one-third of whom were Jewish. Initially the younger male peasants migrated to these centers to work in new positions and learn new trades within the Soviet system. Entire villages disappeared. By 1941 Ukrainians constituted 60 percent of the urban population in Zhytomyr and this growth represented a threefold increase in the number of Ukrainians in cities since 1926. They entered the professions of teaching, bookkeeping, carpentry, printing, and mechanics, and they took up half of the positions in the state and Communist Party offices. Stalin's attempt to rapidly industrialize Ukraine's agricultural economy forced more peasants out of the countryside; thousands were deported and many more died during Stalin's collectivization drive. During the Great Famine of 1932–33, the Zhytomyr and Vinnytsia oblasts lost about 15 to 20 percent of their peasant population to starvation-related illnesses. Despite the seemingly urban features of the New Soviet Men (and women), Ukrainians in Zhytomyr's larger towns were only one generation away from the farm and rural traditions.[16] And despite intense Soviet repression of religious institutions, many Ukrainians, especially those in the countryside, secretly observed their Christian Orthodox beliefs.

Among the region's population of minorities, the Russians composed the political elite for two centuries, a status that was challenged briefly during the collapse of the tsarist empire and Bolshevik revolution.[17] In 1918–19 the embattled Ukrainian movement for independence under Symon Petliura was forced to move the seat of its government (the Directory) to various towns in Right Bank Ukraine including Zhytomyr and Vinnytsia. While the fledgling Directory tried to establish Jewish national autonomy within Ukraine, the political and economic upheaval of the time let loose armed militias, government troops, and anti-Semitic hooligans who attacked and killed thousands of Jews, and many acted in the name of Ukrainian nationhood. Some of the worst pogroms occurred in Zhytomyr, Vinnytsia, and Berdychiv. Jewish businesses, farms, and homes were ransacked. Hundreds of Jews were beaten and harassed; women and girls were raped. In Zhytomyr proper, Petliura gangs killed 317 Jews on 22–26 March 1919. Twenty-three died in Berdychiv. Jewish self-defense units prevented more fatalities in Vinnytsia and in Berdychiv.[18]

According to the 1939 Soviet census of the Jewish populations in Zhytomyr, Vinnytsia, and parts of Polissia, there were about 266,000 Jews residing in the region; an average of 30 percent lived in the cities or larger towns. Indeed, the Zhytomyr region contained some of the highest concentrations of Jewish communities in all of Ukraine.[19] For centuries the Jewish shtetls in these parts were hit by waves of anti-Jewish violence. Yet this area was also a haven for Jews of the Russian empire, officially designated the Pale of Settlement. Berdychiv, a center of Hasidism, was known as the little Jerusalem of Volhynia. Here and in Zhytomyr, Jewish cultural, intellectual, and religious life abounded at eighty synagogues and *battei midrash* (houses of prayer and study), seminaries, printing shops, and theater houses. In the early twentieth century, thousands of Jews moved from the shtetl communities into the larger towns; many continued on to America. The migration was sometimes forced under tsarist laws of Russification. Others left the countryside to seek refuge from the pogroms of October 1905 and January 1919, or to find new livelihoods in the expanding state bureaucracies and industries. In general the Jewish population of the Zhytomyr region decreased dramatically between World War I and World War II; on the eve of World War I, there were 55,876 Jews in Berdychiv, and in 1939 there were 23,266.[20]

The Polish (largely Roman Catholic) minority enjoyed power in the region between the fourteenth century and the eighteenth century as owners of some of the largest estates in Europe. After the partitions of Poland and failed Polish insurrections of the mid-nineteenth century, the tsars pursued intense Russification of the region, exiling Poles to Russia's interior, confiscating their land and peasants (serfs), and banning the Polish language. The former Polish aristocracy became a landless minority. In Right Bank Ukraine, many migrated to Zhytomyr, Berdychiv, and Kam'ianets'-Podil's'kyi, but most settled west of the region in Podolia and Volhynia. A few Polish communities remained intact in Soviet Ukraine until the mid-1930s, most notably the community at Markhlevsk in the Polissia section of the Zhytomyr region. But with the start of World War II and the Red Army advance into Poland, most Poles in the Soviet territories of Ukraine were deported to northern Kazakhstan, Siberia, and other desolate parts of inner Russia.[21]

The ethnic German minority in Zhytomyr consisted of over 70,000 East Volhynian Germans, mostly Mennonites who began arriving in the early nineteenth century from Prussian-occupied Poland.[22] They worked as foresters and tenant farmers and formed settlements near Zhytomyr, such as Neudorf and Alter Hütte, which the Soviets later destroyed and the Nazis tried to revive. As a minority they had enjoyed some privileges under the tsar but were later persecuted by Ukrainian anarchists and nationalists in the wake of World War I. They died in disproportionally high numbers during the Great Famine of 1932–33 and suffered waves of deportations in 1935, 1937–38, and 1941.[23]

Even before the German Army and its allies conquered Zhytomyr in July 1941, Nazi officials expected the region's population of ethnic Germans to serve as the empire's peripheral leaders and frontier defenders. German irredentist claims on behalf of ethnic Germans living outside the Reich's borders had been the cornerstone of Weimar and Nazi foreign policy during the 1920s and 1930s, and indeed Hitler's strongest pretext for initiating the war in 1939.[24] Already in 1934 ethnic Germans in the Zhytomyr region received food aid from the Reich in the form of "Hitler certificates" as part of the Nazis' "Brothers in Need" welfare program for ethnic Germans abroad.[25] These recipients then found themselves the target of Stalin's deportation raids in 1935–36. In January 1935 Stalin initiated the mass deportation of ethnic Germans across the Soviet Union, beginning with the Volhynian Germans from Zhytomyr (Novohrad-Volyns'kyi); at least half of the population was transported to the frigid gulags of Murmansk and desolate camps in Kazakhstan.[26] In the Nazi-Soviet pact of August 1939, Stalin agreed not to deport ethnic Germans, but allowed them to cross the Nazi-Soviet line into German-occupied Poland. Hundreds of thousands of ethnic Germans from the former Polish-held region of Volhynia, which fell under Soviet rule, streamed into German-occupied Poland; but very few of these Volksdeutsche came from the Zhytomyr region and even fewer from regions east of the Dnepr.[27]

A Note on Sources and Languages

The bulk of primary research material collected for this book stems from the captured German records held in former Soviet archives. The Zhytomyr State Archives collection forms the core of the study's source material. The most top-secret German administrative documentation that survived the war, especially concerning Hitler's and Himmler's presence in the region, was transferred to restricted repositories outside the region and eventually reached the Special Archive in Moscow, the former October Revolution Archive in Kiev, and KGB archives. Additional high-level orders from the commander of the Order Police, the Higher SS and Police leaders, the Reich minister for the Occupied Eastern Territories, and other senior officials are scattered in archival collections, primarily in Minsk and Prague. The United States Holocaust Memorial Museum has microfilmed a good portion of this captured German material from the major archives of the former Soviet Union; the museum's collection serves as an outstanding complement to the extensive collection of wartime material held at the U.S. National Archives and Records Administration in College Park, Maryland.

The massive quantity of captured German records presents scholars with research challenges. As is typically the case, quantity is no measure of quality.

The cold, bureaucratic style of the Nazi documents failed to provide a human dimension to the story. To compensate for this lack of material about the individual victims of Nazi policies, I turned to additional sources such as postwar testimonies from war crimes investigations, memoirs, letters, photographs, and oral histories. In Zhytomyr, Ukrainian and Jewish survivors welcomed the chance to finally provide a candid account of the occupation, free from the constraints of the official Soviet wartime history that played down the Holocaust, lionized Soviet partisans, and vilified Ukrainian nationalists. These postwar recollections can be problematic because of memory lapses and other historical inaccuracies, but the survivors provided valuable insight and information about individuals, families, and particular villages. Often their stories can be corroborated with secondary sources or the Nazi documents.

One final note regarding the research and presentation of this study concerns the issue of languages. Most of the primary documentation was written in German; however, Nazi leaders were inconsistent in their transliterations of Ukrainian names and locations. I have used, whenever possible, the contemporary Ukrainian spellings. The transliterations, which are based on the Library of Congress system, have been simplified by the omission of diacritics. Only some of the familiar places, such as Kiev and Crimea, appear in their more common English forms. Use of "Zhytomyr" will refer to the entire region as the Germans conceived it unless otherwise specified as the capital, center, or town of Zhytomyr.

Chapter 1 Nazi Colonialism and Ukraine

In twenty years the Ukraine will already be a home for twenty million inhabitants besides the natives. In three hundred years, the country will be one of the loveliest gardens in the world. As for the natives, we'll have to screen them carefully. The Jew, that destroyer, we shall drive out. . . . Our colonizing penetration must be constantly progressive, until it reaches the stage where our own colonists far outnumber the local inhabitants.
—Adolf Hitler, October 1941

Like its neighboring European powers, Germany pursued imperialist ambitions in the late nineteenth century that were colonial by definition: they settled in the conquered territory, exploited or developed its resources, and attempted to govern the indigenous inhabitants of the territory.[1] Between 1884 and 1900 specifically, the Kaiserreich acquired about 1 million square miles of territory in Africa and Asia with roughly 12 million inhabitants. By 1914 Germany controlled the third largest empire. For Germans in particular, colonies offered much needed space to accommodate an expanding population at home. Adopting the American model of the farm, Wilhelmine population planners and government officials, who were deeply concerned about the mass migration of Germans who lost their völkisch identity or "Germanness" through assimilation, looked east as well as south for territorial solutions to the so-called emigration problem.[2]

A quarter century later, Adolf Hitler too sought space for the Third Reich, although in a significantly different fashion than previous German heads of state. Blending geopolitical theories of empire, Germany's own history of conquest and migration to Eastern Europe (for example, the Teutonic Knights and Hanseatic League), and racial, anti-Semitic theories of the day, Hitler conceived of the world in terms of geographical power blocs and racial struggles. Accordingly, as a Great Power of superior *Volk*, Hitler believed Germany was destined to rule a considerable portion of the Eurasian land mass. Once conquered, this land would be thoroughly Germanized through a long-term system of economic exploitation and revolutionary population changes. Mass deportations, forced labor, and mass murder were the accepted means for achieving his colonial aims. As new and chilling as Hitler's ideas for "inner colonization" were, his concept of German imperial expansion did not develop within a historical vacuum.

In general, historians of the Third Reich and the Holocaust have been reluctant to view Nazi rule in the East as a colonial endeavor, and those who follow historian Fritz Fischer's narrative of German expansionism tend not to connect this history to the Holocaust. Only a few works, such as Raphael Lemkin's *Axis Rule in Occupied Europe* (and his unpublished history of genocide) and Hannah Arendt's *The Origins of Totalitarianism* (1951), have explored the relationship between European imperialism, Nazism, and the Holocaust.[3] Recent sociocultural studies have developed this notion by showing that colonialist ideas began to take shape in eighteenth-century Germany and took on extreme forms in the Nazi era. This emerging narrative of German colonial fantasies does not represent another deterministic version of Germany's *Sonderweg* (special path) toward Nazism; rather, it is understood within a broader European context of exploration, conquest, migration, and mass destruction of indigenous peoples.[4]

Thus one finds in Hitler's, Himmler's, and Rosenberg's imaginings of the new Aryan paradise references to the North American frontier, the British Empire in India, and the European exploitation of Africans in the late nineteenth century. In Heinrich Himmler's SS propaganda publication, *Der Untermensch*, one reads about the life-and-death struggle between Germans and Jews alongside Nazi claims to Eastern European territory depicted as "black earth that could be a paradise, a California of Europe."[5] Propaganda efforts by the regime, including photos and films, showed ethnic German settlers driving covered wagons adorned with portraits of their Führer.[6] The name given to Ukrainian auxiliary policemen who were active in the destruction of the Warsaw ghetto was *Askaris*, a term applied earlier to Germany's African mercenary troops.[7]

More than simply mimicking or exploiting the language and practices of European colonial history and the American frontier, Nazi officials inhabited a world of imperialism within which they defined themselves, their expansionist aims, and their non-German "subjects." As Raphael Lemkin argued decades ago, genocide was linked to centuries of imperialistic warfare, forced migrations, frontier violence, and the displacement of non-Europeans in the Americas, Australia, and Africa. Yet only after Europe itself was destroyed by Hitler's Reich did this historical pattern come to light. The Nazi occupation of Eastern Europe demonstrated that such practices were not strictly overseas forms of conquest and rule, and that the worst aspects of colonialism—forced population movements, slave labor, and mass murder—could be combined and carried out on an enormous scale, in a matter of a few years, and in the heart of "civilized" Europe. This chapter traces the history of ideas that drove this destructive German course in Ukraine, and especially the intersection of colonialism and genocide there.

Roots of Nazi Colonialist Thinking

Nazi colonialism was first and foremost about race and space, or as the Germans termed it *Blut und Boden*. Nazi ideologues such as R. Walther Darré and the Reich's "Raumforschung" and "Raumordnung" specialists opposed the pre–World War I policy of overseas colonies of trade and instead pursued what they believed was a revolutionary land policy of a Germanized and economically developed Eastern and Central Europe.[8] The lure of the East had its historical antecedents in the medieval migrations of Germans to Poland and then to the Russian empire under Peter and Catherine the Great. Additional waves of Germans fleeing religious persecution—foremost among them Mennonites, Baptists, and Catholics—followed in the nineteenth century. This migration history and the German gaze to the East came to be known in cultural and political terms as Germany's *Drang nach Osten*. Its underlying assumption was that Germans were welcome as colonizers; indeed their presence was part of an ineluctable civilizing process.[9]

Above all the frontier metaphor, as historian Alan Steinweis has discerned, appealed to Hitler because, according to racial and geographic studies of the day, the "superior" white pioneers were not only most able to survive on the frontier but also positively transformed by the frontier experience.[10] According to Steinweis, the frontier fantasies of Hitler and his ilk were shaped mostly by the ideas of nineteenth-century thinkers such as Friedrich Ratzel, Frederick Jackson Turner, and Halford John MacKinder. Ratzel, who coined the concept of *Lebensraum*, published an influential study, *Politische Geographie* (1897), that stressed, with a Social Darwinistic slant, the importance of human migration into new spaces. In Ratzel's view, such expansionism revitalized the people by opening up new social, economic, and cultural opportunities that might otherwise be contained within static borders. His ideas derived in part from a late-nineteenth-century transatlantic dialogue that included Turner's frontier thesis about American westward expansion, and they later spawned geopolitical concepts such as those espoused by Karl Haushofer.[11] Haushofer's theories of imperialism, space, and power relations were taken very seriously by Nazi ideologues, who incorporated them into Hitler's *Mein Kampf*. In an important way Haushofer reframed the traditional German focus on eastern expansion by placing it within a global, Eurocentric perspective of empire.[12]

Just prior to World War I, völkisch thought moved in a similar expansionist direction by melding race and space in a new movement for utopian settlements. Unlike the romantic utopian socialists in England, France, and North America (for example, Charles Fourier and Robert Owen) who tried to create rural havens away from the squalor, materialism, and crime of the first smokestack factory towns of the early nineteenth century, the imitators of the German utopians, such as the Social Darwinist Willibald Hentschel, were steeped in racialist thought of the late nineteenth century. In Hentschel's popular book, *Varuna* (1907), he argued that the driving force of history was the spirit or energy inherent in the evolutionary process of race purification. Aryans, he posited, were among the purest race and could ensure their high standing in the "völkisch nobility" if they concentrated themselves into a Germanic colony. According to George Mosse's intellectual history of völkisch thought, Hentschel's "colony was to constitute a new beginning for the race." It was supposed to protect the race "from the corrupting effects of modernity." Women played a special role in Hentschel's colony—they were the "breeding stock of the race who tended the children and the settlement gardens."[13]

Already during World War I, German colonialist fantasies began to materialize in the form of the Second Reich's occupation policies in Eastern Europe and Ukraine. In 1918, the Central Powers established a puppet regime in Ukraine (led by Ukrainian nationalist Hetman Skoropodskyi) and negotiated control over the largest concentration of ethnic Germans (more than 700,000) in the tsarist empire in southern Ukraine. Backed by Kaiser Wilhelm II, the Pan-German League, and the former secretary of the German Colonial Office Friedrich von Lindquist, General Erich Ludendorff established a military occupation administration that treated the eastern territories not as "a complicated weaving of lands and peoples (*Land und Leute*), but as spaces and races (*Raum und Volk*) to be ordered by German mastery and organization."[14] From an ideological, technological, and ethnographic standpoint, World War I revealed a European veneration of violence and capacity for total war, and within German circles specifically a budding interest in Ukraine as a colony.[15]

In the interwar period Nazi Party ideologues developed these trends further by combining the racism, völkisch nationalism, utopianism, and anti-Semitism of the day with Germany's long-standing romance with the frontier. Hitler's generation expressed outrage over the Versailles Treaty's seizure of German colonies because this act as the Germans saw it was a humiliating Diktat, not because they held a special attachment to Africa or Southeast Asia. Rather than champion imperialist ventures, early Party leader Gregor Strasser advocated a socialist revolution at home. The Nazi Party rallied for a consolidation and strengthening of the Volk and stressed Germany's vital need to expand within Europe, not overseas. Hentschel reemerged onto the scene with a more inflammatory pamphlet entitled *Was soll aus uns werden?* (What Shall Become of Us?) (1923), which incited youth to band together under the God of the Aryan race, Artam. Describing the youth as a knighthood whose duty it was to protect the Aryan race, Hentschel provided young men with some ideological rationale for joining the borderlands movement of the Weimar period. This movement mobilized youth to secure Germany's eastern border with Poland by settling there, pushing the Poles out and assisting the Germans who resided there. Among the young men drawn to Hentschel's Artamanen utopian movement and his promotion of eugenics and agricultural, völkisch colonies were Heinrich Himmler and R. Walther Darré.[16]

The Nazis brought all of these elements together, creating a lethal concoction of racial anti-Semitism, völkisch nationalism and geo-determinism that first appeared in the Twenty-five Points of the German Workers' Party Program (1920), the founding document of the Nazi Party. For example, Point One highlighted Germany's right to self-determination of all its peoples, in other words, the expansion of Germany's borders. The third point was more overtly migrationist and colonialist. It demanded "land and territory (colonies) to feed our people and to settle our surplus population," while Point Four declared, "No Jew may be a member of the nation."[17] At this time, the *Eiserne Blätter*, a typical völkisch propaganda leaflet, asked its readers, "Where is the German Colonial Land?" and answered forcefully, "In Eastern Europe!"[18] German territorial aspirations abroad did not disappear in the 1920s, but for pragmatic and strategic reasons they lost their widespread appeal to the more pressing matter of Germany's economic struggles and political survival in Europe.

Though in the short run the Nazi movement prioritized its racial and spatial aims "at home," their Weltanschauung was literally a "worldview" of racial showdowns. The central dynamic in this global conflict, the Nazis argued, was the German-Jewish conflict. Without the Jews, there was (in Nazi thinking) no struggle, no global threat, and no enemy to be vanquished. Just as he was candid about his territorial quest for Lebensraum, so Hitler did not conceal his intense hatred of the Jews, who appeared in *Mein Kampf* as the Aryan's archenemy in a zero-sum game for hegemony.[19] Once in power, the Nazis effectively spread their anti-Semitic propaganda and marginalized the Jewish population through various destructive policies: economic boycotts; "Aryanization" of the civil service, professions, and business; forced emigration and physical intimidation, including beatings and incarceration in the concentration camps.

On the foreign policy front, Hitler and his supporters were as systematic and determined but had other ideological hurdles to overcome. For example on the eve of Hitler's appointment as chancellor, Alfred Rosenberg published an editorial in the *Völkischer Beobachter* about Germany's future challenge. In his view, Germany had to combine its otherwise divergent *Ostpolitik* and *Weltpolitik* trends in order to satisfy the "peasant" and "Viking" drives of the German Volk. Historian Woodruff Smith summed up the point when he wrote that Hitler and the Nazi leadership "had to solve the Weltpolitik-Lebensraum dichotomy in the German imperialist tradition." They bridged the migrationist and economic driving forces for expansion by developing an ambitious program of re-settlement and economic autarky within a Nazi-dominated Europe. The merger of these two expansionist currents—one focused on population policies, the other on economic extraction—centered on Eastern Europe.

When Hitler unveiled his plans for seizing Czechoslovakia and Austria to the Reich's military leadership and his foreign minister in November 1937, he explained that the territorial conquests fulfilled Germany's urgent need for living space and economic self-sufficiency. In order to feed the growing population of Germans, to ensure its future existence, Hitler argued that Germany must acquire fertile land in the East. As he put it:

> The space needed to ensure it [food supply] can be sought only in Europe, not as in the liberal-capitalist view, in the exploitation of colonies [abroad]. It is not a matter of acquiring population but of gaining space for agricultural use. Moreover, areas producing raw materials can be more usefully sought in Europe, in immediate proximity to the Reich, than overseas; the solution thus obtained must suffice for one or two generations. Whatever else might later prove necessary must be left to succeeding generations to deal with.[20]

Irredentist arguments that sought to undo the Versailles Treaty's seizure of "German" territory appealed to most Germans. In particular Weltpolitik advocates and colonial revisionists, foremost among them Reich Minister of Finance Hjalmar Schacht, endorsed war as the only means for regaining Germany's lost territories and needed economic markets abroad.[21] For the economic imperialists of Schacht's generation who espoused an expansionist Weltpolitik, Ukraine did not have the exotic allure of Africa, but it was appealing as a new agricultural and industrial marketplace.[22] Meanwhile Darré's Blood and Soil advocates, who argued that the distant, uncultivated, foreign land of Africa was not fertile ground for Germans, held up Ukraine as the natural place to expand. Thus in the outstanding example of Ukraine, we see the disastrous unfolding of the Nazi concept of empire-building that drew its strength from völkisch utopian fantasies, the Lebensraum tradition of continental migration, and the imperialistic Weltpolitik tradition of economic exploitation.

Nazi Imaginings of Ukraine as a Colony

According to Nazi thinking, Ukraine was populated by inferior Slavs who were racially unfit to rule themselves. Besides its unrivaled natural resources and supposedly compliant population, Ukraine fit perfectly into the bellicose plans of Nazi leaders as the ideal bulwark against Bolshevized Russia. Hitler relished the idea of a contiguous German colony in Ukraine, a "Garden of Eden" where the German settler, described as "the soldier-peasant," tilled the soil with a weapon at his side, ready to defend the farm from the "Asian hordes." As for the Ukrainians, Hitler remarked that the Germans would supply them "with scarves, glass beads and everything that colonial peoples like."[23]

Just over one month into the Operation Barbarossa campaign, when the German leadership assumed that victory was inevitable, Hitler spoke openly about his plans for the conquered territories. He had just completed a brief tour of Ukraine, including a stopover near Zhytomyr at Berdychiv on 6 August 1941, and was thrilled about Germany's new prospects there: "The German colonist ought to live on handsome, spacious farms. The German services will be lodged in marvelous buildings, the governors in palaces. . . . What India was for England the territories of Russia will be for us. If only I could make the German people understand what this space means for our future! Colonies are a precarious possession, but this ground is safely ours. Europe is not a geographic entity; it's a racial entity."[24] Hitler realized that the ordinary German did not share his appreciation for colonies and his vision of a Germanized Russia. Yet, as the "emperor" and self-proclaimed savior of the German people, Hitler forged ahead with his megalomaniac, criminal plans, bolstered by the expanding popular support that his charisma had drawn. The task of Hitler's generation, as he explained it, was to instill in the younger German settlers a feeling of pride in being invited to the East, where they will be expected "to build up something truly magnificent" and will find ample opportunities for promotion.

The following summer, Hitler returned to Ukraine and his imaginings of empire were rekindled. The Führer's personal architect and minister of armaments, Albert Speer, recalled an encounter with Hitler one late afternoon in August 1942. He found Hitler resting in the shade of tree outside his private hilltop bungalow at Vinnytsia. As they both looked out over the expansive sky and surrounding farmland, Hitler expounded on his imperialistic ambitions. In contrast to the British, Hitler argued, the Germans were not only exploiting

Adolf Hitler visits with German Red Cross nurses in Berdychiv, Ukraine, 6 August 1941
(Ullstein Bild #31686)

the conquered areas economically but also introducing new population policies by resettling the areas with Germanic types and suppressing the growth
of non-German populations.[25] At this time and on previous occasions, Hitler
spoke about the prestige that the ordinary Briton garnered from the empire.
He admired the British ability to rule their colonies with a thin layer of officials.
The economic prospects in Ukraine also excited Hitler, who was determined
to avoid famine on the home front in Germany by plundering all the produce,
grain, and livestock for the Reich. On other occasions he described Crimea as
the German Riviera and the proposed autobahns in Ukraine as the routes for
German tourists in their Volkswagens.

Hitler's vision of Ukraine as Germany's "New Indian Empire" was not ignored by his underlings as the delusion of a madman.[26] During his summer
1942 stay in Vinnytsia, Hitler read Ludwig Alsdorf's *Indien*, a history of British
rule in India, and urged that "every German going abroad be compelled to read"
it, especially every German diplomat.[27] One of the underlying concepts of Alsdorf's interpretation, which is worth pointing out, was his distinction between
two types of colonial possessions, later qualified by some as "negative" and
"positive" colonialism. Alsdorf described them simply as the economic type to
be totally exploited (*Ausbeutungskolonie*) and the settlement type for European

migration (*Siedlungskolonie*). India, Alsdorf argued, was the purest example of the Ausbeutungskolonie.[28] In Ukraine, a myriad of Nazi-controlled private and public agencies combined both types of colonialism.

What did Hitler find especially worthwhile in the Alsdorf text? In Hitler's view, Alsdorf correctly pointed out that "it was not the British who taught Indians evil ways; when the first white men landed in the country they found the walls surrounding many of the towns were constructed of human skulls." Likewise, Hitler continued, "it was not Cortez who brought cruelty to the Mexicans—it was there before he arrived. The Mexicans, indeed, indulged in extensive human sacrifice . . . as many as twenty thousand human beings at a time! In comparison, Cortez was a moderate man."[29] Thus, in Hitler's binary formulation, the European white colonizer was a "moderate" man without evil instincts and the Indian was his opposite, excessively cruel. According to his logic, Jews, Ukrainians, and other non-German natives in the East were inherently barbaric, and the history of Bolshevik-led crimes served as a threatening display of this potential.

Most likely, Hitler learned about Alsdorf's study from Alfred Rosenberg. Dr. Georg Leibbrandt, one of Rosenberg's deputies in the Reich Ministry for the Occupied Eastern Territories and an émigré scholar from Ukraine, coedited the book for a Nazi publication series in global history. As the senior official in the political policy department, Leibbrandt also represented the Rosenberg ministry at the Wannsee Conference.[30] In fact, prior to Hitler's promotion of the book, Rosenberg's political policy department endorsed the Alsdorf text as recommended reading for the regional functionaries (known as commissars) in Ukraine. Regional German leaders were also encouraged to read Kurt Freber's *Mit dem Rucksack nach Indien* (With My Backpack to India), Paul von Lettow-Vorbeck's *Um Vaterland und Kolonie* (For the Fatherland and Colony), H. Schulz-Kampfhenkel's *Im afrikanischen Dschungel als Tierfänger und Urwaldjäger* (In the African Jungle as Animal Collector and Primeval Forest Hunter), and Hermann Esser's *Die jüdische Weltpest* (The Jewish World Plague).[31]

Reich Leader of the SS and Police Heinrich Himmler also picked up on the India comparison. He exhorted his regional SS-police subordinates during a speech at his Hegewald compound in Zhytomyr to "learn not only from the theory but also the practice of how Englanders ruled in India." As Himmler stated more concretely than Hitler, a Germanic person could rule over a population of 100,000 natives because there were certainly 50,000 able-bodied workers among them. Plus there was stone, wood, straw, produce, and cattle there, out of which one could create a paradise.[32] Thus Hitler, Himmler, and Rosenberg tried to instill in their officials in the East a heightened sense of empire and German superiority that was suggestive of Britain's India.[33]

Nazi policies and practices in Ukraine took a course that veered dramatically from British rule in India.[34] As patronizing as Germans leaders were, they totally ruled out a "civilizing mission" of peoples they deemed racially inferior. They destroyed the local elites and depopulated the territory.[35] The Ukrainians and other Slavic "Untermenschen" who did not exhibit Germanic features provided a necessary labor force but were to fade away during the next few generations. Again Hitler set the tone, declaring that "we must keep the German colonies strictly separated from the local inhabitants." He argued against educating Ukrainians, providing them inoculations, and improving any life conditions that might foster non-German population growth.[36]

According to the racial hierarchy of Nazi ideology in which the Germans ranked supreme, Ukrainians fell under the Baltic peoples but above those slated for immediate destruction — the Jews, Gypsies, and other "Asiatics," followed by Poles and to a lesser extent the Great Russians and Belorussians. Some Ukrainians with "Aryan" characteristics could be Germanized, while others of purely Slavic origin could not. In Zhytomyr, the German police forces were trained to view the Ukrainians as a docile, peace-loving group who valued work, land, and family. As the police guidelines put it, the Ukrainians' nature stemmed from their "tranquil-tolerant blood elements."[37] Hitler put it more crudely: the Slavs, having no notion of "state," "duty," or even "cleanliness," were destined to be ruled. The Nazis' strident attachment to hierarchical racial taxonomies meant that once one was identified with a race, one's fate was largely sealed. Assimilation was unthinkable, and the ban on miscegenation, which had also been decreed a criminal offense in the Kaiser's colonies, was now fully enforced in Hitler's Lebensraum.

Though Hitler's immediate priorities differed from that of the Wilhelmine generation of imperialists and conservatives like General Franz Ritter von Epp who led the Reichskolonial Bund (Reich Colonial League), he did not totally marginalize this movement and its leaders.[38] Their experience in overseas economic exploitation was brought to bear in Ukraine. A good example of this transfer of experience and ideas is found in the Togo-Company, which pursued one of the more famous capitalistic cotton plantation systems in Africa during the pre–World War I era. It is worth noting that this "progressive" economic system developed from collaboration between the Kaiser's Colonial Economic Committee and Booker T. Washington's Tuskegee Institute. They transferred the racist ideas of "Negro labor" from the American South to the Africans in the

Togo. Remnants of this transfer resurfaced in 1942 and 1943 when the reconstituted Togo-Ost set up its headquarters for exploiting Ukrainian agriculture in Nazi-occupied Zhytomyr.[39] In a similar vein, Rosenberg established a Dutch Trading Company in Ukraine during 1943; the Dutch were not only supposed to help with the draining of swamps in Ukraine but also expected to lend their expertise as colonial economic developers. In another telling development in Poland, in September 1943 regional officials brought in German East Africans to serve as model farmers in the Warthegau. The Colonial School for Women in Rendsburg, Germany, continued until the Third Reich's final days, preparing girls and women for all " 'domestic and agricultural women's careers' with an eye to 'settlement purposes both at home and abroad.' " [40] Most likely, if the Germans had had more time to colonize Eastern Europe, they would have continued to apply European models of colonization, German migrationist history in Eastern Europe, and Wilhelmine imperial history to the making of their own "Aryan" Lebensraum.[41]

The Nazi invasion of the Soviet Union occurred at the same time of year that Napoleon's armies advanced into tsarist Russia 129 years earlier. On the eve of the 22 June 1941 invasion, Hitler could hardly avoid the Napoleon comparison, but he reassured his coterie of generals and his Romanian ally, Ion Antonescu, that the Nazi campaign would be different.[42] In addition to the technical superiority of the modern, motorized forces of the Wehrmacht, the Nazi fighting forces were equipped with a lethal total war ideology that understood the campaign as a Vernichtungskrieg against Judeo-Bolshevism. The retreat of the Red Army into the Russian hinterland would not suffice as a victory for Hitler. Red Army prisoners and matériel were to be annihilated. The Bolshevik threat was not to be given any chance of reemerging. The conquered areas were to be totally "cleansed" and reordered along racial lines. The Nazi pursuit of Lebensraum in the East was a multipronged campaign: a genocidal war against racial and political enemies and a colonization campaign of German migration, total economic exploitation, and subjugation of the "native" population and its culture. In places such as Zhytomyr one sees Nazi notions of progress, humanity, and utopia not as the glimmering landscape that Hitler envisioned but as the grisly reality of his violently racist, imperialistic ambitions.

In hindsight the Nazi colonial venture was short lived. However, Hitler and his subordinates did not develop and implement policies expecting to lose the war, let alone their hegemonic position in Europe. When they invaded Soviet Ukraine in late June 1941, they embarked on what they believed was the first phase of a twenty-year process of Germanization. The Nazi extension of power into the Eastern Territories went far beyond the structures of rule found in an imperial protectorate. Instead it was an aggregate of various far-reaching economic, political, and socio-demographic campaigns. The intent was to transform the land and its peoples more radically than any of Germany's imperialistic neighbors had attempted before in overseas colonies or in Europe itself. The Nazis arrogantly pursued a new racial concept of colonialism on European soil that turned out to be one of history's most destructive and lethal attempts at empire-building.

Chapter 2

Military Conquest and Social Upheaval, July–August 1941

The struggle for the hegemony of the world will be decided in favor of Europe by the possession of the Russian space. . . . The essential thing, for the moment, is to conquer. After that everything will be simply a question of organization.
—Adolf Hitler, 17–18 September 1941

When Nazi officials arrived in central Ukraine in the summer of 1941, they were shocked by the poverty. Sovietization had changed the rural landscape with the erection of machine tractor stations, large grain repositories, and livestock stables. However, many of the collective farmers and villagers still lived in subsistence-level conditions; their thatch-roofed cottages and simple wooden houses often lacked plumbing, electricity, and windows.[1] To the racist German conquerors, such "backwardness" only confirmed their view of the Slavs as inferior as well as fueled the Nazi colonizing mission of bringing order and progress to the region. One German intelligence official in Ukraine went so far as to claim that Stalinism provided the Germans with a convenient base from which they could build their own empire. The Ukrainians, he wrote, were accustomed to imperial rule and living in wartime-like conditions; therefore they would simply accommodate the Germans.[2]

Meanwhile, Zhytomyr's population viewed the arrival of the Nazis through their own distorted lens of recent history and prejudices about westerners. Few if any among the Ukrainians, Russians, Poles, Jews, and ethnic Germans could have imagined what lay ahead. They naively handed over demographic reports that sealed their own fate; they appeared in town centers and German headquarters looking for work assuming that the Germans would be fair rulers and would bring economic prosperity to the region. Many of these job seekers never returned home to their families. Within a matter of days and weeks of the occupation, the local population realized that the German occupiers of the First World War were not those of this Nazi-led war and that German "Kultur" and inhumanity were no longer mutually exclusive terms.

Among historians and laymen alike, the prevailing image of the Nazi military conquest of Ukraine has been of a blitzkrieg sweep eastward that afforded little time for the Wehrmacht to establish and implement policy in the civilian zones behind the battlefront. In the Zhytomyr region, however, the German army and Himmler's SS and police established an administration that remained the leading authority from early July until the arrival of the civil leadership in November 1941. It was during this critical period that the Nazis introduced their genocidal campaign against Jews, Soviet prisoners of war, and other so-called racial and political undesirables. The first months of Nazi rule have also been portrayed as a honeymoon period in German-Ukrainian relations. With the Soviet yoke lifted, Ukrainians were able to practice religion, and Ukrainian nationalists rallied support for their cause of independence. As for the ethnic Germans in the region, they suddenly found themselves within a new caste of Aryan elites. By contrast, the Jews quickly learned that there was no place for them in the New Order, and few could escape their horrible fate. The following chapter on the military administration of Zhytomyr examines how Nazi population policies and genocidal practices took shape in the chaos of the first months of occupation. It shows how regional German conquerors and inter-ethnic relations within the local population fueled the terror and destruction. After starting with the military conquest of Zhytomyr, the chapter explores the varied indigenous reactions to the new German rulers and the establishment of the military administration over the region.

The German Vernichtungskrieg in Ukraine

The leading German military and SS-policemen who first administered the region were armed with an arsenal of lethal ideas as well as modern weaponry. The Nazi Weltanschauung viewed the attack against the Soviet Union as a war of annihilation in the racial-political struggle against Judeo-Bolshevism. In early 1941, if not earlier, Hitler, Himmler, Heydrich, and Göring briefed leaders of the Armed Forces (OKW), SS-police, and Foreign Office about the impending mass murder that would accompany the anti-Soviet campaign in the East. They worked out a division of labor reflected in such documents as the Heydrich-Wagner agreement over the activities of the Einsatzgruppen in the military battle zones and rear areas. Military personnel were also expected to play their part in the campaign behind the lines. On 13 May 1941, Hitler decreed that the army should use all measures to destroy civilian threats or attacks. Army personnel would not be brought before the courts for actions against civilians in the East unless "these actions effected a loosening of discipline or of army security." The High Command instructed the troops to destroy on the spot the followers and relatives of any civilian who attacked the army in any way. If individual perpetrators could not be identified, then collective measures against entire villages were to be carried out. German soldiers who committed crimes against civilians and soldiers of the Soviet Union did not have to worry about possible legal prosecution, because the Hitler decree suspended courts-martial for such acts.[3]

A few weeks later, on 6 June, Hitler issued his more famous "Commissar Order": a demand for the swift execution of suspected political leaders found among Red Army prisoners. Although this written order appeared in June, Hitler held earlier conferences with the High Command during March when he spoke of commissars who were not to be viewed as soldiers and thus could be executed as criminals. There were some objections to the executions that Hitler desired. One source, Major Bechler, testified to the Russians later in the war that Hitler had wanted to order the immediate liquidation of not just the commissars but also all Russian officers and the intelligentsia, yet he settled, at least explicitly, for the commissars.[4]

The Commissar Order and a memorandum that appeared just days before the invasion, titled "Guidelines for the Conduct of Troops of Russia," represented one aspect of the Nazi leadership's campaign to enlist the military in the destruction of Soviet Jewry, which was promoted under the popular banner of anti-Bolshevism. Unlike previous instructions, the "Guidelines" to the troops explicitly linked the Jews as a racial group to a broader category of political enemies.[5]

The "Guidelines for the Conduct of Troops in Russia" described Bolshevism as the deadliest threat to the German people's existence, which justified the ruthless attacks against Bolshevik agitators, armed insurgents, saboteurs, and Jews and the total elimination of active or passive resistance.[6] The chief of General Staff distributed these "Guidelines" to the infantry and security divisions, including three security divisions (Security Divisions 444, 454, and 213) that were active in the military occupation of the Zhytomyr region between July and October 1941.[7] Thus leaders in the German military helped prepare for the invasion by drafting and distributing orders for the ruthless isolation or elimination of individuals broadly defined as Bolsheviks and resisters and more narrowly identified as Jews.

Two days before the attack, at a briefing on 20 June, leaders of the army security divisions assigned to Ukraine reviewed upcoming procedures for securing the conquered territory. They expected no unusual hostility from most of the civilian population of Ukrainians, whom they considered "German friendly,"[8] but they passed on the order to deal with armed insurgents and political commissars swiftly and brutally. At this point it was clear that individual officers and not military courts were empowered to decide the fate of perceived political and racial enemies. The army and SS-police leadership embraced the inevitable bloodshed of the war as the only means to the New World Order.

The German attack against the Soviet Union commenced in the early hours of Sunday, 22 June. Field Marshal Gerd von Rundstedt (1876–1953) commanded the invasion of Ukraine with Army Group South, consisting of the Sixth Army led by Field Marshal Walter von Reichenau (1884–1942), the Seventeenth Army led by Colonel General Karl-Heinrich von Stülpnagel (1886–1944), and the First Panzer Group led by Colonel General Ewald von Kleist (1881–1954). Hungarian, Slovakian, Italian, and Romanian troops joined the German forces and were also supported by Himmler's Waffen-SS divisions Adolf Hitler and SS-Viking. The first ground troops to reach the city of Zhytomyr on 9 July were from the First Panzer Group (XXXXVIII Army Corps); they were followed by Reichenau's Sixth Army, while south of Zhytomyr the Seventeenth Army captured Vinnytsia.[9]

The German army and its allies roared through the Ukrainian cities and villages of the region like the violent thunderstorms that army personnel reported at this time.[10] Foreboding clouds hung over Zhytomyr when the German bombs began to fall on the city. "We were running to the train station," one survivor recalled. "Everyone was trying to leave by train but the Germans were bombing the station and railway cars, bodies lay among the rubble, children cried out for their mothers."[11] In Mohyliv-Podil's'kyi people quickly gathered their belongings while the loudspeaker announced that the last train of evacuees was departing. With the railways bombed and no cars, horses, or bicycles in sight, many trudged on foot eastward. Eventually they confronted the Germans, who had overtaken them and who then forced them to turn back.[12]

North of Vinnytsia, at Khmil'nyk, evacuees from western Ukraine arrived in early July. The local population became increasingly fearful of a German attack and rushed to the "raispolkom" (the executive committee of the district soviet) with the hope of learning some evacuation procedure, but the committee refused to release them from work and denied them transportation to flee. Some Jewish residents who approached the local soviet leaders were told, "You've got nothing to fear; you're not Party members."[13] Soviet leaders announced that L'viv had been retaken by the Red Army in a desperate attempt to control the panicked population, while they and other elite Party members secretly packed their bags and arranged for transport East. Meanwhile, Stalin ordered the destruction of industries and agricultural equipment that the Germans would exploit.[14] Even in the smaller towns around the region Stalin's henchmen managed to destroy hundreds of homes and brutally murdered prisoners deemed potential Nazi collaborators.[15]

In the Zhytomyr region, Soviet military defenses were scattered in pockets near Berdychiv, Korosten', and Vinnytsia. On 7 July 1941, German parachute brigades landed in the town of Liubar near Berdychiv, where they faced Soviet infantrymen.[16] The German Luftwaffe first raided the city of Zhytomyr as early as 9 July 1941. Meanwhile, the Sixteenth Motorized Infantry Division reported from Chudniv (about forty kilometers southwest of the city) that they had captured 2,000 Soviet prisoners and deserters.[17] The First Panzer Group broke through what was left of the Stalin Line near Novohrad-Volyns'kyi (about fifty kilometers northwest of Zhytomyr) and took Novohrad-Volyns'kyi on the ninth and Berdychiv on the thirteenth.[18] Along the way, two heavy artillery battalions (the Eighty-sixth and Fifty-sixth) reported to the First Panzer Group that political commissars and commanders had been shot and there were cases of suicide among commissars.[19]

In addition to bombs, Germans propaganda leaflets fell from the sky and littered the fields and roadways. One popular appeal stated that the holder of the leaflet was guaranteed a friendly reception by the German army and that the real enemy of the Germans was the Jews, the so-called bearers of Bolshevism. In the Zhytomyr region Red Army deserters approached the Germans with this leaflet, asking for more "passes" for their comrades. According to German intelligence reports, the anti-Semitic content of the leaflet was especially "effective."[20] Trusting that the leaflet was a ticket to safety, local women and children collected and distributed them to Red Army deserters.[21]

On the march into the Zhytomyr region, the First Panzer Army reported that thousands of Red Army soldiers surrendered; on 11 July alone the Germans captured 18,779 prisoners. In the battle for Berdychiv (8–12 July) more than 5,260 Red Army prisoners were taken, and another 1,500 surrendered after the city was taken. More than half of these men carried the German propaganda leaflet.[22] The XXXXVIII Army Corps in Liubar encountered about 7,000 POWs, many of whom requested "more leaflets so we have something in our hands."[23]

German intelligence interrogators learned from the POWs that after the commissars fled from their units, Soviet officers distributed the leaflets. Many of the POWs were streaming in from Kiev, over 100 miles west of the front line. These deserters complained of poor rations and training in the Soviet army. They apparently believed in a German victory, not a Soviet one.[24] In the German battles for Zhytomyr, Vinnytsia, and Berdychiv, more than 72,000 Red Army soldiers surrendered.[25]

German flyer offering "passes" for Red Army deserters. The text at the top reads: "Beat the Jew-Commissar, his mug asks for a brick! Your struggle is useless! Your situation is hopeless." The text at the lower left reads: "How can it be permissible that your leadership out of stubbornness is mercilessly driving you to inescapable death? GO OVER TO THE GERMANS! HURRY!" The text in the box, which is headed "Permit," reads: "Bearer of this wishes no senseless bloodbath in the interest of the Jews and Commissars. He abandons the defeated Red Army and goes over to the side of the German Wehrmacht. The German officers and soldiers will treat the deserters well, taking care of them and protecting them. The permit is valid for an unlimited number of officers and soldiers of the Red Army who come over to the German Wehrmacht." Russian text translated by Vadim Altskan. (Anti-Jewish Nazi and Collaborationist Leaflets and Announcements Made and Posted during the Nazi Occupation of Ukraine, 1941–1943, RG 31.023, U.S. Holocaust Memorial Museum, courtesy of the Judaica Institute, Kiev)

By 12 July General Kleist's First Panzer Group had converged on the city of Zhytomyr. While the Red Army had defended Berdychiv, it abandoned Zhytomyr with the priority of establishing a strong defense of Kiev.[26] Air reconnaissance reports described the main roads around the city as deserted. Already on 9 July, German tanks of the First Panzer Group had rolled triumphantly into Zhytomyr's main square and fired artillery down Chudnivs'ka, a main boulevard radiating from the center to the outskirts of the city. Among the columns of tanks that entered Zhytomyr were two vehicles of a special security police unit, Sonderkommando 4a (SK4a, a detachment of Einsatzgruppe C). The Wehrmacht and SS-police arrived in the city together and initiated a reign of terror that would last two and a half years.[27]

Initial Responses to the Nazi Invaders

Although brief, the power vacuum during the summer of 1941 when the Soviets had retreated and the Germans began to establish their rule over Zhytomyr offers an unusual aperture into the social and political history of the region, as well as a dramatic view of the upheaval of war. Amid the chaos, Ukrainian nationalist leaders from the region and elsewhere tried to further their political goal of Ukrainian independence. Many others vied for positions under the Germans with more diverse motives. At the same time, the population reacted and behaved in certain ways that give one a vivid picture of the state of Ukrainian society in the wake of 1930s Stalinism. This "snapshot" offers a basis on which to chart the transformation of Zhytomyr during the Nazi occupation.

The composition of Zhytomyr's population when the Germans arrived consisted primarily of the elderly and female agricultural workers who headed households of children. It was not atypical that women dominated the home front during wartime; however, this demographic situation was also the result of Stalin's policies in the 1930s when many young men went by force or voluntarily to the distant industrial "boomtowns" in eastern Ukraine or were deported or killed during the Communist Party purges. Then in the spring and summer of 1941 several million men from central and eastern Ukraine were drafted into the Red Army or evacuated with it.[28]

The remaining middle-aged men were mainly those unfit for military service and those in lower-level positions and jobs, such as building caretakers and tractor drivers; in addition, a small but significant number of men deliberately stayed behind the lines to work covertly as Soviet intelligence operatives. After the Germans released Ukrainian POWs, the male population expanded and included more skilled and educated workers such as agronomists, land surveyors, and machinists.[29] In addition to the imbalance of men and women, the major changes of the revolutionary period created wide generational gaps; a clear social divide existed between the older generations who identified with the days of the tsar and the younger ones who were tied to the Soviet experiment. Ukrainian men and women who came of age in the 1930s had more schooling and urban-related skills than previous generations, but, like their ancestors, they retained a provincial outlook.[30]

The vast farmland was marked off by dirt roads and strips of houses, which were mostly rough wooden constructions, whitewashed stone blocks, or older huts with thatched roofs. A railway system connected the region's major towns and cities with major hubs in Zhytomyr and Koziatyn, but not far from these centers farmers continued to make their way to the fields and between villages by foot, bicycle, and horse-drawn carriage. The Germans quickly discovered how terrible the roads were as their tanks and trucks got bogged down in the mud during the summer thunderstorms. Except for some telephone and radio communications in the larger towns, the primary means of spreading and exchanging information remained newspapers, public announcements, village and collective farm assemblies, and rumor.

When Nazi forces first penetrated the region during the summer and fall of 1941, with their Luftwaffe bombers, columns of motorized divisions, and streams of soldiers, Ukrainian farmers viewed these "invaders" with awe and uncertainty. Some Ukrainians perceived the Germans literally as a "godsend."[31] Many who hoped for land reform and a better life approached the Germans with friendly offerings of bread and salt.[32] The Germans also effectively exploited the anti-Bolshevik basis of their crusade by presenting themselves as the "liberators." Ukrainians in Zhytomyr believed that the defeat of Stalin's forces would bring their suffering to an end.[33] To a Ukrainian who had survived a decade of famine and terror under Stalin and just witnessed the devastation caused by Stalin's "scorched earth" retreat, it seemed that things could not possibly get worse.[34]

In fact for Ukrainians there was reason to believe that German rule might bring more freedom and prosperity. In the first days of the war, Wehrmacht propaganda units also dropped leaflets and put up posters that were aimed at the civilian population. One that fell in the region was titled "A Call to the Ukrainian People." In it the Germans declared that the Ukrainians were liberated from the tyranny of Jewish-Bolshevik elements.[35] They encouraged Ukrainians to express their religiosity, which German leaders believed would foster peace and order, by announcing: "The time of atheism is gone. The German authorities give you the opportunity to pray in freedom again."[36] Pious Ukrainians rejoiced. Even before rebuilding their wrecked homes, Ukrainian peasants traveled to the nearest churches and began to restore them. Priests who had been working in different occupations under the Soviets came out of hiding. With icons and Bibles in hand, they went to German headquarters requesting permission to reestablish local parishes. In and around the town of Zhytomyr, 106 clergymen refurbished the churches and opened six in the city itself and fifty-four in the surrounding districts. Ukrainians flocked to the churches and local cemeteries and participated in baptismal, funeral, and prayer services. In Korosten' a priest baptized dozens of youngsters and adults in the Uzh River.

Such religious services occurred a few days after the Germans had arrived, and some even just before the Germans arrived.[37]

In 1941 (and indeed throughout the Nazi occupation), religious ceremonies became a political tool of anti-Semites and nationalist activists. For example, in August 1941, the Ukrainian Orthodox bishop Polikarp (Sikorsky) from Zhytomyr, who was an outspoken anti-Semite, traveled to Luts'k for the burial ceremony of over 3,000 victims of an NKVD massacre. The ceremony gave the German military and SS-police a chance to foment anti-Jewish sentiment and local support for pogroms. The Jews were presented as NKVD killers of Ukrainians. Ukrainian nationalists also tried to channel the high emotions of such burial services to swell the ranks of their own movement.[38]

Ukrainian Nationalist Activists
Pokhidni Grupy and the Wehrmacht

In the first weeks and months of their rule, the Germans gave Ukrainians the false impression that the Ukrainian nationalist movement would be tolerated. Ukrainian nationalists of both leading factions established ties and even trained with Wehrmacht and SS intelligence personnel in preparation for Operation Barbarossa.[39] Such German-Ukrainian cooperation signaled to the Organization of Ukrainian Nationalists (OUN) that their goal of independence might be condoned, if not supported. While the OUN leaders organized their own expeditionary forces (pokhidni grupy), German military and police leaders assumed that this relatively small and internally divided nationalist movement could be easily controlled.

The two factions of the movement, one led by Stepan Bandera and the other by Andrii Mel'nyk, formed task forces, each of no more than ten men and women, which spread out across the Zhytomyr region in the summer of 1941. They operated in the Wehrmacht's rear areas, mostly in rural villages where most Ukrainians lived, not the cities where the German forces were headquartered. Each task force leader oversaw about twenty to thirty villages.[40] They usually moved from place to place at night by foot, occasionally by bicycle, and rarely by car or motorcycle.[41] Many secured German army identifications at first officially and later illegally from a secret printing shop they established in the city of Zhytomyr.[42]

Typically, one of the nationalists who arrived at his post in the region began his work by seeking out sympathizers; many had already been identified through the underground as former Petliurists (supporters of Symon Petliura's Ukrainian National Republic and Army, 1918–21). Myroslav Prokop, one of the

more prominent OUN-B leaders who later became the editor of the underground Banderite paper, *Ideia i Chyn* (Idea and Action), arrived in the Koziatyn
district in the summer of 1941. After the war he recalled how he approached
Ukrainians there and elsewhere:

> In my trip from L'viv to Kiev I stopped in villages in the Zhytomyr region;
> I avoided the cities where the Germans were concentrated. I stayed with a
> contact man in the village, a local supporter who was usually a leader of cul-
> tural activities in the village and the most educated. I would clear my identity
> by addressing my contact first as my "Druh" (friend, not comrade) and then
> state that I had arrived from such and such a place from the West. [If I had
> no predetermined contact] I usually approached the younger ones who were
> easier to co-opt by asking a broad question like, what do you think of the
> treatment of the Ukrainians by the Soviets or Germans. If he did not respond
> sympathetically then I would disappear into the night. We used pseudonyms
> for personal and village names. In our written communications we wrote
> on thin cigarette paper; it could be eaten if we were captured; we relied on
> locals and the underground to obtain food and supplies.[43]

The OUN-B activists who penetrated Zhytomyr's countryside with the Wehrmacht brought with them a bold plan to reorganize all aspects of village life, beginning with the formation of youth groups (Sich), military training sessions,
reading clubs, church programs, drama troupes, music groups, new schools,
and the like. Their main goals were (1) to set up an OUN administration overseeing all aspects of Ukrainian life; (2) to incite rebellion against the Germans
and Soviets with the goal of creating a Ukrainian State made up exclusively
of Ukrainians, and (3) to build a Ukrainian Revolutionary Army.[44] The activists distributed the "Act of Proclamation of the Ukrainian State," a declaration
that had been made public at L'viv on 30 June 1941.[45] They read aloud from
their pocket-sized history of Ukraine, titled *Istoria Ukrainy* (*The Little History of
Ukraine*), and formed choirs that sang the anthem "Ukraine Is Not Dead Yet."[46]

Bandera's representatives compiled their own surveys of the villages, carefully listing the ethnic groups, religious affiliations, ages, occupations, names
of former Petliurists, and suspected communist enemies. They also wrote about
Zhytomyr's cities and towns, describing the breakdown of authority, looting,
and alcoholism—a mixture of chaos, crime, and despair. One nationalist (in the
Cherniakhiv district), code-named "Kornienko," revealed that the commander
of the local militia, a former officer in the Petliura army, was constantly drunk.
As Kornienko put it, "If he is not drinking vodka then he is drinking cologne
water so he has no authority over the militia."[47] The commander allowed the

plundering of Jewish homes, and the city militia of twenty-five men was bully-
ing the locals and trying to control all of the Jewish property. Although the
local Ukrainian administration requested that the items be handed over to
the German authorities, the Ukrainian police refused to cooperate and even
bragged about their new booty.[48]

Kornienko and other Bandera agents described the dire economic situation
in Ukraine's villages. In Kornienko's territory, the retreating Soviets had destroyed the local porcelain factory, where 2,000 workers had been employed.
Many of the unemployed went to the collective farms, where they worked the
fields in the hope of securing food.[49] From the village code-named "Milka,"
another nationalist reported that during August 1941 he and twenty-two other
activists set out to organize a number of villages around Zhytomyr, covering
a total population of 21,222 Ukrainians, 2,649 ethnic Germans, 132 Russians,
7 Jews, and 9 "others." The population did not have enough to eat. Instead of
potatoes and bread, the locals survived almost entirely on milk. This OUN-B
leader, code-named "RR," wrote with regret that the local people required significant help and encouragement; when they were not given the means to help
themselves, then they "retreat[ed] like mice into holes."

The Ukrainian nationalist campaign to educate and improve conditions for
Ukrainians clashed with the German program to privilege local ethnic Germans. By placing the local Volksdeutsche into positions of mayors, village
elders, collective farm leaders, shopkeepers, militia chiefs, and school direc-
tors, the Nazis obstructed the Ukrainian nationalist quest for control over the
region.[50] Equally frustrating for the Ukrainian leaders, the ethnic Germans,
who were one of the most oppressed minorities in the region, were by and large
the least qualified for such leadership posts.

Initial Nazi Support of the Volksdeutsche

During the planning stages of Operation Barbarossa, Himmler established
special task forces to rescue the Volksdeutsche in Russia (Sonderkommando
Russland), which were led by SS Brigadier General Horst Hoffmeyer.[51] Hoffmeyer's commandos followed on the heels of the advancing Wehrmacht, and,
with the help of the Sipo-SD, they began to register the Volksdeutsche coming
under Nazi control.[52] Hoffmeyer's first destination in the East was the city
of Zhytomyr, where Nazi population planners hoped to find Volhynian Germans.[53]

Before Hoffmeyer's staff arrived in Zhytomyr in early September 1941, a
subunit of Einsatzgruppe C (Sonderkommando 4a) began to register the eth-

nic Germans there. Members of this secret police unit also reported the first news about the state of the Volksdeutsche who had survived Stalin's terror. They found that the ethnic German population, which was scattered across the region, was generally "friendly but reserved" and could not grasp what the "sudden political change meant for them." The Soviets had deported 150 ethnic Germans from the city shortly before the Germans arrived,[54] and a much smaller number were deported from the region's other centers, such as Berdychiv. The rest of the ethnic German population had escaped Stalin's August decree that all ethnic Germans be evacuated with the Red Army. (By the time this decree was issued, the Wehrmacht had been in Zhytomyr for well over one month.)[55] During the fighting, however, some ethnic Germans were killed by NKVD and Red Army soldiers. According to German reports, in Novohrad-Volyns'kyi, home to about 7,500 Volksdeutsche, the NKVD demanded that they come out of hiding during the two-day battle with the Wehrmacht; those who appeared were shot.[56] Before the Soviets left Berdychiv in early July 1941, they aggressively searched for and murdered the remaining Volksdeutsche. Caught in this killing spree, Volksdeutsche women and children tried to hide in stables and dugout holes, and they sought refuge with Ukrainians.[57] Staff of Himmler's Sonderkommando 4a registered the Volksdeutsche according to the German People's List (DVL) and then offered them hot meals from the field kitchens. Although 40 percent of the ethnic Germans in the region were day laborers who lacked skills, regional German commanders began to place them in leading administrative positions, much to the ire of the rest of the population of non-Germans.[58]

The few ethnic Germans qualified to work in the German administration were passed from one Reich agency to the next, and placed in a number of influential positions. For example, the German field commander in Vinnytsia employed a Volksdeutsche baker named Theodor Kitzmann in his office; then Kitzmann worked for the SS and police, and he finally moved up in the commissariat administration to be a district leader. As the highest-ranking district leader in the native administration, Kitzmann supervised forty villages with about 30,000 inhabitants. The new mayor of Berdychiv was a Russian German named Reder. A leading adviser on the staff of Sonderkommando 4a was the neurologist Arthur Boss, an ethnic German originally from Odessa but residing in Zhytomyr.[59] Many more Volksdeutsche proved immediately useful by filling the military administration's lower ranks of police auxiliaries and translators, especially in the rural outposts across the region. They communicated Nazi orders to the local population. Many helped identify local Jews and also participated in anti-Jewish massacres.[60]

Yet Ukrainians still greatly outnumbered the ethnic Germans employed in local administrative offices. Many Reich officials simply favored the Ukrainian collaborators since they were considered more diligent and reliable than the Volksdeutsche.[61] In the setting of a regional German office, where a handful of administrators were charged with seemingly insurmountable demands from their superiors and had limited resources, ad hoc measures and short-cut solutions were the order of the day. In other words, local officials did not immediately grant ethnic Germans privileged positions because most of their "racial brethren" were simply not qualified. Consequently, Nazi leaders had to convince German officials across Reich agencies that the ethnic Germans were not to be shunned or undervalued, but rather embraced as the quintessential German victims of "Judeo-Bolshevism."

Ukrainian nationalist activists, civil servants, and collective farm leaders perceived the ethnic Germans to be a nuisance and a threat. Yet they vehemently believed that the other ethnic minority in the region, the Poles, posed an even greater danger because historically they had dominated the region and in more recent times had persecuted Ukrainians and Ukrainian nationalists in the interwar Polish republic.[62] One Bandera activist wrote that where his supporters had dug a hole to place a cross, the Poles—who in his words organized themselves "like the devil"—placed their cross there instead.[63] He "had a serious word with them," but he then found a better place to erect the Ukrainian Orthodox cross. When the first groups of pious Ukrainians gathered in Zhytomyr and approached the German army priest about resuming church services, they discovered he was a Roman Catholic. Many of these locals were prepared to convert to Catholicism, but when they realized that the Catholic services would be taken over by the Polish population of Zhytomyr, they stopped attending the services. In fact, in the summer of 1941, Ukrainians in Zhytomyr openly expressed more anti-Polish and anti-Russian sentiment than anti-Jewish or anti-German feelings.[64]

Interethnic tensions surfaced amid the uncertainty and carnage of the Nazi invasion. To a large degree these rivalries were the product of Stalin's contradictory approach of supporting local cultures while unleashing a violent sovietization of society. Most in the region who greeted the Germans in the summer of 1941 welcomed the defeat of Stalinism and hoped their material conditions would improve. As soon became evident, the Nazi notion of "liberation" was not what Zhytomyr's population expected. The haphazard, seemingly sympathetic approach of regional German commanders who tolerated religious and nationalist activities was eclipsed by the more common German method of rule: systematic intimidation and mass violence. When the Wehrmacht city commander, Colonel Josef Riedl, arrived in Zhytomyr, he immediately ordered that everyone be registered by street and district.[65] Within days German military and police administrators had lists at their disposal showing who was Ukrainian, Polish, Russian, ethnic German, or Jewish and where each lived. In Berdychiv, the Wehrmacht plastered posters on buildings in Ukrainian, Russian, and German stating that anyone found on the street between 8:00 P.M. and 6:00 A.M. would be shot without warning, and that "for every assaulted German soldier, 20 male civilians will be shot."[66] All livestock and farm equipment were also registered and taxed; no one was allowed to travel beyond his or her village without permission; trade and commerce could not continue without German approval; and anyone who plundered or inhabited an abandoned dwelling faced the death penalty. Local military commanders demanded that all firearms be turned over to the mayor or village elder within twenty-four hours. If weapons were found near a village, then that village was held responsible and subjected to mass arrests and executions. Ukrainians were prohibited from public transport and certain shops; and food rations were only available to workers and their families.[67] German soldiers grabbed livestock and wheat; some took a household's one and only cow or pig.[68] One of the first German notices to appear in the local paper was a call for the formation of a Ukrainian militia of no more than "100 men armed with clubs and knives."[69] The plan was to create a force of Ukrainian guards with a ratio of one guard per ten households and to enlist the local population in the most urgent of Nazi policies: "security" measures.[70] Such German orders and decrees, which appeared in Ukrainian and Russian and were often signed by local Ukrainian and ethnic German collaborators, were not empty threats issued with the sole purpose of frightening the local population into submission. Their enforcement by the military, SS leaders, and local collaborators was far reaching.

Between July and October 1941, the period of military occupation of the region, tens of thousands of Soviet prisoners of war and civilians (mainly Jews) were executed by army and SS-police forces. The genocide began under the cover of war and in the "euphoria of victory." German occupiers established an administrative division of labor for these programs at a remarkable pace, driven by an extreme concern for order and coordinated action, as well as a desire to put the "unpleasant" but necessary work of the regime behind them. The speed and scope of the action paralyzed the victims, who suddenly realized the sinister intent of the self-proclaimed Nazi "liberators."

Chapter 3

The Wehrmacht Administration of Zhytomyr

Food is given out in the evening. . . . Instead of leading us into the kitchen, they [the camp guards] shout, "To the canteens! Run!" The [guards] appear and start up . . . a line using sticks, rods, rubber truncheons—anything they can beat you with. The usual results are head injuries, nearly broken arms, or the murder of an emaciated and weak prisoner. The beatings go on for hours.

—Motel'e, Soviet prisoner of war, Zhytomyr, fall of 1941

During the first months of the German occupation of Zhytomyr, an administrative structure emerged across the region's towns and villages, a structure that in its basic hierarchical form and ideological content remained consistent until the Nazis were finally pushed out of the region in 1944. Its defining features, which will be explored in this chapter, were numerous indigenous collaborators, an emphasis on security measures, economic exploitation, and systematic mass violence or "punitive" measures against civilians. In both the military and civilian administration of the region, Himmler's SS-police forces played a central role and in some instances a dominant one.

The military occupation structure consisted of two distinct administrative areas. The battle zones and their immediate rear areas were controlled by regional army staffs, such as the Sixth Army and its Rear Army offices. In the vast areas west of these zones, the Germans established a much larger temporary administration headed by the commander of the Rear Army Group Area South, General Karl von Roques, whose power extended over the Zhytomyr region as of 16 July 1941. The regional hierarchy under Roques consisted of a Security Division staff and their subordinates posted at field commands (Feldkommandanturen), city commands (Stadtkommandanturen), and town commands (Ortskommandanturen).[1] To secure the remote rural areas behind the lines, the German commandants relied on indigenous collaborators, who were assigned to the positions of raion leader, mayor, and village elder.[2]

At first the German military and SS-police concentrated its manpower in the most populated areas, along main transportation routes and in selected towns where supplies and foodstuffs were readily available, as in Radomyshl', where a large dairy, slaughterhouse, and brewery still operated.[3] German uniforms were most visible in the cities of Zhytomyr, Vinnytsia, and Berdychiv, where the Sixth Army and Seventeenth Army held their temporary headquarters in July and August. Heinrich Himmler's deputy, Higher SS and Police Leader for Russia South (Ukraine) Friedrich Jeckeln, and Heydrich's Einsatzgruppe C, led by Dr. Otto Rasch, also set up headquarters in the region at Berdychiv and Zhytomyr respectively. While the Wehrmacht established its strategic command posts in the rear areas, the SS-police officials remapped the cities and major towns into police districts. The town of Zhytomyr had four police districts, each one with a police station where three to five (Ukrainian) guards and their German superiors worked. SS-police units as well as agents of Göring's Four-Year Plan supported the army's effort to secure the newly conquered areas and to extract as many economic resources as possible for the troops. Additional construction and technical units also arrived in the rear areas to assist with these operations and to repair damaged bridges, roads, and other necessary facilities.

The Feldkommandantur German Rule in the Towns

In Vinnytsia, Senior Field Commander Markull established the military's occupation administration during August and September 1941. Since at this time there were so few Germans to staff the administration, Markull retained most offices within the Soviet oblast's administrative structure while appointing new ethnic German and Ukrainian leaders and some Russian experts to manage the offices and implement German orders. Among his appointees was the new mayor of Vinnytsia, Professor Aleksandr Sevast'ianov, the former director of the city's medical institute who was of Russian-Ukrainian descent. Markull was impressed with his education and languages skills: Sevast'ianov had studied medicine in Germany and spoke German well.[4] The mayor's deputy was the ethnic German Kezar Bernard. The Germans selected their aides using diverse and ad hoc criteria, which only complicated the enormous task that everyone in Vinnytsia faced: rebuilding a war-ravaged city whose basic infrastructure lay in ruins.

From the start, relations between the Germans and their appointees were tense. German officers complained that the Ukrainians were poor leaders and incapable organizers. They contended that while the Ukrainian police auxiliaries (members of the Ordnungsdienst) were very useful, they were not reliable, and often "unruly." The Ukrainian police or those posing as the police

German road signs in the center of Zhytomyr, summer of 1941 (Ullstein Bild #00438222)

often engaged in plundering. Corruption (black marketeering) among the Germans and their Ukrainian aides was rampant. Field Commander Markull warned that Ukrainian militia were not to be used for private errands; their main tasks were, instead, to supervise the Jews, patrol the streets and market-places, and guard military storehouses and camps.[5]

The army's reliance on Ukrainian leaders from western Ukraine also strained relations. In Vinnytsia the chief of the Ukrainian staff was a lawyer named Luts'kyi who arrived with the Wehrmacht from western Ukraine. Likewise, the Germans appointed as chief of the regional Ukrainian administration an émi-gré named Kucharovs'kyi who was originally from the Vinnytsia (Lityn) area and returned with the German army. The army and SS-police exploited the émi-gré leaders from western Ukraine to help in the purging of the old adminis-tration and the securing of a new one. They had no intention of fulfilling the émigrés' dream of an independent Ukrainian state. Consequently, during the transfer from military to civilian administration most Ukrainian nationalists were arrested, interrogated, and incarcerated. Very few were able to conceal their nationalist sympathies and remain in the German administration beyond the spring of 1942.[6]

Yet in the first months of military rule over the region, the Germans tolerated and indeed depended on the émigrés in the administration. German and Ukrainian leaders discussed how to resume electrical and water service and reopen about fifty produce markets in all parts of the city. They created a fire department and a city transport service for the army. The daily food supply situation was dire, though due to the successful pressure tactics of the army's agricultural leaders and requisition units, daily bread rations for non-Germans were raised to 400 grams per person (less than one pound). The field commander's office assigned local civilians to clean up the rubble at the train station and the city's large sugar factory. By the end of August 1941, the post office, telegraph office, and main bank were functioning again, but the streetcar and railway systems were not in operation.[7]

According to Nazi racial theories and colonial aims, the ethnic Germans were supposed to take on leading positions in the New Order. But this policy had not been clearly spelled out in the military preparations and guidelines for administering the newly conquered territories. In mid-July 1941 Roques, the commander of the Army Group South Rear Area Administration, presented his own plan for the Volksdeutsche. He ordered that ethnic German POWs not be released from the camps since they had not taken up the offer in the past year to resettle in Germany and, therefore, were deemed racially worthless.[8] But Roques's approach did not go over well. He had to rescind this order a month later when he was instructed by the Army High Command to release certain groups of POWs, first and foremost reliable ethnic Germans. Meanwhile, in a special report to Roques, Karl Stumpp (who was attached to an army intelligence unit) stressed the usefulness of ethnic Germans in the administration as informers and translators. Apparently swayed by Stumpp's argument, Roques ordered all army offices to support the "needy" ethnic Germans by placing them in administrative positions and by establishing community credit and loan programs. Subsequently, the army published an October 1941 order in the local newspaper, *Holos Volyni*, requiring that all ethnic Germans report to the labor office for work at military bases.[9]

When the rear area commanders and their collaborators confronted problems that inevitably arose, such as food and housing shortages, they assumed that the "disposable" racial or political sectors of the population were to be exploited as part of the solution. They assigned trash collection and street cleaning to the Jews and collected a "contribution" from the Jewish community since, Nazi leaders claimed, the Jews had plundered many wares in order to barter with the farmers for agricultural goods. In fact, Markull and his associates turned a blind eye to the welfare of the entire Jewish population by relegating the complete care, feeding, and health of Vinnytsia's Jewish population to the newly formed Jewish Council (the Sipo-SD massacred the first Jewish council in early August). The mentally ill and physically disabled in Vinnytsia did not receive rations or proper care. Some died of famine-related illnesses and others were killed in mass shootings and by lethal injections.[10]

The Ortskommandanturen German Rule in the Countryside

The tentacles of the German administration stretched out to the region's smaller towns where German military commanders established twenty-five rural command posts (Ortskommandanturen). Like their counterparts in the more populated areas, the army commanders in the villages concentrated on three areas of administrative priority: security interests, economic measures, and local administration. To start with, the village commanders notified the population that they must surrender all weapons immediately; anyone found hiding arms was treated as an insurgent—that is, killed. Then, with the help of local Ukrainians and ethnic Germans, the Wehrmacht's village commanders conducted the registration of the population, "especially the Jews," who were forced to wear armbands. Economic-related duties were limited to two priorities: the securing and guarding of valuable resources, and the reporting of the status of these resources to the nearest field commander and the economic inspectors' outposts.[11]

The German village commanders and security forces ventured out on patrols and raids to the smaller towns on a fairly regular basis, but they lacked the manpower to actually implement orders in the villages. Thus in these first weeks and months of military rule over the region, the army commanders constructed an administrative hierarchy of Ukrainian and ethnic German raion leaders, village elders, and militiamen.

The German field commander from Vinnytsia, Markull, became directly involved in the search and appointment of Ukrainian district leaders. From 2 to 6 August, Markull traveled by car and horse-drawn cart southwest over Zhmerynka to Bar, Kopaihorod, Kurylivtsi, Murovani, Ivanivka, Mohyliv-Podil's'kyi, Iampil, Chernivtsi, Sharhorod, and Stanislavchik to find "suitable" Ukrainian district leaders.[12] In his travels over partially paved roads and through open fields, he came across very few Reich Germans, except for the Wehrmacht commanders posted at Bar, Zhmerynka, and Mohyliv.[13] When Markull arrived in a town, he was greeted by the Ukrainian mayor and leading intelligentsia (doctors, agriculturalists, engineers, and the like). After a three- to four-hour discussion with these local representatives, Markull selected a district leader (*Rayonchef*) and presented him with his special identification papers in German and Ukrainian. He told the leader that he would be held fully accountable for the implementation of German orders. He was not permitted to carry a gun, but only a club, knife, or pointed weapon. His name would be publicly posted as the authority approved by the Germans.[14] The new leader's contract with the Germans was sealed with a handshake. Markull appointed twenty-five district chiefs around the city of Vinnytsia. Across the entire Zhytomyr region, the Germans posted about seventy-five Ukrainian (and some ethnic German) district leaders.

One of the first administrative requirements of the local leaders was to gather extensive information about the ethnic and political composition of the population, in particular providing the locations of Jews, Roma, POWs, and other targeted groups.[15] In Vasilevichi (where Red Army deserters were presumed to be hiding) Ukrainian district chiefs were also asked to submit reports about any persons who had not been residents of their respective areas before the war; they were to be identified under four categories: (1) families with children; (2) POWs with proper release papers; (3) POWs without papers; and (4) stragglers without a fixed place of residence who took up local residency during the invasion. Such reports included detailed lists of the populations, ethnic groups, and their whereabouts. The lists were based on prewar Soviet nationalities surveys. Thus Soviet records were used to implement Nazi policies, including the Holocaust.[16]

Indigenous Collaborators in the Wehrmacht Administration Auxiliary Police

In carrying out their tasks, the local administrators were allowed to employ very few assistants besides the militia. One of the first acts of the local elders and mayors was to form a Ukrainian "Order Service," or militia. The elders and mayors submitted lists of Ukrainian police candidates to the Germans for approval.[17] The size of the militia groups usually did not exceed fifteen men; militia members were on average twenty-five years old. By contrast, in the region's centers, such as Vinnytsia, hundreds of auxiliaries serviced the more numerous Reich officials and their offices as well as enforced German orders on the entire population. Markull relied on seventy Ukrainian Order Service men. In both the towns and the villages, the auxiliary police did not wear full uniforms; usually just an armband marked their official status. They carried clubs; in 1941 very few if any were trusted with guns.[18]

The Wehrmacht and SS-police also recruited policemen from among the prisoners of war. These former Red Army soldiers had much to offer. They were young, able-bodied men with some military training, and given the deteriorating, desperate conditions in the POW camps, they could hardly refuse the German bid to join the security and police forces. A minority of these recruits became the worst and most notorious of the indigenous SS-helpers, the Trawniki guards and the "Askaris" (who would later help the Germans destroy the Warsaw Ghetto).[19]

Before the invasion and in the summer of 1941, Heinrich Himmler (whom Hitler charged with all security and police matters in the newly occupied territories) worked out an elaborate plan for utilizing Ukrainian, Lithuanian, Latvian, and Estonian policemen (known as *Schutzmannschaften*). But Himmler's orders for the *Schutzmänner* applied to the civilian zones, not the military. Wehrmacht employment of indigenous police aides was done on an ad hoc, as needed basis. Thus in Zhytomyr on 30 July 1941, the German military commander announced in the local newspaper, *Ukraïns'ke Slovo*, the formation of a new police force. The announcement specified that there should be one policeman for every ten households. Many Ukrainians responded to the offer, even though the job was unpaid. Within a two-month period the Germans selected and deployed 6,000 Ukrainian *Hilfspolizei* in the northern half of the region alone.[20]

Mayors, District (Raion) Leaders, and Villages Elders

There existed some similarities among the appointed indigenous leaders. Nearly all of them had a middle school education and were among the local professional class of teachers, doctors, priests, and bookkeepers. They were mostly over forty years of age, so they had grown up in the tumultuous years of World War I and the Bolshevik revolution. Many had held a leadership position comparable to a mayor or a deputy mayor. A few of the older ones were middle-ranking civil servants during the tsarist period. Not all were from the region they presided over. Field Commander Markull described the typical local leaders as *umsichtig* (willing to help), but he also disparaged them as apathetic, lazy "natives," whose work ethnic had been destroyed by the repressive Soviet system.[21]

To the Germans' disappointment, Ukrainian district leaders and village elders were not always willing to implement their orders with the expected enthusiasm. So German leaders used certain methods to test the reliability of the district leaders and elders. Shortly after the Germans arrived in Popil'nia in the summer of 1941, they approved a Ukrainian named Vytovts'yi to be the elder. In order to demonstrate his commitment to the Germans, the local German agricultural leader asked Vytovts'yi to beat one of his "neighbors."[22]

The Germans were not hard pressed to find Ukrainian and ethnic German aides to fill the administrative positions. Each day locals arrived at the village commander's post or the city labor office with the hope of finding a job. These job seekers presented handwritten requests to the Germans, often detailed letters that described their suffering and losses under the Soviets and included desperate pleas to help feed their children who lacked shoes and clothing.[23] Some joined the German administration because they wanted to use their position to rescue friends and relatives who were held in Nazi prisons and camps. At the end of August, a Ukrainian administrator working for the Germans named Liuboms'kyi used his position to request that his son be released from the POW camp in Vinnytsia.[24] Leading Ukrainian administrators in Zhytomyr, many with a nationalist orientation, tried to establish Ukrainian self-help committees and cooperative organizations, including a regional Ukrainian Red Cross.[25]

The war created massive unemployment. Local industries had been destroyed during the Soviet evacuation and the German bombing raids.[26] The German military and SS-police assigned all those capable of working to road and railway construction, prison camp operations, farming, forestry work, and other tasks.[27] According to German labor policy, Ukrainians who did not work were not provided with ration cards.[28] Prisoners of war in the camps and all Jews performed forced labor for the Germans, receiving no wages and inadequate food rations. For those who were eligible and willing to take them, the jobs in the German administration seemed to be the best. Even the lowest-level office jobs paid at least double the monthly wage of a factory worker or agricultural laborer. Ukrainians and ethnic Germans in the higher-level positions such as raion leader received between 1,000 and 3,000 rubles per month, which was considerably more than the Soviets had paid.[29]

With their Ukrainian and ethnic German administrators and police aides in place, Nazi military leaders issued a stream of decrees to establish German rule in the region: collect all munitions, establish curfews, register livestock, impose new taxes, restrict the use of public transport and roadways, and prohibit contact with POWs. The militia enforced a number of anti-Jewish regulations, such as the distribution of armbands, closing of Jewish businesses, and formation of Jewish labor battalions. Militiamen also pressed collective farmers and peasants to cultivate more land.[30] Any elder or raion leader who did not comply with German orders was, according to Nazi policy, treated as an enemy of the Reich and therefore executed.[31]

The Germans needed indigenous helpers to administer and exploit the newly conquered territory. Their short-term and long-term colonial aims of racial Germanization and economic autarky could not be achieved without local accomplices, auxiliaries, and laborers. Although they were able to find a sufficient number of indigenous administrators and policemen to assist them, German leaders increasingly confronted other shortages of labor and supplies. Rubble needed to be cleared and bridges to be repaired; roads were impassable; and electricity, clean water, and basic building materials were scarce. These kinds of shortages and construction demands persisted over the entire German occupation period. What is striking is that despite basic deficiencies, German military leaders and the civilians who succeeded them allocated enormous manpower to "pacification programs" and "security measures."

When conflicts arose over economic or more pragmatic needs and the regime's ideological aims, usually the ideological ones prevailed. In this regard the Nazis broke with their forefathers who conquered and colonized parts of Africa. In the Wilhelmine era, the genocidal impulses of the army and its regional administrators were sometimes tempered by a strong consensus that the colonies must be profitable and that the "natives" were valuable as a labor force. Plus biological racism, although historically rooted in European encounters with non-Europeans during the nineteenth century (if not earlier), was in theory and practice more systematically developed and operative in the Nazi empire than in the Wilhelmine one.

Consequently, in the Nazi case, Hitler's chief of staff of the Armed Forces High Command, General Wilhelm Keitel, implored his subordinates not to employ Jews despite the acute labor shortages, arguing that "the struggle against Bolshevism demands ruthless and drastic action, especially against the Jews, the bearers of Bolshevism."[32] Either by choice or under pressure from above, German regional leaders prioritized racial aims over economic ones. Markull complained about the lack of available manpower while he simultaneously approved the executions of civilians — at least 1,550 persons who by and large were not guilty of a crime but considered racially worthless or politically threatening to the Germans.[33] The prevailing Nazi view was that the Germans would not be able to secure their presence in the region and begin the necessary transformation of it without first destroying their biggest threats: Judeo-Bolsheviks as well as other "racial defects."

Wehrmacht Security Measures
Roques, Stülpnagel, and Reichenau

Scholars such as Alexander Dallin and Timothy Mulligan have elucidated the conflicts among the various German agencies sent to govern and exploit the Soviet territories. There was one area, however, in which all agencies consistently cooperated and dedicated their resources: "security" measures. To this end, agencies shared manpower, matériel, and information. For example, Himmler's police leaders trained the Ukrainian police, and the individual recruits were checked by the SD; but the Wehrmacht village commanders actually enlisted them, outfitted them, and assigned them to their routine tasks of guarding buildings, roadways, and transports of prisoners. For the largest "cleansing" campaigns in the northern Pripiat' marshland, Wehrmacht commanders called in the First SS Brigade to assist in the joint SS-army raids. District agricultural leaders, economic units, and armed Ukrainians in the Polissian Sich also worked closely with the army field commanders and police by patrolling the rural areas and reporting the presence of "suspicious" persons hiding in the forests and fields.[34]

Besides SS-policemen, units of the army's Security Divisions were the most active in the pacification measures around Zhytomyr. Entire Security Divisions, with their foot soldiers numbering in the thousands, descended on small villages and scoured the countryside for "saboteurs" and "insurgents." Women were not spared in these German rampages. On the contrary, they were considered especially dangerous. The Seventeenth Army near Vinnytsia captured women among the Soviet troops and ordered that all uniformed women be treated as POWs and nonuniformed women as insurgents—that is, killed.[35]

Not long after Zhytomyr fell into the hands of Commander Karl von Roques's Army Group South Rear Area Administration, he issued a memorandum about "pacification measures" being carried out under his purview.[36] A veteran of World War I and the Reichswehr, Roques wrote about the involvement of Wehrmacht soldiers in "excesses that are being instigated against certain sections of the civil population." The German soldier, he wrote, "who participates in Jewish pogroms etc. damages to the utmost the reputation of the army and displays an unsoldierly attitude." While Roques expressed some disapproval of a soldier's direct involvement in anti-Jewish massacres, he did not object to the massacres. He referred to Hitler's order explicitly allowing soldiers to ruthlessly kill enemy civilians *in the course of fighting action* (underlined by Roques). As for prisoners of war, they too were to be killed if they escaped from the POW camps and the Germans were able to capture these "insurgents."[37]

Furthermore, Roques wrote that soldiers who commit excesses outside the realm of regular warfare "should be brought to trial" and that "commanders who do not make it a point to find and bring these persons in for trial are not the right persons for their position." Roques seems to have disapproved of the rampant killing of civilians in his area, but he phrased his "protest" in terms of the chaos that the killings created and, in deference to Hitler, reiterated that such killings were to be carried out as part of the warfare.[38]

Roques's memorandum reveals several significant developments. First, the mere existence of this and similar high-ranking orders about "excesses" confirms that the German army did participate in varying degrees in the atrocities committed against POWs, Jews, and other civilian "threats" in occupied Ukraine. Second, certainly not every German officer or soldier approved of the mass executions of Jews, but the few objections that did emerge on paper were critical of the lack of order such actions precipitated. It remains unclear whether this concern for order represented an attempt to criticize Nazi-style warfare against civilians, or an attempt to distance army personnel from what might have been viewed as Himmler's "messy" tasks. Third, Roques's memorandum implicitly raised the issue of accountability. He warned that dismissals and legal prosecution were still possible responses to those who behaved "excessively" or "unsoldierly." As stern as his warning sounded, in reality very few soldiers who plundered or committed "excesses" were brought before military courts. However, those who were prosecuted could and did receive the death sentence.[39]

Like Roques, General Karl-Heinrich von Stülpnagel (commander of the Seventeenth Army) admonished his troops not for the murder of civilians but for their arbitrary methods or disobedient approach. Stülpnagel, who was later executed for his association with the July 1944 plot to kill Hitler, criticized the then-current practice of seizing hostages prematurely for future denunciations and disapproved of random collective measures. He condemned the "wild" behavior that was being displayed by his subordinates who participated in the pogroms against Jews.[40] To institute a more efficient punitive measure, Stülpnagel instructed his troops to blame the Jews and communist civilians for local acts of resistance. After all, he explained, the remaining communists were mostly young Jews and they were to be sought out anyway.[41]

While conducting a murderous policy against the Jews, Russians, and other so-called Asiatic elements, the army tried to promote "peaceful" German-Ukrainian relations. Stülpnagel asked that his subordinates give Ukrainians the impression that German rule was fair. Nazi persecution and reprisal measures were not to be directed against the "helpful" Ukrainians.[42] Even in the rare cases of a Ukrainian act of sabotage, one local army officer of the Zhytomyr region wrote, the Jews would still be held responsible and not the Ukrainians because, according to this officer, the Ukrainians had been especially cooperative.[43]

In a formal communiqué to the soldiers of the Seventeenth Army, headquartered in Vinnytsia, Stülpnagel disclosed how the army leadership struggled to uphold traditional notions of soldierly conduct while unleashing widespread violence behind the lines. He wrote that the real civilian danger lurked among the Jews and POWs who were dressed in street clothing. It was in the Germans' best interest, he believed, to maintain favorable relations with the Ukrainians who might be persuaded to support partisans and who were working the land for the Germans. Stülpnagel criticized the German soldiers who pillaged Ukrainian farmers' homes during the day while they worked in the fields, and he sternly warned that plunderers would be brought before a court. In fact, Stülpnagel argued, "*the fight against a loosening of discipline must be as strong as the fight against resistance efforts of all kinds found among the populace.*"[44] There were some shades of difference among the military leaders, with some more starkly supportive or resistant to atrocities against POWs and civilians. Yet they coalesced around the policy of murdering Jews.

During August 1941 the Wehrmacht's concern for discipline and order within its own ranks, combined with the realization that the number of victims was expanding, prompted the leadership to refine their task-sharing system with the SS-police, as well as to strive for more efficient security operations. The local military and SS-police intelligence offices shared information, but regional commanders of both agencies still needed to work out a division of labor for carrying out the mass murder.[45] The High Command of the Sixth Army ordered that army soldiers should not get involved in executions of Jews unless ordered to do so, because it was primarily the task of the SD. According to this order: "In the different villages of the region where organs of the SD and SS carried out the necessary executions of criminal, Bolshevik elements, mainly Jews," off-duty soldiers had volunteered to assist the SD with executions. They were also taking photos of the executions. Soldiers could continue to participate in mass executions but only with an officer's approval; the SD could also rely on Wehrmacht village commanders to provide guards for sealing off execution sites from observers.[46] In early August the head of Einsatzgruppe C, Otto Rasch, reported that in the Zhytomyr region relations between the army and SD were "cordial" and that "army circles show a steadily growing interest in and understanding of tasks and matters concerning the work of the Security Police . . . particularly during the executions." Moreover, this SD report continued, the army was pursuing the tasks of the Security Police, arresting communists and Jews.[47] Thus soldiers were not forbidden to participate, and the executions themselves were not questioned; rather, the degree of the army's participation was more clearly defined and coordinated with the SS-police.

More than Roques and Stülpnagel, Field Marshal Walter von Reichenau directly shaped the army's involvement in the mass murder that occurred in the rear areas. As commander of the Sixth Army, Reichenau argued that army involvement in atrocities against Jews and other civilians was necessary for securing Germany's rule over the conquered areas. In his infamous October 1941 memo, which was widely circulated with Hitler's blessing, Reichenau wrote that the German soldier be "not only a fighter according to the rules of the art of war, but also the bearer of a ruthless national ideology. . . . The struggle against the enemy ['Jewish subhuman elements'] behind the front is still not being taken seriously enough. . . . The soldier must fulfill two demands: (1) the complete destruction of the Bolshevik heresy, the Soviet state, and its army; (2) the merciless extermination of alien treachery and cruelty and with it the securing of life for the German army in Russia."[48] Reichenau, who had distinguished himself as a devoted Nazi during the Polish campaign of 1939, requested the use of the First SS Brigade for "mopping-up operations" in the Sixth Army areas. Friedrich Jeckeln, who was commander of the First SS Brigade, complied. The brigade did such a thorough job, that Reichenau awarded them combat medals for carrying out atrocities against civilians and POWs near Zhytomyr.[49]

While senior commanders like Reichenau and Roques arranged joint SS-army pacification campaigns, units of the Wehrmacht's Security Divisions established a routine of patrolling the streets and searching the villages labeled partisan nests.[50] Three Security Divisions swept through the Zhytomyr region during the summer and fall of 1941.[51] Security Division 454 was composed of regular army troops and police units: Infantry Regiment 375, Police Battalion 82 (formerly of the Breslau Order Police), and the army secret field police units (Geheime Feldpolizei 708, 721, and 730 and Landesschützen Battalions 286, 416, and 566 and Regiment 102).[52] The Security Divisions coordinated their pacification campaigns with the available units of Higher SS and Police Leader for Ukraine Friedrich Jeckeln. In the area of Novohrad-Volyns'kyi and Berdychiv, Security Division 213 collaborated with members of Order Police Battalions 318 and 45; in Vinnytsia, Security Division 444 worked with staff from Order Police Battalions 45, 311, and 314. The Security Divisions' primary assignment was to pacify areas behind the front and protect military installations and transportation routes. They pursued the "enemy" in remote areas, carrying out arrests, reprisals, and executions. Security Division officers at the battalion level were briefed on the eve of Barbarossa about the "Commissar Order" and "Guidelines for the Conduct of Troops in Russia."[53] In many respects, their security activities overlapped with the secret police tasks of Himmler's forces.[54] When the Rear Area occupation officials arrived in Zhytomyr on 19 July, City Commander Riedl ordered members of Order Police Battalion 82 (attached to Security Division 454) to begin the "pacification" of the inner city and its surrounding areas. They conducted their "systematic manhunts" with the small commandos of Einsatzgruppe C.[55]

During the course of the military occupation the numbers of policemen and soldiers assigned to the divisions increased significantly, which from the Nazi perspective created the possibility for more extensive "cleansing operations" behind the lines. Security Division 454's fighting strength when it arrived in Zhytomyr during the last week of July was 156 officers, 958 noncommissioned officers, and 5,845 enlisted men, and by October it had grown to 279 officers, 1,387 noncommissioned officers, and 7,182 rank-and-file soldiers.[56] Actually these figures represent only a fraction of the security presence in Zhytomyr during August and the first half of September because additional Wehrmacht soldiers and technical personnel traveled through the area and assisted with security measures along with thousands of SS-policemen.

At first the army's security forces (like Heydrich's secret police commandos) focused their raids around German headquarters and the Wehrmacht's main transit routes.[57] But when the military's rapid advance suddenly slowed in August, they found themselves quartered in the area for a longer period. They had the time and manpower to expand their operations. Often their searches were incited by Ukrainians who lodged an overwhelming number of complaints about "armed Russian gangs" roaming the villages and forests. In response, units of Security Division 454 fanned out along the main roads and into the smaller villages around Zhytomyr, Berdychiv, and Biela Tserkva.[58]

In 1941, however, while there were large numbers of Red Army deserters and civilian refugees, there were very few organized partisan groups operating in the region, and so-called antipartisan warfare became a German cover for carrying out atrocities against civilians and Red Army stragglers. At this stage in the war, "antipartisan warfare" was a mendacious slogan for securing territory where little resistance to German rule existed. For example, near Levkovychi soldiers from Infantry Regiment 375 responded to Ukrainian reports of roaming bands. The soldiers disguised themselves in civilian clothing and searched the nearby forests on 29 July. Anyone found hiding in the woods was placed in an enemy category at the discretion of the German officer. The lowest-ranking German officers were empowered to shoot "insurgents" on the spot.[59] In mid-August, Ukrainians in Emil'chyne reported to a local German commander that 2,000 Russian soldiers who were disguised in civilian clothes were working in the fields. To fight the "partisans," Roques deployed Security Division 213 and the First SS Brigade to the area. On 15 August 1941 they opened fire on them, taking 862 prisoners, and killing 272.[60] The First SS Brigade tersely reported that this raid in Emil'chyne was a "success": a few prisoners were taken and a number of Jews shot.[61] Sipo-SD commandos of Einsatzgruppe C also routinely responded to Ukrainian reports. Rasch, the commander of Einsatzgruppe C, wrote that the exaggerated reports of partisan attacks from Ukrainians made it "possible to ferret out the places of Bolsheviks, Jews and asocial elements following the reports."[62] Thus the paranoia about "enemies behind-the-lines" spread throughout the German ranks as well as within the local population. The German field commander in Vinnytsia and intelligence officials in Zhytomyr admitted that the Ukrainian reports of "Russian gangs" were inaccurate or distorted. Commander Markull stated that the locals spoke fearfully about bandits, but without any particular details. "Personally," he wrote after touring the area, "I do not think that the bandits are very dangerous."[63] Still the persistent rumors about bandits fueled the machinery of destruction by providing the Germans with a popular rationale for "cleansing" more remote areas outside the cities of Zhytomyr, Berdychiv, and Vinnytsia, often by a combined force of army and SS units.[64] The exaggerated nature of the Ukrainian denunciations reflected the widespread paranoia.[65] In at least one recorded incident, it is clear that the "bandits" that Ukrainians feared were actually Jews, probably refugees who were trying to avoid captivity or death at the hands of the Germans. An Einsatzgruppe C official observed that the locals frequently withdrew their reports when they realized that they had placed the lives of these individuals in danger.[66] Still, as Hitler had advised in his private remarks of 16 July 1941, the Germans were to exploit this turbulent atmosphere. For local commanders, arrests and executions became a standard response to Ukrainian fears of threatening gangs lurking in the woods. Thus the real or imagined threat of guerrilla attacks intensified the German search for and killing of "suspicious" persons, and it provided local officials with an acceptable rationale for destroying Red Army POWs and civilians.[67]

One outstanding incident further illustrates this development. In the territory of Polonne-Horodnytsia, Battalion 3 of Infantry Regiment 375 carried out a security raid that reportedly was a "success," to the extent that another company of the battalion was called in. In the first week of August, German troops or officials had yet to infiltrate this area. According to the German version of events filed in an after-action report, when a company of Infantry Regiment 375 reached the town of Volodars'k-Volyns'kyi on 3 August, it found that many of the Ukrainians and ethnic Germans had fled because Russian soldiers had taken over the town, and (the Germans claimed) the local Jewish community had assisted the Russians. The regiment had little success in ferreting out the Russian partisans from the surrounding forests; three partisans were in German custody.

The commander added at the close of his report that this operation was an especially exhausting experience and the men should be relieved.[68] It was exhausting for a battalion of about 500 men to bring in three prisoners? A few weeks later, when the First SS Infantry Brigade was mistakenly assigned to "cleanse" this same area, it found neither Jews nor Bolsheviks because, according to the brigade's report, Infantry Regiment 375 had done a "thorough job."[69] And on the morning of 19 August, the Soviet Information Bureau broadcast that unheard-of tortures had occurred in Volodars'k-Volyns'kyi. According to this bulletin (which was published after the war), German officers and Ukrainian nationalists in "drunken bands" herded civilians into a barn, plucked out their eyes, broke their limbs, chopped them into pieces, and burned them alive. Despite the propagandistic tendency of the Soviet reports, the bulletin at least establishes the occurrence of massacres at Volodars'k-Volyns'kyi in the first half of August 1941.[70] This gruesome massacre seems to hint at a Jedwabne-like outburst in Ukraine. Ukrainian involvement in the Holocaust will be taken up in chapters that follow, but it should be mentioned here that no evidence has emerged from the Zhytomyr region that compares with the concerted Polish attacks against Jews in Jedwabne, Poland. In the Zhytomyr region, Ukrainians did not collectively plan and carry out the mass murder of their Jewish neighbors independently of the Germans.[71]

The Wehrmacht's Camp System and the Fate of the Prisoners of War

By the end of August 1941, commanders of Security Divisions in Zhytomyr realized that the prisoner population was far greater than they could manage. Generally the Germans used the existing Soviet prisons and NKVD buildings for their interrogations and incarcerations. But the repeated orders to seize just about anyone within grasp resulted in a prisoner population that exceeded the region's prison and camp space. Around Vinnytsia, all unmarried males between the ages of sixteen and fifty-five were deemed suspect and arrested.[72] A "mass arrest of the people has to cease," one frustrated official wrote.[73] To remedy this problem, Roques's administration ordered that "those without some grounds for arrest should be released if their village is nearby and free of partisans,"[74] but those who "seemed disagreeable" should be left in the internment camp or given over to an SD commando; the military was not to dump them across the border into the General Government, as apparently some German leaders had attempted to do.

While the number of civilian internees was growing, the more pressing issue at hand was the enormous number of POWs. Tens of thousands had been cap-tured in the Zhytomyr region during the fighting of July and August 1941, and more continued to stream in as the Wehrmacht advanced eastward. Additional Red Army soldiers who hid in the forests of the region were swept up in the security raids and crowded into the camps. The deplorable conditions of the camps alarmed local commanders, who feared the spread of disease and so-cial unrest but expressed no remorse over the high mortality rates among the prisoners. The tragic fate of the POWs, however, was not solely the result of unforeseen circumstances or regional conditions.

In May 1941, shortly before the invasion, perfunctory plans were drawn up to build a limited number of POW camps and to use the prisoners as forced laborers. The Soviet POWs were not to enter the German Reich but were to re-main in camps where they could not "infect" the German race with their Slavic Bolshevism. The German leadership did not concern itself with the basic care and nourishment of the millions of prisoners it predicted would be captured in a blitzkrieg defeat of the Soviet Union.[75] In the event that the international community protested their maltreatment of Soviet prisoners, legal experts in the Armed Forces High Command came up with the rationale that the Soviet Government refused to sign the 1929 Geneva covenant on the treatment of pris-oners of war so the Reich could treat them as it saw fit, as "Untermenschen."[76]

All food supplies were channeled to the Reich and armed forces, and in principle were not available for the "superfluous" population of non-Germans. Cutting off the food supplies to the POW camps was, as Christian Gerlach has recently argued in his research on the fate of Belorussians, a *Hungerpolitik* with genocidal intent and consequences. Quartermaster General Eduard Wagner, who was in charge of the distribution of supplies including food rations, ar-gued that nonworking POWs "should starve." As he and the majority of the Nazi leadership saw it, "The more prisoners that die, the better off we are." Their subordinates adopted a similar attitude and implemented the policy of starvation, inhumane neglect, and mass murder of POWs.[77] Instead of plan-ning for the proper care of POWs, the German military poured its energy into a massive propaganda campaign to induce Soviet soldiers to desert to the Ger-man side, leaving the fate of these deserters to local army administrators and their meager resources.[78]

Shortly after the Wehrmacht broke through the Stalin line at Vinnytsia and most of the Zhytomyr region was in German hands, the Army High Command issued an order about the "processing" of POWs. First of all, the directive em-phasized, the German soldier must keep his distance from these dangerous types. Any POW who attempted to flee was to be shot without warning. For the vast remainder, the German military established collection points, which were also internment sites for "roaming civilians," since, the Germans claimed, "most of the former soldiers disguise themselves in civilian clothes." POWs in the rear areas who did not turn themselves in to the nearest Wehrmacht post or who tried to conceal their identity were "treated like insurgents and handled accordingly"—that is, shot.[79]

Collection points existed in each town and were the responsibility of the corps-level officers. From the collection points dotting the landscape of the Zhytomyr region, the POWs were taken, usually through forced marches, to the main transit camps (Durchgangslager, Dulags) located in Zhytomyr, Berdychiv, Novohrad-Volyns'kyi (Zviahel), and Vinnytsia.[80] The transit camps were temporary collection points that fed into the stationary camps (Stammslager, Stalags), which became permanent camps in the military rear areas and later in the civilian zones. In the Zhytomyr region some of the larger camps were established at Liubar, the city of Zhytomyr (Dulag 170 and Stalag 358 and 201), Berdychiv (Dulag 205 and a branch of Stalag 358), Vinnytsia, and Haisyn (Dulag 152).[81] The Stalag at Vinnytsia became well known during the Nazi occupation as the camp for "Prominente," high-ranking Soviet internees who might be politically useful, such as Andrei Vlasov, who commanded a German-sponsored Russian Liberation Army during the last stages of the war.[82]

Those who had been assembled in the collection points and sent on to camps at Novohrad-Volyns'kyi, Zhytomyr, and Berdychiv were then separated into groups, defined by race and ability to work. Army camp administrators, Sipo-SD commandos, and their collaborators sorted the prisoners into five groups: (1) ethnic Germans, Ukrainians, Lithuanians, Latvians, and Estonians; (2) Asians, Jews, and German-speaking Russians; (3) commissars, agitators, and other suspicious elements; (4) officers and noncommissioned officers; and (5) others.[83] The ethnic Germans, Ukrainians, Lithuanians, Latvians, and Estonians were screened by army intelligence for possible release and given special work assignments inside and near the camps. Senior officials in the army and SS-police determined the fate of the second and third groups during the prewar planning and in the first months of the campaign. In the summer of 1941, Chief of the Security Police and SS–Security Service Reinhard Heydrich provided detailed instructions for his Einsatzgruppen leaders whose units were assigned the task of "cleansing" the POW camps as well as finding potential collaborators among the prisoners; these instructions included the segregation of all suspected Bolsheviks, Communist Party officials, and Jews.[84]

In the official military records, certain categories of prisoners—namely, Jews and "Asiatics"—appeared to have been released, but actually these prisoners were given over to the SD and killed.[85] Hans Fruechte, a medical doctor assigned to Dulag 160 in the summer of 1941, observed that from the start Jews, Mongolians, and "other Asiatic races" were segregated; "in most cases commissars had been liquidated before the prisoners arrived in the camp." Fruechte and other camp personnel learned "from the soldiers who had accompanied transports to Zhitomir, that in Zhitomir at the beginning of August 1941, all incoming Jews who had arrived together with the prisoner transport had been shot."[86] In a December 1941 conference, Reich labor, army, and SS leaders discussed how those who were "segregated" for release were mostly shot; in General Reinicke's area (mainly Ukraine), of the 22,000 segregated POWs, Gestapo chief Heinrich Müller (Berlin, RSHA) reported that 16,000 had been liquidated.[87]

From among those who survived the segregation process and were capable of labor, the German military then identified the carpenters, engineers, building masters, and other specialists and assigned them to the operational areas or to the local commanders' offices. After the specialists were separated and deployed, the nonskilled but "able-bodied" POWs were formed into companies of about 250 to 300 men who were sent on construction jobs, generally near the camps.[88]

Many of these POW labor battalions received their assignments from the Organization Todt, which was actively pulling laborers out of the POW camp at Zhytomyr and in Vinnytsia and assigning them to road construction.[89] The biggest network of Nazi-run labor camps in the region centered on the joint army and SS-police construction of the autobahn, planned as the major transit route for military supplies and personnel. The "Durchgangsstrassen," or highways, ran through Vinnytsia (DG IV) and Zhytomyr (DG V).[90] About every fifteen kilometers, POW labor camps for road construction workers were to be set up along the planned routes.[91] Under the direction of OT, prisoners were worked to death hauling stones from the Hnivan' quarry, which were used for the roads as well as the construction of Hitler's elaborate Werwolf field headquarters and bunker. Even after the arrival of the civilian administrators, army village commanders remained posted along the highway and continued to manage the exploitation of POW laborers on the autobahn.[92]

Those who were not fit to work were marched by foot in a "relay system" or, if available, by railway in open cars normally not used for transporting humans.[93] Following the orders and guidelines of the High Command, staff of the Security Divisions managed the movement of prisoners from the transit camps to the permanent camps situated in the rear areas.[94] In August the numbers of POWs in Zhytomyr's camps were already so high that they came close to the popula-

Soviet POWs handing out bread in a Vinnytsia POW camp, 23 July 1941 (U.S. Holocaust Memorial Museum, courtesy of the U.S. National Archives and Records Administration, #10992)

tions of the towns where the camps were situated; at Novohrad-Volyns'kyi, a town of no more than 12,000 inhabitants, the POW transit camp (Dulag 172) contained 8,000 prisoners.[95] To reduce the overcrowding, the German military forced them westward to the Shepetivka Stalag in Podolia. But after the German victory at Kiev, where about 600,000 Soviet soldiers were captured, tens of thousands of these POWs were then transported or were forcibly marched to the Zhytomyr camps, which—despite the August and early September deaths and deportations of POWs—were overflowing with starved prisoners.[96] Many POWs from Kiev who were destined for Zhytomyr died in the transport. The military's Landesschützenverbände (defense units) shot those who collapsed or tried to flee. As the hungry and often wounded prisoners trudged westward, German guards goaded them like animals with whips, clubs, and pistol shots.[97] In a rare report by an incensed intelligence official of Security Division 454, the author wrote that the physical condition of prisoners in Berdychiv who had traveled from Kiev "counter the most basic notion of humanity."[98]

On paper, the existence of German plans to employ skilled POWs as laborers or to form labor battalions obscures the reality that in the fall and winter of 1941 thousands of POWs in Zhytomyr's camps died from starvation, shooting, and disease. When the autumn frost set in earlier than usual, the cold weather took its toll on the poorly clothed and emaciated prisoners. Some resorted to cannibalism. Camp guards treated the prisoners in ways that were not only "harsh but often unnecessarily cruel." [99]

By November 1941, 5 to 10 percent of the prisoners who arrived at the camps were already on the verge of death from starvation and exhaustion.[100] Many thousands died alongside the roads to the camps, but these deaths were not registered in the German reports. In mid-December Reich Minister Alfred Rosenberg reported to Hitler that about 2,500 POWs were dying each day in Ukraine's camps. He explained that many more would die because of malnutrition, but he reassured Hitler that the loss of life would not impair the necessary labor supply.[101]

For the local population, the thousands of POWs who were held in open-air camps across the region and marched through their towns and villages became a troubling, disheartening display of German intentions. At first, the Germans forbade the burying of prisoners who lay dead along the roads and in plain view of the population. Ukrainian women imagined the same fate for their fathers, husbands, and brothers who had been drafted into the Red Army. Ukrainians who sought work at German labor offices found themselves paired up with POWs and formed into labor units. Seeing how poorly nourished and abused these prisoners were, local Ukrainians began to gain a clearer sense of Nazi methods.[102]

The largest and most visible POW camp near Zhytomyr was Bogun'ia, situated about five kilometers from the city. Here the German army cordoned off a former collective farm with barbed wire and herded the POWs into an exposed area where they were subjected to Zhytomyr's climate of steamy summers and bitterly cold winters (comparable in North America to the weather found in Toronto, Canada).

At Bogun'ia the German camp commandant announced in the local paper, *Holos Volyni*, that civilians should bring food and clothing packages to the prisoners between 9:00 and 11:00 A.M. Many Ukrainian women responded to this call; they hoped to find their sons, brothers, or fathers among the prisoners. Instead they discovered that they were the objects of a German ruse. The commandant collected the parcels and then handed them out to the camp guards, not to the prisoners. At Vinnytsia the Russian mayor, Aleksandr Sevast'ianov, announced in the paper that thousands of prisoners would march through town and the locals should come to their aid with food. Hundreds (mainly women and children) waited by the roadside with carts of apples and bread. When the approaching prisoners saw the food they broke through the line of guards to grab it. A convoy officer ordered the guards to shoot. In the chaos and panic that followed, POWs and civilians were shot and trampled to death.[103] In another more extreme example of maltreatment of POWs, the Sixth Army staff doctor, Dr. Gerhart Panning, collaborated with the SK4a chief, Colonel Paul Blobel, in a murderous experiment. They tested the effect of captured Soviet dum-dum explosives on Jewish POWs. Panning's analysis of this experiment and gruesome photographs of the victims were published as a research piece in the journal *Der deutsche Militärarzt* in January 1942.[104]

Through German practices of torture, forced labor, mass shooting, and inhumane neglect, more than 100,000 POWs died at Bogun'ia, around Berdychiv, and in the northern districts of the Zhytomyr region.[105] At the Berdychiv Camp (Dulag 205), where 9,271 prisoners were left in December 1941 (3,320 were Ukrainian), the mortality rate was over 82 percent, and the camp's remaining food supply was sufficient for about eight days. On the outskirts of Berdychiv, the German SD and local Wehrmacht units executed thousands of POWs at Krasnaia Gora.[106]

This particular Nazi campaign generated some conflicts among German military leaders in Ukraine. The more pragmatic types, who also may have been tacitly expressing their disapproval of army "excesses," complained that the prisoners constituted a valuable labor force in industry or agriculture.[107] There was also concern about seeding anti-German sentiments among the Ukrainian population. High Command orders identified Ukrainian POWs as a "privileged" group to be treated less severely than Russians.[108] If a Ukrainian POW's hometown was within a three- to four-day walk from the camp, then the prisoner was allowed to leave for home with the proper identification and release papers. In some cases, a friend or relative from the prisoner's hometown would have to vouch for the prisoner's identity. According to Karel Berkhoff's research, Ukrainian women often claimed prisoners as "husbands" to rescue them from starvation in the camps. The Ukrainian Red Cross was also actively pressuring local German authorities to release and care for Ukrainian POWs.[109] However, before the Nazi leadership announced a formal release policy, regional commanders had already been treating the Ukrainian POWs more favorably by providing them with rations and recruiting them as skilled laborers and as auxiliaries to the police forces.[110]

Of the 280,108 Soviet POWs released by the German military in 1941, Ukrainians constituted 270,095 (235,466 from camps under Army Group South in Ukraine.)[111] German military and police leaders perceived Ukrainians (and Baltic peoples) to be, as a racial-political category, of a higher standing than other "Asiatic" groups.[112] Another important factor encouraging the release of Ukrainians (and Baltic nationals) was the presumption made by the

Germans and nurtured by émigrés that these peoples would be hostile to the Soviet Union and therefore good collaborators. Yet these "Slavs" were still considered an inferior race and a potential political threat. Nazi leaders, including Hitler, disapproved of the release of POWs. Like Hitler, Reich Commissar for Ukraine Erich Koch protested that the freed POWs would avenge the Germans by joining the partisans. Released POWs were also deemed a health hazard because of the possible spread of epidemics from the camps.[113]

In the Zhytomyr region, relations between the Army High Command and the SS over the fate of POWs were not always smooth. The Wehrmacht had agreed to cooperate with Heydrich's policy of purging the POW camps by commandos of the SD, but in at least one documented incident in Vinnytsia the army camp commandant refused to comply with the SD routine.[114] He refused to hand over 362 Jewish POWs and started a court-martial process against his subordinates because they defied him by turning over the Jews to the SD. This conflict prompted army headquarters at Vinnytsia to ban the SD from entering the Dulag, a ban that was promptly overridden by higher levels who pressed for better SS-army cooperation.[115]

The few cases in which army officials resisted Sipo-SD demands for Jewish prisoners, expressed disgust about the "inhumane" condition of the POWs, or argued that labor demands should take precedence over the genocide demonstrate that not all local military commanders approved of Nazi methods. There may have been more expressions of disapproval that were not voiced on paper. But most formal complaints were directed at problems of mismanagement and general disorder. Any glimmer of uneasiness that managed to make its way up the ranks was effectively suppressed by senior-level "assurances" and "explanations" about the German struggle against Judeo-Bolshevism. By the end of summer 1941, if not at the outset of the Barbarossa campaign, most local military leaders came to accept brutality and terror as part of their everyday routine and the general atmosphere in the East.

Summing Up Colonial-Style Warfare and Hitler's War in Ukraine

As practices or features of war, punitive expeditions, collective reprisal measures, and intense paranoia about enemies behind the lines were not Nazi inventions. They had their historical antecedents most recently in the guerrilla-style warfare of the late nineteenth century and total warfare of World War I. In the Franco-Prussian War, the colonial wars in Africa, and World War I, the general staffs of the Prussian and then German Imperial Army sanctioned collective reprisals against civilians in France, Africa, Belgium, and Poland. In part historians attribute these atrocious policies to the military's reading or mis-reading of Clausewitz's notion of a rapid, decisive victory through total anni-hilation of an enemy—the enemy being depicted as the soldier as well as the nation that supports him.[116] Unlike the British and the French, as historian Isabel Hull has argued, the German military developed a "propensity for final, violent solutions," most markedly in the German military's destruction of the Herero and Nama (1904–7) in Southwest Africa. This propensity did not fade over time. On the contrary, for a growing number of conservative Germans it was reaffirmed by the extreme violence of World War I and the existential crisis that the Great War engendered.[117] To what extent does Germany's history of colonial warfare fully explain the brutality that occurred in Hitler's Vernicht-ungskrieg?

To be sure, in the general history of warfare, civilians have always been sub-jected to the brutality of warriors who raped, plundered, pillaged, and mas-sacred. Yet there was something unprecedented about the Nazi case. The newly appointed German (and Austrian) rulers over Ukraine were convinced that not only on the front lines but especially in the rear areas army security was con-stantly in jeopardy. Unlike the similar paranoia found in the guerrilla warfare in the colonies, in Ukraine and the Eastern Territories generally, German officers and regular troops did not understand the war as an isolated regional campaign against a particular group of "unruly natives." For the Nazis, the ideological stakes in the East were much higher. They believed that their entire existence as a political entity (nation) and more decisively as a race hinged on the outcome of this conflict. A German-led victory over Judeo-Bolshevism would demon-strate to the world Germany's racial superiority and ensure the future survival of the German Volk. War and conquest were political instruments as well as transformative ideological experiences. Was the frontier experience a "revital-izing" one for ordinary Germans, as theorist Friedrich Ratzel (the man who coined the term Lebensraum) had promised? To be sure, the initial euphoria of victory emboldened most Germans. As well, perceptions of the conquered ter-ritory as a "Wild East" incited extreme lawlessness and brutality. Armed with modern tools and the ideology of Nazi-style warfare, ordinary German sol-diers and SS-policemen aggressively implemented a policy (which had been defined by the High Command and senior Nazi leaders) to eradicate anyone who stood in the way of a German victory, specifically "suspicious elements" among the Red Army prisoners, civilians, and above all within the Jewish popu-lation, the Communist Party, and the Soviet state apparatus. Local reports and rumors stemming from the local population, which by and large was also unsure of a Soviet defeat and expected severe Soviet reprisals, also became a significant catalyst for planning additional and more far-reaching Nazi "security" raids.

The indigenous population believed or at least hoped that the massive violence wrought by the German military would soon dissipate as the army moved eastward. But this was not to be. Nazi-style warfare proved more than a limited series of military conflicts or isolated acts of frontier violence confined to the battlefront. In Zhytomyr, Wehrmacht soldiers participated in atrocities during the first months of Barbarossa when a German victory seemed certain. The army's involvement in massacres "behind the lines" was not caused by the mental and physical attrition of warfare in the East; rather, it was an assertion of Nazi power in its heyday.[118]

These first months of rule were chaotic. German regional leaders faced many challenges in the field, from severe housing shortages to everyday administrative deficiencies. Many of the problems they brought upon themselves, such as the overcrowding and atrocious conditions of the makeshift POW internment sites and the haphazard ghettos. The recognizable Nazi fanatics, like General Walter von Reichenau, teamed up with the more numerous pragmatists who were willing to use extreme force and terror as a solution to any problems they faced in the field.[119] The genocidal bloodbath that marked the onset of German rule over Zhytomyr developed from a lethal mix of Nazi racial policies, Prusso-German militarism, and an arrogant "Final Solution" approach to problem-solving and empire-building. Nowhere else was the convergence of these historic developments more apparent than in the German response to the so-called Jewish question.

Chapter 4 **Making Genocide Possible**
The Onset of the Holocaust,
July–December 1941

In 1941 I witnessed when all the Jews were gathered. Nearly
1,000 appeared with their suitcases. They were given the prom-
ise that they would go to Israel. They were deprived of all of
their things and forced to strip naked. My friend and classmate was there. His family name was Cantor. He was twelve
years old, and they shot him in the eye. My chemistry teacher,
his wife, and their two kids were also shot—the entire family.
That's how the Jews were treated.
—Iurii Alekseevich Kiian, Zhytomyr, 1996

The Nazi mass murder of Jews began in Eastern European
towns such as Zhytomyr. Of the more than 2 million Jews who died in the Baltics, Ukraine, and Belorussia, the vast majority died at gunpoint. They were
not deported to distant locales; instead, they perished in or near their hometowns. Often neighbors, schoolmates, and colleagues watched as their town's
Jewish population was marched to the killing sites. Some neighbors not only
witnessed the mass shootings but also pulled the trigger. There was nothing
impersonal about the Nazi killing process here, in contrast to the factory-style
gassing facilities of Auschwitz-Birkenau. In the intimate setting of Ukraine's
towns and shtetls, questions about the motivations of the perpetrators, the indifference or silence of bystanders, and the experiences of the victims take on
an extremely profound socio-psychological dimension. Moreover, the human
butchery that occurred in the killing fields of Zhytomyr and other parts of the
former Soviet territories shares more in common with other historical cases
of genocide that have taken place around the globe. Thus an in-depth study of
how the mass murder occurred here tells us much about the distinctive, unprecedented features of the Holocaust as well as casts light on other cases of
genocide.

From the very first days that the Nazis occupied Zhytomyr until their final
withdrawal in early 1944, German soldiers, policemen, and administrators,
along with their non-German collaborators, relentlessly hunted down Zhyto-

myr's Jewish men, women, and children. No other sector of the population was singled out and destroyed with such unabashed and calculated cruelty. In fact, according to Holocaust historian Dieter Pohl's recent study of Ukraine, "events in Zhytomyr show most clearly the transition from a selective policy of destruction to one of total eradication."[1] The Germans did not perceive of the Jews in colonially racist terms comparable to the Ukrainians. There was no place for the Jews in the Nazi utopian vision of a Lebensraum; thus the Jews were denied even the lowest status of a colonial subject. In Zhytomyr the Germans and their local collaborators killed as many as 180,000 Jews between the summer of 1941 and the autumn of 1943—most of the women, children, elderly, and infirm died in August and September 1941. The Nazi drive to annihilate the Jews was so intense that in most cases German officials found it "not useful" to establish ghettos here and in eastern Ukraine. After one year of occupation, the general commissar of the region rushed to declare his districts "free of Jews," although this was not entirely true.[2]

As a regional case study, Zhytomyr provides an in-depth view into the different administrative structures, personalities, and social conditions that made the genocide possible. Given the presence of Hitler, Himmler, Göring and their security retinues, the region also offers an unusual perspective on the interaction between the central and peripheral leaders. Nazi leaders presented their subordinates with a broadly defined aim of a "Final Solution" and left it to their underlings to adapt the policy to local conditions. The "success" of the policy depended largely on the local commanders and their ability to anticipate and meet the demands of superiors. To make their localities "free of Jews," regional and district leaders had to marshal all the manpower and resources within reach to "settle" this so-called racial-political problem. In short, the driving force behind this campaign—the SS, the SD, and the police—needed the full cooperation of other German agencies in the region and the assistance of the local population. They received both.

Other than some familiarity with the destruction of Kiev's Jews at Babi Yar, most scholars and laymen know relatively little about Ukraine's significance in the history of the Holocaust. Given Ukraine's prominence in the history of Jewish life in tsarist Russia, and the fact that the loss of Jews there (1.2–1.4 million) far exceeded other parts of Europe except for Poland, it is surprising that such little attention has been paid to this area. Although Philip Friedman and Shmuel Spector made important early contributions to this field, only recently, with the opening of Ukraine's archives, has more scholarly work started to appear, notably by Dieter Pohl.[3] But there is much more to be done on the topics of collaboration and resistance, and other subjects have barely been touched, such as Jewish forced labor in Ukraine. Thus with few exceptions, our knowledge of the Holocaust in Ukraine has not progressed much beyond Babi Yar, or, at best, the summer and fall of 1941, thereby missing important developments in 1942–44, including the involvement of German civilians outside the SS-police forces, the various forms of Ukrainian participation, and the Nazi use of Jewish forced labor, developments that are explored in chapter 6 of this study. The present chapter — on the first phase of the Holocaust in Zhytomyr — examines how the mass murder actually began, not as it was planned in the meeting rooms of the Nazi leadership but as it developed in the field. What were the radicalizing forces that made it possible? How did the Jewish population respond? And in what ways did Ukrainians participate in the Holocaust?

Recent interpretations about the onset of the Holocaust have stressed that the apparent jump from the Nazi killing of male Jews to the destruction of entire communities manifests the outcome of a Hitler decision to pursue a genocidal course, a step that Hitler apparently took in July 1941. The dramatic increase in the numbers of Jews killed as of August of that year is indeed startling and indicates a change. But the source of this change is still unclear. Was a fundamental decision taken in conjunction with Göring's famous 31 July 1941 memo in which he commissioned Heydrich to conduct a feasibility study for a European-wide "Final Solution"? Was it the euphoria of empire, or as Germans at the time termed it *Ostrausch* (a colonizing high or intoxication with the East), that emboldened Nazi leaders and their underlings to opt for genocide? What conditions incited Nazi leaders in the center and periphery to intensify their murderous campaign? Events in east-central Ukraine reveal several facets of this historically devastating moment when Nazi genocidal intent was first realized on the ground.[4]

The escalation of anti-Jewish violence reflected what Nazi leaders at the center and periphery believed they could get away with at each stage in their revolutionary quest for racial purity and imperial domination of Europe. After November 1938, Hitler and his cohorts learned from the Kristallnacht pogrom, the euthanasia program, and then the Polish campaign how far they could go, where they could act, and who could be relied upon for the more extreme measures. Indeed, two of the leading perpetrators in Zhytomyr, Otto Rasch and General Walter von Reichenau, committed atrocities against Polish and Jewish intelligentsia during Operation Tannenberg, the Nazi invasion of Poland.[5]

During the plans for Operation Barbarossa, Nazi leaders in the army and SS-police continued their systematic approach by moving step by step toward ever more radical "solutions" to the Jewish "problem." Initially the Einsatzgruppen, the first SS killing units to arrive in Ukraine, concentrated their intelligence, police, and security sweeps against male Jews (17–45 years of age). They considered the male Jews the most dangerous immediate threat and potential source of resistance. Moreover, Nazi leaders assumed that the small, mobile killing units would have neither the time nor the manpower to carry out large-scale massacres. For the expanded killing actions, Himmler deployed additional SS-police forces under Higher SS and Police Leader Friedrich Jeckeln.[6]

While most leaders in Hitler and Himmler's inner circle came to accept mass murder as the only "solution" to the Jewish problem, in the field the transition from killing male Jews to killing Jewish women and children did not occur automatically. Reich leaders and their regional deputies had to place extra pressure on their subordinates to kill more Jews. They also had to provide the necessary manpower and matériel to do it. According to the testimony of the former commander of Einsatzkommando 5 (EK5), Erwin Schulz, he was summoned in early August from Berdychiv to Zhytomyr, where his superior, Otto Rasch, informed him that the higher-ups were displeased because the SS-police was not acting aggressively enough against the Jews, in particular, by not killing women and children.[7] Prior to August, some individual SS-police leaders had killed women and children, but apparently these sporadic massacres were not sufficient to meet broader Nazi aims. The Nazis' July and August 1941 reports of anti-Jewish massacres often specify precise Jewish death tolls in the hundreds and thousands, but rarely do they detail the age and gender of the Jewish victims. Likewise, the age and gender of other victims, such as the mentally ill and disabled, are usually not specified in the secret reports. In his postwar testimony, Ernst Consee, who was in charge of the war diary of SK4a, recalled the "shooting of forty Jewish children, but not the details because it was an issue that was not to be recorded in the war diary."[8] When Higher SS and Police Leader Jeckeln met with Himmler on 12 August 1941, he was also urged to act more aggressively, and to report daily about the killings. At first the reports were written; then they were given orally.[9]

The dramatic increase in killing during August and September stemmed from high-level orders to kill as many Jews as possible. But the exact origins and precise date of this decision have not turned up in the documentary record. Certainly Hitler biographer Ian Kershaw is correct in asserting, "No Hitler, no Holocaust." Yet rather than search for a Hitler order that may not exist, it may be more worthwhile to reconstruct how the increase in killing actually happened on the ground, and how leaders and subordinates interacted in order to push through a state policy of genocide.[10] The remainder of this chapter explores the ways in which regional leaders contributed to the radicalization of anti-Jewish measures, and particularly how their interaction with superiors and exploitation of local conditions made the Holocaust possible.

The most prominent regional leaders in the 1941 phase of the Holocaust in Zhytomyr were General Reichenau, Higher SS and Police Leader Jeckeln, Einsatzgruppe C Commander Rasch, and SS-Colonel Paul Blobel. Between late July and early September, the Wehrmacht advance halted before Kiev, allowing for the accumulation of thousands of SS, Order Police, and army security personnel who were based in the region. Together they obliterated the Jewish populations of Vinnytsia, Zhytomyr, and Berdychiv, pursuing a "Final Solution" with unprecedented aggression and violence. After mid-August, regional army, SS, and police leaders planned and carried out massacres with the intent of destroying entire Jewish communities, rather than the Communist Party and the state apparatus per se.[11] It was at this turning point that the Nazis' racial aims overtook their political goals.

From the Center to the Periphery Blobel's Sonderkommando 4a and Jeckeln's SS-Policemen

The first SS unit to spearhead the drive into the region alongside the army was an advance commando of Einsatzgruppe C, a subunit known as Sonderkommando 4a, which was led by SS-Colonel Paul Blobel. Additional subunits of Einsatzgruppe C quickly followed; SK4b and Einsatzkommandos 5 and 6 arrived in July and early August 1941 and set up headquarters at Zhytomyr, Vinnytsia, and Berdychiv. The Einsatzkommando staffs consisted of SD criminal investigators, Waffen-SS men, Order Police, drivers, and clerks; each commando amounted to no more than 100 men.[12]

When the advance squad of SK4a entered Zhytomyr among the First Armored Division's tanks on 9 July, it immediately set about its callous routine of securing quarters, locating the Soviet secret police archives, apprehending Soviet functionaries, and persecuting the Jewish population. They announced that the Jews of the city of Zhytomyr must move immediately into the historic Jewish residences along Chudnovskaia. Less than a week later, when the rest of the commando joined the advance squad, the ground was laid for the first major killing action. SK4a's chief, Paul Blobel, who had on more than one occasion demanded that all members of his staff—including cooks, drivers, and clerks—take on the role of executioner, warned that any objections to the murder would be dealt with severely. He assigned about four shooters to the first massacre. Rumors were circulated and eventually published in the local Ukrainian newspaper, *Ukraïns'ke Slovo*, that the burned buildings of Zhytomyr were ignited by Jewish arsonists, who should be held responsible for the homelessness of Ukrainians. With their pretext in place, the German police prepared a "retaliatory" campaign against the Jewish population—the execution of 100 male Jews who were seized and on 19 July marched along the main square, forced into trucks, and transported to the edge of the city. They were herded into a hollow that was cut by a winding stream. A circle of Ukrainian Hilfspolizei sealed off the ravine. Groups of Jews were ordered to lie face down on the ground and then shot in the back of the head with pistols. As compensation, the marksmen were provided with schnapps, kept in ample supply by Blobel, who nearly fell into the stream in a drunken stupor.[13]

This incident was soon followed by a series of mass shootings of Zhytomyr's Jews, bringing the total to 1,200 victims as of mid-August. Three more "actions" in August and early September took the lives of an additional 600 Jewish males (including youths and the elderly). The massacres took place in a wooded area about nine kilometers west of the city. In early September regional SS-police and army leaders turned their attention to the remaining population in the ghetto. On 10 September 1941, Zhytomyr's Feldkommandantur met with staff of Einsatzgruppe C, and they decided "definitively and radically to liquidate the Jewish community." SS and police forces, indigenous auxiliaries, and army personnel combed every corner of the city for Jews who had not been concentrated on Chudnovskaia; they even checked the local orphanage, where as many as eighty Jewish children were found and placed in a truck, never to be heard from again. The final blow came in the early morning hours of 19 September 1941: "Starting at 4:00 o'clock [A.M.], the Jewish quarter was emptied after having been surrounded and closed the previous evening by 60 members of the Ukrainian militia. The transport was accomplished in 12 trucks, part of which had been supplied by military headquarters and part by the city administration of Zhitomir. After the transport had been carried out and the necessary preparations made with the help of 150 prisoners, 3,145 Jews were registered and executed." The "transport" refers to the movement of Jews to the outskirts of town where prisoners had prepared a mass grave. After members of SK4a grabbed the most valuable Jewish property and currency, they gave the remaining twenty-five to thirty tons of Jewish linens, clothing, shoes, dishes, and other items to the Nazi Party's "People's Welfare Agency" (NSV).[14] In the rubble of the ghetto, the Germans established a prison for 240 Jewish laborers, who were later killed in 1942. Of the more than 5,000 Jews who were unable to evacuate the city with the Red Army, fewer than twenty survived the Nazi occupation.[15]

At this time, the leader of all SS-police forces in Southern Russia was Himmler's deputy, Higher SS and Police Leader Jeckeln. However, in the field the various SS-police units operated within a multiple command structure. The Einsatzgruppe units, such as Blobel's SK4a, received orders from Sipo-SD chief Reinhard Heydrich (and his deputy, Gestapo chief Heinrich Müller) located at the Reich Security Main Office (RSHA) in Berlin. Their geographic targets and security measures were coordinated with and supervised by regional military and SS-police leaders such as Sixth Army general Reichenau and Higher SS and Police Leader Jeckeln. By contrast, the much larger units of Waffen-SS and Order Police received few direct orders from Berlin. Instead, they were under the command of Jeckeln, Himmler's Field Command Staff, and Field Army headquarters.

Within this hierarchy of headquarters and field offices, the key link between the army and SS-police in the Soviet territories (as elsewhere in Nazi-occupied Europe) was the higher SS and police leader. Known collectively as "Little Himmlers," the higher SS and police leaders were the most senior SS-police authorities reporting directly to Himmler. They were responsible regionally for all SS and police tasks in the military and civilian zones, including security and population policies such as resettlement actions, as well as the construction and administration of concentration and labor camps. They traveled throughout the military and civilian zones and directly supervised their subordinates in the mobile and stationary units. In short they were the intersection of the center and periphery. Jeckeln, Himmler's choice for Southern Russia (which was largely Ukraine) turned out to be one of the most aggressive Holocaust perpetrators in the Third Reich. After the war he did not escape the hangman's noose, but he did manage to slip into the margins of most scholarship on the Holocaust.

Unlike his subordinate Otto Rasch, the chief of Einsatzgruppe C, Jeckeln did not hold a university degree. Instead, his educational background and history with the Nazi Party was comparable to that of the other unsavory "Little Himmlers" — Hans-Adolf Prützmann (in Northern Russia) and Erich von dem Bach-Zelewski (in Central Russia). After having earned the Iron Cross (second class) as a pilot in World War I, Jeckeln spent most of the Weimar years unemployed until he found financial security from his second wife and the "career" possibilities that the Nazi Party and the SS offered someone of his type. The reasons for the breakdown of his first marriage are revealing and worth briefly recounting. Following his 1918 marriage to Charlotte Hirsch, Jeckeln had a run-in with his father-in-law who denied him a significant position in the prosperous family business. A humiliated and angry Jeckeln accused his father-in-law of being a war profiteer. Such a person, Jeckeln reasoned, must have Jewish blood in his background. He divorced his wife on the grounds of "racial contamination," and a custody battle over the care of their three children ensued.[16]

Jeckeln joined the Nazi Party in 1929 and the SS in 1930. He quickly climbed to the rank of SS-general lieutenant (SS-Gruppenführer) by the middle of 1933 and was named higher SS and police leader for Middle Germany in 1938. Besides his good relations with Himmler, he had an excellent rapport with Kurt Daluege (chief of the Order Police) and Theodore Eicke (commander of the Waffen-SS Death's Head Division), with whom he shared a virulent anti-Semitism and extreme devotion to the SS-police. Jeckeln's career reached its high point in the Nazi system when, after lobbying for action in the East, Himmler appointed him higher SS and police leader for Southern Russia. For Jeckeln, this assignment was a great honor. He was to lay the foundation of the Nazi empire in the East through the ethnic and political "cleansing" of the territory. To this end, he had at his disposal Waffen-SS, Einsatzgruppen, and at least nine Order Police battalions. His anti-Jewish massacres in Ukraine made the first Sipo-SD sweeps seem relatively small in scale.

Jeckeln was by no means a desk murderer. Flying from killing site to killing site in his Storch plane, he was notorious for "getting the job done." In fact the evident Nazi leap to genocide that occurred in Ukraine was mainly his doing and occurred while he was in the Zhytomyr region between late July and mid-September 1941. He was responsible for the first massacre of Jewish women in the region. On 25 July Jeckeln ordered his First SS Brigade to "cleanse the Rivne–Novohrad-Volyns'kyi stretch of Soviet stragglers of the [Red Army's] 124th Division and of other enemy groups"; he wrote that "until now the areas could only be superficially searched by the Wehrmacht; the villages will be searched between the main streets, and in the villages, and we will connect with the Ukrainian militia if on hand." Consequently the First SS Brigade massacred 1,658 Jewish men and women at Novohrad-Volyns'kyi (Zviahel) at the end of July 1941. Jeckeln personally supervised one mass shooting of 800 Jewish men and women (sixteen to sixty years old), who were killed along the banks of the Sluch' River.[17]

By the time Jeckeln arrived in Berdychiv, known among Nazi leaders as a Jewish capital of the former Russian empire, the city's military commander had already overseen massacres of at least 1,000 Jews carried out by Waffen-SS (SS-Viking) and EK5 units.[18] They tortured and killed the Jewish elders in the synagogue, and shot several thousand men, women, and children in the Brodetski forest on the outskirts of town. More than 15,000 remained. Jeckeln's first move was the formation of a ghetto on 26 August. German SS-police, army personnel, and local auxiliary police drove thousands of Jews into, as Vasilii Grossman described it, "ancient shacks, tiny single-storied houses, and crumbling brick buildings. . . . Everywhere were piles of junk, garbage and manure. . . . People lived five and six to a room." This poor section of town was known as Jatki.[19] But, according to Jeckeln's plan, the Jews would stay here but briefly. The next day Jeckeln told his men to take 2,500 Jews from the ghetto and to shoot them in the forests nearby.[20] Outside the ghetto, people could see and hear what was happening to the Jews; most remained silent. In a memorable, courageous gesture, the bishop of the Berdychiv Cathedral, Father Nikolai, contacted the Jewish leaders in the ghetto and tried to help them, but German officials in Zhytomyr threatened the bishop, warning that if he aided the Jews then he would be executed.[21]

On 1 September Jeckeln met with the new commander of the Order Police for Ukraine, Otto von Oelhafen, who was flown to Berdychiv for this private briefing. During lunch Jeckeln told him that already during that week a number of Jews had been killed.[22] In fact, that week Jeckeln had personally directed and observed the mass shooting of 23,600 Jewish men, women and children near Kam'ianets'-Podil's'kyi (about 200 kilometers southwest of Berdychiv). Jeckeln also instructed Oelhafen that future requests from the Security Police to employ Order Police battalions in the executions of Jews were to be communicated orally.[23] When his longtime colleague Kurt Daluege, the chief of the Order Police, arrived in Berdychiv on 4 September, Jeckeln ordered the execution of 1,303 Jews, including 875 Jewish girls over the age of twelve. According to Vasilii Grossman's account, these young people had been told that they were being sent to do agricultural work, and ended up digging their own graves at the edge of town in the village of Khazhyn. Perhaps the timing of this massacre with Daluege's arrival was purely coincidental. More likely, the zealous Jeckeln sought to show his dedication to the Nazi cause. The liquidation of the Berdychiv ghetto began about one week later, when between 10,000 and 15,000 Jewish men, women, and children (including the elderly and the infirm) were forced to walk four kilometers to the town's airfield, where they were shot in mass graves on 15 and 16 September.[24] The new ethnic German mayor of Berdychiv, a man named Reder, and his Ukrainian chief of police, named Koroliuk, "took an active part in organizing and conducting the execution."[25] Units of Jeckeln's own Staff Company as well as Order Police Battalion 45 participated in the action along with subunits of Einsatzgruppe C.

Jeckeln was not only the most influential SS leader in Ukraine at this time, second only to Himmler, but also the source of strong regional ties that developed between the military and SS, a partnership that permeated the lowest levels. Units of his Russia Regiment South routinely went on joint cleansing operations with the Wehrmacht's Security Divisions. Order Police Battalion 45 worked with Security Division 213 in Berdychiv and Security Division 444 in Vinnytsia. Order Police Battalion 314 collaborated with Security Division 444 in Vinnytsia, and Order Police Battalion 82 with Security Division 454 in Zhytomyr. Meanwhile Waffen-SS Infantry Regiments 8 and 10 (the First SS Brigade) joined forces with the Sixth Army in the northern part of the region.[26]

The "official task" of Jeckeln's First SS Brigade was, as in the case of the Wehrmacht Security Divisions, the suppression of pockets of Red Army resistance and partisans. Yet such "threats" were minimal at this stage. Instead, in addition to apprehending POWs and liquidating Soviet functionaries and "political commissars," the Waffen-SS descended on the villages of the region and shot Jewish men and women, whom Jeckeln branded Soviet agents. In the first two weeks of September, Higher SS and Police Leader units operating in the northeastern sections of the region around Ovruch wrote of their "successes" — the "liquidation" of 3,353 Jews, noting that they were killed along with a few partisans.[27]

The Division of Labor SS-Police and Wehrmacht Collaboration in the Holocaust

It is generally known that collaboration between the SS, the police, and the army was formalized in the pre-Barbarossa agreement between Sipo-SD chief Reinhard Heydrich and Quartermaster General Eduard Wagner. The various forms that this collaboration took once the invasion was under way are less well known.[28] SK4a personnel under Blobel and officers in the Sixth Army became comrades on the front lines as well as in the rear areas during the racial-political cleansing of POW camps and conquered territory. They also bonded socially during meals and late-night meetings in their quarters. Their collaboration in the executions of Jews, POWs, the mentally and physically disabled, "gypsies," and other so-called undesirables was preplanned and well coordinated, but it also exhibited ad hoc, even spontaneous features that were part of the dynamic conditions and context of war. Cross-agency collaboration developed from deliberate Nazi administrative plans that were bolstered by personal networks, military-style camaraderie in the field, and shared ideological beliefs. Most striking is the systematic division of labor that Sipo-SD men and military officials jointly devised in the field. It was demonstrated very clearly in Zhytomyr's Holocaust history, and especially on one day in early August 1941.[29]

On 7 August the entire staff of SK4a joined with the staffs of the Sixth Army and of Zhytomyr's Rear Area Field Command Post in the planning, staging, and implementation of a public execution in Zhytomyr's marketplace, followed by the shooting of 400 male Jews on the town's outskirts.[30] The incident began when members of SK4a arrested two Jewish men from Cherniakhiv (twenty-five kilometers north of Zhytomyr). According to the German reports, the villagers had accused the two men, Wolf Kieper and Moishe Kogan, of being "blood-thirsty agents of the NKVD."[31] After extracting a "confession" from them, security police commanders from SK4a brought Kieper and Kogan to Zhyto-myr. Meanwhile, the Wehrmacht's city commander at Zhytomyr, Colonel Josef Riedl, supervised a brutal "round-up" of about 400 of Zhytomyr's Jews (includ-ing many elderly men), who were escorted to the marketplace and guarded by the military field police and indigenous auxiliaries.

The Wehrmacht Propaganda Unit 637 drove through the city with a loud-speaker announcing in Ukrainian and German that a public execution would be held in the marketplace, where the Germans had erected a gallows.[32] Under the two dangling nooses of the gallows stood a truck that served, at first, as a stage. SD commandos led Kieper and Kogan to this platform, which was al-ready prepared with posters written in German and Ukrainian: "The Cheka Jew Wolf Kieper, the Murderer of 1,350 Ethnic Germans and Ukrainians" and "The Aide to the Jewish Cheka, the Executioner Moishe Kogan." In a rallying cry to the hundreds of curious and cheering onlookers, SS Hauptsturmführer Albert Müller asked aloud in Ukrainian, "With whom do you have to settle a score?" "With one or another Jew," the crowd replied. At which point, some of the 400 gathered Jewish men were beaten with clubs, kicked, and mishandled for about forty-five minutes. Behind the gallows, Wehrmacht soldiers sat perched on the roof of a small building; some looked on pensively while others casually ob-served the scene like any recreation on a day off. According to one eyewitness account, the crowds cheered as the truck drove forward and "Ukrainian women held their children up high." Infantrymen hollered, "Slowly, slowly so we can get a better photograph."[33] After Kieper and Kogan were killed, German guards drove the 402 Jewish men to a prepared shooting site outside of Zhytomyr (the Horse Cemetery).[34]

At the cemetery Germans and their Ukrainian auxiliaries forced between ten and twelve Jews to line up facing the firing squad, a platoon of Waffen-SS men who shot them with rifles. But according to the SS and army participants, this method was ineffective; not every victim who fell into the pit was dead. So an impromptu meeting was held between members of SK4a (including Paul Blo-bel) and two officials of the Sixth Army, a judge named Dr. Arthur Neumann and a doctor named Dr. Gerhart Panning. It was decided that each victim be

SD officers prepare to hang Moishe Kogan (left) and Wolf Kieper on the market square in Zhytomyr, 7 August 1941 (U.S. Holocaust Memorial Museum, courtesy of Zydowski Instytut Historyczny Instytut Naukowo-Badawczy, #17540)

Jews rounded up by the Wehrmacht and Sipo-SD in Zhytomyr watch the hanging of Moishe Kogan and Wolf Kieper on the market square, 7 August 1941 (U.S. Holocaust Memorial Museum, courtesy of Dokumentationsarchiv des Österreichischen Widerstandes, #17549)

first shot in the head, but then this approach also proved inadequate because it was too "messy"—the brains of the victims were spraying the killers.[35] According to another account of this shooting, two Wehrmacht officers, an officer of the Luftwaffe, and SS officers observed, while SD and Order Police units fired rifle shots from a distance of about six meters to the victims who sat facing the pit. The army doctor and SS officials looked into the pit to make sure all were dead. As many as 25 percent were not; but the executions continued, and many of the half-dead victims were covered with more bodies and soil. Later that evening the SS-police and army officials convened again to discuss the way the mass killing was to be done; at least one person present complained that it was "intolerable for both victims and firing squad members."[36]

Collaboration between the army and SD was demonstrated again in Zhytomyr when Blobel and army officials experimented with explosives as an alternative to shooting. In August 1941 the senior staff doctor with the Sixth Army, Dr. Panning, approached Blobel with a special request. During the time that the Sixth Army had been stationed in Zhytomyr (if not earlier at Luts'k), close relations had developed between SK4a and members of the army medical staff. Blobel and some of his fellow killers sought medical attention from the staff. They received injections to calm their nerves after the massacres. Panning, who had learned about the German capture of certain Russian explosives (dum-dum bullets) was investigating the possible injuries German soldiers might suffer from this illegal ammunition. To determine the possible effects of the Soviet ammunition on German soldiers, Panning decided that the explosives should be tested on live humans. Panning asked Blobel for some "guinea pigs." They agreed to use POWs, probably Jews pulled out of the camps by Blobel's units.[37]

Oberstabsarzt Panning did not have the official authorization to order Blobel's men to carry out this murderous experiment, yet Blobel was willing to oblige. The experiment offered Blobel the possibility of advancing the implementation of the "Final Solution," and of maintaining "smooth" relations with the Wehrmacht. Additionally, Blobel handpicked certain men for this gruesome job so that they would become the increasingly hardened killers that he needed to carry out the genocide. Panning, on the other hand, acted under the guise of conducting medical research. In fact, Panning's local reputation as a "researcher" spread to Berlin a few weeks later. On 12 September Helmuth James von Moltke, the Abwehr's international law expert and later a central figure in the resistance group known as the Kreisau circle, wrote to his wife about Panning's experiments, stressing that the incident was "the height of bestiality and depravity and there is nothing one can do."[38]

The Blobel-Panning collaboration reveals several facets of the implementation of the "Final Solution" under the military administration. In particular, their partnership demonstrates how the otherwise independent interests of two agencies converged around the Holocaust. On the face of it, such cooperation between a killing commando chief and a doctor from the Prussian military establishment seems rather odd. Blobel was a notoriously well-connected Nazi and vicious anti-Semite. He was an SD careerist who demanded that all of his underlings bloody their hands in the murder. His superiors praised his total loyalty and reliability. In fact Himmler later recognized Blobel by granting him the task of covering up the genocide as head of the top-secret Sonderkommando 1005. Yet Blobel, who was also known for choleric outbursts, held a degree in architecture from one of the best art schools in Germany. In other words, he was not only, as his personnel file stated, a "geborner Kriminalist" (born detective) "von unbedingter Zuverlässigkeit" (of unconditional loyalty) but also a technically minded architect, "very predisposed to the practical." Thus Blobel appreciated pragmatic solutions, and in this regard he saw eye to eye with the senior staff doctor Panning, who was director of the Forensics Military Institute in the Military Medical Academy in Berlin. Panning was part of a new generation of medical experts who applied their forensics research to the state's "crime-fighting" apparatus. Basically unrestrained by institutional and legal structures, Blobel and Panning were free to "refine" killing methods and to conduct heinous experiments with Jewish "guinea pigs."[39]

As these incidents show, the desire at the lower levels to further Nazi execution methods was a joint army/SS-police endeavor that took on various forms.[40] In the mass shootings that followed the Kieper-Kogan hangings, and in experiments with explosives on POWs, officials from the two agencies sought to "refine" the killing process and demonstrated their inhumane regard for efficiency. In many other cases of "on the spot" collaboration, SS-police and military personnel devised sadistic amusements. For example, at Tul'chyn in August 1941, an SS commando and the local Ortskommandantur forced elderly and infirm Jews to gather in the marketplace. They were made to stand and hop on one leg. At Khmil'nyk the Germans cut the beards of the elderly Jewish men and then forced their grandsons and other Jewish youth to eat the hair. Jews were also brought to the destroyed glass factory and made to dance barefoot on shards of glass.[41] In addition to devising a "reibungslos" division of labor for carrying out large-scale massacres, army and SS personnel initiated such torture, stripping the Jews of their dignity in their last moments of life.[42]

Rationalizing, Legitimizing, or Resisting the Mass Murder

There is scant evidence of lower-level German officials in the military and SS-police who resisted outright the order to kill Jews. Instead, there were some individuals, including Otto Rasch, the seasoned killer and head of Einsatzgruppe C, who voiced concern about the economic results and political backlashes of the policy. In an "Event Report" of 17 September 1941, he made some relatively bold statements about where the genocidal policy was headed:

Even if it were possible to carry out the immediate, 100 percent elimination of the Jews, with that we would still not have done away with the hotbed of political danger. The work of Bolshevism is supported by Jews, Russians, Georgians, Armenians, Poles, Latvians, Ukrainians; the Bolshevik apparatus is in no way identical with the Jewish population. In this state of affairs, the aim of political and police security would be missed, if the main task of the destruction of the communist apparatus were relegated to second or third place in favor of the practically easier task of eliminating the Jews. Concentrating on the Bolshevik functionary robs Jewry of its most able forces, so that the solution of the Jewish problem becomes more and more a problem of organization.

In western and central Ukraine, Jewry is almost exclusively identical with urban workers, artisans, and the merchant class. *If the Jewish labor force is entirely done away with, then an economic reconstruction of Ukrainian industry as well as the development of the urban administrative centers will be almost impossible.*

There is only one possibility, which the German administration in the General Government has neglected for a long time:
Solution of the Jewish Question through the extensive labor utilization of the Jews.
This will result in a gradual liquidation of Jewry—a development that corresponds to the economic conditions of the country.[43]

In September 1941, SS-Brigadeführer Rasch (like his counterpart in Belorussia, Einsatzgruppe B leader Arthur Nebe) stood at the crossroads of his career in the Nazi system. Rasch, who was born in East Prussia in 1891, spent most of his years in battle on Germany's eastern frontiers. In World War I he fought against Polish nationalist groups as a member of the 12th Border Guard Regiment, and continued to fight following the war as a member of the Von Löwenfeld Freikorps. After earning doctoral degrees in law and political economy, Rasch joined the Nazi Party in 1931, the SS in 1933, and the SD in 1936. He enjoyed a swift ascent up the SS-police hierarchy, first as chief of the Gestapo in Frankfurt am Main, then as inspector of the Security Police for Upper Austria, and thereafter as chief of the SD office in Prague. In the Polish campaign of September–October 1939, Rasch served as commander of the Security Police of a special Einsatzgruppe tasked with the eradication of Polish and Jewish intelligentsia.[44] By 1941 he earned the rank of SS-Brigadeführer. According to Rasch's postwar testimony, he hoped that after "paying his dues" in the Barbarossa campaign he would land a nice sinecure in Berlin's RSHA. Instead, as he claimed in the dock at Nuremberg, he was called back to Berlin because of conflicts with Himmler and Erich Koch, the Reich commissar for Ukraine. As of October 1941, his career in the RSHA effectively ended. Rasch assumed the unlikely position of manager in the Continental Oil Company until the conclusion of the war. The reasons for his career shift remain murky. However, his critical statements in the widely circulated "Event Report" quoted above are revealing for other reasons. Rasch, who was fifty years old in 1941, and thus older than most of his counterparts and superiors in the SS-police, apparently felt confident enough in his position to criticize state policy. At the same time he carried out his orders to kill as many Jews as possible in a thorough manner. Indeed, he placed extra pressure on his subordinates to comply with the leadership's demand to step up the killing. Yet even as he held the critical middleman role of enforcing a genocidal "Final Solution," Rasch argued that the total destruction of the Jews was not the best way to stamp out Bolshevism.

Rasch's subordinate, SS-Standartenführer Erwin Schulz, who was the oldest of the Einsatzkommando chiefs, also expressed some ambivalence about killing all Jews. Schulz (b. 1900) had a long career in the Schutzpolizei (he joined in 1923) and then switched to intelligence and political police work in 1935. He detested communism and believed that the Jews were to blame for Bolshevism. When Rasch pressured him to kill more women and children in early August 1941, Schulz claimed after the war that he did not want to carry out this order because the massacres were dreadful for his men. Schulz sent a letter to Bruno Streckenbach, who was the Sipo-SD chief in charge of personnel matters in Berlin, requesting that he be called back from the front. Schulz left Zhytomyr at the end of August. This move did not damage his career. In fact, by November 1941 he was considered competent enough to teach a training course for Gestapo and SD-chiefs being posted abroad. The subject of his course was "Die Haltung eines SS-Mannes" (the attitude of an SS man). Moreover, on 9 November 1941 Schulz was promoted to the rank of SS-Oberführer for his "besonderer Verdienste im Einsatz" (special service in action).[45]

Neither the outspoken Rasch nor his less prominent colleagues disputed the genocide on moral grounds. Instead, even the loudest critics of Reich policy maintained a pragmatic stance, warning about the immediate negative economic and political repercussions of the Jewish losses. The men in the field such as Schulz and even Himmler observed that members of the shooting squads experienced psychological trauma. Yet Rasch articulated what most were unwilling to see or openly admit to, namely, that the Jews, women and children in particular, were in no way to be identified exclusively with Bolshevism. As he observed, most of his colleagues pursued the "easier" task of total destruction of the Jewish community rather than deal with the intricacies of rooting out Bolshevism across the multiethnic Soviet society and state apparatus. Rasch was not the only senior SD official to express some skepticism at this juncture in Nazi anti-Jewish policy. Like Erwin Schulz, Einsatzgruppe B chief Arthur Nebe also voiced his concerns, and he was not penalized for his outspokenness.[46] Some, such as Rasch, Nebe, and Schulz, may have secretly or openly questioned the policy, but they did nothing to slow or obstruct the killing. Shortly after Rasch wrote his mid-September critique, he and his colleagues planned for the destruction of Kiev's Jews at Babi Yar.[47]

As of the summer of 1941, a growing number of SS-policemen and other German personnel in the field found themselves cast in the role of executioner or of accomplice to mass murder. They adapted to the role, in large part by allocating certain "unpleasant" tasks to non-Germans and by "improving" their mass-shooting methods, which in turn enabled them to expand the killing. SK4a executioners such as subunit leader Heinrich Huhn, who joined the Ukrainian militiamen in the killing of the children at Radomyshyl', recounted after the war that at the ghetto liquidation at Zhytomyr (which occurred almost two weeks after the Radomyshyl' incident) the women were allowed to hold their children in their arms ("Die Frauen durften ihre Kinder auf den Armen halten").[48] Huhn and his colleagues believed that this was a more efficient and even "humane" approach. Thus with each killing action, regional officials in the army and SS-police advanced their genocidal methods and overcame organizational and psychological conflicts with the full support of their superiors. Even those who argued for the more economical approach of excusing Jewish laborers from the mass shootings were not trying to stem the violence against women, children, the elderly, and the infirm. The labor rationale for keeping some able-bodied Jews alive was accepted because it was still based on a common understanding that the Jews would die anyway. Besides more efficient shooting methods and forced labor, another Nazi strategy for carrying out the Holocaust crystallized in the summer of 1941: ghettoization.

Facilitating Genocide Ghettos in Zhytomyr

In the pre-Barbarossa guidelines for ruling the conquered territory, German military and SS-police leaders did not plan for the establishment of ghettos. In Roques's Army Group South Rear Area Administration, the regional Kommandanturen (commanders) concentrated on four tasks related to the Jewish question: (1) confiscation of Jewish property, (2) marking of Jews, (3) exploitation of Jewish labor, and 4) registration and listing of the Jewish population. The formation of ghettos is noticeably absent from this official list.[49] Indeed, one of the few pre-Barbarossa references to ghettos appeared in a May 1941 memorandum by the Reich minister for the Occupied Eastern Territories, Alfred Rosenberg, who advised his Ukrainian deputy that "after the customary removal of Jews from all public offices, the 'Jewish Question' must undergo a decisive solution through the establishment of ghettos or labor battalions." Rosenberg, who was not at the forefront of Nazi anti-Jewish policy-making and implementation in 1941, assumed that the same pattern of destruction in Poland would be applied to Ukraine, and that ghettoization would occur in the civilian administered zones, not in the military ones.[50]

From the Nazi point of view, the region's high concentration of Jews in the major towns and on Jewish collective farms, such as the Romanov Settlement of about 1,000 Jews in Dzerzhyns'k, actually "facilitated" the German goal of a rapid destruction of all Jewish communities. Even in the open countryside the

Jews felt trapped, being surrounded by hostile neighbors. According to a Jewish survivor, Michael Rozenberg, his friends and family tried to flee on foot from the Nazis, but they could not find hiding places in the open fields and lacked means of transportation.[51] The Goykher family from the vicinity of Vinnytsia trudged eastward with the Soviet army but soon the German army overtook them and forced them into a schoolhouse with the rest of Illintsi's Jews.[52]

The Nazis' use of schools and other makeshift sites to confine Jews marked a major shift in their ghettoization practices. In general, regional leaders found that the formation of ghettos along the Polish model was neither necessary nor useful. During the first weeks and months of the occupation, both military and SS-police officials utilized the term "ghetto" mainly as a ruse for assembling the population shortly before it would be murdered. Describing the SS approach in the Zhytomyr region, Rasch related how the conditions of the population were connected to the Jews' fate in a curious way. On 25 September he reported that "the procedure against the Jews is necessarily different in the individual sectors, according to the density of their settlement. . . . In the northern sector a great many Jewish refugees have returned to the villages. . . . [There is no food or shelter for them.] . . . The danger of epidemics has thus increased considerably. For that reason alone, a thorough clean-up of the respective places became necessary." At Radomyshyl' the SD crowded the Jews from the outlying areas into an old school; they began to die of hunger and disease. According to the Einsatzgruppe C chief's "official" reasoning, given that conditions were so bad and the Germans could not supply them with food, 1,668 Jews were *therefore* killed by the SK4a and Ukrainian militia. In this and other top-secret SD reports, Rasch "explained" that large concentrations of Jews engendered problems of sanitation, housing, and epidemics, so the population "had" to be eliminated. While that was Rasch's formal rationale for destroying entire communities, the Germans in fact confined the Jews to sites without care or provisions until the date of the mass shooting could be arranged.[53]

General Commissar Klemm's driver observed in his travels during 1941 and 1942 that there were no closed ghettos in Zhytomyr akin to those found at Cracow and Warsaw.[54] The Polish "model," which was the common Nazi point of reference, contained some historically familiar features—such as some degree of independent Jewish life evident in a Jewish Council, Jewish police forces, sociocultural institutions, economic activity, and relatively intact family households. During the late summer and fall of 1941, the Nazis avoided the formation of Jewish ghettos, either because they lacked the resources to establish them or they found that the genocide had turned ghettos into obsolete or, as they put it, "unnecessary" structures. The commander of the Rear Army Group Area

South, Karl von Roques, had ordered at the end of August 1941 that the establishment of ghettos in heavily Jewish-populated towns should be pursued only when necessary or at least "useful."[55] In his guidelines for administering the region, Koch stated that in villages with fewer than 200 Jews, no ghetto should be formed.[56] In the bordering town of Bar in Podil'ia, which was over 50 percent Jewish, the term "ghetto" was used in the public order for Jews to gather, but a ghetto was not formed. On 15 December the local Ukrainian administration ordered that the Jews of Bar report to three separate locations within five days. Of the three locales one housed craftsmen only, whereas the other two sites housed the elderly, women, and children, who were deemed "useless" and therefore annihilated.[57]

As elsewhere, at Voronovytsia, in the Nemyriv district, ghettos were absent from the killing process. The Germans gathered 900 Jewish men, women and children, and then twenty-five Jews were selected as laborers; the rest were placed in an abandoned building for a day or two while the execution site was prepared. The remaining 875 Jews were brought to a pit by EK5 on 10 November 1941 and shot.[58] At Cherniakhiv Jewish families were crammed into a freight car shortly before they were gunned down. In Vinnytsia the much larger population was confined to a bombed-out factory. In Berdychiv, the ghetto existed for less than a month. Jewish workers and their families who survived the September–October massacres were imprisoned in a Carmelite monastery, where they were tortured and killed; the few hundred who survived were then transferred to a labor camp.[59] And at Koziatyn the Germans placed the Jews in barracks and after killing the Jews turned the barracks into a "workers educational camp."

Thus, instead of being domiciled in ghettos, Jews across the region's villages and towns were crammed into barns, schools, and freight cars or restricted to other areas for brief periods, while SS, military, and civil leaders determined how many marksmen would be needed, identified a killing site, obtained possible truck transport to the site, and prepared the pits.[60] Military and SS-police leaders concentrated the Jews into camps and other locales with the intent of creating unlivable conditions for them, to isolate and therefore weaken the Jewish population, to better organize the population for forced labor, and to acquire better housing for German personnel. Yet all of these short-term remedies were pursued with the understanding that the entire Jewish population was dispensable, hence the massive loss of life that often accompanied the relocation.

In the rural areas with Jewish populations that did not exceed 200 persons, the military and SS-police commanders found alternative methods for controlling the population. They pursued a series of anti-Jewish measures that amounted to, in Shmuel Spector's words, "ghettoization de facto." After registering the population, the local village Kommandantur ordered the Jews to move away from the main streets and to the back streets. Jews could not relocate to another residence or leave the village without permission. They were not allowed on the streets except when going to and from the workplace. Unlike the rest of the indigenous population, the Jews were banned from the marketplace for most of the day. They had to register their property, businesses, and financial assets. They were forced to wear a white Star of David or an armband as a prominent, humiliating label of their "pariah" status, which further alienated them from the Ukrainians. Such restrictions coupled with the unpredictable Nazi assaults against Jews created a life-threatening atmosphere that discouraged most Jews from leaving their homes at all.[61]

Beyond Ukraine's borders, the genocidal approach to ghettoization was also applied to Western European Jewry. At the Lodz, Riga, and Minsk ghettos, for example, German Jewish deportees stayed briefly before being shot or gassed. Koch and Higher SS and Police Leader Hans-Adolf Prützmann (Jeckeln's successor) considered Ukraine as a possible dumping ground for Europe's Jews. In a joint memorandum of 12 January 1942, Koch and Prützmann stated that the policy for establishing ghettos was still not defined, but they asked the regional commissars as well as the SS-policemen to identify possible future ghettos near railway links where Reich Jews could be brought.[62] As it turned out, Reich Jews were not deported to Ukraine, but the Koch-Prützmann memo reveals that by late 1941 or early 1942 ghettos in Ukraine and elsewhere in Eastern Europe had been transformed into something unprecedented in Europe's long history of anti-Judaism. Under the Nazis ghettos became transit centers and holding "pens" for facilitating the mass murder.[63]

The 1941 period was essentially a combined SS and military assault against the Jews who were within reach along the major transit routes and in the larger towns of the region. As of August, the number of SS and SD forces around Zhytomyr, Berdychiv, and Vinnytsia under the command of the higher SS and police leader and the army had reached nearly 8,000 men. This figure does not include thousands of police in the military's Feldgendarmerie (military police), Geheime Feldpolizei (army secret field police), and Ukrainian militia as well as the sharpshooters and infantrymen of the regular army troops, who also became involved in anti-Jewish manhunts and massacres.[64]

In Zhytomyr and the neighboring district of Cherniakhiv, SD officials reported a few instances of Jewish resistance. Jews had attacked Ukrainian militiamen and had also established an underground operation of printing false identifications.[65] Near Novohrad-Volyns'kyi a small group of about five Jews, male and female, managed to escape the shooting actions there and later joined the Soviet partisan movement, carrying out acts of sabotage and terror against the German administration. Jews also joined the communist resistance movement in Vinnytsia. However, these brave Jewish acts of resistance were no match for the enormous power of German and non-German anti-Semitic forces in the region. Thus there was an accumulation of "security" units in August and September that created a possibility—or, as some German officials saw it, the "opportunity"—for large-scale killing actions against entire Jewish communities.

Interethnic Relations and the Holocaust
Ukrainians, Ethnic Germans, and Jews

The majority of Ukrainians sought to preserve their own livelihood, which, from the perspective of the peasants, was continually being threatened by outside forces. However, among the thousands of Ukrainians who did work in the German administration—that is, the mayors, collective farm supervisors, postal workers, messengers, and clerks—a minority, albeit an influential one, did systematically hunt and brutalize the Jews: the Ukrainian police. As historian John Paul Himka has recently argued in his work on Ukrainian collaboration in the Holocaust, "In normal historical situations, active sadists would be marginalized as criminal elements and latent ones would not become active. . . . But during the Nazi occupation of Ukraine, criminality moved from the margins of society to its center, and individuals with an inclination to rob, extort, and kill were not lost in the larger crowd of humanity, but rather stepped to the fore." [66] While the Germans did not tolerate Ukrainian criminal activities outside the administration, they did try to mold some of the more unsavory types into obedient policemen by recruiting them for police training programs in the region.

Not surprisingly, the clearest case of a Ukrainian role in the "Final Solution" can be found among the German records of their Ukrainian auxiliary police units. Himmler realized that his security goals exceeded German manpower and introduced in one of his first decrees as the chief of SS and police forces in the East a plan for employing non-German auxiliaries, Schutzmannschaften.[67] According to Himmler's July 1941 order, these police collaborators were chosen from the local militias that had sprung up under the military occupation and from the screening of acceptable racial groups among the POWs, first and foremost the Volksdeutsche and then the Ukrainians.[68]

German military commanders and officers of the SD commandos used these Ukrainians (and ethnic Germans) in a number of so-called security tasks, including the identification of the Jews from among the local population and subsequent anti-Jewish measures. For example, in Shpykiv, south of Vinnytsia on the Romanian border (the Bug River), the very first order issued by the Ukrainian commander of the "Ukrainian National People's Militia" (who wore the nationalist trident on his uniform) was that all Jews over seven years of age must wear the white star. Forcing the Jews to wear the white star was one of the persecutory measures spelled out in the German Ortskommandanturen's guidelines issued from Berlin.[69]

Although German leaders found a sufficient number of Ukrainian volunteers to carry out their anti-Jewish measures, pogroms were not widespread in the Zhytomyr region, to the disappointment of SD officials. According to the Einsatzgruppe C reports from August and early September 1941, "Almost nowhere could the population be induced to take active steps against the Jews."[70] In order to involve the people in the action against Jews, the Jews were first marched through town, and members of the Ukrainian militia were assigned to the executions. So the Einsatzkommando and Sonderkommando leaders thought up ways to provoke pogroms, and the Ukrainian militia helped the Germans foment the violence by publicly seizing, beating, and even murdering Jews. Jewish survivors and contemporary German reports concur that when pogroms did occur in the region, they broke out after the German army or SS arrived. At Bilopil'e, near the railway juncture of Koziatyn, Jewish survivor Nina Borisovna Glozman lost her father when Ukrainians beat him to death in a pogrom at the beginning of September, one month after the German army arrived there.[71] In a village near the city of Zhytomyr, members of SK4a discovered the mutilated remains of Ukrainians and others who had allegedly been massacred during the Soviet retreat; the German police publicly blamed the local Jews for the atrocities, sparking a pogrom that was followed by a German "action" of mass shootings.[72] In a village near Chudniv, the Jewish survivor Galina Efimovna Pekerman recalled, the Germans arrived at the end of July and enlisted local Ukrainians to massacre first the Jewish children of the village and then the rest of the Jews (about 800 persons), who were seized and gunned down at the local park.[73] In general, German officials instigated the pogroms, but they preferred not to bloody their own hands since local militiamen (Ukrainian and ethnic German), anti-Semites, and plunderers were so obliging.[74]

Most Ukrainians viewed these collaborators with suspicion because of their excessive brutality. Next to the stiffly uniformed Nazi secret police, who were assumed to be "cultured," the rather ragged local thugs in many ways posed a greater threat to the local population; they could identify individual Jews and carry out personal vendettas with force. In some cases the Germans found that the Ukrainian militia acted against German interests.[75] In the city of Zhytomyr in 1941, the Germans hanged a Russian named Briukhanov because his sadistic attacks against the Jews and others in the population could not be contained. The Germans needed help from the indigenous population, but they also expected obedience and a controllable level of mass violence. Heydrich, Rosenberg, and other Nazi leaders had instructed their subordinates in the field to allow and even incite pogroms, but the massacres, they stressed, must not spiral into the kind of social chaos that Germans associated with the "less" civilized peoples of Ukraine. Applying whatever resources were available to them, German leaders in Zhytomyr pursued the "Final Solution" in an atmosphere of expediency and with a constant regard for order and efficiency.

Local police and civil commissars relied on the Ukrainians to assist them with nearly every step of the "Final Solution" leading up to the point of execution. They needed the locals to identify the Jewish population, to distribute the armbands, to collect special anti-Jewish taxes, and then to go from house to house, seize the identified Jews, guard them, escort them to their execution, and beat any who tried to resist.[76]

Several thousand Ukrainians in Zhytomyr's German administration (largely in the police) carried out anti-Jewish measures under the watchful eye of their German supervisors. There were also cases in which Ukrainians in and outside the administration came willingly to the Germans and denounced Jews, whose fate no one could doubt after the summer of 1941. As more than one of Zhytomyr's Jewish survivors remarked, for every one Ukrainian who helped a Jew, there were many more who denounced Jews to the Germans. Nina Glozman and her younger brother survived the Holocaust in hiding—not in one place but in many different locations. As Glozman described it after the war:

My mother, my younger brother, and I managed to escape the death pits. We hid in a small village near our hometown until a policeman recognized us. He took us to Koziatyn, since there were no German killing squads in Bilopil'e. We had to stay in the ghetto, chopping wood, cleaning toilets. When the ghetto was liquidated we were able to run to Berdychiv where we hid with another Jewish family. But that was not safe so we ran to Ruzhyn and hid in a barn. After some time there, we heard shots so we fled again this time to the small village of Sestrinaka. It was early 1943. One man named Semen Tkatchuk hid us for two months; he was alone because his son had just been hanged as a partisan the month before we arrived. But someone in the village betrayed us. My mother was arrested and killed. Semen helped my younger brother and me escape from the village. Later we found an abandoned house. My brother and I found work. I was working in a sugar factory one day when the Germans came in and their interpreter turned out to be my former classmate. She recognized me and immediately denounced me. With the help of an engineer in the factory, I fled through the back door.[77]

Glozman was first betrayed by a local non-German policeman, rescued by a grieving perhaps vengeful father whose son had been brutally murdered by the Nazis, and then denounced again by a former classmate. Glozman and her younger brother narrowly escaped death on several occasions, and their lives were largely in the hands of local non-Jews. Her odyssey helps to explain why the few Jews who managed to escape the German killing actions of 1941 ultimately did not survive the occupation; more often than not the individual choice of a non-Jew who also lived under extreme, life-threatening conditions determined a Jew's chances of survival. The Germans tended not to write up extensive reports about non-Jews who helped Jews. Instead, German officials in the Zhytomyr region, who may have been seeking some ideological affirmation from the local population, did report that both the ethnic Germans and Ukrainians vilified the Jews, calling them agents of Satan. Upon the massacre of the Jews in Khmil'nyk, German observers noted, Ukrainians held a church service to thank God for the removal of the Jews. As prevalent as anti-Judaism was, however, there were additional motives that drove Ukrainians and other locals to attack or denounce their Jewish neighbors.[78]

One particular case illustrates the role that interethnic strife played in furthering German anti-Semitic policies in Zhytomyr. In December 1941 the SD and civil administration began to formally develop the Ukrainian police from among the existing militia and new recruits. In the process, the Germans released many militiamen whom they considered unqualified to serve or, if the men were associated with the Ukrainian nationalist movement, a possible threat to German rule. One of the Ukrainian militiamen who lost his job at this time was Mark Koval's'kyi. Koval's'kyi was not a Ukrainian nationalist activist, so he was evidently released for other reasons, which are not altogether clear. In any case, Koval's'kyi was not pleased and promptly went to the local SD office to denounce his former colleagues in the police administration. First Koval's'kyi claimed that the wife of the Ukrainian examining judge, Kersh, was a Jew who held false ID papers. Then he identified Ukrainian nationalists in the administration and told of Ukrainian policemen who secretly traded seized Jewish property, including a Jewish leather coat valued at 3,000 rubles. The SD investigated his allegations by interrogating staff of the police administration as well as friends and neighbors of the accused. One of the Ukrainian witnesses testified that the judge, Kersh, had helped a Jewish man (named Fatzstein) by having him released from police custody. The witness generously provided Fatzstein's address—7 Dmitrii Street. In addition, this witness argued, Kersh's Ukrainian adjutant (named Sherei) employed a Jewish tailor, whom he had placed in the militia with false identification papers.[79] Another disgruntled ex-militiaman also testified that the chief of the Ukrainian Police Department, the ethnic German Alexander Kulitzki, concealed Jews in the administration. As he put it, Kulitzki fired Ukrainians from the militia and replaced them with "communists and Jews."

After numerous interrogations, the Sipo-SD arrested the Ukrainian judge Sherei, the ethnic German police chief Kulitzki, and their alleged Jewish coconspirators.[80] In a desperate appeal to the Germans, Sherei pleaded that he faithfully carried out their orders to "clean up Zhytomyr from its dirty elements." But the SD did not release Sherei or the arrested Jews. Of all those under investigation, only the ethnic German Kulitzki was spared and continued to work as a district police chief in Zhytomyr.[81]

This incident demonstrates how Ukrainians and ethnic Germans exploited Nazi anti-Semitism as well as their own prejudices to curry favor with the Nazis, improve their own conditions, and settle scores with foes. Ukrainians and ethnic Germans competed for coveted positions within the Nazi administration, and they quickly figured out how to play the "Jewish" card in this lethal game. The case also reveals that some Ukrainians and ethnic Germans in the administration tried unsuccessfully to help Jews.

Whether or not individual attempts to assist Jews were altruistic, they were almost always sabotaged by those who sought to exploit the Nazi system, feared Nazi punishment, or were simply anti-Semitic. Do these "accomplices" to the Holocaust have anything in common? Can one particular political, social, or ethnic group be singled out? Survivor Nina Glozman condemned "sadistic" Ukrainians and ethnic Germans as the local perpetrators and collaborators in the German's "Final Solution."[82] Soviet historiography and some polemical Jewish accounts of the Holocaust blamed Ukrainian nationalists as the leading sector of the population that collaborated with the Germans.[83] Ukrainian nationalists did infiltrate the German administration, but were they the largest number of Nazi collaborators who persecuted and even murdered the Jews?

Both factions of the Organization of Ukrainian Nationalists espoused anti-Semitism, and their concept of a Ukrainian state was not a multiethnic one. In April 1941, Stepan Bandera's Second General Congress at Cracow issued a resolution to fight the Jews, whom he branded as the "vanguard of Muscovite imperialism in Ukraine." A month later, as Bandera's leaders trained their task forces for their role in Operation Barbarossa, they prepared a seventy-page set of guidelines titled "Struggle and Activities of the OUN in Wartime." According to scholars Karel Berkhoff and Marco Carynnyk, the OUN-B document states that "at a time of chaos and confusion liquidation of undesirable Polish, Muscovite, and Jewish activists is permitted, especially supporters of Bolshevik-Muscovite imperialism." The guidelines also identified the main props of Soviet power in Ukraine as certain western Poles and Muscovite Russians as well as Jews, who were censured "both individually and as a national group." According to the OUN-B's prewar instructions, these enemies should be made "harmless when the new revolutionary order is being established in Ukraine." In the future autonomous Ukraine, assimilated Jews were also not welcome.[84] In July 1941, the head of the newly declared Ukrainian state, Iaroslav Stets'ko, wrote in his autobiography: "Although I consider Moscow, which in fact held Ukraine in captivity, and not Jewry, to be the main and decisive enemy, I nonetheless fully appreciate the undeniably harmful and hostile role of the Jews, who are helping Moscow enslave Ukraine. I therefore support the destruction of the Jews and the expedience of bringing German methods of exterminating Jewry to Ukraine, barring their assimilation and the like."[85]

Stets'ko's writings and recently discovered documents from Ukrainian nationalists attached to Bandera's movement demonstrate that OUN-B leaders supported Nazi anti-Jewish actions. Yet they also shared the German concern for social order by warning against the outbreak of wild pogroms. Thus Nazi leaders assumed that Ukrainians would start pogroms, but Ukrainian nationalist activists who infiltrated the rural administrations instructed their sympathizers to avoid disorganized massacres of Jews.

With the Germans taking the lead in the Holocaust and facing little or no resistance from the local non-Jewish population, there was actually little need for the Ukrainian nationalists to wage an anti-Semitic propaganda campaign. Their anti-Russian propaganda was sufficient. Since the nineteenth century, the Jews of Ukraine had tended to ally themselves with Russian, rather than Ukrainian, culture; hence, from the local Ukrainian perspective, the Jews had entered into an alliance with the "enemy" camp of Russian, Muscovite oppressors. Thus in 1941 the OUN saw the Jewish and Polish threats as ancillary to a Russian-centered Bolshevik threat.[86]

It is striking however that Bandera's task forces in the Zhytomyr region rarely commented in their reports about the atrocities, nor did they indicate that local nationalists instigated pogroms. One Bandera agent only noted in a perfunctory way that "on Sunday, 8 September, all the Jews of Miropol were shot." In the nationalists' accounts of village life in Zhytomyr in 1941, there were no criticisms of the German-led atrocities against the Jews, at least none made by the nationalists themselves and none that the nationalists observed.[87] If not outright support, then a general indifference seemed to prevail.

The Jews of the Zhytomyr region who managed to survive the 1941 period of SS and army occupation were those in hiding, those whose locales had not yet been "cleansed," and those who were shunted into ghettos and forced labor. Near Vinnytsia the longest-standing ghetto in the region at Khmil'nyk (which was liquidated in June 1943) contained about 3,000 Jews; this was the remnant population that survived a massacre of an estimated 6,000 Jews on 9 January 1942.[88] The largest population of survivors was in Vinnytsia proper; about 5,000 Jewish laborers and their families were confined to the sewing factory and the brick works. Individuals whose villages and towns had been raided by the killing commandos but were able to escape the "roundup" roamed the countryside, hiding in barns and hovels.[89] When Rosenberg's commissars arrived in November 1941 fewer than 100 Jews remained in the city of Zhytomyr; German officials in the police, army, and civil administration employed them as printers, shoemakers, tailors, and carpenters.[90] In the more remote villages that the commandos and other German army and security forces were unable to reach in 1941, the rural German gendarmerie, Ukrainian and ethnic German Schutzmannschaften, and a variety of non-SS agencies introduced the genocide under the rule of the commissars.

Hitler desired the rapid transfer of newly occupied territory from military to civilian administration. With the German-Soviet front about 100 miles from Zhytomyr outside Kiev, he ordered on 20 August 1941 that the western half of Ukraine, including part of the Zhytomyr region, be placed within the borders of the civilian government as early as 1 September.[91] A flurry of decrees set this transfer in motion. The position of military commander (Wehrmachtsbefehls-haber) was created as the supreme military authority over the civilian zones of occupation. Göring's role as chief of the Four-Year Plan was extended to economic matters of the entire occupied East. By October 1941 the Sixth and Seventeenth Armies along with units of Einsatzgruppe C and General Roques's Rear Army administration had advanced eastward to the Dnepr and beyond. Under Wehrmachtsbefehlshaber Karl Kitzinger, the military's presence in the Zhytomyr region continued with forced requisitions of food and clothing for the army, the transport of troops to the front, the management of military hospitals, bordellos, field and town command posts, and the roughly seventeen stationary POW camps scattered around Zhytomyr and the neighboring commissariat of Volhynia.[92] Göring's Four-Year Plan and the Wehrmacht's General Quartermaster's Office maintained a network of agricultural leaders and economic commandos to ensure that the troops could "live off the land" in Ukraine. Yet Wehrmacht and SS-police agencies lost their unchallenged control of the region to a new caste of civilian rulers, known as "commissars."

Chapter 5

**The Zhytomyr General Commissariat,
1942–1943**

As regards the Eastern Territories . . . I wish only broad instructions to be issued from Berlin; the settlement of day-to-day
issues can safely be left in the hands of the respective regional
commissars.

—Adolf Hitler, 22 July 1942

Although the German war against the Soviet Union had long
been in the minds and on the planning tables of the Nazi leadership, it was only
after the campaign was well under way that Hitler held a meeting to determine
who the new leaders of the conquered territory would be, define the administrative structure and its boundaries, and establish the official terminology for
the occupied territories and its leaders. On 16 July 1941 Hitler convened Alfred
Rosenberg, Heinrich Lammers, Wilhelm Keitel, Hermann Göring, and Martin
Bormann at his headquarters. At the start he reminded his top brass that Nazi
plans for the East were to be kept secret; as he put it: "We are not to publicize our objectives to the world; instead the main thing is that we ourselves
know what we want." To the outside observer, Hitler continued, it must seem
that Germany had been forced or obligated to liberate the territory in order to
bring order and security. As Hitler explained it, the German conquest of these
areas had been done in the interest of the local inhabitants. Once power over
the area was achieved, then Nazi plans could be carried out without having to
provide "superfluous" explanations to the world. Then Hitler bluntly remarked,
"Regardless, we are taking all necessary measures—shootings, resettlement,
etc.—and can do so nevertheless."[1]

With what seemed to be a crumbling Europe at his feet, Hitler elaborated on
his secret strategy for controlling and Germanizing the vast territories under
Nazi domination (including plans for Germany's allies in Slovakia, Hungary,
and Romania). What matters, he stated, was "to break the giant [Soviet] cake
into manageable pieces so that we can, first, *govern*, secondly *administer*, and
thirdly *exploit* it." As for Ukraine, Hitler ordered that the Crimea be totally
cleansed of foreign elements and settled by Germans. Likewise, the old Austrian territory of Galicia was to be a Reich territory.

Then Hitler brought up one of his favorite topics: British rule in India. He asked his coterie to learn from England and to follow the example of British relations with Indian princes. He praised the Englishman's "consistent pursuit of *one* line and *one* aim." In this regard, he urged his deputies to remain focused on their secret long-term objectives in the East and not get tangled up in the opinions of others, including the indigenous leaders. "Out of the newly-won Eastern Territories," Hitler declared, "we must make a Garden of Eden; they [the Eastern Territories] are vital to us; [overseas] colonies, on the other hand, play an entirely subordinate role."

In the discussion over the appointment of the Reich commissar for Ukraine, Rosenberg nominated Fritz Sauckel; however, Göring insisted that Erich Koch was the better candidate. He argued that Koch was most capable of exploiting the territory economically and displayed the strongest initiative and best background to do the job. In other words, Koch would be the most ruthless and least sympathetic to Ukrainians who desired autonomy. Being relatively pro-Ukrainian in his outlook, and fearing that the headstrong Koch would undermine his authority, Rosenberg objected to Koch's nomination, but he lost this battle. The Führer asserted that "the most important region for the next three years is undoubtedly the Ukraine. Therefore, *it will be best for Koch* to be appointed there."[2]

The meeting closed on the topic of security issues. Hitler reassured his deputies that should an uprising occur in the new territories, Göring could always bring in his Luftwaffe to bomb the area. But even this might not suffice. Thus, he urged, "the enormous area must, of course, be pacified as quickly as possible; the best way for this to happen will be if *anyone who even looks askance is shot dead.*" Field Marshal Keitel added, "The inhabitants would have to know that anyone who did not work would be shot and that they would be made liable to arrest for any offense."[3] The day after this meeting, Hitler issued two decrees: one concerning the administration of the East under Alfred Rosenberg, who was named Reich minister for the Occupied Eastern Territories; and the other concerning the police security of the occupied East, which was assigned to Reich Leader of the SS and Police Heinrich Himmler.[4]

How removed was this discussion from events taking place in the field? From the standpoint of the regional commanders in Zhytomyr, there existed a common understanding about how to treat the Jewish population and Soviet intelligentsia. However, there was ambiguity about how to treat the rest of the local population. In the short run, colonial-style exploitation of the region's resources and people seemed appropriate for the war effort and Germany's economy, but it remained unclear how these practices over time would lead to the creation of a "Garden of Eden." As long as Germany continued to expand its territory, population, and economy, it mattered little to Hitler's followers that his utopian dreams of a perfect Aryan existence in Europe were inherently irrational, nebulous, and criminal. Instead they devised rationalized systems and procedures for exploiting the new Nazi empire and destroying any perceived threats or impediments to their hegemony.

The decrees that established Nazi rule in Ukraine were no more specific than designating who was in charge. Hitler's minions had to determine how their respective agencies functioned, and they pursued independent courses from the beginning to the end. Himmler and Rosenberg began to devise their structural frameworks before the invasion: Rosenberg planned for a sprawling bureaucracy of administrative commissars, statisticians, Slavic specialists, and indigenous committees, a plan that never reached the scale of his grandiose vision. Himmler and Heydrich started with a smaller hierarchical staff of senior SS and police leaders and special task forces that later multiplied into a vast network of German SS, mobile Order Police, and stationary gendarmerie supported by battalions of Ukrainian, Lithuanian, and Latvian auxiliaries. Meanwhile, Göring's plan for controlling the eastern economy with technical inspectors, businessmen, and agricultural overseers represented only one of several highly competitive organizations that ravaged Ukraine's economic resources; others included the food and agricultural ministry, the army's armament economy office, and private concerns.

All of these agencies coexisted independently, and their representatives in the field operated under an evolving structure. Inasmuch as Nazi leaders and their subordinates believed in a permanent German presence in the East, if not a thousand-year Reich governing the territory, the everyday reality of ruling the conquered land and its peoples was not simply, as Hitler had predicted, a matter of organization. The administrative apparatus with its extended agencies was unstable, and in many ways self-destructive. The protracted war meant that lower-level administrators lived with the constant threat of being sent to the front. Even within the senior ranks of Nazi officialdom one's position was never secure because of Hitler's autocratic power and the encroachment of Himmler's expanding SS-police empire. The fly-by-night atmosphere of the regional administration was exacerbated by the motley assemblage of peripheral leaders, who were granted substantial ruling power within their fiefdoms and charged with the most criminal colonization aims in European history.

As Hitler saw it, his "viceroys" controlled the everyday affairs of policy implementation from the practical issues to the political repercussions. Rosenberg echoed Hitler's concept of colonial rule when he wrote that the district commissar directs the local administration of the region and "therefore in him lies the weight of the entire administration."[5] Instructions from Berlin were broadly defined so that the lower levels had to devise methods for their speedy and efficient implementation. Thus when it came to realizing Nazi aims, it was up to the local leadership to figure out how to best meet their superiors' demands with the resources at hand. To this end, the commissars could choose to cooperate or compete with the various German agencies in their districts. There was also ample room for peripheral leaders to pursue their own self-interests. Like most regional functionaries in the East, the officials in Zhytomyr felt removed from the Reich: they experienced time lags in reporting, poor telephone connections, slow mail delivery, broken ties with family members and sweethearts, and a physical surrounding that simply did not feel like home. However, unlike their counterparts in the Baltics, Belorussia, and other parts of Ukraine, regional leaders in Zhytomyr also felt the direct presence of Hitler, Himmler, Göring, Bormann, and other powerful Nazis who frequented the region with their security entourages. The local leaders needed to demonstrate to their superiors that policies were being implemented with the expected results, despite the constraints of local conditions.

The Administration of Hitler's Garden of Eden

The German regional administration consisted of a thin layer of about 870 German commissariat officials who were responsible for a population of 2.9 million persons and an area of 65,000 square kilometers.[6] In addition to the twenty-five (later twenty-six) rural districts of the commissariat, the Germans created two city district administrations in Vinnytsia and Zhytomyr. The district leaders or *Gebietskommissare* reported to General Commissar Kurt Klemm (and his successor Ernst Leyser) in the region's capital, the city of Zhytomyr.[7] In the outlying district offices the Gebietskommissare worked with an army commander who was situated in the same town or nearby. The typical Gebietskommissar oversaw a geographic area of 2,300 square kilometers with about 108,000 inhabitants. These rural overlords were assisted by a small German staff with four departmental chiefs (Administration, Finance, Economy, and Labor), at least two agricultural and forestry specialists, and one female typist-stenographer.[8] For example, the district commissariat office in Novohrad-Volyns'kyi had twenty Reich Germans supported by at least seventy Ukrainians and ethnic Germans, who worked as administrators, translators, typists, couriers, stable hands, chauffeurs, cooks, cleaning women, land surveyors, veterinarians, agronomists, and other positions. The smaller villages that lay beyond

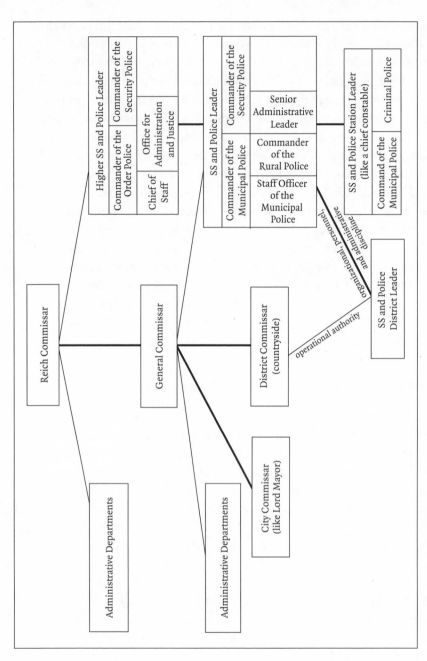

Organizational chart of the Reichskommissariat Ukraine

(U.S. Holocaust Memorial Museum, Acc. 1996.A.269 Zhytomyr Oblast' Records, reel 5, 1465-1-1)

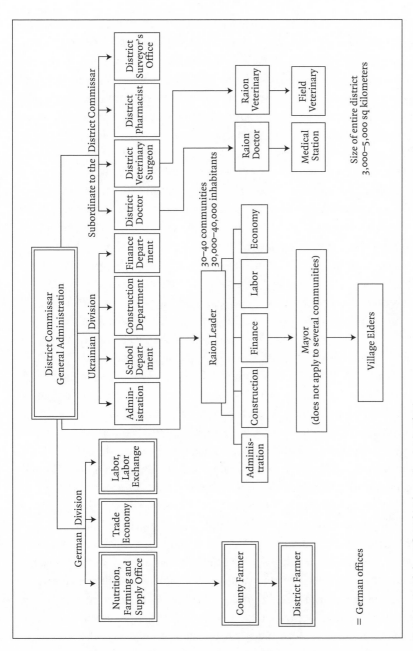

Organizational chart of a Gebietskommissariat in Ukraine

(U.S. Holocaust Memorial Museum, Acc. 1996.A.269 Zhytomyr Oblast' Records, reel 5, 1465-1-1)

the Gebietskommissar's headquarters were supervised by indigenous collaborators, who were known as *Rayon* (raion) leaders (district leaders) and *starosty* (village elders). Each German Gebietskommissar employed about three full-time Ukrainian raion leaders, who in turn relied on about forty village elders to communicate and carry out German orders. Hundreds of additional Reich officials from private business firms, special labor-recruiting commissions, Organization Todt, or other government offices were scattered across the region, such as representatives of the Reichpost, the railway, and the ZHO (Zentralhandelsgesellschaft Ost, Central Trade Company East). They were required to register with the commissar's office when they arrived in the region, but these individuals were not directly subordinate to the district commissar.

To each Gebietskommissar, Himmler assigned a gendarmerie platoon that was distributed across the district. There were eighty gendarme stations (an average of three per district), each headed by a German commander ranking no higher than a lieutenant and supported by two more German policemen, a translator, and between fifty to eighty Ukrainian auxiliary police (*Schutzmannschaften*).[9] The gendarme station leaders reported to the SS and police district leader, who was technically on a par with one of the department heads of the Gebietskommissar's main staff. There were six Sipo-SD offices (*Aussenstellen*) in the region (in Zhytomyr, Berdychiv, Vinnytsia, Ovruch, Mazyr, and Haisyn). Einsatzgruppen personnel, including the most seasoned killers, were used to establish the new stationary Sipo-SD offices in the commissariat; for example, members of Einsatzkommando 5 were among the staffs of the Vinnytsia and Zhytomyr offices.[10] The entire SS-police apparatus fell under the control of the higher SS and police leader, SS General Hans-Adolf Prützmann, who had his headquarters in Kiev, not in the commissariat's capital of Rivne.

The German civil administration in Ukraine was not meant to be a temporary, ad hoc form of rule but the beginning of a long-term colonization process. Like Britain's India, Hitler argued, Ukraine would be governed by a handful of German imperialists. But they would be aided by a steady flow of German (and Dutch) settlers, farmers, entrepreneurs, retired soldiers, engineers, horticulturists, and others who would transform the otherwise daunting open space of the East into Nazi Germany's frontier paradise. There would be no indigenous elites besides the Reich and ethnic Germans. Ukrainians, who were to be denied any education beyond the fourth grade, were deemed useful as long as they supplied the Germans with everything demanded, supplying grain to all of Europe, slaving on a plantation-style collective farm, and performing all the necessary but unpleasant grunt work that was considered beneath the superior Aryans. In the triumphant atmosphere of Hitler's headquarters in September 1941, when Kiev had just fallen to the Wehrmacht, Hitler proclaimed that in Ukraine "the Germans—this is essential—will have to constitute amongst themselves a closed society, like a fortress. The least of our stable-lads must be superior to any native."[11]

Later in April 1942, Hitler offered his views on non-Germans in the administration: "As an administrative organization," Hitler stated, "the most we can concede to them is a form of communal administration, and that only in so far as it may be necessary for the maintenance of the labor potential, that is to say for the maintenance of the basic needs of the individual." Hitler opined that the system should be strictly hierarchical down to the village level and should not encourage any cooperation among neighboring communities, but rather "every form of dissension and schism."[12] According to Hitler's vision, regional leaders in Zhytomyr constructed an indigenous administration that started at the top with a General Commissariat–level advisory and self-help committee composed of Ukrainians. The committees were not supposed to encourage any independent Ukrainian political activity, but they were meant to provide food, medical treatment, shelter, clothing, and other forms of relief for the local non-German population. The committee in Zhytomyr was managed by the chief of Zhytomyr's city administration, Bürgermeister Pavlovsky.[13] Beneath the Ukrainian mayor's office, the raion and village elders (starosty) provided the Germans with a network of local supervisors and informers; the weight of Nazi demands fell on their shoulders directly as they were held personally responsible for the population's fulfillment of German orders in the most remote locations. Ukrainian advisory boards, mayors, raion leaders, and elders were not connected into a unified framework; rather, they remained isolated extensions of the German city and district administrations.

Rarely did a Reich German official venture out to the countryside to directly supervise the Ukrainian and ethnic German raion leaders and elders.[14] But the Nazi terror permeated society. Anyone who defied or obstructed the implementation of Nazi orders was deemed a saboteur and subject to the death penalty. Thus it was very clear to the non-Germans who worked for the Nazis that their existence lay in the balance, depending often on the individual whim of a German ruler. Under these uncertain conditions, Ukrainians in the local administration perpetuated a system that promised them nothing in the long term.[15]

Although most Ukrainians may have felt powerless, numerically they dominated the system. By 1943 there were about 18,400 Ukrainians working in the rural German police stations and commissars' outposts. At least 2,000 served as village elders. Hundreds staffed various German administrative offices in the cities of Zhytomyr and Vinnytsia. These figures do not include the Ukrainians who kept various charitable organizations and schools running, as well as a separate Ukrainian court system that mostly settled civil disputes between Ukrainians. It is difficult to precisely tabulate the figure of Ukrainian functionaries and civil servants, but their numbers were significant and strongly suggest that Ukrainians wielded more influence over the everyday operations of the Nazi system than postwar accounts would dare to admit.[16]

What the Germans lacked in numbers, however, they made up for in the power of their presence, which was a potent mixture of hubris, terror, and violence. Ukrainians mocked the commissars who strutted about like "Golden Pheasants" in their brown uniforms. Wartime critics and postwar scholarship have branded the entire Rosenberg commissariat an "administrative monstrosity," led by a group of "egotistical hyenas," "carpetbaggers" and "Ostnieten" (eastern losers).[17] Who were the commissars that ruled over the Zhytomyr region and how did they conduct themselves?

The Commissars "Golden Pheasants," "Egotistical Hyenas," "Carpetbaggers," and "Ordensjunker"

The recruiting of commissars for the Zhytomyr region began in early September 1941 when Rosenberg's deputy, Alfred Meyer, who was the former Gauleiter of Westphalia, contacted one of his fellow Westphalians, the *Regierungspräsident* (governor) from Münster, Kurt Klemm. Meyer asked him to take the position of general commissar over the Zhytomyr region. The forty-seven-year-old Klemm, the only *Berufsbeamte* (professional civil servant) found among the other five general commissars who were appointed to lead the regional administrations of Ukraine, moved to a new temporary office in Berlin, where he began to select department chiefs for his staff and district commissars for the Zhytomyr region. A decorated veteran of World War I and a member of the Nazi Party since 1931, Klemm distinguished himself as a chief constable in the Ruhr (at Recklinghausen) and early on earned a place within new elite of the Third Reich, which was recognized by his inclusion in a "Who's Who" of German leaders, *Das Deutsche Führerlexikon 1934/1935*. With a requirement that 60 percent of his personnel hold Nazi Party membership, Klemm began compiling lists of names, drawing from the *Ordensjunker* (graduates of the Adolf Hitler Schools for Nazi political training), SA captains, chiefs of Gauleiter departments, Nazi Party district leaders, and government officials with some Party affiliation. Connections to the Party were important for pragmatic and ideological reasons. For example, the man chosen to serve as the German city commissar of Zhytomyr, Fritz Magass, also served as the Nazi Party leader for the district. To his

**Klemm,
Kurt,
Polizeipräsident,
Recklinghausen,
Polizeipräsidium.**

Geboren: 19. Januar 1894 zu Mühlhausen i. Thür. (Regierungsbezirk Erfurt). — *Bildungsgang:* Vorschule, Gymnasium; sechssemestriges Studium der Rechts- und Staatswissenschaft in Göttingen, München, Freiburg und Marburg. — *Militärzeit, Kriegsauszeichnungen:* 1915/18 Teilnahme am Weltkrieg als Kriegsfreiwilliger; später Leutnant d. Res. beim Jäger-Regt. z. Pf. Nr. 2 und Garde - Grenadier - Regt. Nr. 2; Juli 1918 schwer verwundet. E. K. I. und II.; Verwundetenabzeichen. — *Berufsgang u. a.:* 1915 Gerichtsreferendar; 1919 Regierungsreferendar; 1921 Regierungsassessor; 1928 Regierungsrat; 28. Februar 1933 Ernennung zum Polizeipräsidenten (zunächst vertretungsweise, später endgültig); bis 1920 parteilos; 1920/31 Mitglied der Deutschen Volkspartei; seit 1931 Mitglied der NSDAP.

Kurt Klemm, *general commissar of the General Bezirk Zhytomyr, September 1941–September 1942. The image was provided by Randall Bytwerk, German Propaganda Archive, Calvin College, with the assistance of Ronald Coleman,* U.S. Holocaust Memorial Museum. (Das Deutsche Führerlexikon 1934/1935)

list Klemm added a colleague from Münster, a mayor who had been in Zhytomyr when the Germans occupied the area during World War I.[18]

Klemm submitted the personnel lists to his superior, Reich Commissar for Ukraine Erich Koch, for approval. Those chosen as district commissars were not told exactly where they would be stationed but were instructed to find a secretary, driver, and translator to accompany them to the East. The commissars were then ordered to meet Klemm and Koch on 13 October at the Falkenburg on the Krössinsee (Pomerania) for briefings about their duties. The Falkenburg at Krössinsee was one of three castles where Nazi elites were groomed based on ancient models of the German Order of Knights.[19] Little documentation has survived from the briefings, but evidently one of the highlights of the Krössinsee orientation was a speech by Koch's deputy, a fellow East Prussian and Regierungspräsident named Paul Dargel. Dargel shared Koch's hard-core Nazi chauvinism and anti-Semitism, but he surpassed Koch as an orator and administrator. In fact, Dargel ended up managing the commissariat administration from its capital in Rivne because Koch spent most of his time at his estate in East Prussia or at Hitler's headquarters in Vinnytsia.

The fanfare and hype surrounding the orientation quickly disintegrated into false starts and administrative bungles as the commissars' rail transport to Zhytomyr was repeatedly delayed by the Reich railway office. After being stranded for some time in Pomerania, the commissars' "special transport" of thirty-nine railway cars with 150 staff members finally arrived in early November to a snow-covered Zhytomyr with bitter, subzero-degree temperatures.[20] In the city of Zhytomyr, which had suffered extensive bombing, Klemm and his departmental chiefs took over the former state museum building for their temporary administrative headquarters. As for the district commissars in the rural areas, each was allotted three vehicles, a typewriter, two or three Nazi flags, a radio set, several thousand sheets of paper, and words of encouragement from Klemm, who declared that the administration "shall fulfill the tasks that have been conferred upon us by the Führer with a cheerful devotion . . . and without bureaucratic formalism."[21]

Ironically, just as Klemm jettisoned "bureaucratic formalism" in Zhytomyr, Rosenberg's staff was completing the first edition of "guidelines" for the commissars in Ukraine, a cumbersome, long-winded manuscript of nearly seventy pages known as the "Brown File." From his distant position in Berlin, Rosenberg instructed Ukraine's district commissars about the strict but "necessary" tasks of German colonization. Among the commissars' most urgent administrative tasks were:

(a) police measures;
(b) exploitation of economy;
(c) welfare of the local population;
(d) property confiscation and plundering;
(e) reestablishment and maintenance of the transport and postal systems;
(f) supervision of civilians through the intelligence services (Abwehr and SD); and
(g) destruction of remaining opposition.[22]

As this list shows, the commissars' priorities overlapped with the work of other agencies, namely Himmler's SS-police apparatus. Unlike the "smooth" division of labor that developed between the Wehrmacht and the SS-police in the military occupation zones, however, in the commissariat the atmosphere tended to be more competitive and confused. For example, Himmler's SS and police leaders were responsible for initiating a reprisal measure, but the commissars had to consent to the measure and approve or order the executions of the hostages. Thus, according to the official design of the local German hierarchy, the German police suggested measures but could only carry them out upon approval of the commissar.[23] At the lowest levels of German rule, the commissar was supposed to wield exclusive power over the population as a whole, more than his counterparts and subordinates in the SS-police. The commissar was nominally the highest judicial authority at the regional and district levels, whereas the Sipo-SD and police forces investigated, arrested, and interrogated those accused of serious racial and political crimes.[24] In practice, the SS-police carried out death sentences without the commissar's approval.

Rosenberg's guidelines, which are mostly representative of his pedantic approach, also reveal his waning influence over the most secret Nazi policies that had evolved at a rapid pace during the summer and fall of 1941.[25] For example, he advised his commissars that "after the war the Jewish question will be generally solved for all of Europe," but in the meantime they should undertake "preparatory measures" such as registration and ghettoization of Jews. More telling in Rosenberg's guidelines for anti-Jewish policy was his statement that "the experiences in handling the Jewish question in the Occupied Eastern Territories can serve as a guide for solving the entire problem since the Jews in the territories together with the Jews of the General Government comprise the largest contingent of European Jewry." His statement captured the Nazi perception of the East as a laboratory for radical anti-Jewish measures and social engineering schemes.[26]

The commissars may have occasionally referred to the "Brown File," but the stream of directives that later poured into their offices, the swift flow of events, and changing conditions in the field eventually made the "Brown File" an obsolete document. Once in their regional outposts, the district commissars carried out their duties in ways that sometimes strayed far from Rosenberg's initial schemes, either by personal choice or because they had to contend with fluctuating conditions and uncertain relations with other agencies in the field.

Not long after the commissars arrived in Ukraine, Rosenberg received conflicting reports from the field about German attitudes and conduct toward Ukrainians. Evidently, the commissars were treating Ukrainians as "Negroes" because, as they asserted, the "territory will be built up like a colony." [27] The commissars' conduct showed that they did what they believed was possible and allowable as satraps in the Nazi empire. Some Nazi regional leaders fancied themselves as overseers in a system reminiscent of the antebellum South in the United States or of the European colonization of Africa. Taking their cue from Reich Commissar Koch, who described Ukrainians as "Negroes" who should be whipped publicly,[28] the regional commissars spoke about Ukrainians as "white Negroes" and wrote home to the Reich that the black marketeering in Ukraine was like trading with "Negerstämmen" who exchanged glass beads for ivory.[29] The Nazis' de-urbanization of Ukraine, a process that conceived of the former Soviet collective farms and the commissars' neofeudal estates as a quasi-plantation system, was consistent with the use of the whip, "carpetbagging" practices, and racist language about Ukrainian "Negroes."[30] Ukrainians understood the role that the Nazis had cast them in. One Ukrainian woman wrote in her diary, "We are like slaves. Often the book *Uncle Tom's Cabin* comes to mind. Once we shed tears over those Negroes; now obviously we ourselves are experiencing the same thing."[31]

As the designated satraps in the Nazi empire, the regional German commissars had a relatively broad understanding of what was possible in their everyday dealings with Ukrainians and the rest of the population, an understanding that occasionally clashed with the expectations of their superiors. Even Koch reprimanded the civil administrators who appeared intoxicated in public. Whipping the civilians was acceptable to the brazenly violent Koch, but not when one was drunk.[32] The Gebietskommissar, one critic wrote, conducts himself as if he is omnipotent and orders the deaths of civilians at whim.[33]

By April 1942, the highest regional SS authority in Zhytomyr, SS and Police Leader Otto Hellwig, had to respond to an overwhelming number of executions that were ordered by the commissars, which the local police forces were unable to carry out. A World War I and Freikorps veteran, Hellwig had risen quickly within the ranks of Heydrich's SD. At the age of thirty-nine, he was made commander of the Sipo's Leadership School in Berlin-Charlottenburg, where he trained the next generation of SD elites. As a Sipo officer in an Einsatzgruppe in Poland, Hellwig led some of his cadets into battle against Polish intelligentsia and Jews during September–October 1939. Given that he was praised by his superiors for his "impeccable" character and solid ideological commitment to Nazism, it is no wonder that Hellwig was sent to Zhytomyr to establish the SS's place on the new frontier. True to form, Hellwig insisted that the commissars pass their orders for executing civilians first to his office for approval.[34]

German-Ukrainian Interaction Fraternization, Black Marketeering, and Plundering

German-Ukrainian relations, which were strained from the start, were far from ameliorated by the commissars' conduct. Fraternization with the local population was considered a serious crime under Nazi occupation regulations, even punishable by death; nevertheless, members of the civil administration and troops quartered in Zhytomyr violated this rule.[35] In order to prevent further contact between the Germans and local Ukrainian women, the army established a bordello in Zhytomyr that they opened to the Reich Germans in the civil administration two days per week. The bordello came at the suggestion of an army doctor, who found that cases of venereal disease were increasing, especially among Reich Germans who were temporarily based in Zhytomyr. More racially acceptable "partners," such as Dutch women, were brought in to serve as prostitutes at the bordello.[36] Nazi Party activists in Zhytomyr's Party headquarters also tried to prevent sexual relations between Germans and Ukrainians by inviting local Volksdeutsche women to social gatherings in the city.[37]

Outside of the official bordello and Nazi Party functions, military personnel and civilian authorities continued to pursue and often raped local Ukrainian women, and these violations were kept quiet. In at least two instances, one in the city of Zhytomyr and the other in Berdychiv, SS-police officials sexually abused Ukrainian women and then murdered the women to keep these racial violations secret.[38] Indeed, property theft and rape were considered more punishable offenses than murder. Since there were many Ukrainian women working in the underground inside and outside the administration, German perpetrators could rationalize the murder of women who were sexually abused not only as a cover-up for the Nazi crime of miscegenation but also as a "precautionary measure" against Soviet espionage.[39]

Occasionally, however, these cases became public: for example, when a German member of the administration was sentenced by a Nazi court for shooting his Ukrainian lover in a drunken state.[40] To be sure, romantic relationships developed between Ukrainians and Germans, and these social ties caused other problems for the local Nazi leadership. In Novohrad-Volyns'kyi, for example, the labor official of the district commissar's office complained that military personnel were safeguarding their Ukrainian girlfriends from deportation and forced labor in the Reich.[41] Often Reich Germans who carried on "illegal" relations with Ukrainians also couriered letters and reports between Ukrainians who worked in the Reich and their relations in Ukraine. These letters revealed the cruel treatment and conditions of laborers in Germany, sabotaging local propaganda efforts to induce Ukrainians to work in Germany.[42] The children of these Ukrainian-German relationships had uncertain futures. Some mothers tried to secure Aryan papers for them, which often resulted in their being kidnapped and taken into German homes and orphanages.[43]

Since the leadership could not prevent sexual relations between Germans and Ukrainians and the leadership's aim was to reduce the non-German population, Hitler, Himmler, and Koch promoted sterilization of Ukrainian women and abortions. On 22 July 1942, after Martin Bormann toured the collective farms around Hitler's Vinnytsia headquarters, he presented his impressions of the Ukrainians' robust physical features to Hitler. Hitler commented that the "fertility" of Ukrainian women threatened to increase the non-German population. The next day Bormann ordered Rosenberg's officials to develop policies and programs for forced sterilization and abortions in Ukraine. Koch was asked to use the local police to seize Ukrainian women on the streets who prostitute themselves, "wearing shorts, cosmetics, and smoking" and to openly denounce at least ten women as whores. In addition to demanding the public shaming of Ukrainian women, Hitler and Bormann insisted that "the reproductive ability of the women must be lowered to decrease the race." Consequently Koch instructed his district officials to make sure that Ukrainian women had every available chance to have an abortion.[44]

German officials were supposed to keep their distance from Ukrainians by establishing their own shops, restaurants, clubs, theaters, and housing settlements. Nonetheless, the commissars and their staff—and certainly other Germans stationed in Zhytomyr—were also actively engaged in the black market and other activities with Ukrainians.[45] In one of the more interesting cases, a German official named Walter Pieper, who headed the general commissar's transportation and commerce department, befriended one of his Ukrainian subordinates, Ivan Shynal'skii, an electrician and mechanic who was also secretly involved in Zhytomyr's underground resistance. According to Shynal'skii, he and Pieper often disagreed about how a particular technical problem should be resolved, and because Shynal'skii often presented a better solution, Pieper grew to respect him and later protected him when he was suspected of involvement with the partisans. Shynal'skii survived the war.[46]

Though there are significant individual cases of somewhat "friendly" relations between German officials and Ukrainians who staffed the administration, local German authorities were more aware and alarmed about the rampant bartering between Germans and Ukrainians that was turning Ukraine, as one German critic wrote, into the Reich's biggest "flea market."[47] The regional SS and police leader Hellwig sent out numerous orders that any Germans found bartering at the Ukrainian markets be punished; German police and Ukrainian auxiliaries patrolled the marketplace.[48] But the illegal trading continued and became central to the local economy. The commander of the Order Police in Zhytomyr, Gotthilf Oemler, reported to City Commissar Magass that German civil administrators were offering black market items to the Ukrainian auxiliary police as a sort of compensation.[49]

Black marketeering of Ukrainian produce for German manufactured wares extended from Zhytomyr back to the Reich. German officials in Zhytomyr sent letters home asking for items to trade, not glass beads for the "natives," as Hitler had imagined, but cosmetics, matches, and toothbrushes. One factory leader in Pohrebyshche, Gustav Höpel, who bribed the local postmaster with bottles of schnapps, sent to his wife in Germany fifteen packages of meat, butter, and flour with a note indicating that when he came home in two months, he would bring 1,000 eggs. After he was arrested in October 1943, he defended his actions with the statement that he was just doing what everyone else did in Ukraine.[50]

One observer revealed that this "Tauschmanie" (barter mania) had taken on an official tone as a normal everyday duty, much like the official "plundering" campaigns that the commissars carried out. In addition to the "requisitions" of produce from the collective farms, the commissars supervised the seizure of private property from the Jews and Ukrainians and then resold or redistributed the material to individuals and other German agencies. While stolen property circulated through official and unofficial channels, the most senior army, civil and police leaders condemned plundering; the military commander of Reich Commissariat Ukraine, Karl Kitzinger, reported that military field courts were sentencing German soldiers to death for stealing and selling goods on the black market to Ukrainians.[51] In the Ukrainian paper *Holos Volyni* (Voice of Volyn'), which was controlled and censored by the occupation authorities, the Germans publicized that no one could inhabit or plunder former Jewish property without the permission of the local German commissar.[52]

Nevertheless, like the army commanders' 1941 response to the atrocities committed by individual soldiers, senior civilian officials disapproved of random acts of self-interest and insisted that their subordinates carry out orders on behalf of the Reich, no matter if the orders were to execute civilians and seize their property; the subordinates' actions simply had to go through official channels in a controlled manner. Thus, while regional leaders in Zhytomyr issued death sentences to individuals who "stole" Reich plunder, these same officials supervised Reich agencies for seizing and distributing personal property.

In Zhytomyr's General Commissariat office, three departments handled official plundering activities: the finance office, the housing bureau, and the inventory commission.[53] Already in the first days of the commissars' rule in November 1941, the housing office in Zhytomyr began the "official" seizure of Jewish and Ukrainian property. Over the next two years, this office handled the transfer of former Jewish and Ukrainian dwellings to Reich and ethnic Germans.[54] The inventory commission sold Jewish property to German personnel based in the area.[55] During the winter, the Army High Command demanded that the commissars collect winter clothing from Ukrainians for the troops and then paid the civil administration for the seized fur coats, hats, wool pants, leather boots, and the like.[56] The finance office, which also collected exorbitant taxes from the population, took in the money from the sale of seized Jewish property and Ukrainian produce. Many items snatched up by commissariat officials were supposed to be given to ethnic German families, but they too ended up on the black market.[57]

Despite formal efforts to control looting through official Reich agencies, it was difficult to distinguish "official" tasks from individual violations. When staff of the commissariat searched around for suitable office space, they simply pulled a truck up to a Ukrainian shop or business, demanded the premises be vacated, took what they wanted, and set up their office.[58] In Berdychiv, Gebietskommissar Erwin Göllner enjoyed Persian rugs, satin bedding, and Viennese tortes.[59] Even with the severe shortage of paper, commissars sent each other memos simply to brag about the "fruits" of their plundering campaigns and black marketeering.[60] Meanwhile, the commissars complained that they could not afford to pay wages to their Ukrainian staff and cut their pay to such levels that one month's salary was worth less than two kilograms of butter.[61] By mid-1943 General Commissar Ernst Leyser (who had replaced Klemm on 29 October 1942) wrote that district commissars and their staff were disgracing the German uniform, and some staff members had to be sent back to Germany.[62]

Not all the commissars drank excessively, fraternized, plundered, and ordered executions at whim. Here and there a Gebietskommissar, like Deputy Commissar Müller in Novohrad-Volyns'kyi, displayed some compassion for the local population and tried to rule in a just manner, but this behavior was rare. Lenient commissars were usually sidelined in the competitive Nazi bureaucracy. After a member of Prützmann's Higher SS and Police staff wrote to Müller's superior in the General Commissariat's office suggesting that Müller be reprimanded for not exploiting more labor and facilities in his region, the SS and police district leader and agricultural leader simply overrode Müller's authority. They marched into "his" district, seized workers and grain, and murdered Ukrainian village elders and mayors along with some hostages they managed to grab during the raids. Thus commissars who appeared to be too "soft" were unable to sustain a moderate approach within the prevailing Nazi system of rule by force and terror.[63]

The Commissars' Ukrainian Policies The Land Question

Although Nazi leaders admonished subordinates for their "indecent," disruptive, or uncooperative behavior, they simultaneously nurtured a frontier mentality that spawned lawlessness, corruption, and brutality. The contradictory notions of proper German conduct in the "Wild East" carried over into the realm of Ukrainian economic and cultural policies. Hitler and Rosenberg had envisioned that the local commissars would take some initiative; but when the policies themselves were not clearly defined by the Nazi leadership, then the decentralization of rule often led to ad hoc and arbitrary methods. Thus the mere absence of uniform political policies toward the Ukrainians not only represented, in the words of sovietologist Alexander Dallin, a "missed opportunity" to marshal the anti-Stalinism of the local population for the Germans' benefit, but also served as an extension of Nazi power into the hands of regional leaders who used whatever means possible to fulfill Reich goals, or to satisfy their own personal desires.

From the beginning of the German occupation, Ukrainian peasants clamored for the privatization and redistribution of land, and yet the commissars failed to implement a unified land policy. The commissars received mixed messages from Koch and Rosenberg about land ownership and, in turn, made vague promises to the Ukrainian collective farmers in order to extract more from them. As early as September 1941, military commanders raised local expectations by announcing (in a Ukrainian newspaper article titled "A New Way of Life") that the first step toward dissolving collective farms in the Zhytomyr region would begin with the registration of all farming equipment, livestock, and land.[64] But the official policy that was carried out was to starve the local population by letting the army live off the land, reducing rations especially for the townspeople, and controlling the local barter economy.[65] The registration process did not lead to more efficient farming or to a breakup of the collective farm system. It was the first step in systematizing the Nazi confiscation of agricultural property in the East. Although more debate emerged within the civil administration about the fate of the collective farms, ultimately the hard-liners who backed the military's approach (Hitler, Göring, and Koch) succeeded in creating an exploitative colonial economy in Ukraine.

Like the military, the civil administration started out with the carrot. In November 1941 Koch's chief of agriculture wrote to Klemm that the privatization of businesses and farming would occur on the anniversary date of 22 June 1942.[66] In March 1942 the commissars announced to the Ukrainians that collective farms would no longer exist and all farmers would receive land. In September 1942, the Germans celebrated the formation of the first *Landbaugenossenschaft* (Agricultural Union) in Ukraine, which was established in Zhytomyr. In actuality the collectives were kept intact with German overseers, Ukrainian agronomists, and ethnic German managers.[67] To the added disgust of the Ukrainian peasants, the Germans forcibly "evacuated" tens of thousands of peasants from their cultivated farms and handed over the produce and land, including private plots, to Volksdeutsche settlers. Meanwhile in the areas not designated ethnic German colonies, Ukrainian peasants faced regular forced requisitions of foodstuffs. In October 1941 Ukrainian farmers (mainly women) who had enthusiastically brought in 100 percent of the harvest with little or no machinery began to face more repeated, systematic raids of the farms.[68] The German military and police seized one-third of the region's cattle.[69] According to a local German ordinance, Ukrainians could neither sell nor purchase milk, bread, and butter; everything was to be given over to the Germans for distribution.[70] The gendarmerie and their Ukrainian and ethnic German auxiliaries arrested individuals who were caught grinding wheat to make flour or slaughtering cattle without German permission.[71] Those who were caught faced the gallows. Indeed, under a Ukrainian-run but German-dictated justice system, farmers received the death penalty for slaughtering livestock or sabotaging the harvest, whereas domestic disputes that escalated into acts of murder were punished less severely.[72]

One of the chief tasks of the commissariat administration was to supply the army and the Reich with wheat, livestock, and particularly sugar from the former Soviet capital of sugar beet farming, Vinnytsia. The most notorious German official who actually toured the farms on a regular basis was the district agricultural leader (Landwirtschaftsführer, La-Führer), referred to by Ukrainian peasants as "Ihr Kommandant."[73] The La-Führer was an agent of Göring's Four-Year Plan administration and trained by the military's economic offices. Across the rural areas he was left to his own devices and conducted himself as a dictator over the collective farm system. Most agricultural leaders were completely unprepared for their assignments; they were typically transplanted from small farms in Germany to the vast stretches of Ukraine and asked to manage large areas, about 80,000 hectares.[74] Thus SS and police leaders assigned Order Police members (mainly Ukrainian Schutzmänner) to the agricultural stations to ensure that Ukrainian farmers complied with the agricultural leaders' demands.[75] Using strong-arm methods and the existing Soviet collective farm system, the Nazis were able to extract 16,802 tons of grain and 90,000 heads of cattle from the region during a six-month period.[76] Their requisitions reminded Ukrainian peasants of Soviet confiscations of grain in the early 1930s, which resulted in the Great Famine. Though by comparison the Germans were not as thorough as Stalin's agents, and famine was more common in Ukraine's cities during the war (not in the countryside), the recent trauma of the Great Famine was clearly in the minds of Ukrainian peasants during the Nazi occupation.

Ukrainian peasants soon realized that German promises about privatizing the land were absurd. So they increased the use of individual, private plots and secretly stored food, indeed more successfully than under Stalin's rule. As the war dragged on, the commissars, such as Gebietskommissar Fritz Halle (in Vinnytsia), continued to propagate the idea that privatization would come in the future; Halle decreed that in the interim state of war the people must secure the harvest for the Germans, and he stepped up the use of German and Ukrainian police to supervise the requisitions. German agricultural policies were a total failure. Ukrainian farmers were given no incentive to work for the Germans and were forced into servitude under the Nazi whip. Productivity declined, and varied forms of resistance increased.[77]

Ukrainian Schools and Popular Culture

Educational and cultural policies were also ill defined, but the commissars dealt with this ambiguity in a variety of ways. Hitler and his sycophant Koch had ordered that schooling only be allowed up to the fourth grade because, they argued, the Ukrainians needed only to learn basic reading and math in order to serve the Germans. By contrast, Rosenberg tried to persuade Hitler and other German leaders to pursue more pro-Ukrainian policies that supported culture and education.[78] The conflicting statements and utterances of Nazi leaders revealed that there was no clear consensus about the immediate future of Ukrainians and their culture. Intentionally or not, they left Ukrainian educational and religious policies to the regional commissars.

At first the commissars reopened the Ukrainian-run middle schools. By the end of 1942, however, the functioning of Ukrainian schools beyond the elementary level had become a farce, because thirteen-year-old children had become targets of labor raids; if they were not working in the field under their parent's supervision, they were being placed in German concentration camps for youths.[79] Based on an "urgent" order of the commander of the Sipo-SD for Ukraine, Max Thomas, youths of both sexes (ages ten to eighteen) were considered either criminally suspect or racially valuable and the lowest-level district offices across Ukraine were to seize them. During November and December 1942, the local gendarme offices began screening Zhytomyr's youths in a systematic kidnapping campaign known in Nazi circles as the "Heu Aktion" (literally, a collective harvesting of hay), a campaign that Heinrich Himmler endorsed in his September 1942 speech to SS-police leaders at Hegewald. Although Thomas had specified that the lowest age to target should be ten-year-olds, the gendarme lieutenant in Koziatyn revealed in his report that "criminal" children under the age of ten were also being held in the nearby youth camp.[80] The only new schools that the Germans established in the region were for the racially valuable, kidnapped Ukrainians and the Volksdeutsche, who were taught useful labor skills and inculcated with the Nazi ideology.

On the other hand, the commissars supported Ukrainian cultural performances. In the capital city of Zhytomyr, Commissar Magass approved the existence of a Ukrainian club that presented a popular cabaret and variety show for German and Ukrainian audiences.[81] In Vinnytsia, City Commissar Fritz Margenfeld promoted Ukrainian entertainment for the German troops by forming a city ballet, orchestra, and theater.[82] In Haisyn, Ukrainian actors performed Gogol, and local artists painted the sets. At the same time, the Germans tried to control the productions by forcing the actors to learn German plays like Hermann Sudermann's *Johannesfeuer*, by placing local German talent in the productions, and by taking over the direction of the Ukrainian productions.[83] Mostly, the Germans allowed Ukrainians to perform because the Germans desired entertainment. In a patronizing way, they found the local folk customs amusing and believed that permitting some forms of cultural expression would go a long way toward placating and motivating the locals. They hardly held sincere hopes for the development of a strong Ukrainian culture, especially one that might lead to an independence movement or harbor other resistance activities.

This type of German-Ukrainian "cultural" interaction coexisted with violent Nazi practices against the population, including the regular public hangings of Ukrainians in Zhytomyr's Haymarket during 1942 and 1943.[84] The persistence of Ukrainian culture prompted one official from Rosenberg's ministry who traveled through the region to comment on the bizarre juxtaposition of a semitolerant attitude toward Ukrainian cultural activities alongside severe German methods of repression, describing the entire scenario a sham.[85]

Religion

Local policy toward Ukrainian religion took a more divergent course during the occupation. Most of Zhytomyr's population identified themselves as belonging to either the Catholic Church or the Orthodox Church. The Roman and Greek Catholic churches were present in the region, though the Roman Catholic was viewed suspiciously as "Polish" and the Greek Catholic (Uniate) Church as a western Ukrainian "outside" movement. Among the various Christian Orthodox factions that sprang up during the war, the two largest ones were the Ukrainian Autocephalous Church centered in Kiev and the Russian Autonomous Church with its patriarch in Moscow.[86] In December 1941 the Germans allowed for the revival of the Autocephalous Church by appointing Bishop Polikarp (Sikorsky) the "Temporary Administrator of the Orthodox Autocephalous Church in the Liberated Lands of Ukraine."[87] The new council at Kiev appointed Bishop Fotii (Tymoshchuk) to Vinnytsia, and placed a second bishop, Hryhorii (Ohiichuk), in the city of Zhytomyr.[88] In May 1942 Koch's deputies in Rivne announced that in addition to the Autocephalous Church under Polikarp that the Autonomous Church was allowed to exist under the leadership of Bishop Aleksii.

At the regional level, Commissar Klemm and the district commissars shut down the former oblast offices of Ukrainian religion and education. The commander of the Security Police for Ukraine, Max Thomas, instructed his SS and police leader for Zhytomyr, Otto Hellwig, that no organized religious activity should grow beyond the regional level because it could serve as a facade for the Ukrainian underground. The Ukrainian Autocephalous Orthodox Church had openly supported the OUN-B's declaration of independence in July 1941, and German policy toward Ukrainian nationalism had changed to a blanket condemnation of the movement, leading to the systematic murder of its local leaders and sympathizers.[89] Klemm, who did not want the police to interfere in Ukrainian religious activities, informed the commissars that they should look out for priests who carried false certificates; they should force other priests to register and sign an oath that only religious, not political, issues would be discussed at meetings. Simultaneously, Klemm asked the commissars to publicly promote religious freedom in order to avoid civil unrest.[90]

Although widespread and powerful, the resurrected religiosity was not a source of broad social cohesion linking the region's villages, towns, and cities. As was true of other aspects of daily life and occupation administration, the religious setting in the rural areas differed significantly from that of the larger towns. While the popular revival of the church continued to develop rather spontaneously and independently in the countryside, Ukrainian leaders in the cities of Zhytomyr and Vinnytsia, who were negotiating their own nationalist and personal agendas with the Nazis, tried to use the popular force of religion to expand their own power base and test the limits of Nazi rule.[91] In late May 1942 Reich Commissar Koch threatened to shut down both churches because of the infighting and decreed that he alone had the authority to appoint bishops. He also empowered the commissars to dismiss bishops and priests if these religious leaders posed a local threat to security and order.[92]

However, beyond Zhytomyr's city limits, the amount of religious freedom that the rural commissars granted to the population varied from district to district. At the time of Easter in 1942, church bells could be heard in one region but not in another; some churches were closed and others were not; some Ukrainians were forced to work on religious holidays and others were not. The dissimulation and contradictions of Nazi policy were especially evident when in June 1942, after months of deliberations and drafts, Rosenberg presented his "Tolerance Edict." This so-called decree of "tolerance" actually placed greater restrictions on religious organization and granted local commissars the power to remove anyone whose religious practices entered into politics.[93] Until Rosenberg's edict, that is, for over a year, most Ukrainians had enjoyed some sense of religious freedom, but after June 1942 the German version of "tolerance" became synonymous with heightened restrictions and regional inconsistencies. In late 1942, when Koch pressured the commissars to search their districts for more forced laborers and war matériel, religious holidays and Sundays became working days, and the commissars confiscated church bells for the war effort and offered churches and cloisters to the Wehrmacht for quartering troops.

The commissars failed to create uniform cultural policies beyond their own districts and harness the full potential of the Ukrainian population to meet German aims. Instead, like their predecessors in the military administration, they turned to brute practices of force and intimidation to extract what they could from the Ukrainians. Even when it seemed as if some concessions were being made, such as religious toleration, the same German authority would not hesitate to lash out at the population for not fulfilling labor quotas or for refusing to hand over all their livestock. From the perspective of the Ukrainians, especially in the year 1943, there was little difference between the Bolsheviks and the Nazis. Indeed, in September 1942 a Ukrainian man in Vinnytsia compared Nazi labor drives to the Reich with Bolshevik deportations to Siberia; by an order of the Gebietskommissar he was publicly hanged for making this anti-German statement.[94]

The civil administration did not enjoy exclusive power over Ukraine. In Zhytomyr the commissars projected a public image of omnipotence, but behind this veneer of total control was a splintered structure that left the day-to-day management and implementation of German policy in the hands of a few Reich officials who represented Rosenberg's ministry, Himmler's police forces, Göring's economic and agricultural specialists, the military, and private business ventures. The multiple command structure under which the local leaders operated was on paper confusing and inefficient; yet most leaders managed their tasks under these circumstances. The power struggles of the Nazi elite materialized in the conflicting orders that they gave to their subordinates, fueling the inconsistent, contradictory regional practices. Yet the polycratic pattern of institutional relations found at the highest levels of Nazi rule was not duplicated at the regional level. Additionally, the occupied territories in the

East were simply too vast for the cumbersome bureaucracy in Berlin, Rivne, or even Zhytomyr to exercise much effective supervision over individual Gebietskommissare.

There are more examples of cross-agency cooperation than of conflict in the Zhytomyr region, examples that add up to more than individual attempts by ambitious commissars and bureaucrats to gain recognition from above with self-congratulatory memoranda. Indeed, the mere shortage of Reich manpower "in the field" necessitated not only the reliance on indigenous collaborators but also a sharing of resources and personnel across German agencies. Often cooperation grew out of the mere fact that, as was the case in Zhytomyr and Berdychiv, staff from different private and public agencies shared the same outpost or office space.[95] Cooperation can be found within most of the leading Nazi campaigns implemented in the region: exploitation of agriculture, the persecution of the Jews, antipartisan warfare, and Nazi forced-labor drives.[96] However, cooperation did not mean that each agency shared an equal role in the implementation of these leading policies. Indeed, Rosenberg's commissars, who initially may have expected complete power over their districts, quickly found that they had only a share of it.

Beginning in the late summer of 1942, Rosenberg's commissars teamed up with Göring's agricultural leaders and Himmler's SS-police to protect the collective farms from Soviet partisan attackers. The commissars and local gendarme station leaders informed the Ukrainian collective farm leaders that the farmers, in addition to working long days in the fields, had to form night patrols to guard the fields and storage houses. If the Germans determined that any damage or theft had occurred, hostages were taken, beginning with the collective farm leader. The Order Police and Ukrainian Schutzmänner escorted the hostages to the nearest SD office, which meant that the hostages were interrogated, tortured, and usually sent to Germany as laborers, or killed.[97] Thus, while the senior Reich policy-makers debated the fate and productivity of Ukraine's collective farms, a combination of local German agencies relied on a now familiar formula for extracting food for the Reich and Wehrmacht soldiers: cooperation with other German agencies, coordination of resources, reliance on indigenous leaders and auxiliaries, and terror tactics.

During the course of the occupation, the Nazi abuse of Ukrainian forced labor became one of the more dominant features of the commissars' rule. Hundreds of thousands of Ukrainians in Zhytomyr, about one in ten (ages thirteen to fifty-five) were deported to Germany as forced laborers. The implementation of this program depended on the rather smooth collaboration of the regional leadership. The commissars played a central coordinating role, one that

Koch had defined from the start. In Koch's first decree as Reich commissar, he ordered all able-bodied persons (no age or gender specified) to register for work with the commissar's labor office. Those who did not work for the Germans were punished and imprisoned.[98]

Ukrainian Forced Labor Inside and Outside the Commissariat

In the Zhytomyr region there were demands for Ukrainian labor from two sources: the regional construction projects, agriculture, and factory work; and outside the region in the Reich. According to Rosenberg's original administrative design, each commissar's office housed a staff of technical experts and engineers who would determine the labor needs for the local construction projects.[99] In June 1942 Klemm's labor chief, Feierabend, complained about the severe shortage of skilled labor in the region, a shortage that Klemm's political adviser attributed to the "resettlement" of Jews. Feierabend determined that a total of 40,462 men and women had been deported to the Reich and 140,000 more were to follow them. With the current regional need for 67,000 workers in the lumber industry and in the construction of airports, bridges, and canals, it seemed unlikely at the going rate of deportation that the commissars would be able to complete local projects. Nonetheless, he added, Klemm's staff was able to overcome the foreseen difficulties surrounding the construction of Hitler's headquarters by the "complete and smooth cooperation of all agencies involved."[100]

Because most of the local laborers were being deported to Germany, the commissars in Zhytomyr were forced to abandon many of the regional construction projects. Local labor was also allotted to the major construction of the autobahn, particularly the stretch of road being built around Hitler's Vinnytsia headquarters. Rosenberg's chiefs still managed to hold onto some laborers who worked on their houses and offices. The scarcity of skilled labor was so great that they also risked retaining Jews as personal dentists, craftsmen, carpenters, draftsmen, and mechanics and in other positions.[101]

In order to meet the outrageous labor quotas for the Reich, however, Hitler's plenipotentiary for labor, Fritz Sauckel, established regional teams of labor recruiters. In Zhytomyr there were five "Sauckel" recruiting commissioners assigned to the labor departments of the commissariat; one of these commissioners, named Groh, was posted at Novohrad-Volyns'kyi (Zviahel). In April 1942 Groh wrote to the SS and police leader of Novohrad-Volyns'kyi that he

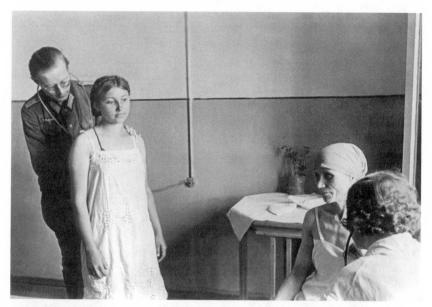

Ukrainian forced laborers being examined by a Wehrmacht doctor prior to their deportation to the Reich, 1942 (Ullstein Bild #0659134)

needed the gendarme posts in Mar'ianivka, Baranivka, and Polianka to be reinforced with more militia. The indigenous collective farm leaders and mayors had not met the latest quota of laborers, so Groh planned for the use of more force to obtain the laborers. After additional exchanges between the chief of the labor department of the commissar's office and the local German agricultural leader (La-Führer), 1,500 persons were seized by the gendarmerie and the entire force of local auxiliaries, in toto about 150 men.

The La-Führer assisted Sauckel's commissioners by informing them of any "excess" labor at the state and collective farms.[102] The district commissar's office, with the help of the police, held hostages from villages until a sufficient number of laborers could be gathered.[103] Meanwhile, the commissariat propaganda office introduced a new campaign, publishing so-called letters from the Reich. In a widely circulated article printed in Ukrainian newspapers, "What Are the Ukrainians Writing from Germany?," the Germans "quoted" from Ukrainian letters that "we all sang to music on the trains to work. . . . There is great camaraderie with the Germans. . . . There is a lot of freedom and shopping"; a Ukrainian *Ostarbeiter* is also reported to have written: "I live in a hotel room where everything is sparkling clean, I eat meat and jam, everything is abundant."[104] But this propaganda effort could not counteract concurrent

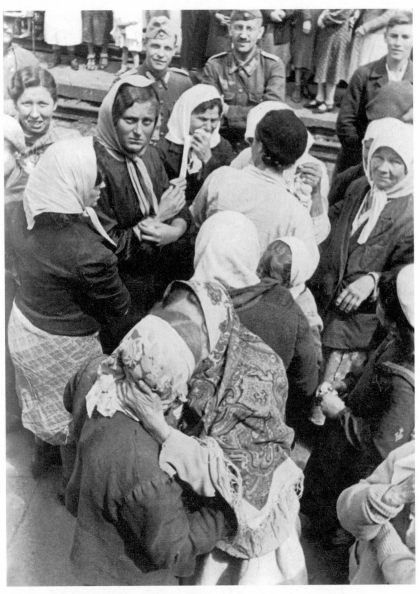

Ukrainian forced laborers say good-bye to loved ones at the train station, 1942
(Ullstein Bild #0659061)

Nazi recruiting methods and the more believable rumors of the time circulating among Ukrainians, such as that workers who were sent from Novohrad-Volyns'kyi to Germany "were shot immediately and turned into soap."[105]

When Sauckel's agents or Rosenberg's commissars received a labor quota for their districts, they employed whatever means available to capture and intern the Ukrainians who were then deported to the Reich. Numerous studies have described the sinister methods used by Sauckel's agents, such as surrounding movie houses and churches and grabbing everyone inside, as well as snatching people on the streets and in marketplaces.[106] Once the laborers had been seized, the commissars worked closely with the SS and police in managing the transit camps in advance of the laborers' transport to the Reich. Klemm's labor leader, Feierabend, also found that camps were the best "solution" for Ukrainians who failed to appear for labor assignments and for "homeless adults." At the "workers' educational camp" at Koziatyn, one of the largest in the region, the district commissar's office of labor assigned "work-shy elements" (of both sexes) to forced labor.[107] The commissar's staff provided a list of the "work-shy elements" to the chief of the gendarmerie who, until 1943, relied largely on Ukrainian Schutzmänner to find them. Any Jews who arrived at the camps were, by order of the commissar, handed over to the district SS and police leader.[108] At the beginning of May 1943, Koziatyn District Commissar Wolfgang Steudel and the SD chief in Berdychiv discussed the future of the Koziatyn camp (Arbeitserziehungslager), and decided that the camp be cleared of its "lazy and work-shy elements." The "unfit" prisoners were given over to the SD and killed—whereas the available skilled laborers were assigned to the German railway and to private firms.[109]

The commissars and SS-police also jointly managed the growing "orphan" problem in the region. The labor camps housed orphans and "suspicious" youths.[110] In August 1942 the Befehlshaber der Sipo-SD (BdS) for Ukraine, Max Thomas, wrote to Zhytomyr's Sipo-SD chief (KdS), Franz Razesberger, that as "preventive criminal measures against youths," children should be seized and placed in hard labor camps that were supervised by the commissar's labor office. The gendarme leader in Koziatyn agreed that police measures needed to be taken against orphans; many under the age of ten years were arriving on trains at the Koziatyn juncture and wandering through the area. In the neighboring district of Ruzhyn, the German gendarme leader also reported at this time that about 235 orphans had been seized.[111] At the youth camps, youngsters who had "racially worthless" characteristics were trained to obey the Germans, work hard, count to 100, read German traffic signs, and learn a manual labor trade. Others became candidates for possible "Germanization."[112]

Though the Nazi terror was systematic, the Nazi apparatus as a whole was unstable, a phenomenon dubbed by some scholars as "organized chaos." The commissars were forced to rely increasingly on Himmler's police forces to secure their power. When the commissars, beginning with General Commissar Klemm, challenged the SS, they were replaced or brought into line. The growing power of the SS and police forces in the region was not unique to Ukraine. In Belorussia the increase of SS power culminated with the appointment in October 1943 of the higher SS and police leader, SS Major General Hans von Gottberg, to the position of general commissar after the assassination of Rosenberg's general commissar, Wilhelm Kube.[113] The district commissars in Zhytomyr who did not immediately cooperate with the SS learned from the fate of their own general commissar, Klemm, that a direct challenge to SS power might result in a "dishonorable" resignation and worse—relocation to the front. Klemm's fate offers an illuminating example of the general outcome of confrontations between regional commissars and the SS-police leaders. It also provides some explanation for the local trend of cooperation or perhaps, in this particular case, of accommodation.

The Case of General Commissar Klemm and the SS-Police

Kurt Klemm's self-image as general commissar was fashioned after the model of highbrow British imperialists in India. But his romantic, naïve hopes of a German "India" in Ukraine were quickly dashed when he arrived and found a city and region ravaged by war and a population that was not quite as docile and diligent as was stereotypically portrayed by the Germans. Klemm was also the quintessential Nazi leader who demanded strict administrative procedures and adherence to the hierarchy. To Klemm's disappointment, he found that his title and rank alone would not secure his authority. Power in the Zhytomyr region was attached to policy, and the commissars were not charged with the leading role in the most high profile campaigns: the ethnic German program, the "Final Solution," the headquarters and autobahn construction projects, and antipartisan warfare. These leading policies were commanded chiefly by the SS-police, the Nazi Party, the Wehrmacht, and Organization Todt. The commissars' authority rested on their willingness to cooperate by coordinating their rivals' policies.

Klemm realized the limitations of his and the commissars' power within the first months of his reign, when he expressed his frustration over relations with the SS-police. He was not a moralist; rather, he resented the fact that the SS could act unilaterally and that the "Final Solution" exacerbated existing labor shortages by eliminating the most skilled sector of the population, the Jews. Klemm and his political and technical advisers wanted to rebuild sections of the city of Zhytomyr, including its streetcars, but they lacked the skilled workers. Klemm complained to his superiors in Rosenberg's ministry about the labor shortage and on more than one occasion indirectly blamed the shortage on the Reich's anti-Jewish policies.[114]

In May 1942 Klemm met with Reich Commissar Koch, Higher SS and Police Leader for Ukraine Prützmann, and Reich Minister Rosenberg at Rivne.[115] Earlier he had written disapprovingly of the independent actions of the SS in Zhytomyr, but at this high-level meeting he decided to voice his complaint again. Prützmann politely expressed his regret about the difficulties or misunderstandings that had occurred in the establishment of the administration, but the issue was dropped. Dissatisfied with this outcome, Klemm circulated a memorandum on 22 May about the local police, who were becoming too involved in "guiding political currents in the region." Prützmann's subordinate in Zhytomyr, Hellwig, responded by ordering the local police to "not get mixed up in leading purely political tasks."[116] At the same time, Hellwig complained to his superiors that Klemm was uncooperative and even too "humane." When Himmler arrived at his newly constructed bunkers at the outskirts of Zhytomyr, he summoned Klemm and sternly reprimanded him. The next month Klemm quietly resigned his position. On 7 September 1942 the official German newspaper in Ukraine, the *Deutsche Ukraine-Zeitung*, published a brief explanation about the personnel changes in Zhytomyr; it stated that Klemm was on vacation, and two of his deputies had moved farther east to Nikolaev, Ukraine. Months later Klemm received official commendations from Hitler for his good work in the East, but was denied permission to wear his general's uniform in public, to his great disappointment.[117]

Just in case there was any lasting confusion among Klemm's subordinates about the relationship between the SS and commissars, two specific actions were taken in the immediate wake of Klemm's departure in August 1942. Klemm's replacement, SS-Brigadeführer and Deputy Gauleiter of Westmark Ernst Leyser (who joined the Nazi Party and SS in 1925), investigated the district commissars' record regarding the "Final Solution"; he found that his subordinates had cooperated with the SS and police in the implementation of this policy. Leyser, who later complained about the local effects of Nazi antipartisan warfare, kept quiet about Nazi anti-Jewish measures. Furthermore, Rosenberg and Himmler issued a joint memorandum to the regional leaders in the commissariat and SS-police defining the official lines of authority between their two respective agencies. Higher SS and Police Leader Prützmann and his regional SS and police leaders (in Zhytomyr, Hellwig) were to carry out Himmler's wishes. The general commissar could issue orders to individual members of the regional police in the Schupo (Schutzpolizei) and gendarmerie but not to the SS and police district leader (SS- und Polizeigebietsführer). Orders to the Ukrainian Schutzmannschaften had to go through the German gendarmes. The commissars could direct the police in labor recruiting raids, but they had to employ them selectively.[118] General Commissar Leyser instructed the commissars to pursue their own duties and to stay clear of SS activities. In effect, the commissars lost direct control over their regional police forces.

In the end, the regional commissars, who had minimal resources and worked under extreme pressure from superiors to meet quotas of all kinds, had little choice but to work with other German government agencies even if there existed some strong emotional crosscurrents of animosity and rivalry.[119] They found that their strength lay in the central coordinating role that they played in implementing Nazi policy at the lowest levels. The commissar's office was not strong enough politically nor was it well enough staffed to enjoy exclusive control over its district; the prestige that the local chiefs sought, indeed their power, depended on the kind of cross-agency cooperation that occurred in Zhytomyr.

Chapter 6 **The General Commissariat's Machinery of Destruction** The Holocaust in the Countryside and Jewish Forced Labor, 1942–1943

We were six in our family. I had two sisters and two brothers. I tried to escape from the Germans. . . . I walked over 500 kilometers begging for food and shelter, from Minsk to Berdychiv, to Koziatyn and then Vinnytsia. Many old Ukrainian women took me in. I was their servant. Some betrayed me. Others did not. I did not look like a Jew, so I survived.

—Eva Abramovna Frankel' (b. Berdychiv, 1919)

In his seminal work on the Holocaust, Raul Hilberg introduced the metaphor of a machine to explain the Nazi administrative process behind the "Final Solution." The key operator of this machine, as Hilberg demonstrated, was the middle-ranking bureaucrat, who "no less than the highest superior was aware of currents and possibilities." Like the Berlin-centered bureaucrats, the regional leaders in Ukraine "displayed a striking path-finding ability in the absence of directives, a congruity of activities without jurisdictional guidelines, a fundamental comprehension of the task even when there were no explicit communications."[1] When it came to Jewish policy, regional and district leaders understood their superiors' wishes, turned Nazi aims into concrete plans of action, and in many instances bloodied their own hands in the implementation of the Holocaust. They developed killing methods and administrative networks in the 1941 massacres of over 60,000 Jews in the Zhytomyr region and continued to refine their mass murder apparatus until the final days of the occupation.

During the second phase of the Nazi occupation, when the civil administration was in place, mass executions of Jews continued, but with very few exceptions killing actions did not reach the scale of several thousands as they often had in 1941. Since it had become quite clear that Himmler and his police organizations had the upper hand in determining the final fate of the Jews, Himmler's SS-policemen and Rosenberg's commissars simply sought a modus operandi in the field. In early 1942 one of the "insiders" among Rosenberg's advisers on

Jewish policy, Erhard Wetzel, corresponded with Himmler's deputies about the need for practical coordination between district commissars and the police.[2]

Himmler's SS and Order Police units maintained overall control of the policy, but its implementation, now that nearly all of the mobile killing forces under Otto Rasch and Hans-Adolf Prützmann (Friedrich Jeckeln's successor) and large army security divisions had moved eastward, required the combined effort of several stationary police and non-police agencies, particularly the gendarmerie, district commissars, agricultural leaders, economic specialists, and foresters.[3] Unlike the 1941 mobile killing sweeps that emanated from Zhytomyr's centers, the massacres of Jews during 1942 and 1943 were left almost exclusively to local German and non-German police as well as other Reich personnel stationed in the region. The outstanding exception to this pattern was the involvement of the Reich Security Service (RSD), Hitler's special forces. To prepare for the Führer's arrival to Vinnytsia, the Reich Security Service initiated and oversaw a thorough "cleansing" of the area in and around Hitler's designated compound. The Reich Security Service drove the timing and intensity of the Holocaust experienced by Vinnytsia's Jews in the spring and summer of 1942.[4]

This chapter explores how the machinery of the "Final Solution" functioned in the commissariat administration. It is organized thematically and roughly chronologically, beginning with an overview of the rural killing machinery of SS-policemen and district commissars, and concluding with case studies of Jewish forced labor in the region, specifically in the construction of the autobahn and the Nazi leaders' field headquarters.

The Local SS-Police Apparatus
Germans, Ukrainians, and Volksdeutsche

The prominent position of the local commissar meant that his involvement in the Holocaust was unavoidable; in fact, some individual commissars distinguished themselves at the execution sites by shooting Jews. However, the shooting squads consisted of personnel from one of the region's six Sipo-SD outposts or the stationary gendarme offices.[5] Some of these "shooters" had firsthand experience in the 1941 massacres. Members of Einsatzkommando 5 (EK5) staffed the Sipo-SD office in Zhytomyr, and the Vinnytsia office. The Sipo-SD officers reported to the region's commander of the Sipo-SD, Franz Razesberger, who arrived in January 1942.[6] The six SD stations that Razesberger oversaw were located in Zhytomyr, Vinnytsia, Berdychiv, Ovruch, Mazyr, and Haisyn. By July 1942 the rural police structure had grown to twenty-five SS-police district stations, one for each Gebiet, with eighty smaller subdistrict gendarme posts. In addition, six mobile Order Police battalions and two horse squadrons reported to the region's four gendarme captaincies at Mazyr, Berdychiv, Vinnytsia, and Zhytomyr.

In the SS and police hierarchy, the Ukrainian auxiliaries were at the bottom of the chain of command structure. Mostly Ukrainians filled the ranks of the rural auxiliaries, known as Schutzmannschaften, led by German gendarme post leaders. In addition, at least six mobile units of auxiliaries swept through the region in 1941–42 (three Ukrainian battalions, one Lithuanian, one Latvian, and one ethnic German).[7]

The German gendarmes and their Ukrainian auxiliaries were responsible for securing the commissariat administration in the rural areas that had not been "cleansed" by the military. On 3 December 1941 General Commissar Klemm ordered the district commissars to dissolve the Ukrainian militia. In his own attempt to assume some direct control over the policemen, he ordered the local German gendarmerie and Schutzpolizei to carry out this task (which they were doing anyway according to orders that came down the SS-police command structure). The new recruits, the Schutzmänner, were given military-style training, including marching and sports. They learned the basics of "Prussian order and cleanliness." The German gendarme commander for the region, Senior Lieutenant Hans Leberecht von Bredow, told his new recruits, "The best training is by doing!"[8]

In early 1942, Bredow's boss, the commander of the Order Police for Ukraine, Otto von Oelhafen, explained more precisely what they were authorized to do. German gendarmes would not need any formal approval to carry out executions, he wrote, in instances "in which it is entirely clear why the execution is to be done."[9] Only a brief report of the event, he wrote, is to be written afterward and circulated to all of the district's SS and police offices. At this time, it was "entirely clear" to Germans leaders in Zhytomyr what was "to be done" with the Jews.

In the commissariat, the administrative machinery of the Holocaust operated at two levels. For the larger actions, such as the final massacres of Jews in Berdychiv, the district SS-police chiefs met with the Gebietskommissare, local army commanders, and an official from the nearest Sipo-SD outpost. They planned the killing action and made the necessary preparations, including the assignment of "executioners." The other pattern involved fewer victims but was geographically more far-reaching and societally more invasive. During the regular patrols of rural areas, or in response to local requests, Ukrainian Schutzmänner and German gendarmes combed the region and uncovered

Jews in hiding. In what became a routine police "matter," district SS-police and gendarme leaders reported the shootings of individual Jews ex post facto to their gendarme headquarters in Vinnytsia, Berdychiv, Mazyr, Korosten', and Zhytomyr.[10]

The Nazi Search for Jews in the Countryside

Among the twenty-six districts that eventually comprised the Zhytomyr region, one of the few surviving collections of gendarme reports stemmed from the Koziatyn and Ruzhyn districts. According to these German reports, gendarmes and Ukrainian Schutzmänner scoured the area for Jews in the summer and fall of 1942 and continued to find and shoot Jewish families and individuals who were found in hovels, fields, and forests in 1943. The Koziatyn district contained three gendarme stations (Koziatyn, Samhorodok, and Pohrebyshche) staffed by a total of thirty-four German gendarmes who arrived between October 1941 and May 1942.[11] The number of Schutzmänner fluctuated, but peaked in September 1943 at 354 men, not including a closed unit of 100 Ukrainian railway guards and trainees who cycled through Pohrebyshche's police school, where they were instructed, according to one lesson title, that "the Jews must be destroyed."[12]

In Koziatyn, as elsewhere in the Eastern Territories, the Germans relied on Ukrainian auxiliaries and ethnic Germans to do the dirty work of the Holocaust. Ukrainian police, most of whom were unmarried, along with former agricultural workers and day laborers, conducted the searching and plundering operations. Reich German SS-police officials, who lacked the personnel and preferred not to subject themselves to the unhygienic, disease-ridden conditions of the camps, assigned Ukrainians to guard the camps. One of the region's Sipo-SD-controlled camps was the so-called workers educational camp in Koziatyn, where about 300 Jews had been confined in 1942 along with other prisoners deemed politically suspect.[13] One Jewish survivor of the camp, Nina Glozman, remembered the excessive beatings by a Ukrainian guard named Godzikovski, who forced her to clean the toilets.[14]

In June 1942, when Koziatyn's SS and police leader, Heinrich Behrens, ordered the execution of Koziatyn's remaining Jews, who were being held at the barracks in Pohrebyshche, the Ukrainian auxiliaries translated the German orders to the Jews, forced them to undress, and stood ready as an SD commando from Berdychiv fired its deadly shots. On 6 July 1942 Behrens sent a memorandum to the gendarme leaders at Pohrebyshche and Samhorodok stating that he was aware of additional Jews hiding in the villages and forests and warned that all villages must report the presence of Jews. If German gendarmes or Ukrainian policemen found Jews, "the entire village should be punished."[15] One month later, in August 1942, after intense searches by the Ukrainian police and German gendarmes, 200 more Jews were gathered at the barracks.

Behrens telephoned the SD post in Berdychiv and agreed to assist the SD in the killing action by providing about forty Ukrainian police and some German soldiers who were stationed nearby. When the SD commando force arrived at the local airfield, Behrens was there to greet them and then drive the killing squad to the Talymynivka ravine, which was the execution site near the barracks.[16]

Ukrainian farmers policed their own villages by telling the Germans the whereabouts of Jews. In the late summer of 1942, a Ukrainian farmer named Tymoshchyk reported to German gendarme station leader Lieutenant Munch in Koziatyn that some Jews were hiding in the village of Kordelivka. Munch immediately deployed to the area a unit of Ukrainian police led by a German gendarme captain. After a futile search of Kordelivka, the policemen departed from the village by foot. As they walked along the road outside of the village, they spotted some people hiding among the corn stalks. The Jewish families Pintel and Bravermann (one man, three women, and four children) tried desperately to elude the police. The Ukrainian and German policemen grabbed them and ruthlessly shot them on the spot.[17] Not long after this incident, at the end of September 1942, Behrens reported to the district commissar that except for those in hiding, the Koziatyn district had been cleared of its Jews; they had just given over the last eighteen Jewish men and three women to the SD for "resettlement."[18]

Yet in 1943 the gendarmes and Ukrainian Schutzmänner continued their intense search for Jews. As in the case of the Kordelivka massacre, SS and police district leaders in Koziatyn and Ruzhyn regularly reported that Jewish families (mainly women and small children) had been found hiding in haystacks and hovels, and were "shot while trying to escape."[19] Meanwhile, the local police pressured Ukrainians to disclose where Jews were hiding. In one outstanding example from Pohrebyshche, a small group of Jews managed to survive for over a year in hiding, though it is not clear how much help they received from villagers. As the German gendarme station leader Bruno Mayrhofer described it:

On 7 May 1943, 21.00 hours, following a confidential report, 8 Jews, that is 3 men, 2 women and 3 children were flushed out of a well-camouflaged hole in the ground in an open field not far from the post here, and all of them were shot while trying to escape. This case concerned Jews from Pohrebyshche who had lived in this hole in the ground for almost a year. The Jews did not have anything else in their possession except their tattered clothing. The few items of food that they possessed and lay strewn about the camp were given to the village poor. As well was the still somewhat usable clothing. The burial was carried out immediately on the spot.[20]

For individual Jews and small Jewish families, who were hunted like animals by the German-led police forces, survival depended almost entirely on the local population. Their only source of food was the local peasantry. Starving and desperate, Jewish fugitives stole the food under cover of night. Some charitable peasants provided food. Others exploited the dire plight of the Jews by demanding large sums of money or valuables in exchange for food or shelter.

Because some German administrators continued secretly to employ skilled Jews, police orders were also circulated in June 1942 and again in early spring 1943 that any remaining Jews must be identified. In the June 1942 order, Berdychiv's district gendarme captain warned that refusing to hand over Jews who continued to work in the administration obstructed their "resettlement" and would result in punishment by the SS and police court for "Befehlsverweigerung" (refusal to follow orders). Then in March 1943 similar instructions were handed down from Berdychiv to Koziatyn, and the local Koziatyn gendarme leader abandoned the "resettlement" euphemism, ordering that the local police must hand over all remaining Jews and then make sure that the "pits were prepared."[21]

Here and there individual Ukrainians did try within their limited means to help Jews, and in doing so they risked their lives as well as those of their neighbors. Indeed, the Germans carried out collective measures against entire villages if Jews had not been handed over to the Ukrainian and German police.[22] In the city orphanage at Zhytomyr, a Ukrainian aide and her superior concealed Jewish children with new Ukrainian identities; one four-year-old girl was adopted by Ukrainian parents who knew she was Jewish.[23] Semen Umanskii's family survived the harsh winters in the forests near Brailov because non-Jewish friends in the surrounding villages gave them food and a place to sleep.[24] Some Ukrainians who lived near the forced labor camps of DG IV brought food to the prisoners and signaled when a massacre was imminent because they saw the death pits being prepared nearby.[25] Only weeks before the Red Army recaptured villages in the Koziatyn district, the local SS and police leader Heinrich Behrens reported that a Ukrainian woman had been arrested for sheltering Jews

Оголошення.

1) Кожний Бургомайстер, староста села зобов'язаний заарештувати через Місцеву Поліцію та передавати Поліції СД в Бердичеві кожну єврейську особу з чужої місцевости, особливо що перебувають тут з 24 грудня 1942 року.

2) Всім місцевим особам забороняється давати притулок чи переховувати єврейських осіб з чужих місцевостей.

3) У кожному випадку, якщо виявиться, що якась єврейська особа перебуває без дозволу, всю сім'ю, що дає таким притулок, буде покарана смертю.

4) Цю ж саму кару буде застосовано до того Бургомайстера-старости села, який не послідує негайно зобов'язанню пункта § 1.

Гебітскомісар

Announcement of the Gebietskommissar of Berdychiv forbidding the sheltering of Jews. Headed simply "Announcement," the text reads: "(1) Every mayor and village elder with the help of the local police must arrest and hand over to the SD-police in Berdychiv each Jewish person from another locality, especially those who remained here after 24 December 1942. (2) All local persons are forbidden to shelter or hide Jews, especially those from other localities. (3) In each instance in which it is found out that Jewish persons stayed without permission, the entire family that sheltered them will be punished with death. (4) The same punishment will be applied to any mayors or village elders who do not immediately follow the obligation under point §1." The announcement is signed "District Commissar." (Anti-Jewish Nazi and Collaborationist Leaflets and Announcements Made and Posted during the Nazi Occupation of Ukraine, 1941–1943, RG 31.023, U.S. Holocaust Memorial Museum, courtesy of the Judaica Institute, Kiev)

in Vchoraishe.[26] These rather few but significant cases demonstrate that some Ukrainians courageously tried to help Jews.

Indigenous Police Forces and the Holocaust
Their Size, Influence, and Ideological Training

How extensive was the local police's role in the Holocaust during 1942 and 1943? The Germans increased the number of Ukrainian auxiliaries in the countryside, most markedly in the spring of 1943. After the big recruiting drives of August 1942 and initiation ceremonies of September 1942, the headcount of Schutzmänner in the entire Zhytomyr region was 5,200.[27] Later in April 1943, after the Germans forced more Ukrainian men to join, it jumped to 16,400 auxiliaries, while the number of German gendarme leaders was about 1,100 men.[28] During 1942 and 1943 the number of Ukrainian police in the region nearly tripled.

The dramatic increase in the number of local policemen in the late summer and fall of 1942 stemmed mainly from a local German policy to employ more Ukrainians in antipartisan warfare, especially in the patrolling of forests and the countryside, where Germans were most vulnerable. This development did not represent a shift in priorities, but rather a German response to local conditions in Zhytomyr and other areas in the East where partisan warfare was on the rise. The primary "enemy" in the minds of the Nazis remained first and foremost the Jews, whom the Ukrainian auxiliaries could continue to uncover during partisan raids and whom the Germans promoted as the core of the Bolshevik insurgency.

Surviving documentation does not reveal exactly who was carrying out the shooting of Jews in the most remote outposts of the Reich. However, Ukrainian policemen were charged with the patrolling of villages without German supervision, and they were empowered to kill persons whom German leaders defined as enemies of the state, for example, Jews. Another case stemming from a Koziatyn district police office sheds additional light on the role of the Ukrainian police. Samhorodok gendarme leader Josef Richter nominated Schutzmann Unterführer Vasyl' Palamarchuk for a service award because of his notable contribution in the "resettlement of Jews" there in June 1942 and in subsequent searches for Jews in hiding. According to Richter, Palamarchuk volunteered for the "special actions" and in carrying them out displayed an exemplary daredevilness and enthusiasm that substantially motivated his fellow Schutzmänner.[29] In the "resettlement" action that Richter referred to (which occurred on 4 June 1942), German gendarmes and Ukrainian police killed the elderly and sick Jews of the Samhorodok ghetto. An SD execution squad gunned down the remainder (about 500 persons).[30]

The Germans did not as a consistent policy place the Ukrainian police in the role of executioners. There were a few controversial cases—for example, at Radomyshl'—in which the Germans used Ukrainian militia to shoot Jewish children, a task that some German shooters preferred to relegate to Ukrainians.[31] Still, German security police and gendarme leaders tended to direct the operation and do the shooting. To be sure, the SS-police effectively trained many Ukrainians (and ethnic Germans) to be reliable ruffians and killers at the death camps and ghettos in Poland.[32] But in general the Germans were wary of arming Ukrainian police auxiliaries in the occupation administration, many of whom had not been carefully screened. The Germans realized that a Ukrainian aide might misuse his weapon or desert his post and join the partisans (and many did). Moreover, armed Germans were not inclined to give over their primary source of power—the gun. Thus the Germans placed themselves in a contradictory position of depending on the loyalty of Ukrainians whom they

increasingly alienated. Both the collaborators and the general populace understood that German leaders were capable of unleashing mass murder to an unprecedented degree, and that upon complete destruction of the Jews the Germans might very well seek to destroy all Ukrainians.[33]

In order to bring the growing force of Ukrainian and ethnic
German auxiliaries into the Nazi campaign and make them more ideologically
reliable, on 24 June 1942 Himmler instructed his subordinates to focus on
the "political training of the Schutzmannschaft." He and Rosenberg agreed to
establish formal educational training schools for the Schutzmannschaft; the
schools were located in Korosten' and Koziatyn. In this agreement they outlined the goals of the indoctrination program, with an emphasis on "stirring
up the strong instinctual anti-Semitism of the eastern peoples" by drawing attention to "the Jewish face of Bolshevism" and other Nazi theories of Jewish
world conspiracies.[34] On 22 August 1942 the chief of the police training office
in Ukraine provided the Order Police headquarters in Zhytomyr with the ideological substance of the program, set forth in an essay entitled *Das neue Werden
im Osten Europas* (The New Development in Eastern Europe):

A large part of the blood sacrifice of the German people was given up over
the centuries in the incessant battles over the borders of Eastern Europe.
What is happening today in the East is already part of the New Order of
Europe. German politics in the East are inspired by the memory of Eastern
Europe as a land of settlement. When the Germanic-German colonists and
merchants penetrated Eastern European countries over the course of centuries, they were called by the rulers of the peoples who lived there. They did
not bring robbery and destruction, fire and murder, death and ruin; instead,
they successfully created from the fertile fields blooming cities, outstanding buildings, and artistic [and] scholarly works of the highest value.

By contrast, the culture-negating and people-destroying forces of Bolshevism have only failed to promote the cultures that were there, and they
have prevented in every way the free development of European peoples in
Russia. Because the Bolshevism that the Lithuanian, Estonian, Latvian,
Belorussian, and Ukrainian people were confronted with was not European,
and also not actually Russian in character, but Jewish and Asian in its nature. The Jews brought Bolshevism to power through a tyranny of terror,
hunger, crime. . . . The current war being led by the Germans and Italians
will mean the destruction of Bolshevism and with it the liberation of the
people of Eastern Europe.[35]

The excerpt of this essay is revealing in several respects. For one, it shows how major themes of Nazi ideology and indeed of Himmler and Hitler's thinking seeped into the minds and indoctrination programs of the regional SS-police offices in the Eastern Territories. Germany's history of eastward migration was distorted to justify Nazi Germany's conquest of the region, and even its application of genocidal policies. The German colonist was portrayed as the source of everything good: a thriving economy, flourishing landscapes, and masterful cultural monuments. This rosy portrait of European superiority as essentially German was contrasted with the destructive other—the "Bolshevik Jew."[36] The German appeal to Ukrainians centered on the notion that the Nazis waged a war of liberation in Eastern Europe by defeating "Judeo-Bolshevism."

Down the chain of command, regional SS-police leaders were asked to report on the results of Nazi ideological indoctrination of indigenous police forces. In October 1942 Reserve Lieutenant of the Schutzpolizei Albrecht in Berdychiv responded. Albrecht trained ethnic German and Ukrainian commanders of the Schutzmannschaften in Berdychiv. The necessity of looking after the political training of the police, he wrote, had been known to the Germans since early 1942 and had been a constant in their program. As part of this program, Albrecht, with the help of the district commissar's office and the German tourist board, distributed colorful posters, picture postcards, and maps of Germany. They observed that the police recruits preferred the images of modern German cities to romanticized rural landscapes. Aside from this, Albrecht wrote, the Germans' handling of the Jewish problem was of special interest to the recruits. They were impressed by the fact that Berdychiv was no longer "72 percent Jewish," adding that here "the Jew is universally rejected. Even the prisoners avoid working with Jews and half-Jews."[37]

German civil and police leaders needed a loyal police corps to secure the remote areas that were coming under increasing partisan attack. They appealed to the desire of the "natives" for a Western way of life, explained their presence as historically justified, and—given the apparent anti-Semitism among Ukrainians and ethnic Germans—claimed that the Holocaust was mutually beneficial.[38]

Thus thousands of Ukrainian policemen provided the commissariat officials with the necessary manpower and local information about the population and terrain. Hundreds in the mobile battalions (#108, 109, 110) and stationary SS-police units participated directly in the killing of Jews. It must be stressed, however, that the Germans initiated and controlled anti-Jewish policies as well as steered Ukrainian involvement in the "Final Solution."[39]

The Commissar as Central Coordinator of Anti-Jewish Policy Interagency Collaboration at the Local Level

Even with the extensive recruiting and training of local police, the regional and district commissars had to enlist other Reich German personnel to carry out the genocide. For example, in the district of Ruzhyn, which was 1,800 square kilometers with 129,000 inhabitants, the gendarme post was equipped with two motorcycles and a motorized bicycle, but no truck. Therefore, individuals ostensibly in non-police functions were expected to provide assistance and to serve in policing roles. It was not unusual for an SD officer to approach a German employee of a private firm, such as a government-contracted engineer attached to Organization Todt (OT), to request the use of his trucks for transporting Jews or of staff engineers to serve as guards in an upcoming action. In July 1942 Higher SS and Police Leader Prützmann decided to train the foresters in Zhytomyr "to carry out tasks similar to the police units." Besides Jewish refugees, a growing number of partisans encamped in the forests were to be apprehended, interrogated, and shot. Like U.S. Park officials, the foresters had law enforcement functions, particularly regarding poaching, vandalism, and the search for missing persons or suspects on their grounds.[40]

The vast involvement of Germans outside of the police hierarchy occurred within the bureaucracy of the civil commissariat, and more directly among individuals who agreed on the spot to assist in the killing actions. Sometimes these two types of involvement overlapped when commissars themselves pushed through the paperwork behind the Holocaust as well as participated in the carnage. In the commissariat structure, the regional and district leaders consulted with a small group of departmental chiefs, five in all. One of these chiefs was the local SS and police leader who advised the commissar on the state of the "Jewish question" in the area. Each month Commissar Klemm (and his successor, Leyser) reported to Rosenberg's ministry in Berlin about whether his respective area was "free of Jews" and the number of Jews killed.

As the primary persons charged with the welfare of the local population, the commissars were responsible for the rations, housing, and general plight of the Jews.[41] According to Koch's ration instructions, Jews received food only if it was available and the caloric allotment was not to exceed the amount assigned to children up to age fourteen.[42] Jews assigned to hard labor who officially should have been allotted larger rations received no more than two "meals" per day in the camps, one at about 5:30 A.M. and the other at about 6:30 P.M. A typical meal consisted of a watery soup and ersatz bread. One Jewish laborer who was among 500 assigned to road construction near Vinnytsia wrote that they received a 100-gram mixture of chestnuts and sawdust.[43] Under the supervision of the commissars' so-called nutrition, medical, and labor experts, non-laboring Jews in the camps were, as a policy, left to die of starvation and disease.

Besides the distribution of food, the commissars controlled the distribution of Jewish property. A subsection of the Political Policies Department, which was led by a Dr. Müssig, tallied the seized currency, gold, jewelry, and other valuables.[44] To some degree, it is possible to connect Müssig's accounting reports to the timing of anti-Jewish massacres, since the district-level SS and policemen were supposed to hand over the most valuable items to Müssig. At the end of July 1942, Müssig ordered that all district and city commissars generate lists of Jewish gold, silver, cash, and other valuables, and that the lists and items be brought to the commissariat's finance department. Müssig reissued this order on 27 October 1942 and added that other items such as clothing should be included for the "urgent" needs of local organizations (for example, the Ethnic German Liaison Office).[45] In the district office at Berdychiv, Gebietskommissar Ernst Göllner levied a special tax against the Jews as part of Erich Koch's demand to raise taxes and seek "other methods for extracting money from the locals." The money collected was carefully counted and entered in the commissar's accounting books as income under the heading "Judenabgabe." The name of each Jewish "taxpayer" was also listed.[46] As of February 1942, the district commissar's accountant in Chudniv stopped tallying a "Jewish contribution," which suggests that the population had been either destroyed or relocated to a camp in Berdychiv.

Given the lack of financial assets held by Jews in Soviet territories, the Nazis concentrated their plundering operation on the confiscation of apartments, furniture, bedding, clothing, and other household items. On 12 December 1941 General Commissar Klemm ordered that all Jewish property be handed over to the commissariat office for disposition. This demand served multiple purposes: it ensured that the Germans skimmed off the best booty; it provided the German commissars with bribery material for manipulating and paying off indigenous collaborators; and it gave the Germans the upper hand in managing the numerous conflicts among Ukrainians who illegally grabbed abandoned Jewish property or made claims to it. When local Ukrainian militiamen plundered Jewish belongings, they violated Nazi decrees as well as stirred up local disputes over the spoils of the genocide.[47]

The commissariat's housing office and inventory commission registered and redistributed Jewish property to local officials, military commanders, and ethic Germans.[48] Assisted by Ukrainian and ethnic German clerks, the commissar compiled lists of Jews who had been "resettled" and the contents of their dwellings. Letters from local OT representatives, ethnic Germans, army officials, and other Reich Germans in the area streamed into the inventory commission's office with requests for beds, tables, chairs, and cupboards. In July 1942 Klemm's deputy in the inventory commission, someone named Plisko, issued detailed instructions about the confiscation of Jewish property, putting a temporary halt to the distribution of Jewish valuables at the booty depot since many local officials were taking items without the proper paperwork. He advised the district commissars not to dispose of the original lists of property registered by the Jews, who were now mostly dead, because these lists were the most complete records available.[49] Plisko wanted to keep these lists in order to maintain financial order and to prevent personal skimming.

The commissars' persecution bureaucracy extended into the realm of public health. In Zhytomyr the chief of public health, Dr. Kuhlberg, reported on the outbreak of epidemics that he attributed to the arrival of Hungarian Jewish construction detachments in the northern districts. No effort was made to provide medical aid to the ill Jewish laborers. On the contrary, typhoid-stricken laborers were quarantined in a barn and burned alive as a "preventive health measure."[50] In another public "hygiene" order of June 1942, the commander of the gendarmerie in Zhytomyr ordered all German police who come in contact with the Jews to bathe and check themselves for lice.[51] The timing of this order coincided with the Nazi liquidations of labor camps and ghettos in the summer of 1942.

While the commissariat officials (many of them with professional and doctoral degrees in law, engineering, and medicine) routinely pursued the implementation of anti-Jewish measures in bureaucratic ways—by calculating lists of Jewish property, distributing starvation-level rations to the camps, and monitoring epidemics near Jewish camps—other German personnel in the civil administration actually participated in the shooting actions.[52] According to Rosenberg's "Brown File," the district commissar had unlimited power to enforce police actions against Jews.[53] Typically, the Gebietskommissar himself, after supervising a roundup of Jews, also arrived with the SD commando at the pits and observed the shootings. In the district of Lityn, Gebietskommissar (SA Standartenführer) Traugott Vollkammer oversaw the action and observed the mass shootings during the "ghetto" clearing on 19 December 1941. One of the commissar's deputies in the political policy department actually carried out the shooting of one or more Jews in October 1942.[54]

In Samhorodok, Gebietskommissar Wolfgang Steudel introduced the Jewish population to the "Final Solution." German gendarmerie and Ukrainian police first began to concentrate the Jews there as late as 16 May 1942; during this "ghetto" action German and Ukrainian police shot the sick and the elderly and those who tried to flee. A few weeks later, on 4 June 1942, the remaining population of about 500 Jewish men, women, and children were killed after Steudel ordered the Ukrainian mayor of Germanivka to assign twenty-five Ukrainians from the nearby collective farm to dig mass graves. Steudel personally inspected the pits shortly before the Jews arrived. He managed the entire action, directing the local gendarme station leader, Josef Richter, and drafting the Ukrainian helpers. Two or more SD men who arrived from the SD outpost in Vinnytsia did the shooting at the pits, however.[55]

Himmler's agencies maintained the leading role over the mass murder apparatus, but the sheer scope and great importance that Nazi leaders assigned to the "Final Solution" meant that the SS-police needed the assistance of virtually all local German agencies. The commissariat's participation, in contrast to other non-police agencies in the region, was imperative.[56] Besides the commissars, local Wehrmacht village and field commanders in the region, as well as Hungarian and Slovakian security divisions, contributed to the Holocaust.[57] The military provided battalions of defense units (Landesschützenverbände), to serve as guards at the POW camps. Throughout 1942, the second company of LS Battalion 351 carried out mass shootings in the sand pits located between the cemetery and horse stables of Stalag 358 (in partnership with Sipo-SD Commander Razesberger's men from Zhytomyr).[58] In the southern part of the region around Vinnytsia, Hungarian officers joined the small planning staffs of commissars and SS-policemen who determined when and how a massacre would occur. For example, on 26 May 1942 in Haisyn (about eighty kilometers southeast of Vinnytsia), a meeting was held in the office of the local Wehrmacht Ortskommandantur. The purpose of the meeting was to plan for the execution of the local Jewish population scheduled for the next day. Gebietskommissar Becher, who had probably received some prior direction from the SD in Vinnytsia, called the meeting and invited two local military commanders, Wehrmacht Major Heinrich and the commander of the Hungarian battalion, along with the station chief of the gendarme post, Dreckmeier.[59] Because they intended to round up the Jews from three villages, Commissar Becher split the action into two transports; one of these was led by Major Heinrich and supported by Ukrainian Schutzmänner and Hungarian infantry. In the early morning of 3:00 A.M. they forced the Jews onto trucks and drove them to the execution site at Teplyk where a shooting commando of SD men stood ready. About 400 Jews were killed in these massacres.[60]

In addition to the collaboration of military units stationed in the region, one of the more unusual developments in Zhytomyr was the involvement of the Organization Todt, a semi-military organization tasked with the construction of military installations and highways. This organization's involvement in the "Final Solution" in Zhytomyr was most evident in the building of Hitler's headquarters and the DG IV project. Typically, OT officials who were employed by private building firms, like Firma Dohrmann, also held staff positions within the commissariat structure and reported up through the military hierarchy. But when the SS began to eclipse the role of the civil administration in the DG IV project as early as 1942, the OT began to work more closely with SS building inspection offices, headquartered in Vinnytsia with outposts near the road construction and camps (such as in Haisyn). The SS formed units of security police who oversaw the forced-labor activities along the highway; they also guarded the projects against partisan attackers. These German SS-police inspectors and their auxiliary guards (mostly Lithuanians) relied on the OT station leaders to identify the Jewish workers who were on the brink of death and therefore deemed no longer useful as laborers.

"Vernichtung durch Arbeit" Jewish Laborers on DG IV and Nazi Headquarters

The Nazi policy of using Jewish laborers, in projects such as road construction, was officially endorsed by Heydrich at the Wannsee Conference in January 1942.[61] But what Heydrich revealed at Wannsee had been put into practice months earlier in Zhytomyr (and before that in eastern Galicia). In August 1941 while stationed at Zhytomyr, Otto Rasch, chief of Einsatzgruppe C, reported that "until the Final Solution of the Jewish problem is achieved across the continent, Jews can be *used up* in the cultivating of swampy areas around the Pripiat', the Dnepr, and the Volga."[62] A month later he reiterated that unlike the procedure in the General Government, the Jews in Ukraine should be killed through the kind of hard labor that was so desperately needed. Since they constituted an entire class of skilled labor, Rasch reasoned, they could be used for special projects and killed when their skills were no longer needed. In order to complete reconstruction work for military operations, he wrote, "it has become necessary to exclude, provisionally, from execution the older Jewish skilled workers."[63]

Already in August 1941, OT officials arrived in the area and targeted the Jews for labor assignments. Since many of these Jews were either beaten or killed on the job, Jews stopped responding to the OT demand for labor.[64] The OT found a less resistant labor force in the POW camps, where captured Red Army soldiers were desperate to flee the abominable conditions of the camps and secure food rations. In early to mid-September 1941, military and OT chiefs in the region began to plan for seven labor camps for road construction to be placed between Vinnytsia and Haisyn.[65] An OT headquarters was established in the city of Zhytomyr for DG V, the proposed highway running north-south from Zhytomyr toward Vinnytsia. The autobahn labor camps were planned for every fifteen kilometers of road. The DG IV route (running in an east-west direction through Vinnytsia) was not a new roadway. In the late eighteenth century, Catherine the Great began to build the road, but in 1941 it fell far below German autobahn standards. The German plan was to reconstruct the existing road by widening it by eight meters, asphalting it, and digging drainage trenches along the sides. With the availability of the needed resources (quarries and laborers) and the proximity of Hitler's headquarters, this particular stretch of DG IV, a highway that was to extend eventually from L'viv to Uman', became a feasible priority.

In the early days of the DG IV project, local German military commanders transferred groups of 150 POWs each from the Stalag Zhmerynka and the Zhytomyr Dulags 201/205 to Vinnytsia; there they were formed into construction detachments and assigned to one of the DG IV camps.[66] Units of the Security Divisions 444 and 454 guarded the workers and the POW camps along the roadway.[67] Organization Todt supplied technical staffs that manned special OT stations along the road. A number of OT engineers arrived in Vinnytsia in April 1942, just after members of the SS Bauabschnittsleitung (Construction Sector Directorate) had received their assignments at the stations.

In January and February 1942 Himmler formalized the SS's role in the autobahn projects of the East. He assigned Higher SS and Police Leader Prützmann and his regional SS-police forces to secure the forced laborers. Prützmann set up a special commission for his assignment, which was called the "Einsatzstab Gieseke," named after the commission's director, Senior Lieutenant of the Gendarmerie Walter Gieseke. Under Gieseke stood four SS Oberbauabschnittsleitungen (Senior Construction Sector Directorates), staffed by SS leaders with the title of inspector. One of these SS offices was located in Vinnytsia and led by SS-Brigadeführer Ludolf von Alvensleben, inspector for road construction. Though initially there existed some conflict among leaders over Himmler's acquisition of the DG IV project, in the field the OT and SS men fell into their respective roles. Essentially the SS took charge of supplying the forced laborers and managing the camps, whereas the OT controlled the engineering and road construction.[68]

The OT stations were situated alongside the SS outposts, such as at Voronovytsia (district Nemyriv) and at the Hnivan' quarry in Teplyk (district Vinnytsia). The OT senior engineers and technicians devised their construction plans and then contracted private firms, mainly from Germany and the Netherlands, to complete the work. Though private firms such as Firma Barkhausen in Lityn paid the SS for the individual laborers and their rations, the SS did not in turn pay wages to the POWs and Jews and forced them to work under the worst conditions. According to the diary of survivor Arnold Daghani, there were eight road contractors hired by OT to engineer the Haisyn-Uman' stretch of road near Vinnytsia. Approximately 3,500 Ukrainian Jews and 3,800 Romanian Jews labored on this project between 1942 and 1944.[69]

By the end of March 1942, the SS Construction Directorates were staffed by two German policemen and guard battalions of Lithuanian, Ukrainian, Latvian, and Cossack Schutzmannschaften. Generally the German civil engineers came up with the work assignments, while the Lithuanian and Ukrainian guards beat the laborers, often in an excessively brutal manner. German Security Police and Order Police served as camp commandants and supervised auxiliary guards over several stretches of road.[70]

Relations among OT men, German police, and the Schutzmannschaften in the DG IV project were generally smooth; however, not all of the OT civil engineers looked favorably upon SS-police methods.[71] For example, when an SD officer from Haisyn approached OT machinist Josef Rader (from Firma Massenberg-Essen) and asked him to participate in a mass shooting, Rader declined. Another OT Stutzpunktleiter (base leader) from Firma Dohrmann helped 200 Jews by allowing them to flee in 1943. In another instance, an OT official from this same firm complained that the shootings near the building sites impaired the productivity of other workers; in response, the SS agreed to carry out the shootings away from the construction areas.[72]

These examples illustrate that some OT representatives were critical of the mistreatment of Jewish laborers, and in rare cases tried to rescue the laborers from their certain death. Most, however, were unable to distance themselves from the SS and police methods, and some even participated in the executions. OT engineers and construction supervisors routinely handed over the Jews who could not work to local SS and policemen. OT engineers and construction leaders did not have the "power of a public office" to carry forth an execution, but occasionally they transgressed this Nazi law. For example, a military court at Proskuriv (Luts'k) sentenced Johann Meisslein to three months in prison for ordering Lithuanian guards to kill two Jewish women. His crime was not the murder of two Jews (or assistance of it); he was convicted of acting outside his official jurisdiction.

Meisslein was an OT foreman. In 1942 he supervised Jewish laborers who worked on DG IV between Luts'k and Vinnytsia. Each day as the columns of Jewish laborers left the Ositna camp to work on his stretch of the road, Meisslein observed that two ill Jewish women were being dragged along. He complained that when the women reached the building site with the others, they were of no use, lying along the side of the road in a trench. He recommended that they be "removed at the next opportunity." It was clear to all what "removal" meant in this context. In fact, a similar situation had previously arisen, and the OT asked that the ill Jews at the construction site be sent to the SS camp Ositna. At Ositna, the German police ordered two Lithuanian guards to shoot and bury the Jews. So when Meisslein then ordered his Polish assistant "to do what he could to remove" the Jewish women from the work site, his assistant brought them to the Lithuanian guards, who then shot and buried them in the nearby woods. Not expecting to be reprimanded for the incident, Meisslein dutifully reported the executions to the local SS office. But shortly thereafter the SS captain Franz Christoffel reproached him for getting mixed up in "police matters"; Meisslein was brought before a tribunal of military, OT, and SS-police officials and sentenced to three months in prison. His case shows that when German officials from different agencies became involved in the execution of Jews, SS and police officials tried to maintain their ultimate authority over the "Final Solution," arguing that only they were empowered to order the execution of Jews. The outcome of the trial demonstrates that overstepping one's authority in the Nazi system was a criminal act, not the murder of Jews per se.[73]

There are extremely few accounts and records about DG IV camp conditions and the experiences of Jews who labored on the road, though a few historians have begun to explore this emerging topic.[74] One Jewish survivor, Vladimir Goykher, published his memoirs about a construction site near Vinnytsia. He wrote that "I and twelve other boys ages 13–15 years dug sand for twelve hours per day. . . . We were beaten regularly" by a German "soldier," who often beat the boys "out of boredom."[75] In another related source, an OT man revealed that the Schutzmannschaft guards had shot all eighteen members of a Jewish labor unit because the weather was cold and the guards wanted to leave their post to find warm shelter.[76] At Mykhailivka, twelve kilometers west of Haisyn, about 500 Jews from Ukraine and Romania were crammed into a stable along with the horses. In such abominable conditions, survivor Arnold Daghani wrote in his wartime diary, disease was rampant, and those who could not get up to work were eventually separated and shot. Besides children, there

Arnold Daghani (1909–85), Work on the Main Road, 1943. Watercolor on paper
(Collection of the Yad Vashem Art Museum, Jerusalem)

Arnold Daghani, a Romanian Jewish artist, was deported in August 1942 to the forced labor camp of Mikhailivka near Haisyn, a town in the Vinnytsia region of German-occupied Ukraine. German officials and Lithuanian guards who ran the camp demanded that Daghani paint their portraits. They supplied him with paper, which Daghani used to secretly document the lives and experiences of the Jewish laborers. He and his wife, Anishora, escaped from the camp in the summer of 1943, a few months before it was liquidated.

were a number of women among the laborers.[77] Starvation was perhaps the workers' greatest form of suffering.[78]

A rare and revealing source, Daghani's diary presents the odd mix and interaction of perpetrators at the road construction sites in Ukraine: German engineers and their families, lowly power-seeking SS men, Lithuanian non-commissioned officers, and high-ranking SS officers. Despite their diverse backgrounds, they devised a brutal system for selecting and killing the "unfit" laborers (mostly women, children, and the infirm); they seemed to relish their power over the laborers, beating them as they worked on the road and in the gravel pits. Their inhumane approach thrived on routine as well as random acts of humiliation, and on murder, which had the desired effect of terrorizing the workers and curbing resistance. Daghani related that at Haisyn, for example, the Lithuanian guards convinced German inspectors to kill two elderly women working on the road. The women (who were friends) appeared to be healthy, but one of them possessed a pair of sturdy snow boots, which the guards wanted. They were simply ordered to march a few hundred yards from the site and were then shot by one of the guards. OT foremen tormented the

Arnold Daghani (1909–85), Back "Home" from Work, 1943. Pencil on paper.
(Collection of the Yad Vashem Art Museum, Jerusalem)

Arnold Daghani (1909–85), Mass Graves, 1943. Watercolor on paper.
(Collection of the Yad Vashem Art Museum, Jerusalem)

laborers with cutting remarks, such as one made by a young OT driver, Ernst Joseph Hennes, who blurted out to Daghani and his fellow laborers: "You're like cattle purchased by the butcher. One of you will be slain today, the others tomorrow. The turn will come to all of you." After hearing this, Daghani reflected in his diary, "That remark passed off for sympathy. Was it?"[79]

Besides the continuous and routine "cleansing" of the camps by German police leaders and their Schutzmannschaften, SS Bauabschnittsleitung leaders joined forces with the nearest Sipo-SD office to "hunt down" Jews outside the camps. Together they carried out mass executions of Jews from nearby villages or from Romanian and Hungarian labor detachments.[80] The German military and SS-police purchased the Romanian Jewish laborers, had them transported across the Bug River (the German-Romanian border), and put them to work in the quarries and camps of the Vinnytsia region. The German "selection" process occurred after the Romanian Jews arrived in Nazi-occupied Ukraine.[81]

One member of the local SS inspectorate office near Vinnytsia distinguished himself as a killer: Karl Klenk. He was Hauptwachtmeister of the Schutzpolizei and camp commandant at Krasnopolka and Tyvriv. Not only did he torture and kill Jews in the camps, but he also went after the remnant Jewish populations in the nearby towns. In the summer of 1942, Klenk assisted the local gendarmerie in the massacre of Hnivan"s Jews. First he forced twenty POW laborers from one of his DG IV camps to level an area into an airfield where the SD killing squad could land its small plane. Then Klenk and his Lithuanian auxiliaries returned to Hnivan', pulled the Jews from their houses, and brought them to a nearby forest. There they met the execution squad of SD men who had been escorted from the airfield by the local Gebietskommissar.[82]

The added presence of SS-policemen assigned to the DG IV project meant that Zhytomyr's Jewish population faced yet another concentrated effort to "clear" the areas along the highways. For most Jews who were assigned to the project, their suffering was merely prolonged and their fate remained the same as their Jewish relatives who had perished earlier in 1941 and 1942. Upon the liquidation of the DG IV camps in late 1943–early 1944, the German SD, Order Police, and non-German auxiliaries had killed, according to one scholar's estimate, as many as 25,000 Jewish laborers in Ukraine.[83] At the DG IV labor camps in Haisyn, about 7,000 Jews were worked to death and killed when the camps were liquidated. Thousands were killed in June 1943 and October 1943 at the former Khmil'nyk ghetto. A recent quantitative analysis of the Holocaust in Vinnytsia estimates that 10,000 Jews died in the labor camps during 1942–43.[84]

Jewish Laborers and Nazi Elite Headquarters

Among the few thousand Jews who were temporarily spared as laborers, more than 1,000 were assigned to a unique project in the Zhytomyr region: the construction of Hitler's and Himmler's headquarters in early 1942. The story of this project reveals more than one facet of the "Final Solution." First of all, the OT officials initiated the use of Jewish labor at Hitler's headquarters, which effectively linked this organization to the Holocaust.[85] Second, the timing of the building and eventual arrival of Hitler and other elites to the region coincided with the major killing actions around Zhytomyr and Vinnytsia. The larger part of Zhytomyr's Jews were killed between September 1941 and July 1942 as local SS and police were pressured to "clear" the area before the arrival of Hitler, Himmler, and other Nazi chiefs. And, third, the use of Jews as laborers fulfilled a short-term German need and also provided SD personnel with an "acceptable" pretext for killing the Jewish laborers who had worked at the sites. They argued that all of the Jewish laborers and their families must die as an extra "security precaution."

In planning the construction of the headquarters, Nazi leaders confronted a problem that became especially acute in the late autumn of 1941. The Germans had destroyed their greatest source of skilled labor in the summer and autumn of 1941. But by January 1942 the priorities of Himmler and Todt converged into another temporary solution to this problem; the remaining Jews from Ukraine, Romania, and Hungary would provide the much-needed skilled labor, and they would be either worked to death or executed upon the completion of the project.[86] At first, local SD authorities were against bringing Jews to the headquarters sites, and they tried to appeal to Reich Commissar Koch, but the army and the autobahn construction chief, Fritz Todt, could not find an adequate number of masons, carpenters, and joiners among the Ukrainian population.[87] In a memorandum to Rosenberg on the handling of the Jewish question, dated 10 January 1942, Himmler had specified that "measures to eliminate Jews should be taken without regard for economic consequences," but (as is evident in the Wannsee Protocol) he also accepted the policy of using Jewish laborers for street building and, more discreetly, in the construction of his own headquarters, and then killing them after the work was complete.[88]

In Vinnytsia especially, where additional Reich security forces were assigned to "Eichenhain" (the code name for the construction of Hitler's Werwolf bunker), massacres against Jews coincided with the preparations for Hitler's arrival in the area. The construction of the bunker lasted from 15 December 1941 to 15 July 1942.[89] Before the builders broke ground on Eichenhain, SS Standartenführer Hans Rattenhuber, who was chief of the Führer's Special Security Forces (Reich Sicherheitsdienst, RSD), contacted the local SS and SD officials to coordinate their security operations around the proposed site.[90] The task of the RSD office near Vinnytsia, staffed by SS men of the GFP Security Group East, was intelligence gathering and control of suspicious persons who "for reasons of their Bolshevik views . . . and their Jewish racial membership" were an espionage and sabotage danger.[91] Since early November 1941 the Geheime Feldpolizei (GFP 721) had been combing the villages near the planned site and began to eradicate all "security" threats, including Jews. Besides the ongoing execution of Jewish POWs who arrived in the region's camps, about 10,000 Jews were killed during October, November, December, and early January in neighboring districts at Khmil'nyk, Lityn, and Brailov. In addition, nearly 1,600 Ukrainian households (about 8,000 Ukrainians) within five kilometers of the site were later "removed."[92] On 10 January the RSD killed 227 Jews at Strizhavka, the actual grounds of the Werwolf site. SS Sturmbannführer Schmidt described the massacre at Strizhavka:

In the village of Strishawka there were 227 Jewish residents. The large number of Jews is explained by the fact that a GPU camp was in that village. Since the Jews were a big danger for the site [Führer headquarters], I made a request to the Gebietskommissar to have the Jews evacuated. Because of special circumstances, an evacuation was not possible. Therefore the Jews were done in on 10 January 1942 between the hours of 8:30 A.M. and 10:30 A.M.

In order to carry out the operation, our office had to provide a pit, and after the "transfer" had to level [the mass grave] in an orderly fashion. With the assistance of OT-men and POWs, the pit was dug out with explosives because of the hard frost. Four officials of the Security Police, twenty officials of the Feldgendarmerie and Schutzpolizei, and all of the officials from the office took part in the operation. The employment of officials was necessary in order to bring the Jews out of their dwellings to the distant pit and to secure the execution site against unauthorized persons.[93]

By mid-January the designated area for Hitler's Werwolf bunker was "free of Jews," and later in March an SS-police unit began to "clear" the areas around the airport and the route leading to the bunker. Local SS-police and RSD officials in Vinnytsia were informed by their SS-police colleagues outside the region about any possible security threats that might infiltrate the area. Lists of Jewish escapees from neighboring regions and from Nazi-occupied Poland were circulated. For example, several dozen Jewish nurses broke out of a POW camp in Luts'k and attempted to rejoin their families in the Vinnytsia region. The Wehrmachtsbefehlshaber for Ukraine instructed the local gendarmerie to hunt down these young women (who were eighteen to twenty years old).[94] The next major task in preparing for Hitler's arrival was the final liquidation of the Jews of the city of Vinnytsia, the largest town just nine kilometers south of the bunker. For this massacre, they needed to draw on several local offices to assist with the planning and implementation.

On 13 January 1942 the SS and police leader for Vinnytsia, Major Kurt Pomme, hosted a meeting with the district commissar for Vinnytsia, Gemeinschaftsführer Fritz Halle; the SD-Sipo chief for Vinnytsia, Theodor Salmanzig; and Rattenhuber's deputy, SS-Sturmbannführer Friedrich Schmidt. They convened to discuss the remaining number and location of Vinnytsia's Jews, the timing of the next killing action, and the number of Jews to be spared as laborers. Johann Bahmann, the chief of the Schutzpolizei in Vinnytsia who had just taken up his position, also attended and was quickly initiated into the local perpetrator network involved in the Holocaust. He and the other SS-policemen who were new to the region learned about the massacres of Jews that had taken place since July 1941 when Sonderkommando 4b had eliminated the Jewish leadership in the first days of the military occupation of the city. Their preferred killing site, where they established a prison for the Jews, was near the brick works. They also placed the Jews under guard in a sewing factory and jail.[95] On 19 September German SS-police and regional military authorities carried out one of the bloodiest actions in the region; between 10,000 and 15,000 women, children, and elderly people were forced to strip naked and stand before pits where they were shot by EK6 and Order Police Battalion 314.[96]

In January 1942 nearly 5,000 Jews remained in the city prison and the brick works, which became an OT-run factory dedicated to the Eichenhain construction.[97] Some worked in the city's essential industries such as electrical and water works. But the SD decided that only 700 of them were absolutely necessary for the local industry while the rest could be simply eliminated in one day.[98] On 16 April City Commissar Fritz Margenfeld ordered all Jews to gather in the sports stadium; they were told that a ghetto would be formed. After 1,000 were selected as skilled laborers for the Werwolf site, the rest were transported by truck to the forest and shot.[99]

About this time there emerged a new "security threat" that local SS and SD officials reported to the RSD commander, Hans Rattenhuber. Some 60,000 Jewish refugees in Romanian-occupied Ukraine (Transnistria) were residing just thirty-five kilometers south of the Werwolf site; they were intolerably close to this top-secret site, so the SS-police argued that they too "had to be killed." The Romanians, a German SD official complained, were not suitably efficient in carrying out the "Final Solution." In order to stem the flow of starved, typhoid-stricken Jewish refugees who were crossing into German territory in search of food, SS leaders in Vinnytsia imposed stricter border controls and pressured the Romanians to follow the current German approach to the "Jewish problem": mass shooting.[100]

About one week before Hitler arrived at his Werwolf headquarters, now barricaded by pine forest, rows of guards, patrols of secret policemen with dogs, aerial surveillance, anti-aircraft guns and barbed wire fencing, Sipo-SD Commander Razesberger in Zhytomyr contacted his SD chief in the Vinnytsia outpost, Salmanzig. He wrote that his boss, the commander of Ukraine's Security Police in Kiev, Max Thomas, had ordered a final, mandatory cleansing action against all the Jews of Vinnytsia. Razesberger added that he knew specifically of sixteen Jews who worked at the Waldhof (a military clubhouse on the Werwolf compound) who should be replaced with Ukrainians "for security rea-

German SS-policeman shooting a Jewish man in Vinnytsia, surrounded by members of the SS-police force and the Wehrmacht (U.S. Holocaust Memorial Museum, courtesy of Ullstein Bild, #00463386)

Hitler with General Field Marshal Wilhelm List and Hermann Göring at Werwolf Headquarters, Vinnytsia, 31 August 1942 (Ullstein Bild #00007695)

sons."[101] After this final massacre, the SS men attached to the RSD were decorated with the Kriegsverdienstkreuz (a distinguished military service medal), for serving as "partisan hunters" in the areas around the Hitler bunker.[102]

The Soviet POWs who worked on the site were also deemed a security threat and killed. As many as 10,000 Soviet POWs constructed the compound, and 2,000 died during the building phase, which occurred mainly in the winter months when the ground was frozen and the Germans insisted on excavating the deep bunker and bomb shelters according to the Führer's wishes. The remaining 8,000 POWs "disappeared" in the summer of 1942 and were not heard from thereafter.[103]

But for some regional officials the immediate need for labor was a strong enough rationale for slowing the machinery of the Holocaust. The story of the use of Jewish labor and the construction of Himmler's headquarters offers an unusual example of how one local SD leader was pressured into complying with the "Final Solution." About 300 Jews were also employed in the construction of Himmler's Hegewald headquarters, which contained an airfield, several houses, barracks, elegant living quarters, and a bunker with thick concrete walls.[104] After the war, Zhytomyr's Sipo-SD chief Razesberger provided

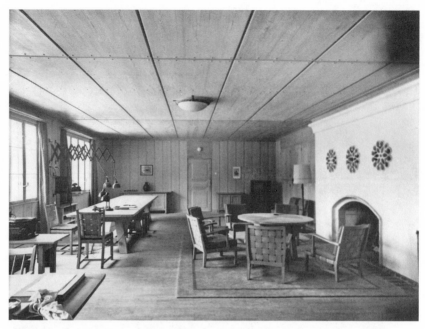

Hitler's office at Werwolf. The photo was taken during Hitler's last stay at the headquarters between 19 February and 13 March 1943. (Ullstein Bild #00038014)

the only detailed description of the compound, referring to an expensive rug on the wall of Himmler's office.[105]

About the time that Himmler arrived at his Hegewald headquarters (on 24 July 1942), the SS and police leader of Zhytomyr, Otto Hellwig, ordered the SD leader in Berdychiv, Hauptsturmführer Alois Hülsdünker, to execute the remaining 300 of Berdychiv's Jews, including eighty women and ten children who had been discovered after the last massacre.[106] Hülsdünker, who had secretly allowed thirty Jews to work in his SD outpost, testified after the war that he felt uneasy about this order. According to his testimony, he had been sent to Berdychiv from the Reich because his superiors suspected his insufficient ideological commitment to Nazism.[107] Service in the East was supposed to toughen him up.

To ensure that the order to liquidate the Berdychiv Jewish camp at Krasnaia Gora would be carried out, Razesberger drove to Berdychiv and presented the order to Hülsdünker in person. Hülsdünker wavered. He asked about the needed laborers and protested that the women and children did not pose a threat, but Razesberger insisted that all the Jews in the area who worked at the Himmler compound or who remained near the site threatened German secu-

Himmler receiving birthday congratulations from SS-police colleagues in his Hegewald office, 7 October 1942 (U.S. Holocaust Memorial Museum, courtesy of James Blevins, #60390)

rity. Hülsdünker complied and began to organize the killing of the 300 Jews in the camp. On 15 June 1942 German SS-police leaders in Berdychiv and their Ukrainian aides brought the Jews to some horse stables and then led them in groups to a pit several hundred meters from there. Several Jews tried to flee but were shot. They were forced to lie face down at the bottom of the pit and were killed by a pistol shot to the head. Ukrainian militia threw sand over them. Hülsdünker telephoned Razesberger to report that the order to liquidate the camp had been carried out. Unbeknownst to Razesberger, the thirty Jews who worked in the SD office were spared. In his postwar testimony, Hülsdünker claimed that some were able to flee when the Sipo-SD closed its office in the autumn of 1943.[108] Vasilii Grossman, who collected testimony in 1943–44 about the Holocaust in Berdychiv, learned that the Germans shot these last Jewish laborers as the Red Army advanced on Zhytomyr. One man, a harness maker named Khaim Borisovich, miraculously survived.[109]

The fact that Hülsdünker and the SD in Berdychiv continued to conceal the Jews in their office demonstrates that at the local level there existed the possibility to disobey official policy and prolong, perhaps even save, Jewish lives. Be it for pragmatic or moral reasons, some of the local German leaders secretly employed Jews. Regional German officials were warned repeatedly to hand these Jews over to the nearest SD office. In addition a small number of Jews continued to work as skilled laborers in various industries. In late October 1942, an economic analyst in Vinnytsia's Stadtkommissariat confirmed that no more Jewish workshops existed since the "Jewish question" had been "clarified" but added that a few individual Jews still worked in various local industries; actually as many as 300 were employed at a local clothing factory.[110] The Nazi exploitation of Jewish labor meant that a relatively small number of Jews had the chance to survive the Holocaust, and many Jews clung to the hope that they might be among those few spared. However, the Nazi use of Jewish labor was not representative of a general pattern "in the field" in which lower-level German leaders in the SS and police, or from other agencies, tried to rescue Jews or resist the "Final Solution." Pressure from superiors and their ardent followers, who gained control over the everyday operations of the Nazi system, was so great that by the end of 1943 nearly all of these remaining Jewish laborers and their families had been killed.

The Nazi implementation of the "Final Solution" was an ongoing invention of central and peripheral leaders. Hitler, Himmler, and Heydrich defined the aim of the policy, and they constructed an administrative framework in order to achieve it. Yet in its realization, the process of persecution and methods of mass murder developed from the ground up, often after "on the spot" decision-making about how to proceed with a massacre in the most expedient manner. In other words, the technicians and operators of the "Final Solution" apparatus—men like Higher SS and Police Leader Jeckeln, SK4a commander Blobel, Sixth Army judge Neumann, and Oberstabsarzt Panning developed a callously efficient, "zweckmässig" approach to mass shooting. As of August 1941, they sought to kill as many Jews as possible. Many written reports specified that male Jews had been executed first because the Germans believed that the men posed the greatest threat of resistance, but Nazi racial anti-Semitism was inherently aimed at the entire Jewish population. There were limitations and contingencies that surrounded the implementation of the policy, such as its psychological effects on the German executioners, and logistical issues in the field. Yet, at a staggering pace, German leaders and their subordinates effectively overcame such barriers and developed a division of labor for carrying out the genocide.

Besides the magnitude of Nazi killing sprees in the region and the approach of German commanders posted there in July–October 1941, the absence of ghettos in Zhytomyr also indicates that Nazi leaders intended to destroy the population as quickly as possible. Generally they found the ghettos "not useful," except as a temporary measure for concentrating larger Jewish populations while the details for planning their mass execution could be worked out. Ghettos in the Zhytomyr region were briefly considered by Nazi elites in early January 1942 as a remote place for "dumping" German Jews from the Reich, not as transit sites for deporting Ukrainian Jews elsewhere. The only basis for temporarily prolonging the lives of Jews, as Rasch and others recommended, was to work them to death.

The timing of killing actions in the Zhytomyr region was directly linked to the arrival and presence of the top leaders, who had numerous security forces at their disposal. Mass shootings occurred in unprecedented numbers against women and children when Higher SS and Police Leader Jeckeln was in the area during August and September 1941. Postwar testimonies concur that a general escalation in killing was prompted by the visits of either Jeckeln or Heydrich to Zhytomyr during the first half of August 1941. A similar more explicit pattern occurred in 1942 before and during Hitler's and Himmler's stay in the region. Local leaders in the commissariat administration and the SS-police tacitly understood or received explicit instructions that the Jews had to be "removed" around the headquarters.

During the second phase of the "Final Solution" in Zhytomyr (and elsewhere in the Reichskommissariat Ukraine), the commissars imposed their own individual styles of terror on the Jews—hence the mosaic of local Holocaust histories across the regions. Commissars like Göllner (in Berdychiv) and Steudel (in Koziatyn) were middle-ranking bureaucrats and former SA men who suddenly found themselves in positions of extreme power. Like the SS-police killing commanders who preceded them during the 1941 sweep, the commissars understood that their local anti-Jewish actions were part of a much larger aim of the "Final Solution." Ultimately the test of a regional leader's success was his ability to seize on all of the local possibilities, especially the use of indigenous auxiliaries, for bringing about the exploitation and destruction of the Jews. When the commissars declared their districts "free of Jews," they sought approbation from superiors for a job "well done."

The most remarkable administrative pattern was one of ad hoc collaboration. Ironically, factors that might have otherwise caused conflicts or resistance to the Holocaust, such as personnel shortages and the isolation of the rural outposts, actually furthered it. Nevertheless, there were certain aspects of the genocide, like the loss of skilled Jewish labor and the distribution of Jewish valuables, that sparked in-fighting among local German officials. The commissars and Nazi elites who had ambitious plans for building up the region's transportation systems, housing, and industry wished to capitalize as much as possible on "free" Jewish labor.

Hundreds of skilled Jewish laborers and thousands of POWs built the Nazi leaders' secret bunkers, and then were killed as a "security precaution" in the first half of 1942. When General Commissar Klemm claimed that his territory was "judenfrei" in June 1942, this was not actually the case. Members of the commissariat apparatus along with Himmler and Hitler's special security forces conducted some of the most aggressive manhunts against Jews. Yet they also continued to bring in Jews from Transnistria, Hungary, and other parts of Ukraine to build a new thruway system. Ultimately, however, the ideological consensus surrounding the "Final Solution" proved stronger than the economic rationale for keeping Jewish laborers alive. Thus, from the Nazi standpoint, a male Jewish laborer might be economically useful, but he was always expendable.

In Zhytomyr the question of "how" the region's Jewish population was destroyed so quickly and brutally can be explained as a combination of factors: (1) a close collaboration of some of the more fanatical SS and army leaders (Blobel, Jeckeln, and Reichenau); (2) sufficient manpower found in the increasing number of Order Police and indigenous auxiliaries; (3) high concentrations of Jews who had little time and means to escape, and who found that their non-Jewish neighbors were by and large indifferent to their plight; (4) the presence of Nazi leaders in the region who either directly or indirectly pressured local leaders to make their regions judenfrei; and (5) the involvement of non-police agencies in anti-Jewish measures and massacres, namely, the General Commissariat and Organization Todt. Because these factors were present in other parts of the Reich Commissariat Ukraine, the Holocaust in Zhytomyr was to a large extent typical of what occurred elsewhere in occupied Ukraine.

The level of consensus and collaboration surrounding the "Final Solution" exceeded that of other top policies of the Nazi regime, such as forced-labor programs, agricultural requisitions, and campaigns to resettle ethnic Germans. In contrast to these policies and programs, the "Final Solution" became embedded in the total administrative apparatus; as one German witnessed at Stalag 358 when Jews were being sorted out and executed, it all ran automatically ("Das Ganze lief sozusagen automatisch ab").[111] Regional leaders and functionaries who felt uneasy about the massacres found ways to adapt to the genocide. Even at the lowest levels of the hierarchy one could play a part in the Holocaust without dirtying one's own hands. In other words, one could avoid officially authorizing murder through oral orders and gestures (nodding and the like), or one could find bloodthirstier types among the Germans and the indigenous population to do the more gruesome and tiresome work, such as killing children and searching for Jews in hiding. The Nazi approach to mass murder was systematic and highly coordinated, but this destructive machine was not operated by "automatons." Rather it functioned in the hands of dedicated professionals who sought to develop a "frictionless" killing process, one that afforded them some psychological distance from the killing, one that was efficient enough for large-scale massacres, and one that would impress superiors.

Chapter 7

Himmler's Hegewald Colony
Nazi Resettlement Experiments
and the Volksdeutsche

Who would have dreamed ten years ago that we would be holding an SS meeting in a village named Hegewald, situated near
the Jewish-Russian city of Shitomir. . . . This Germanic East ex-
tending as far as the Urals must be cultivated like a hothouse of
Germanic blood. . . . The next generations of Germans and history will not remember how it was done, but rather the goal.
—Heinrich Himmler, 16 September 1942

On 16 September 1942 Heinrich Himmler, Reich leader of the
SS and police and the commissioner for "the strengthening of Germandom,"
gave a sixty-minute speech to an audience of senior SS and police leaders. The
conference was convened at the secret field headquarters that he named "Hegewald," a term roughly meaning "game reserve" but in this context referring
to an SS-Volksdeutsche colony.[1] For historians of Nazi Germany, Himmler's
speech and its historical context reveal several significant aspects of the Nazi
colonial vision of race and space in Ukraine. First, on this occasion Himmler
announced to the SS and police leaders of the East that 10,000 Volhynian Germans would be concentrated in the Hegewald settlement. The project was inspired by Hitler, who had observed many "Aryan types" laboring in the fields
and villages around his Werwolf bunker. In Hitler's eyes, these peasants were
the descendants of Goths; he therefore reasoned, "Only German should be spo-
ken here."[2]

Like many German imperialists and ideologues at the time (if not earlier),
Hitler looked to Germany's eastern frontier as the "natural" space for expansion.[3] However, unlike his predecessors, Hitler wedded the forces of the traditional Drang nach Osten to a radical, racial worldview, forcefully arguing that the
push to the East was a biological imperative for Germans. In Hitler's Weltanschauung, race and nation were one in the same. Wherever Germans resided,
he argued, the Third Reich had claims to these individuals. In other words, the
borders of the German nation were not fixed by common political, social, or

cultural institutions, but instead by a vague combination of pseudoscientific and mythic notions of race.

Like their racial theories and practices, Nazi utopian notions of a Ukrainian or eastern paradise contained their own ambiguities and prejudices. For the Nazis, soil held two meanings. It was the source of economic—primarily agricultural—wealth for the empire as well as a metaphor for the cultivation of the German race. The proposed German-only rural paradise was also to be the site of modern industrial enterprises, labor camps, autobahn networks, and defense fortifications. There was, as historian Alan Steinweis has stressed, "an inherent contradiction in this marriage of racial utopianism and modern technology. Romantic notions of self-sufficient, racially superior pioneers moving east to settle the frontier were hard to reconcile with centralized planning and direction, technocracy, and big industry."[4] Another feature of Nazi colonialism was its gendered stereotyping and roles. As historian Elizabeth Harvey has elucidated in her study of Reich female agents of Germanization in Poland, Nazism "simultaneously exalted womanly concerns as national concerns, lauded women's caring energies, and harnessed them to a racist and chauvinistic pan-German vision of expansion and domination."[5] Such ideological contradictions and gendered visions were revealed when German central and peripheral leaders implemented experimental colonization programs in Zhytomyr.

In his Hegewald speech, Himmler presented a new spatial concept that differed from the larger ethnic German settlements being created in Nazi-occupied Poland. In Lublin, for example, Himmler's loyal henchman SS and police leader Odilo Globocnik carried out the most aggressive operations to transform his district into the European center of Volksdeutsche farms, Nazi death camps, and SS-run industrial enterprises.[6] By contrast, Himmler's own pet project at Hegewald was conceived of as, in his words, a settlement "pearl."[7] This "pearl" was actually a cluster of ethnic German-run farms and SS garrisons that would eventually expand like a "string of pearls" into a defensive line that would protect Germans from the "Asiatic hordes." Himmler's decision to create Hegewald was as pragmatic as it was ideological. The location had been a former Soviet air base with useful railway and communications connections. In early October 1941 Himmler surveyed the site, and about a month later plans were under way to turn this air base into his own elaborate SS-police compound, housing over 1,000 SS men and extensive security installations.[8] To Himmler, it made perfect sense to consolidate the region's Volhynian Germans around this area: here they would come under SS control and cultivate the richest black soil in Ukraine, as well as the German race.

The timing of Himmler's Hegewald speech was significant as well. It marked a turning point in the history of Nazi resettlement experiments, which had been gathering momentum during 1942. An increasing number of Nazi Party activists had descended on the Zhytomyr region to establish educational and relief programs, especially schools and birthing facilities. More numerous were the SS and police forces and Sonderkommando Russland officials. The 272 SS men who worked for the Sonderkommando Russland in Ukraine stemmed from at least five of Himmler's agencies (the Reich Commission for the Strengthening of Germandom, the Race and Settlement Office, the Economic Administration Main Office, the Volksdeutsche Liaison Office, and the SD).[9] Many came to Ukraine with two years of experience in Poland managing the movement of Jews, Poles, and ethnic Germans there. Altogether his staff represented a diverse grouping of "experts" in demography, cartography, population movement, agricultural economy, forced labor, industry, and policing. They headed to the Black Sea region of Odessa and Crimea to assist the so-called Black Sea Germans, but they kept headquarters in the offices of Higher SS and Police Leader Prützmann in Kiev and near Himmler in Zhytomyr.[10] By September 1942 Himmler had at his immediate disposal ideological campaigners and the manpower, expertise, and matériel needed to implement a resettlement program like Hegewald.

Another factor that influenced the timing of the formation of Hegewald was the increase in Soviet partisan attacks against ethnic German farmers in the region. These assaults alarmed Nazi leaders, including Hitler and Himmler, who often discussed strategies for dealing with the "partisan menace" during meetings in their headquarters. In order to protect ("hegen") the German race, they concentrated the Volksdeutsche in defense settlements near their headquarters. Himmler agreed with local leaders that the best time to carry out such a disruptive population transfer would be in the late autumn of 1942, after the harvest had been brought in.

Most importantly, Nazi leaders believed that the necessary "preparatory work" for resettling the region was basically complete. By August 1942, they had totally destroyed the Jewish communities in the designated resettlement space and "cleansed" it of other so-called undesirable elements, including a small population of Roma. Ukrainians were also deported by the thousands to forced labor camps outside the area and in the Reich. In Himmler's Hegewald speech, he referred obliquely to these criminal acts when he stated "how" the

"Jewish-Russian" city of Zhytomyr became German. He reassured his men that future generations and history would not remember these acts, but rather applaud their outcome. Thus the German momentum behind the formation of Volksdeutsche settlements like Hegewald climaxed in the latter half of 1942. Flushed with the prospect of victory in the East, Himmler boldly pursued his colonial dreams with a presumptuous eye to the future, envisioning his Aryan successors full of appreciation for the "sacrifices" of his generation.[11] Many of the local leaders outside the Nazi "inner circle," however, doubted the ultimate success of these Lebensraum schemes.

The formation of Hegewald was a controversial affair that exposed the real centers of power among the Nazi elite as well as the chimera of Nazi racial-colonial dreams. Many of the contradictions and tensions that lay beneath Hitler's vague theories about an Aryan "living space" in the East revealed themselves at the local level, the level of praxis. The local commissariat and economic leaders disagreed with their superiors, who ordered them to grant ethnic Germans leading positions as mayors, policemen, and collective farm leaders, because the Volksdeutsche constituted the most impoverished and least skilled sector of the population. To many Germans posted in the region, the ethnic Germans seemed to fit the pejorative European notion of an "Easterner" rather than the Nazi image of a cultured Aryan.[12] The regional commissars in the civilian zones of occupied Ukraine argued that full-scale colonization should occur after the war.

The constraints of war thwarted Nazi colonial experiments, but the course of these experiments was not steered entirely by the war. The story of Hegewald, one of the most celebrated colonies in its day but largely unknown to postwar scholars, casts light on some of the more significant aspects of Nazi and Holocaust history. It demonstrates how the German administration in the East functioned, particularly how the realization of Hitler's ideological vision of Lebensraum was hampered by pragmatic concerns, institutional rivalries, and mixed German perceptions of the "East." Why has so little been written to date on this topic, especially given Hegewald's wartime significance as a top-secret headquarters and center of resettlement planning in Ukraine?[13] Certainly the lack of available documentation has hindered scholarly research, an obstacle that has been recently overcome partially by the opening of former Soviet regional archives. But source material has not been the only inhibiting factor. The history of the Volksdeutsche has been further complicated by the fact that the ethnic Germans were both the blatant beneficiaries of Nazism as well as its victims. As the new local elites in the regional apparatus of the Nazi

Lebensraum, they also played an instrumental role in the Holocaust by identifying their Jewish neighbors, translating anti-Jewish decrees, and even assisting in the mass murder. During the Cold War, German scholars, politicians and Russian-German émigrés in America lobbied on behalf of the ethnic Germans who suffered under the Soviets, while they ignored the significant role the Volksdeutsche played as collaborators in the "Final Solution" and other Nazi occupation policies in the East.[14]

Only recently has the topic of Nazi resettlement schemes in the East attracted the attention of Holocaust scholars, thanks largely to Rolf-Dieter Müller's and Götz Aly's work on the planners, technocrats and regional SS-police leaders involved in Generalplan Ost.[15] Few would dispute that the essence of Nazi power was destructive, but the "logic" of this brutality is oversimplified by scholarship that describes "the Holocaust of the Jews, genocide of Soviet POWs, euthanasia, and criminal occupation policies in Poland and Russia altogether as elements and consequences of Generalplan Ost."[16] For the "social engineers" discussed by Aly, the dilemmas of space and material shortages served to push Nazi anti-Jewish policy toward genocide. While this may have been a motivating factor in Poland, in Nazi-occupied Ukraine (home to over 200,000 ethnic Germans) the links between the Holocaust and resettlement schemes were more tenuous. Regional leaders, like the commissars and SS-police district chiefs, approached these two occupation policies very differently and they rarely made causal connections between the two.[17] Why did local leaders, on the one hand, "succeed" in bringing about the Holocaust, but, on the other hand, fail at the task of rehabilitating their "racial brethren?"[18] What do Volksdeutsche colonization schemes in Ukraine tell us about the varying levels of ideological commitment that local Nazi leaders held toward the regime's racial goals?

Initial "Germanization" Effort

Over the years, as Himmler built up his police empire, he also acquired a sprawling bureaucracy of offices dedicated to the cause of ethnic Germans abroad. Shortly after the outbreak of the war in 1939, Hitler named Himmler, who was already in charge of the SS Race and Settlement Office (Rasse and Siedlungs-Hauptamt, RuSHA), the Reich commissioner for the strengthening of Germandom. With this appointment, Himmler took over the Ethnic German Liaison Office (Volksdeutsche Mittelstelle, VoMi), which was the leading agency coordinating Nazi Party, SD, and Foreign Office campaigns for ethnic

Germans residing across Eastern and Southeastern Europe. VoMi was one of four SS agencies dedicated to ethnic German and resettlement affairs in the occupied territories.[19] In 1940, this agency combed the newly conquered Polish territory for ethnic Germans and categorized them in a register known as the German People's List.[20]

During Operation Barbarossa, a VoMi field office was set up at Zhytomyr (led by Obersturmführer Erwin Müller) under the auspices of the secret Sonderkommando Russland operation. The aims of this special task force were, first, to determine who within the local population was racially valuable and, then, to survey and designate the best space for later SS colonization, and to combine this work with the establishment of regional SS-police offices. In its first few months of work, Himmler's ethnic German Liaison office registered over 40,000 ethnic Germans in the region, the largest number ascertained in German-occupied Ukraine until that time.[21] Although Horst Hoffmeyer's Sonderkommando R forces would later find a larger number of ethnic Germans residing in Dnipropetrovs'k and Romanian-controlled Transnistria, they maintained their headquarters near Himmler at Hegewald.[22]

Yet as influential as Himmler was, he did not achieve supreme control over the Volksdeutsche. Away from Hegewald, less prominent Nazi resettlement and Germanization initiatives were carried out by Nazi Party and commissariat officials. The Reich minister for the Occupied Eastern Territories, Alfred Rosenberg, set up a special Volksdeutsche commission under Karl Stumpp, the established scholar and demographer of ethnic Germans in Russia.[23] Stumpp arrived in Zhytomyr with the Rear Army's intelligence office at the end of August 1941; he screened the POWs for ethnic Germans who could serve as informers and translators. While Stumpp supplied the military with ethnic German collaborators, his main objective was to compile lengthy surveys about the composition and recent history of the ethnic German population. By the time he arrived in Zhytomyr, Stumpp had assembled a staff of nearly ninety ethnic Germans, whom he used to investigate the ethnic German villages around the city, concentrating on the districts of Novohrad-Volyns'kyi and Korosten'.[24]

While Stumpp and his men were busy surveying the ethnic German communities and filling out lengthy questionnaires, Nazi Party leaders attached to the National Socialist People's Welfare Agency (Nationalsozialistische Volkswohlfahrt, NSV) also arrived in Zhytomyr during September and began their "charity" work.[25] One of the NSV's immediate goals was to secure foodstuffs and material goods for the ethnic Germans. They found ample material in the SS storehouses of Jewish belongings, first from Zhytomyr's massacred Jews, then from Kiev's Jews. Later, in July 1942, they arranged for shipments of Jewish belongings to Zhytomyr from as far away as France. Nazi Party activists in the Zhytomyr region who worked on behalf of the ethnic Germans also relied on Gauleiter in Germany to conduct charity drives, and made appeals to private German business firms to donate material.[26] Their greatest source for outfitting the Volksdeutsche, however, was the Jews. In fact, the NSV began its campaign in Ukraine by distributing about thirty tons of linens, clothing, shoes, dishes, and other items that the German police confiscated from Zhytomyr's Jews after the massacre of 19 September 1941.[27]

The work conducted by Stumpp (a Rosenberg agent) and the NSV (under the aegis of the Nazi Party) differed significantly from that of VoMi (associated with Himmler's SS). Under the leadership of Hoffmeyer and Erwin Müller, the VoMi commandos pursued their "urgent task to consolidate and protect the ethnic Germans in order to prevent further decay of the race." They focused on the largest ethnic German villages and communities, not on the remote areas where individual ethnic Germans lived among Ukrainians. VoMi teams also sought to activate the ethnic Germans on the spot by registering them, classifying them into racial categories, distributing German identification papers, and establishing or reopening German schools. VoMi leaders picked out the "reliable" youths and inculcated them with Nazi propaganda, discipline, and obedience. Those who passed muster had a "bright" future in one of Himmler's organizations. Usually their first assignment was as an informant to the SD.[28] For those youngsters under ten years of age, immediate Nazi educational training began with language instruction because the Soviets had closed German schools in 1938. Local VoMi leaders forced the children to learn the Nazi greeting, the history of the Nazi Party, and "the life of the Führer," to sing German songs, and to listen to Hitler's speeches. Boys in particular were singled out for paramilitary exercises and the Hitler Youth. One of VoMi's goals was to make the school the center of the village and therefore of Nazi-style Germanization.[29]

In their effort to complete the initial registration and "reeducation" of the region's Volksdeutsche, the three main organizations—VoMi, the Stumpp commission, and the NSV—worked side by side, but not in unison. They vied for the support of the local commissars, who could provide them with much-needed resources, and they competed with one another for recognition from Nazi headquarters in Zhytomyr, Vinnytsia, and Berlin. Their biggest common obstacle in the first months of the occupation, however, was the ambiguity surrounding the German policy toward the ethnic Germans, and the general apathy among civil and military leaders who thought that the ethnic Germans were more of a burden than an asset.

Sowing the Seeds

In March 1942, after about three months of commissariat rule in Zhytomyr, the chief of the regional civil administration, General Commissar Klemm, wrote his first memorandum on ethnic German policy to his city and district commissars. "According to Koch's instructions," he wrote, "the ethnic Germans, who had no chance to resettle to Germany and suffered as victims of the Soviet regime, should be treated with respect and appreciation; they should be valued." He continued, "It is known that there are ethnic Germans who are not willing to work and are not assiduous; therefore, steps will be taken in order to provide them immediately with the needed schooling and education."[30] Intensive German language instruction was certainly a priority, but Nazi officials had other educational goals in mind.[31]

Regional campaigners in the commissariat administration, the NSV, and VoMi agreed that educational efforts were best directed at those children whose minds and manners could be most easily molded. They also reasoned pragmatically that if the children were cared for in Reich-style schools, then the parents would be free to labor in the fields. The first tasks Nazi leaders confronted in this plan for Germanization were to establish a kindergarten and to secure teachers from the Reich.[32] In fact, the "experimental" kindergarten programs for ethnic Germans in the Eastern Occupied Territories began in Zhytomyr. The schools were run largely by Reich German women whom the Nazi Party mobilized for service in the East. In contrast to their female counterparts in the German commissariat offices who worked as secretaries, the educators worked rather independently in the field.[33]

Following Hitler and Himmler's arrival in the region in July 1942, these female Reich welfare workers (ages eighteen to twenty-one) flowed into the area. They traveled to remote rural areas around Zhytomyr, establishing schools, birthing centers, and nursing stations.[34] By the end of September 1942, these efforts had led to the creation of forty-one permanent and seasonal Volksdeutsche kindergartens in the region, and had resulted in the training of eighty-six local Volksdeutsche girls to serve as schoolteachers.[35] In addition, midwives and nurses from the Reich set up infant care stations where they taught ethnic German women about the "racial hygienic" principles of nutrition and cleanliness in order to increase fertility and reproduction.[36]

The Nazi Party–led kindergarten and infant care programs reveal two significant aspects of this regional campaign of Germanization. First, German officials sought to assimilate the youth according to Nazi racial tenets, hence the large number of kindergartens and ethnic German orphanages in Zhytomyr. Once in these schools, Nazi educators taught the ethnic Germans that the Jews had set out to destroy the German people, and that the war was being fought against the Jews who surrounded and threatened to starve the Germans. To protect the German race, they advised young ethnic Germans to follow the Führer's example and neither smoke nor drink. They were warned to avoid mixing with non-Aryans because mixed marriages were a violation of racial purity. During medical examinations, Nazi doctors and nurses looked for the presence of certain hereditary diseases, and as a "protective racial measure" made plans to have these "diseased" youth sterilized.[37] And though the educational emphasis for both sexes was the loyalty to the Reich and obligation to work, Nazi courses revealed the more gendered roles that were to be filled. Boys learned paramilitary exercises, while girls took infant care and homemaking courses. Simply put, the boys were to become soldiers for the Reich, while the girls were to serve as "baby machines."

These Nazi missionaries sought to convert Zhytomyr's "racially acceptable" ethnic Germans into productive workers in a manner that was reminiscent of the Wilhelmine era's Protestant-run workhouses and "Erziehung zur Arbeit" campaigns. Yet the targeting of children and the ideological content of the Nazi campaign more closely resembled the fascist, totalitarian movements of its day. Volksdeutsche children came home from school with photos of Hitler, Swastika flags, and Nazi songs.[38] Raising the racial consciousness of the Volksdeutsche, these educators argued, could not be forced but could only come through the Party.[39] They propagated notions of German racial superiority that were virulently anti-Semitic, nationalistic, centered on loyalty to the Führer, and based on a work ethic of extreme proportions.[40]

On the other hand, those ethnic Germans who failed to accept or conform to the Nazi worldview, or who physically did not meet Nazi racial standards, received no sympathy from the Reich German campaigners. For example, a deputy commissar in the political department of the Zhytomyr city administration advised VoMi in February 1942 to strike an ethnic German female from the German People's List. She had applied for a marriage license at the commissar's office, but since she wished to marry a Ukrainian whom she had come to know after the Nazi occupation and "her attitude is not of the kind that one must demand of an ethnic German," then, this official wrote, "she will be denied that status and treated like an inferior Ukrainian."[41] In another case, Herbert Hafke, an ethnic German who joined the Schutzmannschaft in Koziatyn, was arrested for stealing produce from some local Ukrainians in October 1942. Hafke was supposed to be deported to Germany as a forced laborer, but he escaped from jail and was caught in April 1943. After an interrogation by the Koziatyn SS and police district chief, Lieutenant Heinrich Behrens, he was sentenced to death, because Behrens argued, Hafke "is a bandit of the worst kind and can in no way be accepted into the German Volksgemeinschaft." Furthermore, Behrens wrote, "he is married to a Ukrainian and in my view feels himself to be more Ukrainian than ethnic German."[42] Reich officials who felt in any way betrayed by the "non-German" conduct of Volksdeutsche thus clearly viewed them as both odious racial defectives and serious threats to the system.

Nonetheless, members of the ethnic German population were granted certain advantages that placed them in a privileged category, seeding resentment within the larger Ukrainian population. Volksdeutsche were supposed to receive at least double the rations of other locals and three times more than the Jews. If available, their rations might include the most sought after items of meat, salt, sugar, and butter.[43] Ethnic Germans were generally protected from the brutality of the Ukrainian Schutzmannschaften and the German Order Police. In the cities and larger towns, the Germans gave them the best living quarters, often former Jewish apartments. In April 1942 Koch's deputy Helmuth von Wedelstädt ordered that in public decrees the Volksdeutsche must be singled out and given special instructions, including exemptions from taxes and forced labor.[44] With few exceptions, the dreaded labor commissioners who raided the villages avoided the ethnic German communities. In the city of Zhytomyr, the VoMi founded two special ethnic German shops where Volksdeutsche could obtain scarce items.[45] Gebietskommissar Hans Schmidt opened a similar shop in Novohrad-Volyns'kyi.[46]

Most of these privileges contrasted with the tragic losses and sacrifices of others. Consistent with Himmler's orders on the distribution of Jewish property and then Commander Roques's order of 28 August 1941, in the Nazi Party's guidelines for work in the Zhytomyr Commissariat, activists were told that available Jewish property should go first to the ethnic Germans and then to Ukrainians.[47] The distribution of Jewish apartments, clothing, furniture, bedding, and other personal items mirrored the Nazis' racial hierarchies, with the Reich officials receiving the choicest items, followed by the Volksdeutsche, and then Ukrainian collaborators.

Himmler's "Garden"—Hegewald

Before Himmler introduced his Hegewald project in September 1942, the district German leaders in and around Zhytomyr had concentrated most of the Volksdeutsche into small communities. They agreed with Himmler that resettlement should occur in order to prevent racial mixing and to further Party-led educational and welfare work, but they were reluctant to undertake a large-scale program that might jeopardize the region's economy and promote social unrest. Despite their misgivings, Himmler—who had the upper hand in ethnic German policy-making and exerted his direct influence over the Zhytomyr region from Hegewald—pushed through the resettlement action around his headquarters. Once Hegewald reached its full population capacity, it was declared an ethnic German district to be governed not by Rosenberg's commissars but by Himmler's SS.[48]

The creation of resettled areas like Hegewald represented a calculated attempt by Himmler to increase his power over policies and local administration in the East. In addition to controlling an empire of SS economic enterprises, police forces, and labor camps, Himmler placed himself at the forefront of "Blood and Soil" social engineering in what was to be a new, thoroughly Germanized land. Yet the creation of a new eastern colony in Zhytomyr was not Himmler's sole concern. An upswing in partisan activity in the region also prompted Himmler to think of Hegewald in defensive terms as an "organic, racial" strongpoint of ethnic German blood. As single-mindedly as he had pursued the destruction of the Jews to this point, Himmler would now force the issue of German colonization in the East by aggressively promoting the Hegewald settlement despite the opposition of rivals like Alfred Rosenberg. Hegewald was in effect his colony, and as he pushed through its creation, he established another similar settlement near Lublin in Poland.

As was typical, Himmler's first step toward achieving his goal was securing the support of Hitler. On 25 July 1942, the day after Himmler arrived in Zhytomyr, he traveled to Vinnytsia to meet with his Führer. During this meeting at Hitler's Werwolf bunker, one of the topics they discussed was the plight and fate of the Volksdeutsche.[49] About two weeks later (probably on 9 August) Himmler returned to Hitler's headquarters for a conference of VoMi and SS officials.[50] During this meeting, Himmler touted the "successes" of VoMi in Transnistria while condemning Rosenberg's commissars as a bunch of overpaid bureaucrats who worked few hours and took long vacations. Himmler argued that VoMi had already proven itself in Transnistria, where VoMi commandos had rapidly resettled nearly 90,000 Volksdeutsche. Furthermore, Himmler warned, partisan attackers jeopardized the ethnic German families in the northern parts of the Zhytomyr region; the Volksdeutsche needed to be "protected." With the fleet of trucks and vehicles at his disposal at the Hegewald-SS compound, SS forces could quickly move the population into a secured area. After successfully convincing Hitler of the value of his plan, Himmler gained the necessary approval to form the Hegewald settlement.[51]

In the evening of 9 August and during the next day, Himmler convened leading SS officials at his headquarters to introduce his scheme. He assigned Ulrich Greifelt (head of the staff headquarters of the Reich Commission for the Strengthening of Germandom) and VoMi commandos to direct the first relocation of 10,000 ethnic Germans from the northern "partisan-infested" areas of the region (Bazar, Malyn, Ovruch, and Jemyl'chyne) into Hegewald. The thousands of Ukrainians to be deported from their homes in the Hegewald area were to be dumped in an area as yet to be determined. The ethnic German families would be resettled in about 100 villages along the main roadway from Zhytomyr to Berdychiv. The central point of the settlement would be Himmler's command post, because Hitler wanted Reich officials to move out of the cities into rural barracks and quarters as a further step toward transforming the region into ethnic German farming settlements and military strongpoints. SS officials planned to bring in an additional 30,000 ethnic Germans who would be placed along the major highways under construction in the area.[52]

One of the participants in the Hegewald planning meeting of 10 August 1942, the senior commander of the Order Police for Ukraine, Otto von Oelhafen, was put in charge of another aspect of the program: the formation of ethnic German police units. Oelhafen ordered that suitable ethnic German men be formed into closed units, known as *Selbstschutz* or Self-Defense/Protection units. Ethnic German police squads, one of the topics of Himmler's conference with Hitler, had already been formed in Romanian-controlled Transnistria where they had been actively involved in the "Final Solution." [53]

In the Zhytomyr region, however, the Selbstschutz played a less prominent role in the Holocaust. Instead, they served as regular Order Police forces over the ethnic German villages, thereby relieving Reich Germans of this duty and also preventing the possible "racial mixing" that might occur between ethnic German female villagers and the much larger native police force, the Ukrainian Schutzmannschaften.[54] Plans for increasing the Selbstschutz materialized later at Hegewald, where Oelhafen placed about 2,500 ethnic German men into police formations, established four Selbstschutz schools, and began training an additional 1,000 men.[55]

As Himmler worked out the technical details of the resettlement action, he also prepared himself for a probable run-in with his rival Rosenberg. First Himmler openly censured Rosenberg for his mishandling of the ethnic Germans in Ukraine, and, in the same breath, he asserted his own role as the master of resettlement schemes.[56] Then, on 9 September 1942, Himmler presumptuously ordered Rosenberg's subordinate, Reich Commissar Koch, "to Germanize with great haste the ethnic Germans living around Hegewald, Eichenhain, and Korosten'" (for example, around his, Hitler's, and Göring's headquarters). His authority over Koch in this matter, Himmler wrote, was based on his appointment by Hitler as the Reich commissioner for the strengthening of Germandom and as the commander of antipartisan warfare in the civilian occupied zones. With Hitler's backing and the powerful SS-police agencies at his disposal, Himmler went a step further by demanding more land from Koch for his SS colony at Hegewald. He specified that the farmland allotted to each ethnic German family be increased from earlier plans of between ten and twenty hectares to between thirty and forty hectares. When Rosenberg found out about Himmler's orders to Koch, he immediately challenged Himmler's authority, and a typical Nazi "paper war" ensued.[57] While this power struggle took its course in Berlin, the actual resettlement moved forward in Ukraine.[58] Koch's chief of food and agriculture, Hellmut Körner, had already been sent to Zhytomyr to meet with Himmler's newly appointed chief of the Special Staff for Resettlement, SS-Oberführer Theo Henschel.[59] Henschel had worked in the Race and Settlement Main Office since the early 1930s and had extensive experience managing property confiscations, deportations, and resettlement schemes in Poland.

In this meeting, Körner, Henschel, and agricultural experts from the local commissar's office determined more precisely who would be relocated and when. First they had to plan for the evacuation of an estimated 16,500 non-Germans (mostly Ukrainians) who lived in the area designated for the first stream of ethnic German settlers (1,450 families, a total of 6,000 ethnic Germans). According to Himmler's proposed increase of farmland, additional areas were to be evacuated along the Zhytomyr-Vinnytsia roadway. Land distribution to the ethnic German settlers depended on their demonstrated productivity. Most would start out with one to six hectares of land until they proved their diligence. Then the holdings would be expanded to no more than twenty-five hectares. Under the management of the Reich agricultural monopoly (Landbewirtschaftungsgesellschaft, LBGU), reserve farmland would be tilled by Ukrainian and White Russian laborers, but it would be controlled by German overseers. Once the Volksdeutsche were relocated, they lost all rights to their former homes and farms. The evacuated Ukrainians would not be moved to the abandoned ethnic German homes in the region, which was an earlier proposal, but brought to labor camps in southern Russia.[60]

On 12 September the chief of the Race and Settlement Main Office, Otto Hof-

Himmler inspecting cotton fields in Ukraine, fall of 1942
(U.S. Holocaust Memorial Museum, courtesy of James Blevins, #60407)

mann, celebrated "a German harvest" with the thirty-five SS farmers stationed near Zhytomyr. He called the men "Pioneers of Germandom in the East" — revolutionaries charged with creating something new. As such, they were to always behave decently, Hofmann stated, and when confronted with important decisions should always ask themselves, "What would the Führer or Reichsführer do in their position." [61]

A month later, on 10 October, the resettlement action began. German police units of Higher SS and Police Leader Hans-Adolf Prützmann, members of the local gendarmerie, and VoMi officials rounded up 10,623 non-Germans from the area and, along with some livestock, placed them on 770 freight cars bound for Dnipropetrovs'k. At the same time columns, or as the Nazis called them, "treks," of ethnic Germans totaling 6,362 persons (1,579 men, 2,371 women, and 2,412 children) moved into Hegewald from various points in Zhytomyr's northern districts. Both the ethnic Germans and Ukrainians were forcibly moved under police guard.[62] NSV leaders provided relief for the ethnic Germans at various stopovers along the way. For the "trek" of 2,500 ethnic Germans from Ovruch, five villages were reserved as overnight and rest areas during the journey to Hegewald; the inhabitants of these villages were simply

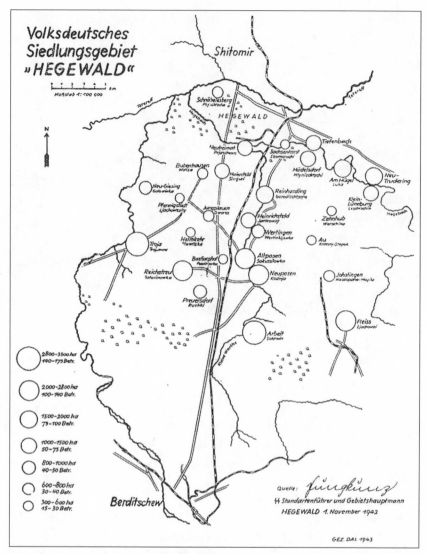

Ethnic German Settlement Area, named "Hegewald" (preservation forest). The circles on the map represent the Volksdeutsche communities, the size of the communities in hectares, and the number of local industries (such as dairies, tanneries, smoke houses, distilleries, slaughterhouses, textile mills). The map was issued by SS-Colonel Jungkunz who was the District Captain of Hegewald, 1 November 1942. Source: Bundesarchiv Koblenz, R/69/215, courtesy of U.S. Holocaust Memorial Museum, RG 14.040M.

pulled from their homes and placed in temporary camps; many were shipped to the Reich as forced laborers. The NSV provided ten nurses from its staff to assist the ethnic German mothers with their infants.[63]

Once the ethnic Germans arrived at Hegewald, SS farming specialists allotted the land and advised the ethnic Germans about farming techniques. The ethnic German farms were subjected to high SS quotas and random confiscations of milk and other produce.[64] The land that was not agriculturally rich was slotted for SS factories, where Ukrainian forced laborers worked under guard. On 20 October Himmler inspected the new ethnic German villages in Hegewald. When he returned to his field headquarters, he ordered the immediate shipment of about 10,000 shoes and textiles to the Volksdeutsche in Hegewald. This was in addition to another shipment, originating from the storehouses at Lublin and Auschwitz, that was scheduled to arrive in time for Christmas.[65] The first step of the Hegewald resettlement action was virtually completed by early November 1942, leaving just one group of 170 families residing in Radomyshl' to be moved into the enclave.

Before it became public knowledge that Hegewald existed, General Commissar Leyser sent a memo to his deputies on 16 November explaining that the area south of Zhytomyr toward Berdychiv was now an independent district for ethnic Germans, to be administered by ethnic German mayors and led by a Reich German SS "district captain," not a commissar.[66] Leyser added that because the area was populated by Volksdeutsche, it would be unnecessary in the future to send memoranda to the Hegewald SS–district captain about Ukrainians or Russians.[67] About a month later, on 12 December 1942, Hegewald was officially declared a distinct administrative unit exempt from the jurisdiction of Rosenberg's ministry; it was 200 square miles in size with a population of 9,000 Volksdeutsche. The last ethnic Germans to be resettled in Hegewald came from Kiev during March 1943,[68] bringing the total population to 10,178 persons. They lived in twenty-eight villages organized around seven SS-agricultural economic bases with names such as Troja, Maienfeld, Neu Posen, and Am Hügel, sixty-three communal industries, and an SS supply house.[69] SS and Party officials initiated training and educational programs for the Volksdeutsche so that the largely unskilled ethnic Germans learned how to be carpenters, auto mechanics, telegraph operators, tailors, and the like.[70] Senior-level Party members made speaking tours of the settlement, which was expanded to nearly 500 square kilometers in early 1943.[71]

The Failure of Nazi Lebensraum Plans

The publicity and fanfare surrounding the establishment of the Hegewald settlement trumpeted its success. Yet the internal government correspondence and reports from across the various agencies involved in the "rescue" of the Volksdeutsche are filled with complaints and criticisms. One Nazi Party activist, Maria Cormann, calculated that the Volksdeutsche rations were as inadequate as those allotted to prison inmates. Months after her alarming report, the Volksdeutsche survived on a paltry diet that was certainly better than a prisoner's but not as hearty as the Reich Germans'.[72] In stark contrast to the German implementation of the "Final Solution" and other criminal policies of Nazi rule in Zhytomyr, the German crusade to "rescue" and "Germanize" the region's Volksdeutsche population was a campaign that created more conflict than consensus within the German administration. The kinds of institutional and ideological clashes surrounding these programs revealed just how "inefficient" the Nazi system could be. In the area of educational efforts the SS, the commissars, and Party leaders generally cooperated, but there was much friction between the commissars and local SS leaders about the social and economic repercussions of the vast resettlement actions that Himmler introduced. At the district level, those commissars entrusted with ethnic German populations were left to carry out their own experimental programs, influenced in varying degrees by the agencies of Himmler, the Nazi Party, and Rosenberg.

German administrators rarely questioned the policy of exploiting and eradicating those deemed inferior, while they remained uncertain of their role in forming ethnic German colonies and in integrating the Volksdeutsche, whom they viewed sympathetically but often begrudgingly as a pathetic group. In the Zhytomyr region, ethnic German policy and programs were centered in the cities of Zhytomyr, Berdychiv, and Vinnytsia and in a few northern districts along the Belorussian border. They did not consume the attention of the Nazi administration in the way that the genocidal campaign against the Jews, the forced labor drives, and, eventually, the antipartisan warfare did.

One of the more revealing aspects of the failure of ethnic German programs in Zhytomyr was the underlying skepticism among local leaders toward Hitler's vision of a Lebensraum in the East and Himmler's colonization schemes. This skepticism derived from the contradictory Nazi images of the East. Nazi leaders portrayed this space as both a hotbed of "Judeo-Bolshevism" and a future Aryan paradise. In carrying out their war of extermination in the East, Nazi leaders effectively marshaled a deep-seated German contempt for the "inferior" peoples of the East. But building a German consensus around a utopian vision of the East as a "flourishing park landscape" and a "garden of Germanic blood" proved to be a much more difficult undertaking in the context of war, especially a protracted campaign that was by no means restricted to the front. The concept of an "Aryan" Volksgemeinschaft and other Nazi appeals centered on the Führer did not effectively integrate Reich and ethnic Germans to the extent that Party propagandists and Nazi demographers expected. The destructive aspects of the Führer's Lebensraum policies proved easier to promote and carry out than the constructive ones. A combination of German prejudices toward the East and "eastern peoples," wartime conditions, and the destructive nature of Nazism sabotaged the Volksdeutsche programs in Zhytomyr. In the end, Himmler found fertile ground in the East not for German colonization, but rather for the Holocaust.

Chapter 8

The Unraveling of Nazi Rule, 1943–1944

> Seven of us gathered in my flat in Liubar: the head of the col-
> lective farm, an agronomist, a bookkeeper, a driver, a school-
> master, a mechanic, and me. We started to organize bombing
> raids of the Zhytomyr-Fastiv railway lines. Women, including
> my wife, were our couriers and helped us identify sources of
> arms and locations of other resistance movements. We had to
> kill two traitors in our village so that we could work freely.
> After that, people were afraid to report underground members
> to the Germans.
>
> —Petr Ignat'evich Iunitskii (b. 1912), Zhytomyr, 1996

For the Ukrainians, Russians, Poles, and Jews in Zhytomyr who managed to survive the German invasion, the Holocaust, the forced labor deportations, and SS-police resettlement actions, it seemed that things could not possibly get worse. The February 1943 German surrender at Stalingrad instilled them with renewed hope. But the year that followed turned out to be the worst of the occupation for all, even the ethnic Germans, who realized that their privileged status placed them in greater danger. Vengeful Ukrainians, Poles, and Soviet partisans attacked them even as they retreated westward upon the collapse of the commissariat administration in November 1943.

Like the rest of Eastern Europe, the Zhytomyr region became a battlefield of brutal partisan warfare that was not solely a Nazi-Soviet struggle. Regional civil wars erupted among various ethnic and political groups (Stalinist, communist, nationalist, Zionist), which on the one hand sought to defeat Nazism and on the other tried to establish power in the areas once occupied by the Germans. These regional clashes derived from competing ideological aims as well as manifested the social backlashes resulting from the Nazi occupation system. By using local leaders and auxiliaries to carry out their criminal policies and by imposing a new hierarchy based on race, the Germans deepened and even created new social divisions within the occupied population.[1] Many local leaders abused their limited power, and their affiliation with Nazi policies aroused additional enmity. Additionally, the commissars themselves ruled in a dilettantish, often brutally impulsive manner that garnered little respect from "their subjects." In the spring of 1943, General Commissar Ernst Leyser's office reported to Rosenberg that the extreme differences across the region in the way that the commissars dealt with matters such as religious policy were now causing civil unrest.[2] The Germans were unable to retain indigenous staff in their offices. In 1943 one-third of the Zviahel district commissariat office staff consisted of ethnic Germans who were new hires. Many Ukrainians stopped working for the Germans.[3] Thus, in contrast to postwar stereotypes of Ukrainians — either as mass collaborators or as pro-Soviet partisans — the history of resistance efforts in Zhytomyr reveals that Ukrainian society was far from unified.

The German reaction to local resistance movements and partisan attacks was characteristically extreme. At Hegewald, Himmler and his SS-police minions took mainly two approaches. They first tried to safeguard the Volksdeutsche by consolidating them into a protected enclave near the secured headquarters. They then planned more sweeping antipartisan raids in designated areas that were to become "dead zones." By depopulating the areas where partisans found a haven and local supporters, Nazi leaders reasoned, the partisan menace would go away. One of the projected "dead zones" in the Zhytomyr Bezirk was in Polissia, the swampy area bordering Belorussia where from the start of the Wehrmacht invasion different Ukrainian nationalist factions, Soviet POWs, and Jews had found refuge and later based their resistance movements against the Germans.

This chapter traces the rise of organized resistance movements in the region and the Germans' radical attempts to maintain their hold over Zhytomyr, first through draconian antipartisan policies and then paradoxically through anti-Soviet propaganda and incentive appeals that were supposed to galvanize everyone under the Nazi victory banner. However, as the Nazi system unraveled in 1943 so did the tattered social fabric of Zhytomyr. Caught in the crossfire of the Nazi-Soviet struggle, groups and individuals were forced to choose different survival strategies as well as pick sides.

The Emergence of Partisan Movements

Although there were cases of indigenous manipulation of and sabotage against the German system throughout the occupation period, acts of resistance that were connected to the partisan movements in Zhytomyr became more widespread in late 1942 and throughout 1943. There are several reasons for the increase in resistance acts and partisan warfare. Foremost among them were the forced labor deportations and the protracted war, which fueled anti-German sentiment and strained the commissars' ability to govern the vast territory.

In the Zhytomyr region the partisan movement was mainly divided among the Ukrainian nationalist factions, roving bands of resistance fighters, and Stalin's larger partisan brigades deployed from Moscow (for example, the Lenin Mounted Brigade).[4] Actually the largest of these movements, the Soviet one, contained few communists and even fewer Party members. Other than the shared belief that the Nazis had to be crushed and pushed out of Eastern Europe, the Soviet movement was not ideologically unified; it was multiethnic and not strongly communist. According to historian Amir Weiner's study of the war in Vinnytsia, in August 1943 there were 25,850 partisans operating in the city and its surrounding districts, of whom only 4,913 (or 19.1 percent) were Communist Party members or candidates for membership. Though the region was between 80 and 90 percent Ukrainian, the Stalin Brigades were only half Ukrainian, whereas the nationalist forces led by Andrii Mel'nyk and Stepan Bandera were, as one might guess, mainly Ukrainian (at least 70 percent).[5]

Independent resistance cells began forming in the initial months of the occupation and were composed of communists, Ukrainian nationalists, and some Jews, who were joined in much larger numbers by Red Army deserters and POWs.[6] At first, these "resisters" were fugitives from the Nazi terror. They were disorganized and lacked arms to launch any effective campaign. Similarly the Ukrainian nationalists possessed few guns and explosives, and the movement itself was divided and therefore vulnerable. To their advantage, however, the Ukrainian nationalists had spent the interwar period in Poland developing terrorist methods and collaborating with German intelligence offices. They arrived in Ukraine with an inside view of the German system as well as an organizational framework. But even so, they had little leverage: the Germans turned on the Ukrainian nationalist movement and crushed its local networks in the fall of 1941 and early 1942.

First, Mel'nyk's top leaders were assassinated on the streets of Zhytomyr, most likely by Bandera's agents, who were assisted by the Germans.[7] A month later, the Germans suppressed Bandera's movement.[8] At the end of November 1941, Einsatzgruppe C members issued a death warrant against Banderites, declaring them "enemies of the Reich" who were to be "arrested and after a complete hearing exterminated in the greatest secrecy as pillagers."[9] The German crackdown intensified in the spring of 1942 when the commissariat's SS-police administration was in place. German secret police found and killed Zhytomyr's OUN-B leader Roman Marchak at the end of March. Sipo-SD interrogators extracted from a prisoner the location of Bandera's headquarters in Zhytomyr. On 8 February 1942 the German police raided the basement of a bombed-out building in Zhytomyr, where they uncovered a false identification printing operation and dozens of secret files about the nationalists' underground activities there as well as in Kiev, Kharkiv, and Poltava. German investigators were incensed by the discovery of receipts that showed that the nationalists had been selling forged papers to the Jews. This was not an altruistic rescue operation to save Jews. In fact, Bandera's agents had been financing their local activities by extorting money from the Jews, and, in at least one case, they blamed the Jews when the Germans uncovered caches of arms belonging to Bandera's underground militia groups.[10]

The nationalists' administrative files containing their treasured lists of supporters had fallen into Nazi hands and facilitated the destruction of the movement. Supplied with names and information on where to find the people in question, the German secret police under Zhytomyr's commander, Franz Razesberger, began to arrest and interrogate hundreds of Ukrainians deemed to be partisan threats.[11] At the beginning of April 1942, Razesberger reported to his superior in Kiev, the Security Police chief for Ukraine, Max Thomas, that in Zhytomyr they had identified 356 nationalist suspects and had arrested 200 members.[12]

By the summer of 1942, Ukrainian nationalists who escaped the clutches of the German secret police were in hiding and waiting for instructions from one of three nationalist factions led by Bandera, Mel'nyk, and Taras Borovets.[13] Like other nascent resistance movements in the region, they sought out followers, more arms, and reliable information channels. Attacks against German headquarters in the region's cities, as well as assassination attempts against German officials and bombings of German offices, occurred sporadically.[14]

The Germans were well aware of the emerging partisan pockets in the region.[15] When the commissars began arriving in November 1941, Roques, the commander of the Army Group South Rear Area Administration, warned them that partisan cells were forming in the villages, and that they consisted of Red Army deserters and Soviet intelligence operatives who were purposely left behind to conduct warfare in the civilian occupied zones. According to German suspicions, these agents had designated informers in the villages, including women and girls who worked as laundry women and maids. The women, he warned, had the task of befriending German officers and soldiers.[16] In this atmosphere of paranoia, the Germans responded to the few initial attacks by embarking on a strict antipartisan policy that was directed against the entire population (although often their reprisal measures served as a cover for carrying out the mass murder of Jews). In December 1941 General Commissar Klemm ordered that for every German who was shot at and not injured or killed, ten civilians were to be executed, and for every German injured or killed by partisans, 100 local civilians would be executed.[17]

During the summer of 1942, instances of sabotage and resistance in the northern terrain of the commissariat (today in Belarus) steadily increased.[18] The German gendarmerie district leader and two gendarmes stationed in El'sk were murdered by partisans. Consequently, the commander of the Order Police for the region, Hans Leberecht von Bredow, instituted new prophylactic measures. First he advised his German gendarmes to avoid using bicycles in fields and forests and to stay on the main roads. Then each month the district police stations in the region began submitting special partisan-attack summary reports that included the times and locations of the attacks; these reports helped them track the size and location of the movement.[19] When the Germans arrested partisans, they took different courses of action. If the so-called partisan was Jewish, he or she was killed on the spot. If the partisan was part of the nationalist or Soviet underground, then he or she was interrogated first and then usually killed.[20] Meanwhile, German SS-police and military reinforcements streamed into the area to fight the partisans. On 18 July 1942 (as part of Operation Bamberg), units in Mazyr, Korosten', and in other parts of El'sk destroyed five villages and murdered all of the roughly 1,000 inhabitants, except for the Volksdeutsche and Schutzmänner living in these locales.[21]

Actually the Germans never had complete control over the northern stretches of the region along the Pripiat' River. Under the leadership of C. F. Malinkov and the command of S. Kovpak (a Ukrainian-born Communist, who claimed to be a descendent of the Zaporozhian Cossacks), Soviet guerrillas who had been parachuted into the region established stationary camps along the border with Belorussia. In the last week of July 1942, Security chief Razesberger reported to his superior in Kiev, Sipo-SD general Thomas, that Russian parachuters were landing in the areas of Mazyr, Bragin, and Ovruch.[22] They attacked river traffic and destroyed military buildings, including a hospital. In response, the SD outpost at Ovruch sent out their Einsatzkommandos and discovered, after apprehending one parachuter, that communications had been established in Ovruch with Moscow's central command center. From an intercepted radio transmission, the SD also learned that a plane with additional men and supplies would be landing in the area. The Germans captured the plane.[23] For the Nazis, the situation did not seem to be improving, despite the increased German presence of Sipo-SD and regular police forces.

During Hitler's and Himmler's stay in the region, they often discussed how to deal with the partisan menace. At the end of July 1942, attention shifted from the "Jewish problem" (which in Zhytomyr was nearly "resolved") to an emerging, real threat—the partisans. On 25 July Himmler, while stationed at Hegewald, addressed the situation during a dinner with senior SS and police leaders. He remarked self-confidently, "As for the partisan danger I will take care of that too. I do not know yet what I will do, but something will strike me. I have been thinking about blinding the captured partisans."[24] To further criminalize the partisans (who had begun to make widespread propaganda appeals to Zhytomyr's population), Himmler later ordered that the term "partisan" be replaced with "bandit."[25]

A few weeks after this meeting, Hitler appointed Himmler the commander of antipartisan warfare in the civilian zones (and rear army areas). On 18 August 1942 Hitler, who followed the partisan warfare closely through Himmler, issued a special directive (#46). In it, he asserted that "the destruction of banditry demands active fighting and the most severe measures against everyone who supports the bandits or participates in the formation of the bandit movement." At the same time, Hitler wrote, the Germans could not avoid relying on the local population to fight the bandits and therefore German administrators were to rule in a strict but just manner. Those who resisted German rule were to be so horribly punished that others would be dissuaded from resisting.[26] Thus Himmler and German regional leaders were given the go-ahead to use the "harshest" combat measures.

In the months that followed this directive, German antipartisan policies resulted in the destruction of 108 villages and the mass murder of more than 2,300 people in the region.[27] In December 1942 Higher SS and Police Leader for Ukraine Prützmann wrote a report about the new Nazi approach to the partisan problem. Owing to the increase in attacks, the SS-police in cooperation with the Reich Commissariat officials would force out all inhabitants in partisan areas and then bring in German militarized forces. Chiefly targeted were the swampy areas deemed economically "hardly useful" anyway. According to Himmler's instructions for this campaign, all civilians living in or near partisan "nests" who were not shot outright were to be deported en masse to concentration camps or to the Reich for forced labor. However, many were not deported as ordered and were immediately killed because the local commissars lacked the transport to send the civilians out of the region; and the commissars feared that any survivors would join the partisans to take revenge on the Germans.[28]

According to a Soviet account, in early 1943 the Germans burned to the ground more than 100 communities and killed or left homeless thousands of civilians from these "dead zones."[29] In March and April 1943, Leyser's commissars specified in their reports 617 clashes with partisans, which left over 600 peasants homeless; plus several hundred more were dragged away by the partisans.[30] Just as the Germans prepared their early 1943 offensives, Malinkov and Kovpak's forces moved deeper into the heart of the region, conducting periodic raids southward from the Olevs'k district. They captured (temporarily) the German district commissar capital of Lel'chytsi and assassinated the German SS and police district leader of Bragin.[31] In the spring of 1943, Kovpak commanded a total of 3,000 Soviet partisans operating in two groups along Zhytomyr's northern border. Attacks on Germans, their facilities, and military transports had increased significantly; in one week, German commanders counted twenty-nine clashes and thirteen attacks on major transport lines.[32] German SS and police commanders complained that because of inadequate forces and matériel, and harsh weather conditions, they could not crush Kovpak's units.[33] Meanwhile, Stalin sent in additional Soviet forces southeast of Vinnytsia with orders to drive northward to meet Kovpak's units.[34]

The Moscow command had learned months earlier from one of their agents, a Schutzmann named Mel'nichenko who had access to the SD office in Zhytomyr, that Himmler's headquarters and vast SS and military installations were located in the city's vicinity at Hegewald. Already in the summer of 1942, underground movements in Kiev and Vinnytsia radioed to Moscow that Hitler had built a bunker near Vinnytsia as well as a "Prominente" POW camp, where Andrei Vlasov and other Soviet commanders were being held. Soviet partisans (renamed by Stalin as Red Army rear units) converged on this important Nazi stronghold. Soviet intelligence operatives in the area attempted to assassinate Hitler while he was based at the compound.[35]

But the Soviet partisans were not alone in their effort to destroy the Nazis "behind the lines." While the Soviet partisans came to dominate the Zhytomyr region and also managed to infiltrate areas near the Hitler-Himmler headquarters, the anti-Soviet nationalist partisans operated in the more vulnerable plains and forested patches found in the central districts and western borders of Zhytomyr.[36] The Mel'nykites in Vinnytsia and Banderites along the commissariat's western border with Luts'k formed smaller mobile units (although some reached battalion size) and waged a small-scale local campaign of sabotage and propaganda. They pursued their own campaigns to "purify" Ukraine of its Russian, Jewish, and Polish elements.[37]

In the Zhytomyr region, another nationalist partisan group sprang up; it was commanded by the son of Zhytomyr's chief Ukrainian administrator, the young Iatseniuk, who was a former Mel'nyk supporter and had fled the Germans in the wake of the Bazar demonstration of November 1941. Indeed, Iatseniuk led the only independent nationalist partisan group to have emerged within the borders of pre-1939 Soviet Ukraine. Iatseniuk and his supporters in Zhytomyr waged an effective propaganda campaign against the Germans that spoke directly to the local conditions and population.[38] In May 1943 the leaders of the disparate Ukrainian nationalist partisan groups connected to Borovets, Iatseniuk, and Bandera considered combining their groups under one single command structure. But these negotiations broke down. They were resumed only a few months later, when the Red forces under Kovpak penetrated western Ukraine and, along with Bandera's forces, threatened the smaller nationalist factions. Borovets, Mel'nyk, and Iatseniuk had little choice but to join their nationalist movements under the most militant and popular of the nationalist leaders, Bandera.[39]

The merger of nationalist partisans under Bandera meant that a unified approach ultimately triumphed.[40] However, this merger also represented a defeat for the moderate nationalist forces. As a native of the Zhytomyr region, Iatseniuk carried out his underground campaign with a concern for the security and livelihood of the peasantry and townsfolk; Borovets also waged his attacks with the cooperation of the peasantry. The Banderites, however, like the Red Army forces, often conducted their partisan campaign in ways that sacrificed the local population to the punitive measures of the Germans.

Relations between Zhytomyr's Population and the Partisans

Before they could gain control over a community, both the Soviet and nationalist partisans found that they had to contend first with the German-appointed village elders. One of their initial tasks was to determine whether the elder could be a trusted sympathizer. Before 1943 resistance fighters often moved to another location if the elder was deemed unreliable, but during 1943 they simply did away with the unsupportive elder (and often killed or abused his wife and children).[41] Such murderous actions complied with official Soviet partisan warfare policy.[42] A former chief of the local Soviet partisan movement around the city of Zhytomyr, Leontii Antonovich Kozaritskii, recalled:

We had many of our own leaders among the starosty, and they were not all Ukrainians. In one case the ethnic German elder proved to be helpful and for that the Germans killed him. His replacement, a Ukrainian, refused to assist us and reported our whereabouts to the Germans, who then planned a major air strike over the forest where we were encamped. So the partisan commander put out a death warrant against the starosta who had moved into a protected German headquarters. The partisans dressed as Ukrainian policemen, entered the headquarters, seized the starosta, and shot him in the forest.[43]

Consistent with Kozaritskii's account and several others found in the German documentation, Soviet partisans attacked uncooperative elders and Ukrainian or ethnic German policemen (and their families), whose mutilated bodies were often later discovered in subsequent patrols of the forests.[44]

By June 1943 resistance forces controlled about 60 percent of the region's cultivated land. They killed 2,568 German officials and administrators and their Ukrainian and ethnic German allies.[45] The commissars panicked, barricading themselves into their offices and homes. They turned to the SS-police for protection and underwent their own police-led defensive training course against partisan attacks. Some went on the defensive; others, the offensive. As Koch observed, commissars engaged in partisan warfare beyond their districts, out of "Abenteuerlust" (lust for adventure). In a joint SS-commissar reprisal action on 22 March, the village of Kazymirivka (district Mazyr) was destroyed, and 500 inhabitants were murdered; 450 of them were women and children.[46] The district commissar in Retchiza, Dr. Paul Blümel, assisted the SS-police forces (including an SS cavalry division) in carrying out Operation "Weichsel." Prior to the operation, Blümel determined who within the population of the designated "dead zone" would be killed and who would be spared. They killed 4,018 persons, deported at least 18,860 as forced laborers, and razed 61 villages.[47]

Leyser, whom Himmler later censured as someone who "understood nothing of the partisan warfare," was so frustrated by his inability to govern and exploit his region's riches that he sent a scathing report to Berlin in June 1943. In it he wrote about the social and political backlashes of German antipartisan warfare. Excessive SS and police raids on villages created homelessness and lack of productivity, a welfare and economic burden on the commissariat that also ended up alienating the entire Ukrainian population. He explained that the loss of Germans in the guerrilla warfare resulted from a broken, corrupt Nazi system. A few months prior to Leyser's report, Koch admonished the commissars for taking up arms against the partisans, ordering them to stay at their desks and write up reports about the attacks. Accordingly, Leyser submitted his June report to Berlin (through Koch's office in Rivne). His critique shocked some Nazi leaders, including Himmler, because besides detailing the failings of the Nazi system, Leyser complained about the self-seeking power struggles between Wehrmacht and SS-police officials who competed over antipartisan operations. Leyser too sought unsuccessfully to control antipartisan policies in his region, but he saw the "problem" as essentially a political one, not strictly a military, strategic one. In many ways Leyser articulated the general skepticism and disillusionment that began to permeate the empire's eastern outpost in the summer of 1943.[48]

As the tension mounted in the German commissariat offices over the partisan warfare that disrupted everyday life, rifts developed among the German personnel. Shortages of resources and manpower became especially acute, and cooperation began to break down. The district commissars across Zhytomyr reported to Leyser that, given the fact that many of their colleagues had already been drafted, it seemed unfair that so many private German business entrepreneurs were still around in great numbers doing useless work. The commissars branded them draft dodgers. Leyser responded by asking the local commissars to investigate the activities of the private German businessmen and report anybody who could be placed in more war-related work.[49]

The commissars who had initially arrived in the region with an arrogant attitude of superiority found that much of their power over the countryside hinged on the loyalty of the very "colonial subjects" whom they terrorized. This instability was recognized at all levels of the German hierarchy. In the summer of 1942, Hitler and General Wilhelm Keitel announced a program that would reward any "eastern peoples" for acts of bravery in support of the Germans, particularly in the "fight against enemies of the Reich."[50] Shortly after this program was introduced, the Reich Commissariat's Abteilung für Ernährung und Landwirtschaft (Department of Nutrition and Agricultural Economy) sent to Zhytomyr 2,000 liters of vodka, 5,000 kilograms of tobacco, and 100 tons of sugar, to be distributed as bribes to indigenous supporters of the Reich. The local German police also offered certificates for up to two hectares of land (including former Jewish property) to those civilians who assisted in denouncing or fighting partisans.[51] Ukrainian police were given fifty German Reichsmarks for every "bandit" whom they captured or killed.[52] When the Germans bribed Ukrainian auxiliaries, the Schutzmänner snatched up the German goods (butter, meat, and bread) and demanded more. When Ukrainian auxiliary policemen abandoned the Germans and joined the partisan movements, they brought the goods with them to the forests.[53] Many farmers did not need the German bribes anyway because they secretly slaughtered their livestock; in 1943 German commissars in the Zhytomyr region reported that 90,000 pigs and 55,000 cattle were missing, and people stopped bringing their produce to the marketplace. In short the Germans were unable to manage the local economy and extract material resources from Ukraine to the extent that they had predicted in 1941.[54]

In early 1943 local German commissars and gendarme leaders were asked to nominate indigenous auxiliaries and administrators for commendation, because thus far the Germans had not identified a significant number of outstanding acts of bravery committed by civilians in support of the Germans.[55] In Monastryshche the Germans were pleasantly surprised by a village elder who fought aggressively against the Soviets and, with a bit of local support, was able to capture and kill some partisans. The Germans left behind few reports about the distribution of rewards to civilians, or the recognition of civilians who assisted the Germans. While Ukrainians seeking to conceal their collaborative role from Soviet authorities may have destroyed these records, this gap in the documentation may also indicate that there were few locals whom the Germans deemed worthy of recognition, and, therefore, few who remained loyal to the Germans throughout the occupation.

Dissension within Ukrainian communities was rife. German policy pitted Ukrainians against one another, and members of the Ukrainian police (the most detested of all) abused their power to no end. In Koziatyn, for example, the Ukrainian mayor observed that a Ukrainian Schutzmann who was not at his designated post was stealing from the locals and amusing himself by shooting wildly at stray animals. The mayor approached the policeman and threatened to report him to the Germans for his wild conduct. The policeman clubbed the mayor to death. In the town of Nepedivka, a gang of drunken Ukrainian policemen started to beat up the village elder. This incensed several of the locals, who decided to take action. Fifteen Ukrainians ran to the nearest German authority, the agricultural leader, and with his help, they rescued the elder and apprehended the drunken Ukrainian police.[56]

Women and the Partisan Movement
Maria Atamanskaia and Maria Kondratenko

In the end, the partisan warfare struck hardest at the local population of mainly women, the youth, and the elderly. They became the pawns in the Nazi-Soviet and local nationalist movements' struggles over Ukraine. Women and children who were drawn into Zhytomyr's resistance movements (forcibly or willingly) provided food and shelter for underground agents, as well as information about the region, the Germans, or other rival partisan factions. In the eyes of the Germans, the local's role, whether central or peripheral to any movement, was cause for severe punishment if not death. Often people were tragically in the wrong place, at the wrong time. For example, in March 1943 the sixteen-year-old collective farmer Maria Atamanskaia was going about her work when Soviet partisans approached her and asked for directions to the house of the village elder. The partisans also demanded food from the collective farm, at which point, Maria recalled, many female peasants wept for there was not enough food to feed the partisans, the Germans, and, most important, their own families. This brief exchange with the partisans came to the attention of the Germans. Atamanskaia was seized by Ukrainian police and brought to German police headquarters in Zhytomyr. There Ukrainian and German police interrogated her and tried to force her to sign a confession of partisan membership or support. But Atamanskaia refused, so they beat her until she was unconscious. When she awoke in her cell, a day had passed. Ukrainian police told her that she would be released, but Atamanskaia was kept in the cell for another week while arrangements were made for her deportation to the Reich. She was placed in a sealed freight car and sent to Germany as a forced laborer.[57]

Family members—usually wives, daughters, and mothers of suspected partisans—were always the first targets of German police investigations into the movement.[58] The gendarme captaincy in Mazyr had ordered in the late summer of 1942 that if the family members of partisans were connected with the movement, then they, too, should be killed.[59] In August 1942 the Ukrainian district leader of Bazar issued an order similar to one that was signed by the Gestapo of Zhytomyr: if a member of a community helped a partisan in any way, then all of the members of the community were to be killed; if a villager did not report the presence of partisans in or near the village, then the entire village would be razed.[60]

In an atmosphere of insecurity and paranoia, Nazi regional leaders suspected everyone of partisan activity, killed "resisters" en masse, and aimed punitive measures against family members of suspects, thereby destroying the Germans' remaining ties to villages and communities. Local SS-policemen killed an ethnic German woman named Frau Wegerer in the town of Mar'ianivka; she was executed for supplying partisans with food. On the morning of 16 September 1943, a thirteen-year-old girl named Hania was standing guard over the harvest. She was hungry and secretly pocketed some of the produce. When a member of the Koziatyn SS-police office approached her, she became frightened and ran. The policeman shot her dead.[61] In September 1943 German gendarmes in Koziatyn went from village to village under orders to kill the wives and family members of Ukrainian auxiliary policemen who had deserted their posts and presumably fled to the partisans. The Soviet partisans had been practicing the same policy against Ukrainian collaborators for over a year.[62]

In what ways did the local population—in particular, women—become involved in the resistance? In addition to supporting the Soviet and nationalist partisan movements by offering shelter and food, women in Zhytomyr served as couriers and sabotaged the German administration and economy by secretly slaughtering livestock, hiding food, stealing supplies, and planting explosives. A few murdered German officials by poisoning their food. German commanders had warned early on that women should be deemed as suspect as men, perhaps trying to counter the prevailing gender stereotype that women were "intellectually limited, emotional, submissive."[63] The prominent role of a female partisan leader in Korosten' named Maria Kondratenko alarmed Nazi leaders and challenged their gendered prejudices about women's capabilities. Since Kondratenko successfully eluded the Germans, they investigated and hunted her with a determination (and frustration) unmatched in other cases against local partisans.[64]

Sometime in 1941 or early 1942, Kondratenko (who was from Iagniatyn) joined the commissar's office in Koziatyn. Before the war, she was employed as a truck driver; therefore, she had a good geographic sense of the roadways and routes in the region. But under the Germans she worked as a translator and also contributed an article to the local Ukrainian (German-censored) newspaper in April 1942. In July 1943, about a year after she joined the commissar's office, German police carried out extensive interrogations of Kondratenko's contacts and friends in Koziatyn. They also circulated a photograph of her, which showed that she had a small child.

The German police search for Kondratenko began after one night in mid-May 1943 when she tapped on the window of her friend Anna Tkachova. She told Tkachova that she was going to hide out in the forests near Ruzhyn, and that she was seeking to "bring into line the guys from the railway." Her task was to persuade the Ukrainian railway guards to help with the planned sabotage of the rail lines. The next day these Ukrainian Schutzmänner fled with Kondratenko to the forest, where they encamped by the forester's house near Ruzhyn. Meanwhile, Tkachova obtained forged travel documents and went by horse-drawn cart to the Ruzhyn marketplace; during her return trip, she stopped by the forest hideout to bring soap, matches, and other items. Tkachova continued to work as a cleaning woman in the Ukrainian courthouse while she secretly brought letters and supplies to the forest hideout. After about two months, at the end of July, the Germans captured Tkachova and interrogated her about Kondratenko and the resistance group. When the German interrogators were finished with Tkachova, the SS and police leaders handed her over to the SD in Berdychiv. She was executed on 29 July 1943.[65]

Besides Tkachova, the Germans arrested and questioned Kondratenko's friends, neighbors, and landlord. They learned exactly where Kondratenko's group was hiding and planned a "cleansing" operation of the forest near Iagnia-tyn. On the morning of 18 August, twelve German SS and policemen, ninety-one Ukrainian auxiliaries, and sixty Hungarian soldiers raided the camp. They identified one woman among the twelve "bandits," but she escaped during the skirmish; and they managed to capture and kill the commander of the group, a Jewish man known as Black Misha, as well as Kondratenko's lover, Fedo-ruk.[66] Two days after the raid, on 20 August, one of the German police chiefs in Koziatyn, Josef Richter, the station leader at Samhorodok who led numer-ous anti-Jewish and antipartisan manhunts in 1943, was assassinated when his truck was stopped on the road near Iagniatyn.[67] Kondratenko successfully hid from her German pursuers. However, her friends who had been arrested, in-terrogated, and later executed told the German police that she had been de-ported to the Reich as a laborer.[68]

The Kondratenko case illustrates that women did join the partisans in the woods, where they carried out a number of important, dangerous tasks. But Kondratenko represented a small number of women who held leading roles in the resistance movement. The majority of women in Zhytomyr labored under the eye of German and Ukrainian overseers, while they were increasingly ex-pected to respond to partisan demands in their villages and homes. When they were not working the fields during the spring, summer, and fall, they were as-signed by the Germans to heavy labor projects, such as digging trenches and clearing roads of rubble, ice, and snow. In the cities and towns, they were em-ployed as maids, factory workers and, more numerously, *Putzfrauen* (cleaning women). They also tried to hold together what remained of their households by concealing their children from forced labor raids and hiding food from the Ger-mans to feed their families. When German or Soviet forces razed their houses, they built shelters in the holes that were once their homes.[69] Whenever pos-sible, they tended the small plots around their houses.

Thus there are important social, indeed gendered dimensions to the history of factious partisan warfare that struck nearly all of the households of Zhyto-myr's northern districts, and in pockets of the central and southern districts around Vinnytsia. By 1943 nearly all Ukrainians, male and female, were united in their anti-German sentiment and desire to remove the Nazis from Ukrai-nian soil. However, the wartime presence of a number of resistance groups— above all the Ukrainian nationalists and the Soviet detachments—also reveals that beneath this common immediate desire to expel the Nazis persisted a society fractured along ethnic, political, ideological, religious, and gendered lines.

German Atrocity Propaganda

A Ukrainian "Katyn" at Vinnytsia

If the commissar's role in the 1943 period of "total war" was not to impersonate the police by carrying out heightened "security measures," it was to champion a new Nazi propaganda campaign that, paradoxically, emphasized the crimes of Stalinism. The goal was to induce Ukrainians to fight against the Red Army and the partisans. In the commissariat apparatus, a new main department was formed for propaganda, which had previously fallen under the department of politics. General Commissar Leyser wrote to the commissars that the immediate objective of 1943 was to use more propaganda in the "service of the German administration and war in the East" because "we must convince Ukrainians that only the Germans will allow free religion and protect people from hunger and Soviet crimes." The new Nazi propaganda effort should, in Leyser's words, "stress Soviet crimes."[70]

At the end of March 1943, Leyser required the commissars to collect and submit to him all photos, testimonies, and documents that revealed the horrors of Bolshevism. He also asked the commissars to publicize in the Ukrainian newspapers a contest for the best essays titled "What Do We Have to Thank the Germans For?" and "Never Again Bolshevism!" Leyser dictated which themes the Ukrainians should write about: "the generous and modern administration of the Germans; a fair justice system; decree on the privatization of agriculture; the expansion of farm plots; employment possibilities; religious tolerance and cultural freedom." As a grand prize in this contest, the Germans offered a trip through the Reich of ten to fourteen days, which given the increasing presence of the Soviets may have seemed especially attractive to some Ukrainians.[71]

The Nazis' biggest propaganda event in Zhytomyr was the unearthing of mass graves at Vinnytsia containing 9,432 victims of Stalin's 1937 purges. Ukrainian leaders had told the Germans earlier about the location of these mass graves, but the Germans chose to exploit the Vinnytsia tragedy in July 1943, after the Katyn massacres were revealed (which Goebbels hailed as a propaganda success). Religious leaders and forensic experts from Nazi-occupied Europe arrived in Vinnytsia, as part of what the Nazis touted was an international investigation. One of the experts on the scene was the former Sixth Army doctor Gerhart Panning who had conducted gruesome experiments on Jewish POWs during August 1941. City Commissar Fritz Margenfeld questioned Ukrainian administrators in his office about who in Vinnytsia might have been an NKVD official in 1937 and could be blamed publicly in a Nazi show trial.[72]

The Ukrainian Autocephalous Church supported the entire Nazi campaign, especially its anti-Semitic content. During one of the funeral processions, the Autocephalous bishop Hryhorii told the mourners that the Jews had tortured and killed the victims of the 1937 massacres. Then he lashed out further: "Well then, my dear ones, rise up at once and, like Christ, ask the bloodswollen torturer, 'the father of all workers,' Stalin, for which of the good deeds that we have done for you and your Jews throughout our lives, you torture us so much? Maybe for our hard labor in the kolkhoz fields, where we worked without straightening our backs, growing high wheat, so that your Jews would have a tasty roll for *shabbas* and Passover? Or maybe for filling our eyes with sweat as we worked on sugar beats [sic] so that your kikes would have sweet things?"[73]

The unearthing of the Vinnytsia site in the summer of 1943 was depicted in a series of propaganda posters that showed an anti-Semitic Jewish figure towering over the mass graves. Thus even after the Germans had killed nearly every Jewish person in the region, they continued to effectively exploit their anti-Semitic aims as a popular mobilizing force against Bolshevism. As historian Amir Weiner's work has shown, after almost three years of Nazi anti-Semitic practices and propaganda, few flinched at or even questioned such grotesque and vitriolic distortions. Indeed, during the war the Nazis reignited smoldering ethnic animosities and introduced new forms of anti-Semitism in Zhytomyr (and the rest of Europe). Meanwhile, within local German circles the commissars and their deputies continued to disparage Ukrainians as "white Negroes" and "colonial peoples," showing that their propaganda appeals to Ukrainians as victims of Stalinist crimes were certainly not inspired by a sudden and sincere empathy for the local population of non-Germans.[74] It was purely a short-term tactic done out of desperation as the Germans tried to maintain power over the region. The Nazi reward program and propaganda efforts failed. It was too little, too late. Moreover, Ukrainians who were caught in the middle of the Nazi-Soviet war naturally threw in their lot with the perceived winner. After Germany's defeat at Stalingrad in early 1943 and the unsuccessful German offensive in the summer of 1943, siding with the Soviets seemed to be the safer bet.

The Collapse of Nazi Colonization Experiments
Hegewald under Attack

The 1943 military setbacks on the Eastern Front compelled Nazi leaders to reduce Volksdeutsche programs to regional initiatives, and then to abandon them altogether.[75] Local leaders continued to fulfill the plans made in the fall of 1942, resettling more Volksdeutsche in Hegewald and in another settlement at Cherniakhiv (named "Försterstadt") in early 1943. But by April 1943 General

Vinnitsa. Vinnytsia, 1943. A Nazi anti-Semitic poster claiming that the source of Soviet terror was the "Jewish-Bolshevik" commissar. The Ukrainian women in the poster are viewing victims of the 1937–38 purges exhumed in Vinnytsia in July 1943. The illustration was obtained with the help of Dr. Amir Weiner, Stanford University. (Vinnitsa. GE 1958. Hoover Institution Archives)

Commissar Leyser declared that all resettlement actions were to be postponed, and only in the severe cases of life-threatening conditions, especially partisan attack, should ethnic Germans be resettled.[76] Later, on 5 July 1943, Himmler's Generalplan Ost was abruptly shelved when Hitler ordered a halt to ethnic German resettlement and land "grants" until after the war.[77]

Although Hitler demanded that large-scale colonization schemes cease, local efforts to "educate" Volksdeutsche and to bestow on them a higher German status continued until the final days of the Nazi evacuation. These efforts were ultimately cut short by the war, but even before the Red Army returned to Zhytomyr in November 1943, other local factors were sabotaging Hitler's Lebensraum goals. As much as local officials spoke of "protecting" the ethnic Germans who had been classified and resettled, the population was in fact subjected to Nazi brutality and the circumstances of war. The SS and the Party's NSV transplanted thousands of ethnic Germans by force, and often under harsh conditions. After the Volksdeutsche arrived in their new settlements, the Nazis failed to provide the types of privileges propagandized in earlier decrees and policy plans. German leaders of the various agencies posted in the region lacked adequate resources and manpower to care for this dislocated population.

Hegewald's Volksdeutsche received the most attention, but many ethnic Germans remained outside the settlement. They were scattered across Ukrainian villages in the northern districts where they fell victim to the brutal Nazi-Soviet partisan warfare. To protect these vulnerable Volksdeutsche, the RuSHA regional chief in charge of special resettlement actions, Theo Henschel, and members of the German People's List began a rapid campaign to classify and resettle over 9,000 ethnic Germans around Hegewald.[78] They formed a second colony in the Zhytomyr region named Försterstadt ("game-keeper's town").[79] During this hasty resettlement action, Himmler's subordinates followed his lead by kidnapping "racially valuable" children from Ukrainian homes (a crime that Himmler promoted in his Hegewald speech of September 1942). In the aftermath of the last SS sweep of Volksdeutsche villages in Zhytomyr's northern districts, the number of orphans under SS-VoMi care in Zhytomyr increased by nearly 600 children.[80]

Himmler's functionaries rushed to expand their local support base among the Volksdeutsche population, so much so that the local chief of the Sonderkommando Russland outpost in Zhytomyr, SS-Sturmbannführer Richard Schill, was fired in July 1943 for the unauthorized enrollment of ethnic German settlers.[81] Hundreds of local Ukrainians and Poles tricked the Nazi racial examiners by falsely claiming German blood in order to secure better rations, better jobs, and possible escape from the advancing Soviets. The SS-police, the Party, and Rosenberg's commissariat offices were unable to manage this growing population of ethnic Germans. In the city of Zhytomyr, where Sonderkommando 4a first registered 963 ethnic Germans in late August 1941, the population reached several thousand by summer 1943. City Commissar Fritz Magass had nominal control over them since they resided in the city, but the leading offices governing ethnic German programs were also headquartered there. Given the high-profile presence of leading SS-police and Party organizations, the Volksdeutsche there should have enjoyed the maximum level of German privileges that the Nazis promoted. However, in the summer of 1943, an official of General Commissar Leyser's office observed that the ethnic Germans in the city still lived in very primitive houses and were unable to obtain food. At one shop that was supposed to serve 3,500 Volksdeutsche, the ethnic Germans stood in line all day and crowded inside where a single clerk tried to stock the shelves and sell the goods. At the shop counter, ethnic Germans fought over produce, and rations could not be distributed; one family had been eating only peas for dinner, while another received only milk. The entire program, this official wrote, is "eine Schweinerei" (an awful mess).[82]

Meanwhile, Nazi thugs who conducted forced labor raids throughout the region began to strike the Volksdeutsche settlements. Ethnic Germans were supposed to be exempt from labor deportations to the Reich, but Nazi leaders like Erich Koch and Fritz Sauckel placed enormous pressure on local authorities to round up as many people as possible. Even at the prized Hegewald settlement, SS leader Henschel complained in one report that "wild" labor recruiters snatched ethnic Germans, forced them onto trucks, and placed them in the reception camps. When General Commissar Leyser later reprimanded the labor recruiters, he explained that "a strengthening of the German peoples, which was the goal of resettlement, will not be possible if the [ethnic German] labor force is deported."[83]

From the perspective of the Soviet partisan movement, the ethnic Germans' "racial" status placed them in the enemy camp of Nazi fascists and "collaborators." Soviet attacks against Volksdeutsche settlements and households, which began in 1942, increased considerably during 1943. It was no secret to the local Ukrainian population that SS-army storehouses kept ample supplies of food and equipment for the Reich Germans in Zhytomyr. In May 1943 partisans raided Hegewald's special SS shops and stole vehicles and goods. Outside Hegewald—for example, in Mazyr—partisans massacred ethnic German families. Across the northern part of Zhytomyr, partisans continually ransacked ethnic German farms for livestock and produce. The SS-police carried out reprisal measures for such attacks; and when units of the ethnic German Selbst-schutz were in place, they took revenge on neighboring Ukrainian villages.[84] Meanwhile, south of Hegewald near Vinnytsia, Hitler visited his Werwolf com-pound for the last time on 27 August 1943 for a meeting with General Erich von Manstein. One month later, his security forces at the compound reported over 1,360 acts of resistance in and around the site, resulting in the arrests of 722 persons. Among the partisans who were arrested and killed were a few Jews from the Vinnytsia region.[85]

The atrocities that accompanied the Nazi retreat have been largely over-looked in military studies of the war. In addition to the enormous suffering and loss of life, the violence had other psychological and political consequences. By further demoralizing Zhytomyr's inhabitants—many of whom were bereft by the loss of loved ones in the partisan warfare or were left homeless—the strongest of the movements, the Soviet insurgency, was able to effectively stifle any Ukrainian resistance to a Stalinist reoccupation of Zhytomyr. Instead, Ukrainians developed a new patriotic attachment to the victorious Red Army, a source of unity that Stalin among others effectively exploited in the postwar period.

Shortly before the Red Army entered Zhytomyr at the end of November, the Nazis hastily implemented an evacuation plan. In the city prison of Berdychiv, the prisoners were gathered in the courtyard and shot; others were thrown into wells. One of the few Jewish survivors of Berdychiv, Khaim Borisovich, described the German evacuation as he experienced it:

> When the Red Army first liberated Zhitomir, the Germans in Berdichev be-
> gan to panic. At this point I was able to escape. I hid in various places looking
> for shelter in cellars and half-ruined houses. I was able to remain in hiding
> until 1 January 1944. On this day, feeling their evacuation was close at hand,
> the Germans started rounding up citizens, indiscriminately sending people
> to Germany. I snuck into an empty house right next to the SD, trusting that
> no one would search this place. . . . During the night of 1 January, I climbed
> up to the attic of the abandoned building. With the Red Army nearby, the
> Germans quickly tried to do away with all of the prisoners. On the morn-
> ing of 3 January, I could see and hear the shooting of the prisoners in the
> SD courtyard from my attic hiding place. They were taken out in groups of
> 5–10 people; their hands were tied behind their backs. About 120 prisoners
> who were shot on that day were also buried in the pit of the SD yard. That
> same night all of the SD men and soldiers fled. Some of the prisoners were
> buried alive since the Germans were in such a hurry to leave. The next day,
> 4 January 1944, Soviet troops entered Berdychiv.[1]

Even in the final hours of their rule, German officials continued to hunt for every last Jew; some feared that Jewish survivors would take revenge on their tormentors. Others seemed to have an insatiable appetite for blood and violence that even the Reich's imminent defeat did not diminish. Ukrainians who tried to help the prisoners, including the few remaining Jews, were also shot.[2] The commissars and the SS and police destroyed top-secret documents. They loaded up trains, trucks, cars, and horse carts with their most prized plunder. Along with the livestock from Hegewald, the ethnic Germans were formed into columns and forced to march westward toward the German-Polish border.

Himmler had waited until the last possible minute to evacuate the ethnic Germans from Zhytomyr, and thus he forced many Volksdeutsche to serve in defensive military operations.[3] On 12 November 1943, the day after General Commissar Leyser fled the city of Zhytomyr, the ethnic Germans departed in four "treks." One of the columns of ethnic Germans, numbering 600 persons (mainly women and children), was massacred by Soviet forces on 16–17 November.[4] To make matters worse, the ethnic German Selbstschutz and Ukrainian auxiliaries who were supposed to act as "security escorts" for the Volksdeutsche treks were (as one SS official put it) "lacking in leadership" and prone to "plundering and other offensive excesses."[5] By 26 November, streams of ethnic German refugees were arriving by foot and wagon in the Polish Warthegau, where they remained in camps run by VoMi.[6] According to historian Doris Bergen's research, the mostly ill, starving, and terrorized Volksdeutsche who arrived in these camps were "crammed into school buildings, guarded by police, and in some cases turned away from local hospitals." Once the pride and joy of Nazi colonial enthusiasts, now they "embodied the failure of the Nazi empire, both inside and outside the Reich."[7] For the ethnic German refugees, the Nazi defeat marked the onset of a new phase of Soviet persecution. When the Red Army uncovered these camps in January 1945 during its advance on Berlin, they rounded up the ethnic Germans, shoved them into sealed freight cars, and sent them to the trans-Ural region. Those who did not die on the journey were forced into "special settlements" for Germans.[8]

Months before the Red Army first pushed the Germans temporarily out of Zhytomyr on 12 November 1943, Ukrainians prepared themselves for the return of Soviet power. They started to secretly collect rubles and devise alibis that would hold up under Soviet interrogations. Many began to stockpile their own arms by trading foodstuffs for weapons with the retreating Wehrmacht soldiers who trudged through the region, emaciated and defeatist. The Red Army liberated the city of Zhytomyr on New Year's Eve, 31 December 1943, and Vinnytsia on 20 March 1944.[9] Yet for most the euphoria of liberation was short-lived. All men in the region between the ages of seventeen and fifty were immediately drafted into the Red Army. Soviet secret police and intelligence units (NKVD and SMERSH) began to round up and shoot collaborators; collective farms were stripped of any remaining foodstuffs. In some cases the Soviets, upon overrunning former labor camps, branded the workers as traitors, and then brutally killed them with their tanks and grenades.

While nearly all Germans feared Soviet retribution and fled westward, the electrician Ivan Shynal'skii, who worked for German officials in Zhytomyr's commissariat office, remembered one contrary example from the final days of the war in the city. One of his German superiors was deeply involved with a Ukrainian woman and fathered more than one child with her. He also sup-

German soldiers during the reconquest of Zhytomyr, December 1943 (Ullstein Bild #00190443)

ported the local Ukrainian underground. When the Germans evacuated Zhytomyr, this commissar decided to stay. Red Army intelligence arrested him. He
pleaded with them that he was a Communist sympathizer, but he was shot on
the spot anyway.[10]

From the perspective of Zhytomyr's Ukrainians, the continuities between
Nazi and Soviet occupation were striking. As had been the case under Stalin's
totalitarian rule, Ukrainians under the Nazis were the objects of a revolutionary reordering of society forged through violence. They often compared the two
regimes. For example, when the Nazis shut down a local Orthodox church in
Zhytomyr and then crammed hundreds of Jewish laborers inside it, Ukrainian
peasants remarked that the Germans used Bolshevik methods. Ukrainians also
frequently complained that German labor raids were like Stalin's mass deportations in the 1930s.

However, what the Nazis attempted to achieve in the region and how they
implemented their imperialistic, criminal policies represented a dramatically
different episode in Ukraine's history, unlike the Stalinist campaigns of the
1930s and the subsequent, relatively relaxed Soviet policies of the postwar period. The Germans introduced familiar colonial forms of rule as well as initiated revolutionary racial programs that were genocidal. The first step, as the
Nazis saw it, in fulfilling their utopian plans for the East was the destruction
of the Jews. This was a policy goal that had been made clear to senior offi-

The Collapse of the Nazi Empire: The Forced Evacuation of Volksdeutsche from Ukraine, 1943. The arrows show the paths or "treks" of ethnic Germans who went (mainly in horse-drawn wagons and on foot) to Nazi-occupied Poland and the Reich. The squares on the map represent the Volksdeutsche colonies and the reception areas or camps where the evacuees stopped along the way or ended their journey. Source: U.S. National Archives and Records Administration, T-81/314/2443669.

Key:
I. General District Kiev
II. General District Dnipropetrovs'k
III. General District Taurida by Crimea
IV. General District Nikolaev
V. General District Zhytomyr
VI. General District Volhynia Podolia

Taganrog
Rostov on Don
Mariupol'
Oriechow
Berdians'k
Dnipropetrovs'k
Stalino
Zaporzhzhia
Nikopol
Melitopol
Halbstadt
Nikolaev
Cherson
Kharkiv
Chortitza
Kriwoj Rog
Orloff-Kronau
Odessa
Balta
Chernivtsi
Kam'ianets'-Podil's'kyi
Proskiriv
L'viv
Shepetivka
Rivne
Novohrad-Volyns'kyi
Vinnytsia
Kalynivka
Berdychiv
Hegewald
Kiev
Minsk
Königsberg
Pr. Stargard
Kulm
Danzig
Neustadt
Kanitz
Poznan
Berlin
Lodz
Breslau
Aussig
Prague
Cracow
Warsaw
Budapest
Vienna

II
I
IV
III
V
VI

cials in the military, SS and police, and civil administration shortly before they arrived in the region. Given the secret and criminal nature of the "Final Solution," however, not all levels of the local hierarchy were made aware of their expected role as perpetrators. While stationed in Zhytomyr, some of the rank and file in the military and even members of the SS-police in the SD special (killing) task forces began to realize the magnitude of this criminal undertaking, but any trepidations that surfaced at the lower levels were suppressed by the reassurances and "explanations" of superior commanders. No other group within the indigenous population was pursued and destroyed in such a systematic, thoroughgoing manner, and with such widespread participation of Germans and non-Germans.

By contrast, when regional leaders approached the more vaguely defined project of "Germanization," they proved to be less capable of realizing the elite's intentions. The history and outcome of the ethnic German programs in Zhytomyr demonstrate that the structures of Nazi power in the field functioned differently depending on the policy. In other words, at the lower levels a typical German official understood how to "deal with the Jews" and was generally willing to do what was expected of him. The ethnic German policy, on the other hand, did not generate the same kind of consensus; it stimulated, instead, improvisation and chaos.

Hitler was well aware that his empire could not be secured though military conquest alone. The Germans had a brief history of imperialism and therefore needed to be taught how to administer and exploit conquered territories as colonial possessions. Nazi leaders, foremost among them Himmler, cherished the Eastern Territories as a laboratory to let loose revolutionary völkisch experiments and agrarian colonial fantasies. Short-lived and ultimately a failure, Himmler's Hegewald experiment manifested these irrational, utopian elements of Nazi empire-building. The tragic paradoxes and delusions of the entire Nazi endeavor are particularly evident in the words of the local SS-police trainer in Berdychiv. He celebrated the genocidal destruction of the Jews while touting the "New Eastern Europe" under the Nazis as a historic continuation of the migration of Germanic colonists "who penetrated Eastern European countries over the course of centuries . . . [who] did not bring robbery and destruction, fire and murder, death and ruin; instead, they successfully created from the fertile fields blooming cities, outstanding buildings, and artistic [and] scholarly works of the highest value."[11] This ironic statement was supposed to convince young Ukrainian and ethnic German policemen, who were mainly conscripts, that German colonialism was civilized and historically legitimate.

The Ukrainian, ethnic German, Jewish, and Polish responses to German rule were not uniform, primarily because Ukraine was a country that had a long history of foreign rule and regional particularisms. No discernible political impulses were expressed by a majority. Instead, most Ukrainians embraced efforts to revive the school system and religious institutions; they clamored for the privatization of the collective farms. Still recovering from the horrors of Stalinism, they earnestly hoped for a "New Way of Life" (as promised by the Germans), one that would genuinely benefit Ukrainians.[12] Although the Germans made overtures along these lines to the Ukrainians, their propaganda promises never bore fruit.

The Germans found an ample number of Ukrainians to serve in the RKU administration. But in contrast to the Nazi occupation of most Western European countries, the Germans did not conquer a Ukrainian government, and this fact made it all the easier for many Ukrainians to join the German administration without feeling as if they were national traitors. Ukrainian nationalists who joined the Nazi administration perceived the defeat of the Soviets as an opportunity to establish an independent Ukraine under German protection. But the most common motivation of the local Ukrainian leader was a desire for power and material improvements, often to the great disadvantage of his neighbor. Ukrainians who took on leading roles in the German administration believed that there was something to be gained, at least in the short term, by cooperating with the Germans.[13]

The revival of Orthodox Christianity, although it too was rife with factionalism, provided a significant demonstration of the power of religion as a coping mechanism for Ukrainians. When faced with total terror, grief, and deprivation, Ukrainians searched for explanations for their plight and sought a spiritual haven from the horror of everyday life. Yet even the shared hatred of Nazism neither united Ukrainians under the banner of nationalism nor instilled a renewed faith in Soviet-style communism. In fact, the destructive years of the Nazi occupation created more ambivalence toward the nationalists and left Ukrainians more vulnerable to Soviet reoccupation; the Nazis actually seeded new antagonisms and strengthened old rivalries. Polish-Ukrainian and Jewish-Ukrainian relations sank to the worst levels of violence, spiraling into civil wars, first behind the lines in the occupied territory and then within the maelstrom of the Nazi-Soviet military conflict as it moved westward.

Ukrainians suffered tremendous losses under the Nazis. Having made terrible sacrifices during the 1930s to facilitate the buildup of the collective farms and the region's industry, they now saw all of that effort gone to waste. The material devastation was enormous, but it paled next to the death toll and the immeasurable grief and trauma that struck all survivors of the Nazi occupation.

Virtually everyone had witnessed the brutalization of friends, family members, and neighbors. With a single, fatal stroke, the Germans and their accomplices erased centuries of Jewish life and cultural achievement. Forced evacuations and migrations of ethnic Germans also resulted in the near disappearance of that minority in Ukraine. According to Soviet postwar investigators and forensic reports, in the Zhytomyr and Vinnytsia oblasts a total of 321,503 persons died during the war; more than half were civilians, and the rest were prisoners of war.[14] Unlike other foreign rulers who had occupied the region, the Germans left nothing of any social or economic value. To Soviet leaders, however, the Nazis bequeathed much more.

Even before the Red Army reoccupied Zhytomyr, Soviet partisan leaders and intelligence officials took note of the behavior and loyalties of people living under German rule. They exacted their greatest revenge on the nationalists and collaborators in the wartime administration. But everyone in postwar Ukraine was subjected to a new kind of "cleansing" of Soviet society. As historian Amir Weiner found in his study of the war's impact on Vinnytsia, "Wartime conduct emerged as the key criterion in the evaluation of 'party worthiness.' Subjected to [Soviet-style inquisitors demanding to know] 'Where were you during the German occupation, and how did you survive?' (which often implied 'Why did you survive?'), thousands of Communists saw their careers and beliefs assessed through the prism of the new legitimizing myth of the war."[15]

For many, the Soviet Union's triumph over Nazism validated the communist experiment and even heralded a new era in the socialist revolution. At the heart of the new patriotic myth of the war was the claim that all "peaceful Soviet citizens" were united in the struggle against fascism and all Soviet nationalities suffered equally under the Nazis. Though ethnic Germans and Poles from the Zhytomyr region had been deported by the thousands in successive waves between 1935 and 1941, it was the war that cemented a Soviet policy of full-scale ethnic cleansing and homogenization. The strength and stability of the Soviet Union and the socialist experiment now depended on republics that contained large ethnic majorities rather than aggregations of potentially disloyal ethnic minorities. The purification of Soviet society meant that all of the enemies from within—namely, collaborators and Ukrainian nationalists—were exposed, often killed outright, or deported. The Holocaust was universalized, since no ethnic group was to be given a special status as the victim of Nazism. The war allowed Stalin to push his crimes into the background while Hitler's took center stage.

The Holocaust became prominent not as the source of empathy toward the Jews but just its opposite. Nazi anti-Semitic practices and propaganda continued to resonate among Ukrainians into the postwar period. In 1944–45 Jews returned to Ukraine from service in the army or evacuation camps in Tashkent and found that their relatives had been killed, their apartments occupied, and their furniture and other belongings dispersed. Jewish attempts to reclaim their dwellings angered Ukrainians who occupied them during the war and who argued that the Jewish returnees had not done their part to defeat the Germans. Such disputes often erupted into fights, and pogroms occurred in Dnipropetrovs'k and Kiev. In Dnipropetrovs'k an angry mob attacked the Jews, yelling "Death to the kikes" and "Thirty-seven thousand kikes [have] already been slaughtered [by the Nazis], we'll finish off the rest." [16] Such outbursts as well as the return of official anti-Semitism across Soviet state and party institutions silenced many Jewish survivors. At the same time, as anthropologist Rebecca Golbert has observed, "private acts of remembrance continued in the face of public silences." Among these private acts were "annual visits to the former camp and mass grave sites." [17]

Since the collapse of the Soviet Union, citizens of the newly independent Ukraine have been grappling with these mixed legacies as they try to build their own nation.[18] In the 1990s, after nearly fifty years of Soviet repression of the Holocaust, wartime survivors and their descendants began to openly come to terms with the war. Many Jews from Israel and North America returned to Ukraine to reclaim their heritage, often initiating the restoration of synagogues and Jewish schools. Former Soviet commemorative plaques meant to honor those killed in World War II have been altered to reveal that among the "peaceful Soviet citizens" were a significant number of Jewish victims.[19] A new Holocaust memorial was erected in Zhytomyr. Yet deep-seated prejudices persist despite the dwindling Jewish population in Ukraine. The memorial in Zhytomyr was vandalized in 2002, and anti-Semitic hooligans desecrated a new plaque at Babi Yar in 2003. As a political movement, Ukrainian nationalism continues to be tainted by its wartime history. Eastern Ukrainians remain suspicious of Galician-based nationalism and condemn the OUN for its collaboration with the Nazis and perpetration of atrocities against Poles and Jews. Meanwhile, the revered "heroes of the Soviet Union" and other medal-adorned Red Army veterans who valiantly defeated Nazism are fading from the scene. And the Soviet empire that they fought for is now discredited—deemed another disastrous political experiment that, along with Nazism, destroyed Ukraine's twentieth century and now haunts its twenty-first.

Appendix
German and Ukrainian Spellings of Place Names

German spelling	Ukrainian spelling	German spelling	Ukrainian spelling
Andruschewka	Andrushivka	Lemberg	Lviv
Baranowka	Baranivka	Lipowez	Lypovets'
Baraschi	Barashi	Litin	Lityn
Basar	Bazar	Ljubar	Liubar
Berditschew	Berdychiv	Lojew	Loiev
Bila Zerkwa	Biela Tserkva	Luginy	Lugyny
Bilopilje	Bilopil'e	Luzk	Luts'k
Bragin	Bragin	Machnowka	Machnivka
Brailow	Brailiv	Malin	Malyn
Brussilow	Brusyliv	Marchlewsk	Markhlevsk (Dovbysh)
Chmelnik	Khmil'nyk	Michailowka	Mykhailivka
Choiniki	Khoiniki	Mogilew-Podolsk	Mohyliv-Podil's'kyi
Czernowitz	Chernivtsi	Monastyrischtsche	Monastyryshche
Daschew	Dashiv	Mosyr	Mazyr
Dschulinka	Dzulinka	Naroditschi	Narodychi
Dsershinsk	Dzerzhyns'k	Narowlja	Narovlia
Emiltschino	Emil'chyne	Nemirow	Nemyriv
Gaissin	Haisyn	Nikolajew	Nikolaev
Gorodniza	Horodnytsia	Nowograd-Wolynski	Novohrad-Volyns'kyi
Illjinzy	Illintsi	(Zwiahel)	(Zviahel)
Januschpol	Ivanpil'	Nowo Miropol	Novyi Muropil'
Jarun	Iarun'	Olewsk	Olevs'k
Jelsk	El'sk	Oratowo	Orativ
Kalinkowischi	Kalinkovichi	Owrutsch	Ovruch
Kalinowka	Kalynivka	Petrikow	Petrikiv
Kamenez- Podolsk	Kam'ianets'- Podil's'kyi	Pliskow	Plyskiv
		Pogrebischtsche	Pohrebyshche
Kasatin	Koziatyn	Polessia, Polesje	Polissia
Komarin	Komarin	Popelnja	Popil'nia
Komssomolskoje	Komsomol's'ke	Potijewka	Potievka
Kornin	Kornyn	Pripjet	Pripiat'
Korosten	Korosten'	Radomyschl	Radomyshl'
Korostyschew	Korostyshiv	Retschiza	Retchiza
Leltschizy	Lel'chitsy	Rushin	Ruzhyn

German spelling	Ukrainian spelling	German spelling	Ukrainian spelling
Schepetowka	Shepetivka	Tschernjachow	Cherniakhiv
Shitkowitschi	Zhitkovichi	Tscherwonoarmeisk	Chervonoarmiis'k
Shitomir, Shytomyr,	Zhytomyr	Tschudnow	Chudniv
Zhitomir		Turbow	Turbiv
Slowetschno	Slovecho	Turow	Turov
Ssamgorodok	Samhorodok	Ulanow	Ulaniv
Ssitkowzy	Sitkivtsi	Wassiljewitschi	Vasilevichi
Strishawka	Strizhavka	Winniza, Vinnitsa	Vinnytsia
Teplik	Teplyk	Wolodarsk-Wolynski	Volodarsk-Volyns'kyi
Trojanow	Troianiv	Woronowiza	Voronovytsia
Tschepowitschi	Chopovychi	Wtscheraische	Vchoraishe

Notes

Abbreviations
BAL   Bundesarchiv Aussenstelle Ludwigsburg
BDC   Berlin Document Center
CSA   Central State Archive, Kiev
GARF   State Archives of the Russian Federation
IMT   Records from the Trial of the Major War Criminals before
             the International Military Tribunal at Nuremberg, War Crimes, NA
KTB   Official War Diary
MHI   Military Historical Institute Archives, Prague
NA   United States National Archives, College Park, Md.
NMT   Records from the Trials of War Criminals before the Nuremberg
             Military Tribunals, War Crimes, NA
RG   Record Group
RGVA   Russian State Military Archive, Moscow (former Osobyi Archive)
USHMM   United States Holocaust Memorial Museum Archives
ZSA   Zhytomyr State Archives

Introduction

1 Magocsi, *A History of Ukraine*, 638.

2 Brown, *A Biography of No Place.*

3 At the end of 1942, there were 870 Reich Germans posted in the region's commissariat offices, divided into twenty-five districts, known as *Gebietskommissariate*. In Feb. 1943 the region was remapped into twenty-six districts. ZSA, P1151-1-26.

4 On Hitler's colonialism as an overseas venture with primarily economic interests, see Townshend's "Hitler and the Revival of German Colonialism," in *Nationalism and Internationalism*, ed. Earle, 399–430. Hannah Arendt's and Raphael Lemkin's early work on Nazism, genocide, and imperialism has been developed by Kamenetsky in *Secret Nazi Plans for Eastern Europe* and W. Smith in *The Ideological Origins of Nazi Imperialism*. Also see Lennox, Friedrichsmeyer, and Zantop, *The Imperialist Imagination*, and Jürgen Zimmerer, "Colonialism and the Holocaust: Toward an Archeology of Genocide," in Moses, ed., *Genocide and Settler Society*.

5 More recent studies of resettlement and the General Plan East include Aly and Heim, *Vordenker der Vernichtung*; Rössler, Schleiermacher, and Tollmien, eds., *Der "Generalplan Ost"*; R.-D. Müller, *Hitlers Ostkrieg*; and Aly, *"Final Solution."*

6 Hitler, *Mein Kampf*, 654.

7 The commissars dressed themselves in light-brown military-style suits adorned with a gaudy display of medals and insignias. See the "Richtlinien für die Aus-richtung der Gefolgschaft: Das öffentliche Auftreten der Deutschen," issued by the HSSPF Ukraine, 22 June 1942, USHMM, RG 11.001m15, reel 83, 1323-2-272. On the expansionist theorists and ideologues, see Haushofer, *Weltpolitik von Heute*, and Burleigh, *Germany Turns Eastward*.

8 On Hitler's remarks about "fertile" Ukrainian women and the sterilization policies that resulted, see entry of 22 July 1942, *Hitler's Table Talk*, 587–88. Bormann order, 23 July 1942, NA, RG 238, NO-1878. In a Koch memo about new rations for Ukraini-ans, he based this policy change on Hitler's remark that wheat grew in abundance around his Vinnytsia bunker while Reich Germans were going hungry. Koch order, in "Vermerk über die Tagung in Rivne," 26–28 Aug. 1942, NA, RG 242, T-454/R 92/000895.

9 Hegewald speech of Heinrich Himmler, 16 Sept. 1942, NA, RG 242, T-175/R90/ p. 22.

10 Paul Albert Scheer testimony, 29 Dec. 1945, USHMM RG 06.025 Kiev. Witte et al., eds., *Der Dienstkalender Heinrich Himmlers*, 498–99. On the famine in Kiev, see Berk-hoff, *Harvest of Despair*, 164–86.

11 On the radicalization process within the Hitler dictatorship, see Kershaw's analy-sis of "working toward the Führer" in *Hitler, 1889–1936*, 529.

12 See Charles Sydnor, "Reinhard Heydrich: Der 'ideale Nationalsozialist,'" in *Die SS*, ed. Smelser and Syring, 208–19, and Wistrich, *Wer war wer*, 161. On Heydrich's deci-sive presence in Zhytomyr, see testimony of former SK4a member, August Häfner, 6 July 1965, Trial of Kuno Callsen, BAL, 207 AR-Z 419/62, 17.

13 See Snyder, "The Causes of Ukrainian-Polish Ethnic Cleansing, 1943," 204–5. Weinberg, *The Foreign Policy of Hitler's Germany*.

14 These figures are based on the Soviet census of 1939. Since the figures include por-tions of the Soviet oblasts of Vinnytsia and of Polissia, which fell within Romanian-controlled Transnistria and the Reichskommissariat Ostland, respectively, they do not correspond exactly with the projected agricultural output of the Generalbezirk Zhytomyr. See the report of the Reich Ministry for the Eastern Occupied Territo-ries, "Der Generalbezirk Shytomyr," 15 Mar. 1942, pp. 15–16, ZSA, P1151c-1-51. The Zhytomyr Oblast (est. 1937) and the Vinnytsia Oblast (est. 1932) were separate ad-ministrative districts within the Ukrainian Soviet Republic. In pre-Soviet times, the region around Zhytomyr, Vinnytsia, and Berdychiv was known as the Podol area of the Right Bank of the Dnepr. See Magocsi, *A History of Ukraine*, 5–8.

15 For an insightful account of Zhytomyr's Polish history and then Soviet "de-Polo-nization" of the region, including Marklevsk, see Brown, *A Biography of No Place*, 18–55, 134–40.

16 Abteilung Statistik, Zhytomyr General Commissar's office, Mar. 1942. District

population reports and occupational breakdowns, ZSA, P1151-1-700. On industrialization's impact on Ukrainian society in the interwar period, see Krawchenko, *Social Change and National Consciousness*, 119–30. On the impact of Soviet nationalities policies on Ukrainians, see Liber, *Soviet Nationality Policy*. The failure of Ukrainization and Russification is well argued by Martin, *The Affirmative Action Empire*, 122–24.

17 Weeks, *Nation and State*, and Snyder, *The Reconstruction of Nations*, 119–22.

18 Potichnyj and Aster, eds., *Ukrainian-Jewish Relations*. See entries on Zhytomyr, Vinnytsia, and Berdychiv in *The Encyclopedia of Jewish Life*, ed. Spector.

19 Liubar, 70 percent; Olevs'k, 42 percent; Chudniv, 46 percent; Korosten', 35; percent; Khmil'nyk, 63 percent; Bershad, 73 percent; Illintsi, 63 percent; Tomashpil', 62 percent; Tul'chyn, 41 percent. These 1939 figures were compiled in 1996 in an unpublished report by the Office of Jewish Affairs and Emigration, Zhytomyr, Ukraine. Also see Altshuler, *Soviet Jewry on the Eve of the Holocaust*.

20 Tsarist policies were aimed at assimilation and secularization of the population by restricting Hebrew printing and rabbinical education to Vilna and Zhytomyr. Raisin, *The Haskalah Movement in Russia*, 15, 186, and 197. The population figures are from the *Encyclopedia of Jewish Life*, ed. Spector; see entries on Berdychiv and Zhytomyr.

21 See Sword, ed., *The Soviet Takeover of the Polish Eastern Provinces*.

22 See Stumpp report covering his activities from Aug. to Sept. 1941, sent to Bfh. rückw.H.Geb.Süd. Ic, NA, RG 242, T-501/R 6/001142-52; also see a VoMi report of 12 Oct. 1941, "Volksdeutsche in Shitomir," NA, RG 242, T-454/R 100/000661-670. According to Buchsweiler, in 1926 there were 76,185 ethnic Germans around Zhytomyr (in 1941 about 44,000 remained); see Buchsweiler, *Volksdeutsche in der Ukraine*, 129. German migration to Ukraine swelled in the eighteenth century when colonists were invited to develop the Volga region under Catherine the Great. By the early twentieth century there were over 300 settlements in Ukraine with more then 500,000 inhabitants. See "Braune Mappe: Die Zivilverwaltung in den besetzten Ostgebieten, Teil II: Reichskommissariat Ukraine," GARF, 7021-148-183, and Fleischhauer and Pinkus, *The Soviet Germans*.

23 On the Soviet records of ethnic German settlements in Zhytomyr during the interwar period, see ZSA, P85-1-490, 491, 661. See also Martin, *Affirmative Action Empire*, 40–45.

24 Weinberg, *The Foreign Policy of Hitler's Germany*, 2:35, 41.

25 During the 1930s, the Nazis' "Brothers in Need" reached Zhytomyr's ethnic German population. See village surveys from the Zhytomyr region in 1941–42 prepared by Rosenberg's agent Karl Stumpp, ZSA, P1151-1-142.

26 According to Stumpp's reports, which were prone to exaggeration, the population of the Volksdeutsche villages of Zviahel, such as Vladyn with 250 persons, was reduced by at least half in 1936. In the village of Makovits, out of a population of 259 ethnic Germans in 1936, 172 persons were deported; in the village of Tesnovka,

the German population in 1934 was 335 persons, 146 of whom were deported in 1935; in Neu Romanowka, the German population in 1935 was 556 persons, 338 of whom were deported in 1936. In the village of Nikolajivka, the German population in 1935 was 300 persons; it was reduced to 151 by 1939. See Stumpp village studies, ZSA, P1151-1-142. On deportations and Hitler certificates of 1933–34, see NA, RG 242, T-501/R 6/001142-52.

27 On the Hitler-Stalin pact and the Volksdeutsche, see Kleist, *Zwischen Hitler und Stalin*, 86–90, 105.

Chapter One

1 Boehmer, *Colonial and Postcolonial Literature*.

2 As historian Woodruff Smith has demonstrated, leading scholars of the Kaiserreich have not stressed enough just how persistent and widespread the emigrationist, settler colonialism idea and movement were in the 1880s and '90s. See Smith, *The German Colonial Empire*, 30; Oelhafen von Schoellenbach, *Die Besiedlung Deutsch Süd-westafrikas*, 114. A major in the Schutztruppe in SWA from 1911 to 1919, Oelhafen von Schoellenbach argued that smart, robust Germans were exceptional colonizers and settlers. Colonies complicated as well as solved the "woman question"; see Wildenthal, *German Women for Empire*.

3 See Lemkin, *Axis Rule in Occupied Europe*, 79–95, and Arendt, *The Origins of Totalitarianism*, 123–25. Lemkin's unpublished manuscript on the history of genocide and colonialism is among his papers at the American Jewish Historical Society, New York, N.Y. I am grateful to John Docker and Ann Curthoys for bringing this material to my attention.

4 Norman Goda, *Tomorrow the World*, and Zantop and Jameson, *Colonial Fantasies*.

5 NMT, NO-1805. Reprinted in Kamenetsky, *Secret Nazi Plans*, 189–92 (appendix 2).

6 Also see Alan Steinweis, "Eastern Europe and the Notion of the 'Frontier' in Germany to 1945," in *Germany and Eastern Europe*, ed. Bullivant, Giles, and Pape, 56–69. Grill and Jenkins, "The Nazis and the American South in the 1930s," 667–94. Gröning and Wolschke-Bulmahn, *Der Drang nach Osten*, 132. For photos of migrating Volhynian Volksdeutschen in covered wagons, see du Prel, ed., *Deutsche Generalgouvernement Polen*.

7 Black, "*Askaris* in the 'Wild East.'"

8 See the chapter in Darré, *Neuadel aus Blut und Boden*, on the Hegehof, which resembled the later farming communities formed at Hegewald in 1942–43. Darré was born in 1895 in a German settlement in Argentina and attended a British public school as well as the *Kolonialschule* at Witzenhausen. See his biography in *Das Deutsche Führerlexikon 1934/1935*, 21–22. See also Corni and Gies, "*Blut und Boden*."

9 Wippermann, *Der "deutsche Drang nach Osten."*

10 Steinweis, "Eastern Europe and the Notion of the 'Frontier,'" 61–63.

11 Ibid., 56–69.

12 Herwig, "*Geopolitik*," 218–41.

13 See the discussion of Germanic utopias in Mosse, *The Crisis of German Ideology*, 113, 114. On women, see Harvey, *Women and the Nazi East*, 1–22.

14 See the most recent analysis of Ludendorff's Ober Ost Administration: Liulevicius, *War Land on the Eastern Front*, 8. See the discussion of Paul Rohrbach's influence in Fedyshyn, *Germany's Drive to the East*, 24–25. On comparisons of the First and Second World War occupations, see Torke and Himka, eds., *German-Ukrainian Relations*.

15 See Ihor Kamenetsky, "German Colonization Plans in Ukraine during World Wars I and II," in *German-Ukrainian Relations*, ed. Torke and Himka, 95–99.

16 Mosse, *The Crisis of German Ideology*, 116–17, and Harvey, *Women and the Nazi East*, 23–44.

17 Noakes and Pridham, *Nazism: A Documentary Reader*, 1:14–15.

18 From DNVP activist Gottlob Traub, cited in Murphy, *The Heroic Earth*, 195.

19 Ibid., 193. On the Reich's Colonial Association, see Hildebrand, *Vom Reich zum Weltreich*.

20 Reprint of the Hossbach memorandum from 5 Nov. 1937 meeting, in Hildebrand, *Vom Reich zum Weltreich*, 682.

21 Schmokel, *Dream of Empire*, 95.

22 German ideologies of expansion—Lebensraum, settler colonialism, and Weltpolitik—are examined by W. Smith, *The Ideological Origins of Nazi Imperialism*.

23 Hitler monologue of 17 Sept. 1941, *Hitler's Table Talk*, 34.

24 Hitler monologues of 8–11 Aug. 1941, ibid., 24.

25 Among the Germanic types Hitler counted the Dutch, Luxembourgers, Danes, the Flemish, Swedes, Norwegians, Alsatians, and the blond-haired, blue-eyed Ukrainian children. According to Speer's account, Hitler also stated that the loss of a few hundred thousand Germans on the battlefield did not play a role, since these losses could be easily made up in two or three years. Speer, *Spandau*, 46–49.

26 Kershaw, *Hitler, 1936–1945*, 400–405.

27 Hitler monologue of 22 Aug. 1942, *Hitler's Table Talk*, 654–55.

28 Alsdorf, *Indien*, 64.

29 *Hitler's Table Talk*, 654–55.

30 Schmaltz and Sinner, "The Nazi Ethnographic Research of Georg Leibbrandt and Karl Stumpp," 28–64.

31 General Commissar Klemm memo to district commissars, 27 Feb. 1942, ZSA, P-1151c-1-21. Books for administrators in the NSDAP library are listed in ZSA, P-1151-1-104.

32 Heinrich Himmler speech at Hegewald, Zhytomyr, Ukraine, 16 Sept. 1942, NA, RG 242, T-175/R 90/p.18.

33 On the general appeal of the British model and transfer of imperial concepts, see Schumacher, "The American Way of Empire," 35–50.

34 Nazi racial theorists were also fascinated with India, which they claimed as their Aryan heritage. See Lixfield and Dow, *Folklore and Fascism*; Poliakov, *The Aryan Myth*; and Kater, *Das "Ahnenerbe" der SS*.

35 On the tabula rasa mentality and anti-Bolshevism, see Dr. Guilleaume's "Gedanken zur Verwaltungsorganisation des Ostraumes," NA, RG 242, T-454/R156/99-498 (MR 336), and Aly and Heim, *Vordenker der Vernichtung*.

36 *Hitler's Table Talk*, 588–89.

37 Informationsblätter Polizeischulungsleiter, Der Befehlshaber der Ordnungspolizei für die Ukraine, "Wie verhält sich die deutsche Polizei der einheimischen Bevölkerung im Osten gegenüber?" 29 May 1942, ZSA, P1151-1-147a, p.5.

38 Epp tried to convince the Nazi leadership and German public of the importance of overseas colonies and contributed to the bitter anti-Versailles sentiment and rationales for remilitarizing Germany. See Epp's *Deutschlands koloniale Forderung*.

39 On passing references to Togo-Gesellschaft and Togo-Ost, see USHMM, RG 31.002M, reel 2 and reel 4, in the selected records from the former Archive of October Revolution, Kiev, now the CSA. The collaboration between the Kaiser's agents in Togo and Booker T. Washington's institute has been explored in Zimmerman, "The Tuskegee Institute in German Togo and the Construction of Race in the Atlantic World."

40 Wildenthal, *German Women for Empire*, 197.

41 I am grateful to David Furber for the information on East Africans in the Warthegau, and additional material about colonialist thinking and policies in Poland. See *Litzmannstädter Zeitung*, USHMM Newspaper Collection. Also see Furber's doctoral dissertation, "Going East."

42 Kershaw, *Hitler, 1936–1945*, 384.

Chapter Two

1 In the northern section of the Commissariat, the Polissia lowlands, the "rate of urbanization actually dropped by 5 per cent between 1926 and 1939," according to Krawchenko, *Social Change and National Consciousness*, 119.

2 An Abwehr official from Army Group South wrote this in Oct. 1941. See "Stimmung und Lage beim Einmarsch der deutschen Truppen," Abwehr II bei Heeresgruppe Süd, 28 Oct. 1941, NA, RG 242, T-77/R 1028/6500707.

3 "Erlass Adolf Hitlers vom 13. Mai 1941 über die Ausübung der Kriegsgerichtsbarkeit," in *Europa unterm Hakenkreuz*, ed. N. Müller, 132, and *Verbrechen der Wehrmacht*, ed. Hamburger Institut für Sozialforschung, 46–49. For the pre-Barbarossa planning of mass murder with a particular emphasis on the complete annihilation of the Jewish population, see Breitman, *The Architect of Genocide*, 145–66.

4 See testimony of Leeb, NMT, High Command Case XII, vol. 10, 1090–91. The Commissar Order is found in NA, RG 238, NOKW-1076. Bechler testified in Dec. 1943. See Breitman, *The Architect of Genocide*, 284 n. 21.

5 On the Hitler address of 30 Mar. 1941 and the orders leading up to the "Guidelines" and Commissar Order, see Hans-Adolf Jacobsen, "Kommissarbefehl und Massenexekutionen sowjetischer Kriegsgefangener," in *Anatomie des SS-Staates*, ed. Buchheim et al., 144–52.

6 This top-secret memo, "Guidelines," was distributed to the division level by Jodl with his instructions for further distribution (to battalion level on 15 June 1941). Jodl "Guidelines" to division commanders, received by Security Division 454 on 8 June 1941, KTB SD454 Anlage, NA, RG 242, T-315/R 2215/000711–13. Additional documentation about the murder of civilians in conjunction with the invasion has been published in Jacobsen, "Kommissarbefehl und Massenexekutionen," 166–94.

7 The "Guidelines" memo was distributed to the company level. The OKW chief, Alfred Jodl, set forth the use of this memo and propaganda measures for the invasion of June 1941. See "Aus den Weisungen des Chefs des OKW vom Juni 1941 zur propagandistischen Beeinflussung der Angehörigen der Roten Armee und der sowjetischen Zivilbevölkerung," in *Die Faschistische Okkupationspolitik*, ed. N. Müller, 153–55.

8 Meeting identified in the war diary of SD454, under 20 June 1941 entry. See specific instructions on the handling of civilians, "Freischärlern usw.," and political commissars in the meeting notes, "Kommandeur Besprechung vom 20 Juni 1941," in KTB SD454 Anlage, NA, RG 242, T-315/R 2215/000393 and 000684–5.

9 Additionally, the Eleventh Army of German and Romanian troops fell under Army Group South and served as the spearhead into Ukraine's southern borderlands (with Einsatzgruppe D). For a complete "order of battle" of Army Group South, June–July 1941, see Militärgeschichtliches Forschungsamt, ed., *Germany and the Second World War*, 4:550–55.

10 AOK 17 Ic/AO, 8 and 9 July 1941, NA, RG 242, T-312/R 674/8038278–9.

11 Former WWII Soviet pilot from Zhytomyr, Pavlo Gorlach, interview by author, 15 May 1996, Zhytomyr, Ukraine.

12 Mordechai Altshuler, "Escape and Evacuation of Soviet Jews," in *The Holocaust in the Soviet Union*, ed. Dobroszycki and Gurock, 94–96.

13 Ibid., 94.

14 Later in July the SD found in Zhytomyr local Soviet orders for the systematic destruction of "the entire property of state, for example, buildings and supplies." According to the SD, the Soviet order also called for the evacuation of political commissars, Russians, and "Jews." Meldungen der Einsatzgruppen und -kommandos, Einsatzgruppe C, Standort Chitomir [sic], 29 July 1941, NA, RG 242, T-175/R 233/pp. 7–10. Some of the material destruction was described in the local newspaper. For example, in the village of Baronivka there were, before the Nazi invasion, 170 houses, but only seven remained. In Yaltsivka there had been 240 houses, but in Sept. only nine remained; see *Ukraïns'ke Slovo* (Zhytomyr), 7 Sept. 1941, ZSA, Newspaper Collection.

15 Near the city of Zhytomyr, German SS and police discovered the mutilated remains of former prisoners; body parts had been crammed into sewers and drain pipes and dropped into wells. The SS took photos of the atrocities, generally for propaganda purposes, and retaliated against the local Jews who were publicly blamed for the atrocities. See interrogation of Viktor Trill, Paul Blobel's driver, 25 June 1960,

BAL, 207 AR-Z 419/62; and article in *Ukraïns'ke Slovo* (Zhytomyr), 17 Aug. 1941, ZSA, Newspaper Collection.

16 See intelligence report of 60 Inf. Div. (Mot) to General Command of 48th A.K., 13 July 1941. NA, RG 242, T-314/R1146/000425.

17 See "Morgenmeldung 16 I.D. (mot)" from Oblt. Holtermann, 10 July 1941, NA, RG 242, T-314/R1146/000277.

18 The Stalin Line, though based on the defensive principle of France's Maginot Line, was in Soviet Russia a disconnected network of fortified districts. In Zhytomyr sections of the Stalin Line were around Zviahel (Novohrad-Volyns'kyi) and Vinnytsia. Clark, *Barbarossa*, 30–31.

19 See report from "Zviahel" (MG Batls 86 and 56) to AOK Panzergruppe I, dated 9 July 1941, NA, RG 242, T-313/R10/7241488.

20 Panzer Gruppe 1, Abt. Ic/AO, 9 July 1941, NA, RG 242, T-314/R 1146/000267–268.

21 60.Inf.Div Ic, to 48th AK Ic, 11 July 1941 NA, RG 242, T-314/R 1146/000340–341 and 000424.

22 A report states that 50 to 60 percent carried the leaflet. Fernspruch 16 Pz.-Div., 14 July 1941, NA, RG 242, T-314/R 1146/000467.

23 48th AK to Panzergruppe 1 Ic/AO, 11 July 1941, NA, RG 242, T-314/R 1146/000315–6.

24 48th AK to Panzergruppe I, 13, 14, and 16 July 1941, NA, RG 242, T-314/R 1146/000424, 000468, 000544–5.

25 See report of AOK 17, Ic from 19 July 1941, section (3), NA, RG 242, T-312/R 676/8310377.

26 AOK 6 Ic reported that around Zhytomyr and in the woods many tanks and planes were abandoned by the Russians. NA, RG 242, T-312/R1406/000299.

27 In addition to the Heydrich-Wagner agreement, their collusion was spelled out in an OKH memo of 28 Apr. 1941 about how the army should support the SS security forces in their "special tasks." See NMT, High Command Case XII, NOKW-2080 and NOKW-3234. These OKH documents about SD-military cooperation are reprinted in *Anatomie des SS-Staates*, ed. Buchheim et al., 2:171–73. Kuno Callsen, a member of the Vorkommando of SK4a, stated that the military column was interrupted by two vehicles of their commando, that the SD arrived in Zhytomyr "unter Panzerdeckung." Interrogation of Kuno Callsen, 28 June 1965, Trial of Kuno Callsen, BAL, 207 AR-Z 419/62; also described in Streit, *Keine Kameraden*, 112.

28 In addition to serving as the heads of household during wartime, young women in Ukraine were often overburdened with three or four children by the age of twenty, a situation stemming largely from the lack of contraception and Stalin's ban on abortions in 1936; see Ereignismeldung Einsatzgruppe C, Standort Zhitomir, 1 Aug. 1941, NA, RG 242, T-175/R 233, 17–18. Ereignismeldung Einsatzgruppe C, 7 Aug. 1941, NA, RG 242, T-175/R 233. Krawchenko, *Social Change and National Consciousness*, 129. On the population trends and increase of women in nonskilled and agricultural work, see Lapidus, *Women in Soviet Society*, 113, 172–77.

29 There were also a number of petty bureaucrats from state and Communist Party

offices who continued to work in the German administration. Abteilung Statistik, Zhytomyr General Commissariat, ZSA, P1151-1-700. *Deutsche Ukraine-Zeitung* (Luts'k), 13 Feb. 1942, 3, Library of Congress, newspaper microfilm 3010.

30 Most could read; fewer among the peasantry could write. The population density was on average forty-eight persons per square kilometer. On the lower end, the population density in Olevs'k was eighteen persons per square kilometer. See surveys dated Oct. 1941, Abteilung Statistik, Zhytomyr Commissariat, ZSA, P1151-1-700.

31 Heyer, *Die Orthodoxe Kirche in der Ukraine*, 170–71.

32 Army officials wrote that the Ukrainians in the Zhytomyr region responded with "surprising friendliness"; see Bfh.rück.H.Geb. 103, 11 July 1941, NA, RG 242, T-501/R 5/000482; and the intelligence report of AOK 17 (Ic) from 16 July 1941, NA, RG 242, T-312/R 674/8308271.

33 Ukrainian refugees interviewed in the early 1950s explained that at first they were unaware of Hitler's racial ideology and the brutal nature of the Nazi regime, and believed that the Germans were good people who "didn't kill." They were relieved that the Germans had forced out the Bolsheviks. See, for example, Human Resources Research Institute, *Harvard University Refugee Project*, vol. 15, Interviews no. 284, A Schedule, 8; and no. 285, 54.

34 See Foreign Office report on Ukrainians 1941–43 dated Mar. 1943. NA, RG242, T-454/R 92/001022-26.

35 This leaflet is among the attachments to the war diary of AOK 17, from mid-July 1941 (it appears in German and Ukrainian). NA, RG 242, T-501/R 674/8308414. In a second leaflet to the mayors or village elders, the army stressed that the Ukrainian leaders were responsible for order in their town and that agricultural quotas had to be met until 15 Oct. 1941. The leaflet closed with an appeal to religious freedoms. KTB Bfh.rückw.H.Geb.Süd., leaflet dated 19 July 1941, NA, RG 242, T-501/R 5/000518.

36 Berkhoff, "Was There a Religious Revival . . . ?," 538.

37 See the OUN-B activist report on Ukrainian activities near Zhytomyr (district Tschernjachow), 25 July 1941, ZSA, P1151-1-13. Similar developments are described in Heyer, *Die Orthodoxe Kirche*, 170–72.

38 Berkhoff, "Was There a Religious Revival . . . ?," 549–50, and *Harvest of Despair*, 83–84.

39 Ilnytzkyj, *Deutschland und die Ukraine*, 173–94; Matla, *Pivdenna pokhidna hrupa*, 1. Matla was the leader of the southern marching group.

40 For lists of sympathizers by village, see the OUN-B file in ZSA, P1151c-1-2.

41 See Armstrong, *Ukrainian Nationalism*, 55, 60–61; and Matla, *Pivdenna pokhidna hrupa*, 9, who describes the activists traveling by night through waterways.

42 The ID printing shop was discovered by the SD in Mar. 1942. NA, RG 242, T-175/R 235/2724106.

43 Myroslav Prokop (b. in Przemysl, 1914) attended L'viv and Berlin Universities. He

was imprisoned by the Poles in his campaign to resist Polonization of Ukrainian schools in Galicia; when he was released in 1938, he fled to Berlin. He was an OUN-B underground leader, moving from L'viv to Kiev between July 1941 and Apr. 1942. In Kiev, he was the editor of the nationalist organ *Ideia i Chyn*. In 1943 he organized the Ukrainian radio broadcast in the Carpathian Mountains, providing news about Ukraine in French, English, and Ukrainian. He also helped organize the Supreme Liberation Council in July 1944. Author's interview with Prokop, 15 Mar. 1995, Shevchenko Society, New York. Prokop's identification with the youth is reflective of the composition of the OUN; in 1941 the movement had nearly 20,000 members, and about half of them were under the age of twenty-one. Krawchenko, *Social Change and National Consciousness*, 157.

44 See the captured OUN-B documents on the goals of revolution, ZSA, P1151-1-2.

45 On the proclamation at L'viv and its suppression by the Germans, see Armstrong, *Ukrainian Nationalism*, 54–59.

46 Matla also describes the distribution of this "history" in *Pivdenna pokhidna grupa*, 28. SD interrogations were led by Razesberger in Zhytomyr between Jan. and Mar. 1942. Many of those brought in were implicated by captured Bandera reports in which their names appeared as sympathizers; some of those arrested had been working in the German administration, such as Mykola Klymenko, who was the Ukrainian mayor of Novyi Muropil', Iwan Petschersky, an active militia and then *Schutzmann* in Novohrad-Volyns'kyi, and Nikita Pyvovar, the chairman of the district administration of Cherniakhiv. ZSA, P1151-1-16.

47 The nationalist "Buiny" also emphasized the heavy drinking among local leaders. ZSA, P1151-1-2.

48 Nationalist reports concur that the local Ukrainian militia plundered, murdered, and molested civilians. See Security Division 454's report "Stand der Militärverwaltung," 4 Oct. 1941, NA, RG 242, T-315/R 2216/000213.

49 Kornienko report of 25 July 1941, ZSA, P1151-1-2.

50 Ukrainians developed strong anti-Hungarian and anti-Romanian attitudes, calling the Hungarians "Austrian Huns" because the Hungarian troops were pillaging the farms and taking away everything that was "not nailed down." Roques to General Staff, 7 Sept 1941, Bfh.rückw.H.Geb.Süd., NA, RG 242, T-501/R5/000848-9.

51 A former official of the Union of Germans Abroad and key negotiator with the Soviets (1939–40) over the resettlement of ethnic Germans from Soviet (East Poland) zones, Hoffmeyer was also named the Führer's deputy for resettlement matters in treaties and agreements with Romania in 1940. Koehl, RKFDV, 64. Heinemann, "*Rasse, Siedlung, deutsches Blut.*"

52 On early Vomi-SD campaigns applying the German People's List, see Fleischhauer, *Das Dritte Reich*, 185.

53 Lumans, *Himmler's Auxiliaries*, 244. Introduction to Klaus Siebert Case, BAL, 45 Js 26/62. Siebert was Hoffmeyer's deputy in Transnistria 1941–42, and in 1943 he was made chief of the VoMi office in Zhytomyr.

54 See Einsatzgruppe C Report, 6 Sept. 1941, "Lage der Volksdeutschen in Shitomir," NA, RG 242, T-175/R 233/2722221-5.

55 Rosenberg responded to Stalin's order about the evacuation of Volksdeutsche and dissolution of the Volga German oblast by asserting that the Jews would be held responsible for the plight of the ethnic Germans under Soviet rule. See Fleischhauer, "The Ethnic Germans under Nazi Rule," in Fleischhauer and Pinkus, *The Soviet Germans: Past and Present*, 83–84.

56 See the situation report of Gebietskommissar Schmidt of Novohrad-Volyns'kyi from early 1942, ZSA, P1151-1-142.

57 Karl Stumpp report of Aug. 1942, from CSA, Kiev, microfilm held at USHMM, RG 31.002M, reel 11. The office of Gebietskommissar Schmidt in Novohrad-Volyns'kyi also reported that Ukrainians concealed ethnic Germans during the Soviet retreat; see the "situation report," early 1942 (date illegible), ZSA, P1151-1-142.

58 See "RR" report of 30 July 1941, ZSA, P1151-1-2.

59 SD case of Mark Koval's'kyi, Dec. 1941, ZSA, P1151-1-3.

60 See Boss statements of 23 June 1965 and 6 July 1966, Kuno Callsen et al., BAL, 207 AR-Z 419/62. On the Volksdeutsche informant network attached to EGC, see the report of 11 Sept. 1941, NA, RG 242, T-175/R 233/2722288. In another case the female ethnic German translator attached to the Khmil'nyk gendarmerie identified Jews and was accused of shooting Jewish children during a ghetto-clearing action there; see "Abschlussbericht," Litin Commissariat Case, BAL, 204a AR-Z 135/67, p. 53. Outside the Zhytomyr region, in the Romanian-occupied Ukrainian territory known as Transnistria, members of the ethnic German "Selbstschutz" were significant perpetrators of the Holocaust.

61 See the reports of Commander Markull on appointing native district leaders, Aug. 1941, Vinnytsia State Archive, 1275-3-662, microfilm held at USHMM, RG 31.011M, reel 92.

62 On Polish persecution of Ukrainians, see German Consul's files from L'viv and Katowice, 1938–39, NA, RG 242, DW Files, Box 24, folder 20a.

63 See "RR" reports, ZSA, P1151-1-13. Later the OUN-B lashed out against the Poles in 1943; the Polish underground retaliated, resulting in a near civil war. The Germans used photographs of these Polish-Ukrainian atrocities to promote themselves as civilized and to portray the Ukrainian nationalists and Poles as savages. See RKU decree about Ukrainian-Polish atrocities, 19 May 1943, ZSA, P1182-1-6; and General Commissar Zhytomyr "Lagebericht," 5 June 1943 (which mentions a meeting with Rosenberg in Rivne to discuss Polish atrocities against Ukrainians), Bundesarchiv Koblenz, R6/310. Armstrong describes Ukrainian-Polish conflicts, *Ukrainian Nationalism*, 131 n. 30. The worst clashes occurred in Volhynia; see Snyder, *The Reconstruction of Nations*, 165–201.

64 See OUN-B reports, ZSA, P1151-1-13; Berkhoff, "Was There a Religious Revival . . . ?," 548.

65 *Ukraïns'ke Slovo* (Zhytomyr), 19 July 1941, ZSA, Newspaper Collection.

66 This order was issued by the General Staff of the 48th AK to Panzergruppe I on 16 July 1941, NA, RG 242, T-314/R 1146/000531.

67 See "Besondere Anordnungen für die Behandlung der ukrainischen Frage," NA, RG 242, T-501/R 5/000482–3. Panzergruppe I, Ic/AO, 16 July 1941, NA, RG 242, T-314/R 1146/000531; KTB SD454 Anlage zum Div. Befehl Nr. 59, "Merkblatt über Sofort-aufgaben der Ortskommandanturen," NA, RG 242, T-315/R 2216/000091–94; AOK 17, Ic/AO, 10 Aug. 1941; NA, RG 242, T-501/R 674/8308394.

68 See report of Panzergruppe I, Ic/AO, NA, RG 242, T-314/R 1146/000606.

69 Division Orders of SD454, 28 Aug. 1941, NA, RG 242, T-315/R 2216/000065–66.

70 The notice to form a Ukrainian police in the city of Zhytomyr appeared in Ukraïns'ke Slovo (Zhytomyr), 30 July 1941, ZSA, Newspaper Collection.

Chapter Three

1 The Wehrmacht field commander in Zhytomyr was Colonel Riedl, who was suc-ceeded by Colonel Kefer (FK 197). By the end of July, field commanders were also posted at Zviahel (Novohrad-Volyns'kyi) and Berdychiv; during Aug. the army posted more commanders in Korosten', Ovruch, Koziatyn, Korostyshiv, and Radomyshl'.

2 As more representatives of German agencies began to arrive, departments of the oblast administration were phased out, and Ukrainians were sent to the German labor office for reassignment. Order to transfer Zhytomyr to Roques jurisdiction, 21 July 1941, NA, RG 242, T-501/R 5/000529–30.

3 According to a member of SK4a, one of the main reasons that they ventured to this town in the first weeks was the operating food industries that lay on a good street about fifty kilometers northeast of Zhytomyr. Kuno Callsen Trial, BAL, 204 AR-Z 269/1960, Urteil, Fall VII Radomyshl', 343.

4 See report of Field Commander 675, Dr. Markull, 14 Aug. 1941. RGVA, 1275-3-662, microfilm held at USHMM, RG11.001M.13, reel 92. Vinnytsia leaders are also men-tioned in Weiner, Making Sense of War, 246, and Armstrong, Ukrainian Nationalism, 195.

5 On militia and plundering, see Ukraïns'ke Slovo (Zhytomyr), 24 Aug. 1941, ZSA, Newspaper Collection. Regarding the Ukrainian police and other aides, see FK 675 report of 1 Aug. 1941, RGVA, 1275-3-662, microfilm held at USHMM, RG 11.001M.13, reel 92.

6 The troop commander established the administration on 22 July 1941. See FK 675 report of 1 Aug. 1941, Osobyi 1275-3-662, microfilm at USHMM, RG 11.001M.13, reel 92. See Armstrong, Ukrainian Nationalism, 195. See reports of Markull, FK 675, "Lageberichte," 14 Aug. 1941 and 30 Aug. 1941 from RGVA, 1275-3-662, microfilm held at USHMM, RG 11.001M.13, reel 92.

7 See FK 675 Abt VII (Mil-Verw.), reports of 11 Aug., 14 Aug., 25 Aug., 30 Aug. 1941, RGVA, 1275-3-662, microfilm held at USHMM, RG 11.001M.13, reel 92.

8 See Roques order of 14 July 1941, NA, RG 242, T-501/R 5/000494–5. "Resettlement

opportunity" refers to the Nazi-Soviet agreement that ethnic Germans in Soviet zones be allowed to resettle to the Reich. On treaties of 1939–40, see Koehl, RKFDV.

9 Roques order of 16 Aug. 1941, NA, RG 242, T-501/R 5/000803; Holos Volyni (Zhytomyr), 30 Oct 1941, ZSA, Newspaper Collection.

10 According to Markull's report, the SD decimated the first "Judenrat" in Aug.; the new Jewish Council was generally cooperating, though one member had to be eliminated for "political incrimination." See FK 675 report of 30 Aug. 1941, RGVA, 1275-3-662, microfilm held at USHMM, RG 11001M.13, reel 92. On the asylum in Vinnytsia, see Alexander Kruglov, Unichtozhenie evreiskogo naseleniia v Vinnitskoi oblasti v 1941–1944.

11 KTB SD454 Anlage zum Div. Befehl Nr. 59, "Merkblatt über Sofortaufgaben der Ortskommandanturen," NA, RG 242, T-315/R 2216/000091–94.

12 These locations are situated between the Dnister and Bug rivers, which were later part of Romanian-occupied Ukraine.

13 A week following this trip, Markull traveled to the north, toward Koziatyn and Berdychiv, where he came across more Reich Germans in building battalions and railway troops. Local administrators under the direction of German town and field commanders had also begun repair work and even the reopening of schools. FK 675 report of 25 Aug. 1941, RGVA, 1275-3-662, microfilm held at USHMM, RG 11.001M.13, reel 92.

14 See the Seventeenth Army Headquarters order on the formation of local administrations, NA, RG 242, T-501/R 674/8308420.

15 See the FK 675 report of 30 Aug. 1941, RGVA, 1275-3-662, microfilm held at USHMM, RG11.001M.13, reel 92. A similar report details the population composition and local leaders found at Lityn, Khmil'nyk, Ulaniv, Machnivka, Samhorodok, Kalynivka, Voronovytsia, and Nemyriv. See the FK 675 report of 25 Aug. 1941, RGVA, 1275-3-662, microfilm held at USHMM, RG11.001M.13, reel 92.

16 FK 675 reports of Aug. 1941, RGVA, 1275-3-662, microfilm held at USHMM, RG 11.001M.13, reel 92; General Commissar's "Lagebericht," 3 June 1942, Bundesarchiv Koblenz, R6/310. Brown, A Biography of No Place, 209.

17 See the German order on the formation of police in Zhytomyr and Berdychiv, signed by Iatseniuk, which specified that there should be one policeman for every ten households. Ukraïns'ke Slovo (Zhytomyr), 30 July 1941, ZSA, Newspaper Collection.

18 See order of Seventeenth Army Headquarters, Vinnytsia, 12 July 1941, NA, RG 242, T-501/R 674/8308420.

19 Black, "Police Auxiliaries for Operation Reinhard." I am grateful to Dr. Black for material on Trawniki guards from Zhytomyr.

20 On the army's formation of Ukrainian Hilfspolizei and militia groups, see 11 July 1941 order, NA, RG 242, T-501/R 5/000482-3; and 14 Sept. 1941 order, NA, RG 242, T-315/R 2216/000098-100. The formation of militias by the army is documented by the OUN-B underground situation reports, July–Nov. 1941, ZSA, P1151-1-13; on 30 July 1941, in Ukraïns'ke Slovo, the army commander announced the formation

of Ukrainian police. See Army Group South Rundstedt order on the formation of Ukrainian Hilfspolizei, which he placed under the command of the army's security divisions and the HSSPF, NA, RG 242, T-501/R5/00916–918. Captain Dietrich of SD454 tally of Hilfspolizei, 4 Oct. 1941, NA, RG 242, T-315/R 2216/000213.

21 Records of the FK 675 Vinnytsia, Aug, 1941, RGVA, 1275-3-662, USHMM, RG 11.001M.13, reel 92.

22 See the SS and police leader from Ruzhyn's "Tätigkeitsbericht" on "Witowzi," Mar. 1943, ZSA, P1452-1-2.

23 See letters, many written by women, in Vinnytsia State Archive, P2383-2-41, microfilm held at USHMM, RG31.011M, reel 9.

24 Letter of 20 Aug. 1941, regarding Cholm POW camp, Vinnytsia State Archive, P1311-1-1, microfilm held at USHMM, RG31.011M, reel 1.

25 See the announcement about a Ukrainian Red Cross in Holos Volyni (Zhytomyr), 27 Nov. 1941, ZSA, Newspaper Collection.

26 See FK 675, Lagebericht, section (2), Arbeitsamt, 14 Aug. 1941, RGVA, 1275-3-662, microfilm held at USHMM, RG 11.001M.13, reel 92.

27 See KTB SD454 Anlage zum Div. Befehl Nr. 59, "Merkblatt über Sofortaufgaben der Ortskommandanturen," NA, RG 242, T-315/R 2216/000094.

28 See the order by Roques stating that anyone who did not register for work would be treated as a partisan and shot. Ukraïns'ke Slovo (Zhytomyr), 14 Aug. 1941, ZSA, Newspaper Collection; also see the German order presented by Bürgermeister Pavlovsky, Zhytomyr, stating that those who did not work would not receive goods and rations. Ukraïns'ke Slovo (Zhytomyr), 17 Aug. 1941, ZSA, Newspaper Collection.

29 Soviet raion leaders received 750 rubles. The Germans promoted these higher wages in the first weeks of the occupation before inflation set in; the wages later proved to be inadequate. See German report on wages for local leaders, 22 Aug. 1941, Bfh. rückw.H.Geb.Süd., NA, RG242, T-501/R 5/000752–3. The Soviet wages are from Fitzpatrick, Stalin's Peasants, 175.

30 The "Dienstanweisung für den Rayonchef" contained broadly defined measures, such as maintaining peace and order; subordinates turned them into specific practices. Compare FK675 Abt VII, 26 July 1941, RGVA, 1275-3-662, microfilm held at USHMM, RG11.001M.13, reel 92, with Vinnytsia State Archives 1417-3c-1, microfilm held at USHMM, RG 31.011M, reel 4.

31 See the Jan Lazar order, from Tul'chyn, 17 Nov. 1941: "Any mayors who do not comply with German orders or who issue false IDs will be treated like spies." Vinnytsia State Archive, P1417-3c-1, microfilm held at USHMM, RG31.011M, reel 4.

32 Keitel memo of 12 Sept. 41, NA, RG 242, T-77/R 1028/6500510. Like Reichenau's memo that followed, the highest-level commanders sought to impress upon subordinates the ideological basis of the campaign and anti-Jewish measures. Reichenau order of 10 Oct. 1941, NA, RG 242, T-315/R 2216/000283.

33 Soviet sources focus on Markull, stating that as early as 29 July 1941 he ordered the killing of twenty-five hostages in the quarry near Pjatnitschany and an additional

350 persons in the beginning of Aug. (most of the victims' names were Jewish). See the Soviet (Russian, Ukrainian, and Jewish) witness statements, investigation of Schmidt and Danner, BAL, 204a AR-Z 122/68 and 136/67, 45, 299, 303, and in *History Teaches a Lesson*, 240.

34 Berkhoff, *Harvest of Despair*, 64.

35 See Chief of General Staff memo drafted to troops, AOK 17 Ic/AO, 8 July 1941, NA, RG 242, T-501/R 674/8308425.

36 One of the first published sources on Wehrmacht crimes was Major Rössler's report concerning the killing of Zhytomyr's Jews; a reprint is in N. Müller, *Okkupation, Raub, Vernichtung*.

37 Roques was born in 1880; he served as a general staff officer in World War I and became a divisional commander in Dec. 1939. He was commander of Rear Area Army Group South from Mar. 1941 until 15 June 1942 (due to illness, he was replaced by Erich Friderici from 27 Oct. 1941 to 10 Jan. 1942). Later he was appointed commander of Rear Army Area Group A (Caucasus) and retired with the rank of lieutenant general in Dec. 1942. Roques was convicted by the American Military Tribunal at Nuremberg. See NMT, vol. 11, 630.

38 See Roques secret order "Befriedungsmassnahmen," 29 July 1941 in KTB Bfh.rückw.H.Geb.Süd., NA, RG 242, T-501/R 5/000476. Secret Order of Commander Rear Army South stated that recently "soldiers and officers have on their own undertaken the shooting of Jews . . . but this is expressly the work of the HSSPF." 1 Sept. 1941, KTB SD454, NA, RG 242, T-315/R 2216/000081.

39 Kriegsgerichtliche Verurteilungen, 5 Nov. 1941–16 Dec. 1941, ZSA, P1151-1-21.

40 As the military commander of Nazi-occupied France, Stülpnagel was later associated with the resistance groups around Halder and Beck and executed at Plötzensee (after a failed suicide attempt). He was responsible for ruthless crimes committed against civilians in Ukraine and in France, and so his association with the resistance was not based on a moral crusade against Nazism but rather a conservative, nationalist attempt to prevent Germany's defeat by Hitler. A critical biography is lacking; see basic biographical information in Wistrich, *Wer war wer*, 350.

41 Stülpnagel order, 30 July 1941, KTB, AOK 17, NA, RG 242, T-501/R 674/8308402.

42 See Stülpnagel order of 16 Aug. 1941, RGVA, 1275-3-662, microfilm held at USHMM, RG 11.001M.13, reel 92.

43 Schräder report on the handling of civilians, July 12 1941, NA, RG 242, T-501/R 674/8308418.

44 Emphasis in the original. "Behandlung der Bevölkerung und Aufrechterhaltung der Disziplin," 24 Aug. 1941, KTB AOK 6, record from AOK 17 Ic/AO, NA, RG 242, T-312/R 674/8308378.

45 An army liaison officer to the SD was posted in the intelligence unit (Ic) of army headquarters. See 30 July 1941 order, KTB AOK 17 Ic/AO, NA, RG 242, T-501/R 674/8308401.

46 AOK 6 order of 10 Aug. 1941, KTB SD454 Anlage, NA, RG 242, T-315/R 2215/

000959. About this time Reichenau also personally stood before a delegation of army and SS leaders of the First SS Brigade and expressed his recognition of the excellent successes garnered from the employment of officers and men of the EK2 in the area of Korosten'. Lagebericht, 16 Aug. 41, 1. SS Brigade, KTB Kommandostab RFSS, Records of the MHI, Prague, microfilm at USHMM, RG 48.004M, reel 1.

47 EGC event report of 20 Aug. 1941, NA, RG 242, T-175/R233/2721995.

48 Reichenau order of 10 Oct. 1941, approved by Hitler and distributed to the battalion level. NA, RG 242, T-315/R 2216/000283.

49 KTB Kommandostab RFSS, MHI, Prague, carton 1, microfilm held at USHMM, RG 48.004M, reel 1; also see Büchler, "Kommandostab Reichsführer-SS," 17–18.

50 As mentioned, one company of Orpo Battalion 82 was used by the city commander of Zhytomyr, Josef Riedl, for police tasks in the first weeks of occupation as of 19 July. The Orpo battalion was joined by Geheime Feldpolizei units and Landesschützenverbände. See war diary entry of 3 Sept. 1941 and Divisionsbefehl of 26 July 1941 in KTB SD454, NA, RG 242, T-315/R 2215/000412–14, 000446 and 000890.

51 See KTB Bfh.rückw.H.Geb.Süd., "10-tägige Meldung," 20 July 1941, NA, RG 242, T-501/R 5/000519.

52 The Breslau Orpo battalion was one of the nine motorized battalions assigned to the army's Security Divisions but not "fulfilling their tasks from the basic orders" of Himmler. The other Orpo battalions in the Zhytomyr region (nos. 318, 45, 311, 314) received orders from Higher SS and Police Leader Jeckeln. The Himmler order of 21 May 1941 regarding Orpo units in the East is reprinted in Der Krieg gegen die Sowjetunion 1941–1945, 99–100. Assignment of Orpo 82 (Breslau) in KTB SD454, 16 May 1941, NA, RG 242, T-315/R 2215/000392.

53 The Security Division 454 briefing about executions of commissars and the conduct of troops in Russia occurred on 20 June and 21 June 1941; KTB SD454, NA, RG 242, T-315/R 2215/000393–394.

54 The commander of Occupied Rear Army South wrote that in "cleansing" operations between Fastiv and Ovruch Jeckeln should work together with units of SD 454; 8 Sept. 1941, KTB Bfh.rückw.H.Geb.Süd., NA, RG, 242 T-501/R 5/000894. See intelligence activity report about military secret field police and HSSPF units' screening and handling of civilians and "smooth" relations with SD; 1–8 Aug. 1941, KTB Bfh.rückw.H.Geb.Süd., NA, RG 242, T-501/R 5 /000663–4. Security Division 213 coordinated operations with HSSPF northeast of Zviahel (Novohrad-Volyns'kyi) and in Rivne; KTB Bfh.rückw.H.Geb.Süd., NA, RG 242, T-501/R 5/ 000681–2, 000694–95.

55 Ereignismeldungen der Einsatzgruppen und -kommandos, 22 July 1941, NA, RG 242, T-175/R 233/p. 3. The SD 454 war diary shows a total of 1,486 civilians and POWs captured between 29 July and 16 Sept. 1941; of these, seventy-eight were Jews who were killed for not wearing armbands, for "assisting" partisans, or for hiding weapons. Infantry Regiment 375 was also active in the Pripiat' Marshes on 3 Sept.

1941 and supported by L.S.Btl 566; KTB SD454, NA, RG 242, T-315/R 2215/000385–469.

56 KTB SD454, NA, RG 242, T-315/R 2217/000222-219.

57 SD444 in Vinnytsia, like SD454 in Zhytomyr, went out on "cleansing" operations in the forests and villages that locals claimed were partisan areas. For Khmil'nyk action, Fernspruch, 5 Aug. 1941, and Roques report to OKH Gen Qu, 10 Aug. 1941, re: "Säuberung des noch unsicheren Gebietes," see KTB Bfh.rückw.H.Geb.Süd., NA, RG 242, T-501/R 5/000639 and 000661–662.

58 Divisionsbefehl of 22 Aug. 1941, KTB SD454, NA, RG 242, T-315/R 2216/00003.

59 In the military reports that refer to "cleansing campaigns," the Germans tended to use interchangeably terms such as "partisan," "insurgent," "commissar," "Bolshevik," and "Jew." The mixed terminology caused some confusion about how to categorize and treat captured prisoners. See Fernspruch of SD444, dated 5 Aug. 1941, KTB Bfh.rückw.H.Geb.Süd., NA, RG 242, T-501/R 5/000639.AOK17; KTB, 30 July 1941, Re: treatment of enemy civilians (partisans, youth gangs) and Russian POWs, NA, RG 242, T-501, r 674, frame 8308400-401. This term, "Freischärler," was used on a list of those targeted for execution, as defined in the pre-invasion "Guidelines" and Commissar Order; see *Anatomie des SS-Staates*, ed. Buchheim et al., 2:192. On the use of vague terminology as a deliberate concealment of crimes, see statements of Ernst Oscar Consee, 19 Mar. 1964, Trial of Kuno Callsen, BAL, 204 AR-Z 269/1960.

60 See Roques to OKH General Staff, "10-tägige Meldung," 20 Aug. 1941, in KTB of the Commander of the Rear Army Area South, NA, RG 242, T501/R 5/000970.

61 The actions of the First SS Brigade under AOK 6 in Zhytomyr best represent the intersection of army and SS goals of "pacifying" areas by killing and interning civilians (nearly all Jews) and POWs. German reports often did not specify whether the Jews were men, women, or children. For these combined SS and military "cleansing" operations, see the war diary of Kommandostab RFSS, MHI, Prague, carton 1, microfilm held at USHMM, RG 48.004M, reel 1; and the war diary of Bfh.rückw.H. Geb.Süd., NA, RG 242, T-501/R 5/000557-60. In his "Einsatzbefehl," HSSPF Jeckeln wrote that during the antipartisan action female agents and Jews should be "handled accordingly"—for example, executed; Jeckeln order of 25 July 1941, in KTB Bfh.rückw.H.Geb.Süd., NA, RG 242, T-501/R5/000559-60.

62 Arad, Krakowski, and Spector, eds., *The Einsatzgruppen Reports*, 134.

63 See Markull (FK 675) report to SD444, 11 Aug. 1941, p. 5, and 25 Aug. 1941, p. 3, RGVA, 1275-3-662, microfilm held at USHMM, RG 11.001M.13, reel 92.

64 After action reports of Security Division 213 and SS brigades in Emil'chyne, 20 Aug. 1941, NA, RG 242, T-501/R 5/000694 and 000970, HSSPF Jeckeln met with Sixth Army officers on 23 July 1941 at Zhytomyr to discuss SS brigade cleansing action scheduled for 24 July in the woods near Shepetivka; NA, RG 242, T-501/R 5/000543 and 000894-5. The First SS Brigade was made available to the AOK 6 for special security tasks in the rear areas; Aug. 1941, NA, RG 242, T-501/R 5/000695.

65 Ukrainians in the villages were also able to identify who was an outsider and asked

the German authorities where these outsiders should go. At first, Ukrainians may not have realized that their inquiries were fatal for the outsiders; but once they did understand, some tried to hide POWs. Panzergruppe I Ic/AO, 20 July 1941, NA, RG 242, T-314/R 1146/000606. Author's interview with Pavlo Gorlach, whose family hid a Russian POW.

66 See the "Operational Situation Report USSR no.86," 17 Sept. 1941, Einsatz-gruppe C, in *The Einsatzgruppen Reports*, ed. Arad, Krawkowski, and Spector, 56.

67 According to Bormann's notes from a meeting of 16 July 1941, Hitler stated, "Dieser Partisanenkrieg hat auch wieder seinen Vorteil; er gibt uns die Möglichkeit aus-zurotten, was sich gegen uns stellt." N. Müller, ed., *Die faschistische Okkupationspolitik*, 161. This is also examined in Büchler, "Kommandostab Reichsführer-SS," 14.

68 See report of Infantry Regiment 375, 9 Aug. 1941, in KTB SD454 Anlage, NA, RG 242, T-315/R 2215/000935-36.

69 Streit, *Keine Kameraden*, 350 n. 193.

70 Document #25, *Zhytomyrshchyna v period*, 74. This "reprint" of the Aug. 1941 bulletin describes German accomplices in these tortures as Ukrainian Petliurists (nation-alists).

71 Gross, *Neighbors*.

72 AOK 17 order of 10 Aug. 1941, NA, RG 242, T-501/R 674/8308393.

73 Attachment Division Order #49 (no date), on handling of civilian prisoners, KTB SD454, NA, RG 242, T-315/R 2216/000063-64.

74 Ibid. The official also specified that no one from the area north of Zhytomyr near the army transport route could be released; this was a critical supply route for the Sixth Army, which was losing momentum in its northern advance on Kiev, and it was also a target of Soviet attacks.

75 Berkhoff, "The 'Russian' Prisoners of War in Nazi-Ruled Ukraine," 1–32. Dallin, *German Rule*, 409–11.

76 OKW Directive of 16 June 1941, NA, RG 238, NOKW-549, and Dallin, *German Rule*, 418.

77 Gerlach, *Kalkulierte Morde*, 44–47.

78 Streit, *Keine Kameraden*, 70–79, 169.

79 OKH order, "Behandlung feindlicher Zivilpersonen und russischer Kriegsgefang-ener im rückwärtigen Heeresgebiet," 25 July 1941, NA, RG 242, T-315/R2215/ 000919–922. Also see Roques's secret order to shoot POWs because they had not complied with German order to surrender to authorities, "Befriedungsmassnah-men," dated 29 July 1941. NA, RG 242, T-501/R 5/000476.

80 See camps identified under entry of 25 July 1941, war diary of Security Division 454, NA, RG 242, T-315/R2215/000415.

81 Stalag 358 was set up in Zhytomyr on 15 Sept. 1941 and remained until the evacua-tion of Nov. 1943. A postwar case against the camp personnel of Stalag 358 was pursued in West Germany, Dortmund prosecution 45 Js 13/69, BAL, 319 AR-Z 11/69, but not brought to trial. The subcamp of Stalag 358 located in Berdychiv was situ-

ated in the former Soviet military barracks at the edge of town. A subcamp of Stalag 329 (Vinnytsia) was also established in Berdychiv, to which POWs from Darnitsa near Kiev were transferred until the summer of 1943. Case against Friedrich Becker (SD office Berdychiv), BAL, AR-Z 129/67, vol. 4, 915–17.

82 Vlasov was brought there at the end of July 1942 to begin negotiations with members of the Nazi elite about the formation of the army. On Vlasov and the "Prominente" camp near Vinnytsia, where "there were about 80–100 prisoners who were relatively well-treated and given German rations," see Andreyev, *Vlasov and the Russian Liberation Movement*, 40–42. Also see OKH top-secret report about POWs in the operational areas and Romania, 1 Feb. 1942, WiID/33, Anlage 3, Bundesarchiv-Militärarchiv Freiburg.

83 OKH order, "Kriegsgefangenen-Arbeitseinsatz und -Abschub," and Anlage, "Russische Kriegsgefangene," dated 31 July 1941. NA, RG 242, T315/R 2215/000651–652 and 000912–14.

84 See Anlage 2, "Russische Kriegsgefangene" (no date; early Aug.?), KTB SD454, NA, RG 242, T-315/R 2215/000912–914. In these instructions Heydrich advised his commandos not to carry out the executions of prisoners in or near the camp, unless executions were necessary for "reasons of camp discipline." Heydrich order from NMT, High Command Case XII (Leeb et al.), vol. 11, 9–11. On the summer and fall 1941 Heydrich orders, see the reprints of his Einsatzbefehle 8, 9, and 14 in *Die Einsatzgruppen in der besetzten Sowjetunion*, ed. Klein, 331–41, 355–60.

85 During the invasion, initial German reports concerning POWs mention on several occasions the high number of Central Asians found in the Red Army ranks. As a racial category, these persons were slated for destruction by the Nazis. They were separated from the other POWs and killed along with the Jews; however, it is not clear from SS and army documents of 1941 how many were captured and killed in the Zhytomyr region. See instructions for the handling of POWs, KTB SD454, Aug. 1941, NA, RG 242, T-315/R 2215/000912; also, 60 Inf.Div Ic to 48th AK, 13 July 1941, T-314/R 1146/000424.

86 Fruechte testified further: "The Jews whom we kept separated in the camps were, without exception, shot by the Security Service commandos that arrived later." NMT, High Command Case XII, vol. 11, 15–17.

87 Memorandum of Dr. Letsch, Advisor, Office of the Reich Minister of Labor, meeting of 5 Dec. 1941. NMT, High Command Case XII (Leeb et al.), vol. 10, 1090.

88 Those working in operational areas were assigned to more lethal tasks such as digging up mines. POW labor in the rear areas was generally related to construction and repair work. See memo from SD454 Ia to Stalag and Dulag Kommandanten, regarding skilled workers and specialists among the POWs, 25 July 1941, KTB SD454 Anlage, NA, RG 242, T-315/R 2215/000889.

89 For example, two labor companies of three hundred POWs were taken from Zhytomyr Dulag for street work under the direction of the Organization Todt. See war diary entry of 12 Sept. 1941, KTB SD454, NA, RG242, T-315/R 2215/000453. Re-

leased Ukrainian POWs who could not be returned to their nearby hometowns were the first to be formed into labor units; see AOK 6 O.Qu., "Befehl zur Bildung von ukrainischen Arbeitskompanien," 23 Aug. 1941, NA, RG 242, T-315/R 2216/000010–11.

90 Reconstruction of roadways was the top priority as the conversion of Russian railway gauges to fit German trains was not progressing fast enough to meet the transport needs. As of 3 Oct. 1941 the only rail route that had German rail gauges was the Berdychiv-to-Zhytomyr line; the remaining routes to Kiev or north to Ovruch were not passable. See map dated 3 Oct. 1941, KTB SD454 Anlage, NA, RG 242, T-315/R 2216/000218. The roadway from Zviahel over Zhytomyr to Kiev, however, was in good condition.

91 On POWs and road construction, see SD454, [illegible day of month] Sept. 1941, SD454 order, NA, RG 242, T-315/R 2216/000106; and von Krosigk memos of 1 Aug. 41, 6 Sept. 1941, KTB Bfh. rückw.H.Geb.Süd., NA, RG 242, T-501/R 5/000608 and 000879–880.

92 On Wehrmacht village commander stations placed near DG camps, see SD454 Anlage, NA, RG 242, T-315/R 2216/000198. On POW camp Hnivan', see interrogation of former camp commandant Karl Klenk, BAL, 204 AR-Z 188/67, vol. 1, 94–98, 260–85.

93 OKH General Staff orders regarding "Kriegsgefangenen-Arbeitseinsatz und -Abschub," 31 July 1941, in KTB SD454 Anlage, NA, RG 242, T-315/R2215/000651–653.

94 Wounded or ill POWs were not treated by the Germans and were left to die among the other prisoners or were executed. They were separated as "unfit" for labor, and some were placed in "military hospitals" or in special sections of camps, found, for example, in Berdychiv. A group of crippled POWs survived in the Berdychiv camp until Dec. 1942 when the SD ordered their execution, but some escaped during the transport to the killing site; see USSR-311, Proceedings 5–19 Feb. 1946, IMT, vol. 7, 406.

95 After these thousands were left for some time in the inadequate conditions of the open air "camp" in Zviahel (Novohrad-Volyns'kyi), the survivors were marched to a stationary camp in Shepetivka. See "Bericht" of Security Division 213 from Major Münchau, 13 Aug. 1941, KTB Bfh.rückw.H.Geb.Süd., NA, RG 242, T-501/R 5/000681. In Haisyn, where the population was about fifteen thousand, the local Dulag contained at least five thousand POWs. AOK 17 report of 17 Aug. 1941, NA, RG 242, T-501/R 5/000707.

96 On 6 Oct. 1941, twelve thousand POWs from Kiev were transported to Zhytomyr; requests for the transfer of more POWs to Zhytomyr were refused by local commanders because of severe overcrowding. KTB SD454, NA, RG 242, T-315/R 2216/000469. The figure of 600,000 Soviet prisoners is from Streit, *Keine Kameraden*, 152.

97 On the Reichenau order of 31 Oct. 41, see Berkhoff, "The 'Russian' Prisoners of War in Nazi-Ruled Ukraine," 6. This order appeared after lower-level security personnel began shooting POWs during the marches in September.

98 These transports ended up in Berdychiv because the prisoners were too exhausted to continue to Shepetivka. The SD454 officer expressed regret that the prisoners in this ghastly state were seen by the local population; it was, he believed, a public embarrassment to the army. See SD454 Abt. Ic to Bfh.rückw.H.Geb.Süd, Betr: "Transporte von Kriegsgefangenen," 19 Sept. 1941, KTB SD454 NA, RG 242, T-315/R 2217/000163. On the death marches, see Berkhoff, "The 'Russian' Prisoners of War in Nazi-Ruled Ukraine," 5-6.

99 See report to General Thomas regarding POWs in civil occupied areas, 29 Nov. 1941, NA, RG 238, IMT, PS-2174.

100 Gestapo Chief Müller telegram on POWs' mortality rate, NA, RG 238 IMT 1165-PS. The Wehrmachtsbefehlshaber for RKU, Lieutenant General Kitzinger, later reported in Dec. 1941 that the death rate for POWs was 2,500 daily. This increased in Dec. to 4,300 deaths per day. See Streit, Keine Kameraden, 113.

101 Rosenberg, "Vermerk über Unterredung beim Führer am 14 Dec. 1941," NA, RG 238, PS-1517.

102 See report of the Sixth Army, "Befehl zur Bildung von ukrainischen Arbeitskompanien," 23 Aug. 1941, NA, RG 242, T-315/R 2216/000011.

103 Berkhoff, "The 'Russian' Prisoners of War in Nazi-Ruled Ukraine," 9.

104 Holos Volyni, 22 July 1941, from a Soviet war crimes investigation of Zhytomyr, reprinted in Klee and Dressen, Gott mit Uns, 37. The Bogun'ia incident is detailed in a Soviet Ukrainian study of the occupation, Zhytomyrshchyna v period, 18-19, 27-40. On the Zviahel experiment, see interrogation of August Häfner, 6 July 1965, and interrogation of Ernst W. Boernecke, 5 Nov. 1965, Trial of Kuno Callsen, BAL, 207 AR-Z 419/62. See Gerhart Panning, "Wirkungsform und Nachweis der sowjetischen Infantriesprengmunition," Der deutsche Militärarzt, Jan. 1942, Library of Congress, microfilm 0184. Panning later returned to the region in July 1943 as part of a forensics commission that examined the disinterred bodies of victims of Stalin's purges in Vinnytsia. Herber, Gerichtsmedizin unterm Hakenkreuz, 274-276.

105 The latest figures for prisoners killed in the Zhytomyr oblast alone (covering about half of the German Commissariat's population) vary between 101,293, and 101,900; that more than 100,000 were killed was determined by a 1988 memorial commission in Zhytomyr. See Stryvozhena pam'iat', 209, 240.

106 On the Berdychiv camp's mortality rates in Dec. 1941, see report of Rear Army Area South, 20 Dec. 1941, NMT, NOKW-1605. A year later this camp, a former Russian barracks, still housed some maimed POWs, about eighty, who were executed by the local SD commandos under the command of SS Hauptsturmführer Kallbach and SS Commander Fritz Knop; see Case no. 490 (Hülsdünker and Knop), Justiz und NS-Verbrechen, vol. 16. Records of Berdychiv's Sipo-SD office on this massacre

are also in IMT, USSR-311. Postwar Soviet investigators discovered in Berdychiv's Krasnaia Gora (= Red Mountain) four mass graves containing 4,832 bodies with their hands and feet tied and their skulls shattered either by a gunshot or a blunt instrument. On the 8,000 POWs shot by the SD at Krasnaia Gora, see testimony of Michail Pekelis, Case against Friedrich Becker, SD Office of Berdychiv, BAL, 204 AR-Z 129/67, vol. 2, 476, and vol. 4, 1024, 1035.

107 See the 29 Nov. 1941 report from the chief armaments inspector in Ukraine, which criticized the massacres of Jews and POWs as a loss of skilled labor. IMT, NA, RG 238, PS-2174. The conflicts over POW policy in the summer and fall of 1941 are described more extensively in Streit, *Keine Kameraden*, 191.

108 See Seventeenth Army headquarters order of 7 July 1941, NA, RG 242, T-501/R 674/8308428; Hitler objected to the release of Ukrainians. Koch later blamed the military for creating the partisan movement with the release of POWs; IMT, NA, RG 238, 1193-PS. The threat of disease was also an argument made against the release. By early Oct. the release of Ukrainian POWs was forbidden; see Division Orders, KTB SD454 Anlage, NA, RG 242, T-315/R 2216/000286.

109 Dallin, *German Rule in Russia*, 413. Berkhoff, "The 'Russian' Prisoners of War," 17.

110 Order of AOK 6, 24 July 1941, NA, RG 242, T-315/R 2215/000888–889. Formation of the Ukrainian police instructions in KTB SD454 Anlage, NA, RG 242, T-315/R2215/000917–8 and T-315/R 2216/000098–101. See Divisionsbefehl, "Entlassung von Kriegsgefangenen," 8 Sept. 1941, KTB SD454, T-315/R 2216/000089, and Quarter Master instructions, Befh. Rückw.H.Geb.Süd., according to OKH orders on release of POWs, dated 11 Aug. 1941, NA, RG 242, T-315/R 2215/000985–6.

111 Figure cited from Garrard and Garrard, *The Bones of Berdichev*, 10–11. I am grateful to the authors for sending me a copy of the German document, OKH General Staff report on POWs dated 20 Feb. 1942. This report also reveals that in Jan. 1942, in the POW camps under Army Group South, a total of 24,861 POWs perished or were shot. Bundesarchiv-Militärarchiv Freiburg, WiID/33, 94.

112 The large number of Ukrainians released, a figure that was tabulated by a Wehrmacht agency, is also a bit misleading because on the records the Germans used the term "released" when a large number of them were seized outside the camps. For example, in Berdychiv, when the formal order to release certain POWs, such as Ukrainians, was publicized near Berdychiv, the commandant of the Dulag also received a verbal order that released prisoners who were found wandering on the roads should be returned to the camp. Apparently many POWs had used false identifications, and members of Orpo Battalion 82 were sent out on patrols to reinvestigate the identity of these prisoners. See SD454 orders to local Dulag and Stalag chiefs, 1–9 Sept. 1941, KTB SD454, NA, RG 242, T-315/R 2216/000449–50.

113 See BdO [Befehlshaber der Ordnungspolizei] Tagesbefehl, 2 Feb. 1942, reprinted in the RKU "Amtliche Mitteilungen," Feb. 1942 issue, p. 13, in CSA, Kiev, 3206-6-2, microfilm held at USHMM, RG31.002M, reel 6.

114 Heydrich Operational Order No. 8, 17 July 1941 (350 copies were distributed to

SS-police and military leadership). Reprinted in NMT, High Command Case XII, vol. 11, 5.

115 See N. Müller, *Die faschistische Okkupationspolitik,* document #52. Arad, Krakowski, and Spector, eds., *The Einsatzgruppen Reports,* 3 Nov. 1941, 211–12, 218–20; and Reichenau memo of 10 Oct. 1941, NA, RG 242, T-315/R 2216/000283.

116 See Jan Philipp Reemtsma, "The Concept of the War of Annihilation: Clausewitz, Ludendorff, Hitler," in *War of Extermination,* ed. Heer and Naumann, 13–35; Rossino, *Hitler Strikes Poland,* 136–37. On World War I, see Horne and Kramer, *German Atrocities, 1914,* 419–31.

117 Isabel V. Hull, "Military Culture and the Production of 'Final Solutions' in the Colonies," in *The Specter of Genocide,* ed. Gellately and Kiernan, 161–62.

118 Bartov, *The Eastern Front, 1941–45* and *Hitler's Army.* Earlier work—first by prosecutors in the NMT High Command Case XII and then by German historians (for example, Streit, Jacobsen, Krausnick, Messerschmidt, and Förster)—elucidated the crimes and ideological disposition of the Wehrmacht. Wehrmacht crimes continue to be the topic of public demonstrations and conflicts in Germany today; see Heer and Naumann, eds., *War of Extermination.*

119 Schulte, *The German Army,* 289–92.

Chapter Four

The quotation used as the epigraph is from an interview by the author, 20 May 1996. Iurii Alekseevich Kiian was born in Ljubar, 1 Apr. 1929. In 1943 he was deported to Leipzig as an Ostarbeiter and worked in an armaments factory.

1 Dieter Pohl, "The Murder of Ukraine's Jews under German Military Administration and in the Reich Commissariat Ukraine," in *The Shoah in Ukraine,* ed. R. Brandon and W. Lower (forthcoming).

2 General Commissariat "Lagebericht," *Judenfrage,* 3 June 1942, Bundesarchiv Koblenz, R6/310, p. 6.

3 Pohl, *Nationalsozialistische Judenverfolgung in Ostgalizien,* and "Schauplatz Ukraine: Der Massenmord an den Juden im Militärverwaltungsgebiet und im Reichskommissariat 1941–1943," in *Ausbeutung, Vernichtung, Öffentlichkeit,* ed. Frei, 135–73. Angrick, *Besatzungspolitik und Massenmord;* Dean, "The German Gendarmerie, the Ukrainian Schutzmannschaft, and the 'Second Wave' of Jewish Killings in Occupied Ukraine," 168–92; Dean, *Collaboration in the Holocaust;* Penter, "Die Lokale Gesellschaft im Donbass unter deutscher Okkupation," 183–223.

4 See Browning, *The Origins of the Final Solution,* 307–14. More recent regional studies follow Browning's basic argument that two fundamental decisions were made sometime between late July and mid-Dec. 1941, one against Soviet Jewry and the other against all of European Jewry. See Herbert, ed., *National Socialist Extermination Policies.* For a contrasting view of the evolution of the policy that stresses the leadership's clear intentions as of early 1941, see Breitman's *The Architect of Genocide.* On "Ostrausch," see Harvey, *Women and the Nazi East,* 125.

5 On Tannenberg, see Rossino, *Hitler Strikes Poland*.

6 On the importance of Jeckeln's units, see Büchler, "Kommandostab Reichsführer-SS," 11–26, and Breitman, *Official Secrets*, 26–68.

7 Affidavit of Erwin Schulz, 26 May 1947, NMT, NO-3644, reprinted in vol. 4, 135–36. Among the oldest within the Einsatzkommando leadership, Schulz was born in 1900, joined the Schutzpolizei in 1923, and then switched to political intelligence work in the SD in 1935. After Mar. 1938, he helped establish Gestapo offices in Austria and became the inspector of the Sipo-SD in the Sudetenland. He was a staunch anticommunist who participated in the crushing of Spartacist revolt and also joined the Freikorps. See Wildt, *Generation des Unbedingten*, 573–78.

8 Consee statement of 6 Sept. 1965, Trial of Kuno Callsen et al., BAL, 207 AR-Z 419/62.

9 See Witte et al., eds. *Der Dienstkalender Heinrich Himmlers*, 191; Commander of the Order Police in Ukraine, Otto von Oelhafen testimony, Nuremberg, May 1947, NA, RG 238, roll 50, m1019.

10 Longerich, *The Unwritten Order*.

11 In *The Destruction of the European Jews*, Hilberg introduced the significant role of the Orpo, and current scholarship has greatly expanded on his work by showing that they carried out the larger "cleansing" actions. On the role of Orpo in Barbarossa, see Breitman, *Official Secrets*, 27–68; Also see Westermann, "'Ordinary Men' or 'Ideological Soldiers,'" 41–68, and Matthäus, "What about the 'Ordinary Men'?," 134–50.

12 The subunits of the SK and EK units were of platoon size—about twenty-five men. Krausnick and Wilhelm, *Die Truppe des Weltanschauungskrieges*, 186–89; Ogorreck, *Die Einsatzgruppen*.

13 Viktor Trill, statement of 25 June 1960 and of 8 June 1965, Callsen Trial, BAL, 207 AR-Z 419/62. Trill was one of the drivers of the three vehicles in the Vorkommando. The executions, explained as retaliation for arson, are reported in *Ukraïns'ke Slovo*, (Zhytomyr), 19 July 1941, ZSA, Newspaper Collection. These killings were also recorded in the Ereignismeldungen of 19 July 1941 and of 22 July 1941; see Arad, Krawkowski, and Spector, eds., *The Einsatzgruppen Reports*, 41.

14 Ereignismeldung, 7 Oct. 1941, NA, RG 242, T-175, R 234/2722808–09. On the conversion of the ghetto into a prison/labor camp, see the statement of the former adjutant to Zhytomyr's commander of the Order Police, Karl Kietzmann, 9 Sept. 1960, BAL, 204 AR-Z 1301/61, 4.

15 According to a German Sipo-SD report, there were about 30,000 Jews in and around Zhytomyr before the occupation, and more than 15,000 in Zhytomyr proper prior to June 1941. Between 25 and 50 percent of the urban Jewish population of central and eastern Ukraine fled eastward; but the rural population remained trapped in towns and villages where there was little access to railways and transport. The Ereignismeldung of 29 July 41 shows a figure of 5,000 Jews in the city of Zhytomyr; Arad, Krawkowski, and Spector, eds., *The Einsatzgruppen Reports*, 55. According

to the local paper at that time, Zhytomyr's population was 40,131, including 4,079 Jews; Ukraïns'ke Slovo (Zhytomyr), 4 Sept. 1941, ZSA, Newspaper Collection. Also see population surveys of the region from the Abteilung Statistik, Zhytomyr Commissariat, ZSA, P1151c-1c-700. The various postwar commissions' figures of Jewish dead differ dramatically. In the six mass graves outside the city, there were 9,323 victims, many of them in civilian clothing and children. See Benz and Langenheim, Mordfelder, 127–28.

16 Himmler transferred Jeckeln to Ostland at the end of Oct. 1941 to carry out the "Final Solution" there; apparently Jeckeln's replacement, HSSPF Prützmann, was on better terms with Reich Commissar Erich Koch. On Jeckeln, see Breitman, Official Secrets, 37–41, and "Friedrich Jeckeln: Spezialist für die 'Endlösung' im Osten," in Die SS, ed. Smelser and Syring, 267–75. Also see Birn, Die Höheren SS und Polizeiführer, 337. The Soviets tried and hanged Jeckeln in the ruins of the Riga ghetto.

17 See Jeckeln's Einsatzbefehl of 25 July 1941 for Novohrad-Volyns'kyi, NA, RG 242, T-501/R 5/000559–60, and Unsere Ehre Heisst Treue, 95–96. Some 4,000 Jews died in the July–Aug. massacres.

18 In addition to the Einsatzgruppe C reports, see testimony of Hans Wilhelm Isenmann, member of SS-Viking, in USHMM, RG 06.025.02 Kiev, records of the former KGB.

19 It is possible that 546 Jews were killed during the ghetto action; one source states that the staff police units of the HSSPF were responsible for this massacre on 26 Aug. 1941. German Police Decodes, ZIP G.P.D. 335, 30 Aug. 1941–10 Sept. 1941, NA, RG 457, Box 1386. This brief description of the ghetto is in Ehrenburg and Grossman, eds., The Black Book, 16. Also see testimonies and segments of the Extraordinary Commission Report in Elisavetskii, Berdichevskaia tragediia, 81–85. I am grateful to Asya Vaisman for assisting with the Russian translations. Also see Garrard and Garrard, The Bones of Berdichev, 23–25.

20 German Police Decodes, ZIP/MSGP.28, 27 Aug. 1941 and 12 Sept. 1941; also for the period 13–31 Aug., see p. 5, "Executions." NA, RG 457, Box 1386. Order Police Battalions 45 and 320 were assigned to the Berdychiv and Kam'ianets'-Podil's'kyi actions along with EK5. "Abschlussbericht" Case against Friedrich Becker, Schupo [Schutzpolizei] Berdychiv, BAL, 204 AR-Z 129/67, 1000.

21 Ehrenburg and Grossman, eds., The Black Book, 17.

22 Statement of Oelhafen, 7 May 1947. After meeting with Jeckeln, Oelhafen returned to Germany to organize his staff, which was headquartered in Kiev. Koch had asked Oelhafen to make Rivne "judenfrei" before his arrival; when asked about this action after the war Oelhafen told Nuremberg interrogators that "Rivne, das war ein kleines Nest, 500–600." Actually the number of Jews killed was 15,000. Oelhafen commanded Orpo regiments 10 and 11. He was BdO Ukraine from 1 Sept. 1941 to Sept. 1942. He was interrogated at Nuremberg on 7 May 1947 and 28 May 1947; NA, RG 238, roll 50, m1019.

23 Jeckeln may have been referring to a number of actions, either in Berdychiv itself

or around the city to the north and south. Most likely he was "boasting" about the largest actions thus far by his units, mostly by Orpo Battalion 320 in and around Kam'ianets'-Podil's'kyi. See Richard Breitman, *Official Secrets*, 64.

24 German Police Decodes, 27 Aug. 1941; ZIP/MSGP.28, 27 Aug. and 12 Sept. 1941; also see the period 13–31 Aug., p. 5, "Executions." NA, RG 457, Box 1386. An SD commando and two Ukrainian policemen, Zelinskii and Mashkovskii, are identified in the Soviet account of this action; see Soviet witness statements, Case against Friedrich Becker, "Untersuchungsbericht," BAL, 204 AR-Z 129/67, 998. Also see Ehrenburg and Grossman, eds., *The Black Book*, 16–17. Members of Orpo Battalion 303, Company 1, may have also been involved. See testimonies of former battalion members Walter Bostelmann and Walter Bötel, Callsen Trial, BAL, 207 AR-Z 419/62.

25 Ehrenburg and Grossman, eds., *The Black Book*, 18.

26 Kommandostab RFSS files, MHI, Prague, carton 1, microfilm held at USHMM, RG 48.004m, reel 1; also see *Unsere Ehre Heisst Treue*, 96–97, 104–5.

27 German Police Decodes, nos. 344–86 for the period 1–30 Sept. 1941; ZIP/MSGP.29/ 22/10/41, p. 4. NA, RG 457, Box 1386.

28 Thanks to Wolfgang Seibel and Gerald Feldman for bringing the "Division of Labor" theme to my attention. See Feldman and Seibel, eds., *Networks of Nazi Persecution*. Information was exchanged between Jeckeln's and Rasch's headquarters, but there is little documentation about how they coordinated their actions. Einsatzgruppen rarely reported on HSSPF actions; in one unusual instance EGC reported on 11 Sept. 1941 that "in Kamenez Podoliia in three days 23,600 Jews were shot by one commando of HSSPF." NA, RG 242, T-175/R 233/2722291.

29 Negotiations between the army and the SD began in Mar. 1941, but were finalized at the end of May between Heydrich and Quartermaster General Eduard Wagner. See Breitman, *The Architect of Genocide*, 149–50, and Hilberg, *Die Vernichtung der europäischen Juden*, 299. Heer and Naumann, eds., *War of Extermination*.

30 This particular period was the heyday of army-SS cooperation in anti-Jewish actions. Jeckeln had the previous day temporarily given over his command of the First SS Brigade (IR 8/10) to Sixth Army general Reichenau. See *Unsere Ehre Heisst Treue*, 24.

31 Though these two may have been connected to the Soviet trial system, the German accusations, which were meant to stir up anti-Semitism, were outrageous. They claimed that "as Jews" Kieper and Kogan were to blame for the famine and deaths of 8 million Ukrainians. See Ereignismeldung of 19 Aug. 1941, in Arad, Krawkowski, and Spector, eds., *The Einsatzgruppen Reports*, 96–97. Statement of J. A. Bauer, 2 Aug. 1965, Callsen Trial, BAL, 207 AR-Z 419/62.

32 According to the statement of J. A. Bauer, driver of Paul Blobel, the commander of SK4a, the newsreel outfit *Wochenschau* was present at the executions. Statement of 29 Jan. 1965, Callsen Trial, BAL, 207 AR-Z 419/62.

33 See eyewitness statements from a postwar trial of a former Wehrmacht soldier,

P.A., Landeskriminalamt Nordrhein-Westfalen, 27 Feb. 1964 and 26 Jan. 1966. This statement, photographs, and an essay on the crimes of the Sixth Army are presented by Bernd Boll and Hans Safrian in "Auf dem Weg nach Stalingrad: Die 6. Armee 1941/42," printed in the exhibit catalog *Vernichtungskrieg*, ed. Heer and Naumann, 270–72.

34 Some army personnel may have also carried out the shootings. Statement of Kuno Callsen, 28 June 1965, Callsen Trial, BAL, 207 AR-Z 419/62. The Callsen judgment is also found in Krausnick and Wilhelm, *Die Truppe des Weltanschauungskrieges*, 234. This event is also recounted in Klee, Dressen, and Riess, eds., *The Good Old Days*, 107–17.

35 See statement of August Häfner of SK4a, 9 June 1965. Häfner also claimed that the Wehrmacht soldiers clubbed the Jews who were awaiting execution, so that when they arrived at the pit, they were covered in blood. Callsen Trial.

36 See Ernst Wilhelm Boernecke statement of 5 Nov. 1965, Callsen Trial, BAL, 207 AR-Z 419/62. According to one account, the brains of the victims were spraying the shooters, one of whom, a person from SK4a named Janssen, returned to the Reich for treatment of a skin rash on his face. Statement of August Häfner, 10 June 1965, Callsen Trial, BAL, 207 AR-Z 419/62.

37 Statement of Kurt Friedrich Hans, 30 Sept. 1965, Teilkommandoführer SK4a, Callsen Trial, BAL, 207 AR-Z 419/62.

38 See Gerhart Panning, "Wirkungsform und Nachweis der sowjetischen Infanteriesprengmunition," Jan. 1942, *Der deutsche Militärarzt*, Library of Congress, microfilm 0184. Panning died in Mar. 1944. See Moltke's letter reprinted in Ruhm von Oppen, ed., *Letters to Freya, 1939–1945*, 160. Also see Streim, *Die Behandlung sowjetischer Kriegsgefangener*, 135–37. Panning's contribution to Nazi "crime fighting" is detailed in Herber, *Gerichtsmedizin unterm Hakenkreuz*, 274–76.

39 See Hans Mommsen, "Preussentum und Nationalsozialismus," in Benz, Buchheim, and Mommsen, eds., *Der Nationalsozialismus*, 29–41. Blobel's personnel file is reprinted in Friedlander and Milton, eds., *Archives of the Holocaust* 11, 70.

40 The more routine army-SD collaboration is illustrated in the actions that occurred in Berdychiv before HSSPF Jeckeln arrived and dominated the scene. See Ehrenburg and Grossman, eds., *The Black Book*, 14. Also see "Abschlussbericht," Case against Friedrich Becker, BAL, 204 AR-Z 129/67.

41 Ehrenburg and Grossman, eds., *The Black Book*, 31.

42 Umanskij, *Jüdisches Glück*, 66–67.

43 Einsatzgruppe C Ereignismeldung, Sept. 17, 1941, USHMM Acc. 1999.A.1096 (also available at NA, RG 242, T-175, R233, frame 2722384).

44 SS Personnel file of Emil Otto Rasch, NA, RG 242, Berlin Document Center Records, A3343 SSO-0007B, 836–846. Also see Rossino, *Hitler Strikes Poland*, 50.

45 See Michael Wildt, *Generation des Unbedingten*, 573–78, and Matthäus, Kwiet, Förster, and Breitman, *Ausbildungsziel Judenmord?*, 201.

46 See Peter Black, "Arthur Nebe: Nationalsozialist im Zwielicht," in *Die SS*, ed. Smelser and Syring, 365–78.

47 On Rasch, see Krausnick and Wilhelm, *Die Truppe des Weltanschauungskrieges*; Headland, *Messages of Murder*; and the entry on Otto Rasch by Shmuel Spector in *Encyclopedia of the Holocaust*, ed. Gutman, 3:1223.

48 Heinrich Huhn statement of 13 Oct. 1965, Callsen Trial, BAL, 207 AR-Z 419/62.

49 (FK 676) records from Aug. 1941, RGVA, 1275-3-661, held at USHMM, RG 11.001M.13, reel 92.

50 The translation stems from Rosenberg's marked-up version. The original typewritten text included this statement (which was crossed out): "Insofar as the Jews have not been driven out by the Ukrainians themselves, the small communities must be placed in large camps and forced to work, like the practice already being carried out in Lodz." NA, RG 238, IMT, Doc. 1098-PS, 12–13.

51 Mikhail Alekseevich Rozenberg, interview by Kira Burova, 25 Apr. 1996, Office of Jewish Affairs and Emigration, Zhytomyr Oblast, Ukraine. The Nazi population survey of Romanov, under Chudniv, shows, under the category of "other" for ethnic group and religion, between 987 and 1,036 persons. Abteilung Statistik, ZSA, P1151-1-700. Nina Borisovna Glozman, interview by Kira Burova, 2 Feb. 1995, Office of Jewish Affairs and Emigration, Zhytomyr Oblast, Ukraine. Glozman was from a village near Koziatyn (Bilopil'e); she was unable to evacuate because there was no access to the railroad in the village. See Mordechai Altshuler, "Escape and Evacuation of Soviet Jews at the Time of the Nazi Invasion," in *The Holocaust in the Soviet Union*, ed. Dobroszycki and Gurock, 91–96.

52 Goykher, *The Tragedy of the Letichev Ghetto*, 5. General Commissar Klemm's "Lagebericht" of June 1942 stated that 434 Jews were killed in Illintsi in May 1942, Bundesarchiv Koblenz, R6/310, p. 6.

53 Ereignismeldung, 19 Sept. 1941, NA, RG 242, T-175/R233/2722427–9, and Ereignismeldung, 25 Sept. 1941, in *The Einsatzgruppen Reports*, ed. Arad, Krakowski, and Spector, 158.

54 Statement of Josef Quante, 24 May 1955, Case against Franz Razesberger, BAL, 204 AR-Z 8/80, Band II, 71.

55 Roques order, 28 Aug. 1941, KTB Commander of the Occupied Rear Army South, NA, RG 242, T-501/R 5/000805. This was in accordance with an earlier OKH order of 19 Aug. 1941, NA, RG 242, T501, roll 5/000805.

56 RKU "Instructions," 1 Sept. 1941, ZSA, P1151-1-22.

57 The German SD oversaw the action, but instructions came from the Ukrainian mayor. This area was later situated outside the borders of the Zhytomyr General Commissariat. Vinnytsia State Archive, 1358-1c-1, microfilm held at USHMM, RG 31.011M, reel 3.

58 "Abschlussbericht," Case against Herbert Sittig, Gebietskommissar of Nemyriv, BAL, II 204a AR-Z 141/67, 373–4.

59 Ehrenburg and Grossman, eds., *The Black Book*, 20–21.

60 This pattern is described in several testimonies from SK4a members. For Cherniakhiv, see statement of Friedrich Wilhelm Ebeling, 11 Aug. 1965, Callsen Trial,

BAL, 207 AR-Z 419/62. For Radomyshl', see statement of Ernst Wilhelm Börnecke, 16 Mar. 1959, Callsen Trial, BAL, 207 AR-Z 419/62. Also in Vinnytsia, a survivor wrote that the Jews were concentrated in a factory; see Israel Weiner letter, 1 May 1944, USHMM, RG 22.003.1. In the interview conducted by Burova (25 Apr. 1996), Rozenberg stated that in Dzerzhyns'k "we were crammed into one building." At Koziatyn the Jews were confined to an area that was described as both a ghetto and a labor camp; see Burova interview of Glozman, 2 Feb. 1995. Koziatyn's Jews were placed in army barracks outside of town, not a ghetto; see file on the Koziatyn camp from Oct. 1942, ZSA, P1182-1-6.

61 On the curfews and other restrictions as well as Koch's 20 Aug. 1941 memo on ghettoization, see ZSA, P1151-1-31a. The restrictions are also described by a survivor in Umanskij, *Jüdisches Glück*, 66–67. Spector's analysis of ghettoization is in *The Holocaust of Volhynian Jews*, 117–19.

62 Plans for deporting German, Austrian, and Czech Jews to the East, where they would be killed, emerged earlier at the end of Sept. and in Oct. 1941. See Aly, *Endlösung*, 350–52, 359–61.

63 See the joint memo from Koch and Prützmann to the Generalkommissare, BdO, BdS, and SSPF. They asked that the information about remaining Jews, their locale, and accessible train routes for Reich Jews be provided by 1 Mar. 1942. Memo dated 12 Jan. 1942, ZSA, P1151-1-137, p. 8.

64 Landesschützenverbände (defense units) were also brought in to support the "pacification" campaign behind the lines; in Zhytomyr these included: L.S. Btl. 416; 466; 286; 566 and L.S. Rgt. 102. In Jan. 1942 at Khmil'nyk, L.S. Btl. 466 was active in massacres, and some members of the battalion volunteered to serve as shooters in the action. "Abschlussbericht," Investigation of Gebietskommissariat Litin (Vollkammer et al.), BAL, II 204a AR-Z 135/67, 600–601.

65 Ereignismeldung, 17 Sept. 1941, NA, RG 242, T-175/R 233/2722375.

66 John Paul Himka, "Ukrainian Collaboration in the Extermination of the Jews during the Second World War: Sorting Out the Long-Term and Conjunctural Factors," in *The Fate of the European Jews*, ed. Frankel, 172.

67 Breitman, "Himmler's Police Auxiliaries in the Occupied Soviet Territories," 23–39.

68 Himmler specified that these auxiliaries would also be used in mobile battalions outside their native countries, thus Lithuanians (battalion 11 stationed in Korosten') and Latvians (battalion 25 stationed at Ovruch) were active in the Zhytomyr region in 1942–43. NA, RG 242, T-454/R 100/699. On the army formation of Ukrainian Hilfspolizei and militia groups, see 11 July 1941 order, NA, RG 242, T-501/R 5/000482–3; and 14 Sept. 1941 order, NA, RG 242, T-315/R 2216/000098–100. Another account, though propagandistic, on the formation of Ukrainian auxiliaries is available in *Deutsche Ukraine-Zeitung* (Luts'k), 2 Oct. 1942, Library of Congress, newspaper microfilm 3010.

69 Orders of Ukrainian elders and militia commanders, July–Sept. 1941, Vinnytsia State Archive, 1358-1c-1, microfilm held at USHMM, RG 31.011M, reel 3.

70 See Ereignismeldung, 12 Sept. 1941, in *The Einsatzgruppen Reports*, ed. Arad, Krakowski, and Spector, 131.

71 Burova interview of Glozman, 2 Feb. 1995.

72 Viktor Trill, statement of 25 June 1960, Callsen Trial, BAL, 207 AR-Z 419/62.

73 Galina Efimovna Pekerman, interview by Kira Burova, 21 May 1996, Office of Jewish Affairs and Emigration, Zhytomyr, Ukraine. Pekerman (b. 1927) is one of three Jewish survivors from Chudniv. After crawling out of the mass grave, she roamed the forests for several months begging for food with another small group of Jewish survivors; they went to Berdychiv (late winter 1942–43); she pretended to be a Ukrainian orphan and was later sent as a forced laborer in a transport of Ukrainians to Auschwitz. She stayed in the Ukrainian barracks, worked in a cement factory and was liberated by the Soviets there. In her account of mass shootings in Chudniv, she described three German police officers who stood near the pits while the Ukrainian police did the shooting.

74 German commissioner Stumpp wrote that, west of the Zhytomyr Commissariat in Luts'k, a Ukrainian woman approached him and whispered in his ear that the Germans should get rid of the Jews, whom she described as "an evil pagan people." Stumpp, Aug. 1941 report on his travels from L'viv to Zhytomyr, NA, RG 242, T-454/R 6/001144–45.

75 See announcement of arrests of Ukrainian police who plundered Jewish homes in *Holos Volyni* (Zhytomyr), 30 Oct. 1941, ZSA, Newspaper Collection.

76 The SD routine of using local village chiefs and militia is described in part in Einsatzgruppe C report, 19 Aug. 1941, NA, RG 242, T-175/233/2722016–7. The district commissars used the local Ukrainian mayors and district chiefs to register the population, implement taxes, relocate Jews to camps and ghettos, and so forth. Anti-Jewish "administrative" measures were outlined in the commissars' "Amtliche Mitteilungen," beginning with taxes against Jews. 3 Nov. 1941, RKU Mitteilungen nr. 4, CSA, Kiev, 3206-6-1, microfilm held at USHMM, RG 31.002M, reel 6.

77 Burova interview of Glozman, 2 Feb. 1995.

78 See Ereignismeldung, 17 Sept. 1941, in *The Einsatzgruppen Reports*, ed. Arad, Krakowski, and Spector, 134; RMfdbO reports and VoMi reports about the anti-Jewish attitude of ethnic Germans and Ukrainians, NA, RG 242, T-501/R 6/001143–4; CSA, Kiev, 3206-255-6, microfilm held at USHMM, RG 31.002M, reels 6, 11.

79 Sherei was from Chernivtsi, Soviet-occupied Romania. At the beginning of Sept. 1941, he and 800 other men were sent to Zhytomyr. Sherei stated that their relocation was ordered by the SD, and under SS Untersturmführer Schlosser of EK5 they were formed into police units of 120 men to be dispersed in the major towns and cities of German-occupied Ukraine; the Kiev unit stayed in Berdychiv until Kiev fell to the Germans. Koval's'kyi SD investigation of 9 Dec. 1941, ZSA, P1151-1-3. On the German secret police transfer of Ukrainians in Romania who were being

persecuted there to German-occupied Ukraine, see Arad, Krakowski, and Spector, eds., *The Einsatzgruppen Reports*, 25 (Ereignismeldung, 14 July 1941 report).

80 One of the issues that was being investigated was the ownership of a Jewish leather coat that was valued at 3,000 rubles. Martha Arndt, an ethnic German, found it when she occupied a former Jewish apartment at Moskaustrasse #30; 9 Dec. 1941, ZSA, P1151-1-3.

81 Kulitzki was born in Kiev, but his family was from Königsberg. His relatives held similar positions—an ethnic German brother was an SD chief at Litzmannstadt; a cousin was Untersturmführer in VoMi Zhytomyr; and two of his brothers-in-law were in the Wehrmacht. ZSA, P1151-1-3.

82 Glozman described a Ukrainian who guarded the Jews in Koziatyn; at night, when the Germans were not around, he tortured the Jews. Later she was betrayed by an ethnic German interpreter who had been a classmate. Burova interview of Glozman, 2 Feb. 1995.

83 On the Soviet and Jewish accounts that brand nationalists as collaborators, see Zvi Gitelman, "Politics and the Historiography of the Soviet Union," in *Bitter Legacy*, ed. Gitelman.

84 Berkhoff and Carynnyk, "The Organization of Ukrainian Nationalists," 153.

85 Ibid., 171.

86 For one of the few scholarly treatments of this topic, see Potichnyi and Aster, eds., *Ukrainian-Jewish Relations in Historical Perspective*, in particular the essay in this volume by Altshuler, "Ukrainian-Jewish Relations in the Soviet Milieu in the Interwar Period," 281–305. I will examine the Ukrainian nationalist factions (OUN-B and OUN-M) and their activities in Zhytomyr in more depth in chapter 6 and chapter 8.

87 ZSA, P1151c-1-2. During the OUN's Apr. 1941 Congress, one resolution was put forth that the OUN "combat the Jews as the prop of the Muscovite-Bolshevik regime." The Nazis viewed the Jews as a racial menace and the source of Bolshevism, whereas the OUN leaders in Cracow defined their anti-Semitism along political, not racial, lines. This distinction is misrepresented in Taras Hunczak's essay "Ukrainian-Jewish Relations during the Soviet and Nazi Occupations," in *Ukraine during World War II*, ed. Boshyk, 42; Hunczak states that neither the Ukrainian underground movement "nor any other organizations thus cultivated anti-Semitic programs or policies."

88 On the Khmil'nyk liquidations, see the Abschlussbericht, BAL, II 204 AR-Z, 135/67, 23–24.

89 One of the two survivors of Dzerzhyns'k, where the Germans destroyed a population of 4,000 Jews, described his ordeal of hiding in old barns and roaming villages in search of food and shelter; Burova interview of Rozenberg, 25 Apr. 1996. Nina Borisovna Glozman also told of her hiding in old barns, abandoned houses, and factories; Burova interview of Glozman, 2 Feb. 1995. Eva Abramovna Frankel walked hundreds of kilometers and had to beg for food and shelter in villages

around Berdychiv; Burova interview of Frankel, 2 Feb. 1995. Vladimir Goykher wrote of similar experiences in his memoir, *The Tragedy of the Letichev Ghetto*.

90 Statement of Karl Kietzmann, 9 Sept. 1960, Case against Kohlmorgen, BAL, 204 AR-Z 1301/61. There were also about 500 Jewish laborers who were held in a camp just outside the city in Apr. 1942. Over the next months the Germans brought in hundreds more from Volhynia and Galicia and kept them temporarily in a few buildings on Mikhailovskaia Street until they brought them to their final destination, the pits of Bogun'ia. Testimony of Josef Kwjatowski (who worked in the kitchen on Mikhailovskaia Street, Zhytomyr), Case against Franz Razesberger, BAL, 204 AR-Z 8/80, Band I, 82. On the removal of Jews from Wehrmacht offices, see Keitel order "Juden in den besetzten Ostgebiete," 12 Sept. 1941, NA, RG 242, T-77/R 1028/6500570. Jews in Zhytomyr were employed by the Sixth Army in the printing shop where they were "allegedly" able to forge documents. Einsatzgruppe C report, 17 Sept. 1941, in *The Einsatzgruppen Reports*, ed., Arad, Krakowski, and Spector, 135.

91 The small slice of the Zhytomyr region that was included in the Hitler order of 20 Aug. lay west of Novohrad-Volyns'kyi. See war diary entry of 20 Aug. 1941, KTB SD454, NA, RG 242, T-315/R 2215/000438, and Commander of Rear Area South to OKH General Staff, "Übergabe an die Zivilverwaltung d. Reichskommissare," 7 Sept. 1941, NA, RG 242, T-501/R 5/000848. The complete transfer of the region to civilian authority under General Commissar of Zhytomyr Kurt Klemm occurred on 20 Oct. 1941, when the RKU was expanded to the Dnepr (East) and the Bug (South); this was according to a Hitler decree of 11 Oct. 41, NA, RG 242, T-454/R 92/000861–62 and T-315/R 2216/000330. Continued military administration was placed under Wehrmachtsbefehlshaber for Ukraine Kitzinger, who was stationed in the RKU capital, Rivne; the army commandants who focused on the passage of troops, POWs, and supplies across the region to and from the front were also drawn into civilian occupation policies. Military Field Commander 811 arrived in Zhytomyr on 27 Oct. 1941; NA, RG 242, T-315/R 2216/000437.

92 His ruling style continued in the manner of Stülpnagel and others in the Sixth and Seventeenth Army leadership. In one of Kitzinger's inaugural decrees as Wehrmachtsbefehlshaber for Ukraine, he demanded that collective reprisals target local Jews and that the indigenous mayor serve as the German's "front man" by publicly ordering the shootings of civilians. Kitzinger order of 10 Oct. 1941, CSA, Kiev, 3206-6-1, microfilm held at USHMM, RG 31.002M, reel 6.

Chapter Five

1 Bormann Meeting Notes, 221-L, IMT, vol. 38, 86–94. Also reprinted in N. Müller, *Die faschistische Okkupationspolitik*, 160–62.

2 Bormann Meeting Notes, 221-L, IMT, vol. 38, 86–94.

3 Ibid.

4 Rosenberg had been forming a staff of eastern experts since early Apr. On 20 Apr.

1941, Hitler officially appointed Rosenberg the central authority on the East; see IMT, NA, RG 238, 865-PS. Himmler and Heydrich had also planned since early 1941 to lead the police and security operations of the occupied East, placing the Einsatzgruppen and higher SS and police leaders' units (including Order Police) within the army areas and civilian zones. On Himmler's planning for the war in the East, see Breitman, *The Architect of Genocide.*

5 "Die Zivilverwaltung in den besetzten Ostgebieten, Teil II: Reichskommissariat Ukraine," "Brown File," RGVA, 7021-148-183, p. 10. I am grateful to Jürgen Matthäus for providing me with a copy of this document.

6 The "Generalbezirk Zhitomir" as a geographic construct was a German creation, whose borders included the former Soviet oblast of Zhytomyr and parts of Vinnytsia (in the South bordering Romania along the Bug River); Polissia (the northern border of Belorussia including a southern section of the Pripiat' marshlands); and Gomel' (the northeast corner). See the overview "Der Generalbezirk Shytomyr," 15 Mar. 1942, RMfdbO, ZSA, P1151-1-51.

7 In Feb. 1942, however, three of the twenty-five districts were still lacking a commissar: Lel'chytsi, Komaryn, and Monastyryshche. CSA, Kiev, microfilm at USHMM, RG 31.003M, reel 3, 14–16.

8 See report by the General Commissar on the structure of the administration, ZSA, P1151-1-42. Also see description of district commissars' offices in Abschlussbericht, Investigation of Zhytomyr district commissars, BAL, ZSL II 204a AR-Z 135/67, and Case against Friedrich Becker, Schupo Berdychiv, BAL, II 204a AR-Z 129/67, Band IV.

9 These figures are based on the composition of the Koziatyn district police, the Zhytomyr city police, and the Ruzhyn district police; ZSA, P1182-1-1, P1182-1-162, and P1182-1-36. Four *Gendarmerie Hauptmannschaften,* a group of about 150 rural or county troopers, were assigned to the region by mid-1942 to support and manage the stationary gendarmerie units around Berdychiv, Vinnytsia, Zhytomyr, and Mazyr. The German police in the urban centers of Berdychiv, Vinnytsia, and Zhytomyr were not gendarmes, but rather municipal police, or *Schutzpolizei,* who were supported by Ukrainian police aides, or *Hilfspolizei.*

10 "Abschlussbericht," Koziatyn Case, BAL, 204a AR-Z 137/67, Band II, 225. Thanks to Martin Dean for the information on the Sipo-SD Aussenstellen, ZSA, 1182-1-26, p. 104.

11 *Hitler's Table Talk,* 35.

12 Ibid., 424.

13 Pavlovsky's first name does not appear in the German accounts. The rest of the committee consisted of an engineer from Vinnytsia named Bernard, a district chief from Korostyshiv, a department leader from the district administration of Mazyr named Miko, and a district medical adviser from Novohrad-Volyns'kyi named Nievidovskii. *Deutsche Ukraine-Zeitung* (Luts'k), 25 Feb. 1942, Library of Congress, newspaper microfilm 3010.

14 On the General Commissariat structure and placement of Ukrainian leaders as raion leaders and village elders, see RKU decree of 14 Feb. 1942. CSA, Kiev, 3206-6-2, microfilm held at USHMM, RG 31.002M, reel 6.

15 See the Jan Lazar order, from Tul'chyn, 17 Nov. 1941: "Any mayors who do not comply with German orders or who issue false IDs will be treated as spies." Vinnytsia State Archive, P1417-3c-1, microfilm held at USHMM, RG 31.011M, reel 4.

16 General Commissar Klemm, "Lagebericht," dated 3 June 1942, Bundesarchiv Koblenz, R6/310.

17 See IMT, NA, RG 238, NO-1897. See also the biased postwar account of Rosenberg's deputy, Bräutigam, Überblick über die besetzten Ostgebiete während des 2. Weltkrieges, 25; and the more balanced portrait by historian Jonathan Steinberg, "The Third Reich Reflected," 621.

18 For the Klemm-Meyer correspondence, see ZSA, P1151-1-19; regarding the credentials of staff and the Party quota, see ZSA, P1151-1-26 and P1151-1-46; for the meeting in Berlin, 23–24 Sept. 1941, and staff appointments, see ZSA, P1151-1-24.

19 The other two castles were in Vogelsang and Sonthofen. See entries in Michael and Doerr, Nazi-Deutsch.

20 Klemm file, ZSA, P1151-1-26; the commissars' arrival is also described by Fritz Margenfeld, the former city commissar for Vinnytsia. See statement of Margenfeld, 17 Mar. 1971, BAL, Sta Stuttgart 84 Js 3/71, 2. Thanks to Konrad Kwiet and Jürgen Matthäus for the Margenfeld material.

21 See Klemm's introductory memo to commissars, 5 Dec. 1941, ZSA, P1151-1-33.

22 "Brown File," RGVA, 7021-148-183, p. 12; also found in Commissar Klemm file 1941, ZSA, P1151-1-31a; and referenced by Dallin, German Rule in Russia, 305.

23 "Brown File," RGVA, 7021-148-183, p. 37. Also see General Commissar orders on relations with local police, see Klemm order to commissars on administrative procedures, 5 Dec. 1941, ZSA, P1151-1-33, P1151-1-42.

24 On the initial line of authority and the establishment of SS and police courts, see Klemm (briefing notes among Krössinsee material), ZSA, P1151-1-31a; and Koch memo of 5 Sept. 1941 from Königsberg, CSA, Kiev, 3206-1-72, microfilm held at USHMM, RG 31.002M, reel 2.

25 By mid-Dec. 1941 it seems that Rosenberg was well aware of a decision to "exterminate" all Jews, at least those in the Soviet territories. None of Rosenberg's earlier writings from spring 1941 indicates his knowledge of a decision. See Rosenberg's "Vermerk über Unterredung beim Führer am 14 Dez. 1941," IMT, NA, RG 238, PS-1517.

26 Rosenberg's "guidelines" for the Jewish question in his "Brown File," RGVA, 7021-148-183, p. 35.

27 RMfdbO memo on the treatment of Ukrainians, 22 Nov. 1941, ZSA, P1151-1-137.

28 Koch reiterated the "proper" use of the whip in an 18 Apr. 1942 order and a memo of 17 Nov. 1942 to the general commissar of Zhytomyr, "Verhalten der deutschen Bevölkerung gegenüber den Ukrainern," ZSA, P1151-1-42, p. 38. There were enough

instances of such abuses that Alfred Meyer, Rosenberg's deputy minister, issued an order to Reich Commissar Lohse of the Ostland and Reich Commissar Koch of Ukraine against the use of cudgels and whips; 9 Apr. 1942, NA, RG 242, T-77/R 1174/001085.

29 NSDAP report of 3–23 June 1942 trip, NA, RG 242, T454, roll 92, frames 000193–000199.

30 Descriptions and critiques of the commissariat with reference to carpetbaggers and colonial agricultural economy in private German letters, NA, RG 242, T-454/R 161/folder 1001; and Reich Minister of Finance Krosigk critique of 4 Sept. 1942, NA, RG 238, Box 38, NO-1897.

31 Berkhoff, "Hitler's Clean Slate," 505.

32 See Koch memo of 17 Nov. 1941, ZSA, P1151-1-42.

33 See Ukraine's armaments inspector report of 29 Nov. 1941, IMT, NA, RG 238, PS-2174.

34 See order of Zhytomyr's SS and police leader, Otto Hellwig, dated 13 Apr. 1942, in the postwar criminal investigation files against the district commissariats, Zhytomyr, Nemiriv district, BAL, 204a AR-Z 141/67, document volume, 125–6, 183. Hellwig (b. 1898, Nordhausen) commanded Sipo cadets in the Polish invasion. Between 1937 and 1941, he directed the Sipo leadership school. See Rossino, *Hitler Strikes Poland*, 50–51, and Hellwig's SS personnel file with Lebenslauf, in NA, RG 242, Berlin Document Center Records, A3343 SSO-083A.

35 See order of 19 Feb. 1943 that anyone caught mixing with locals will be sentenced to death, ZSA, P1182-1-162.

36 In Vinnytsia, the SD had reported in July 1941 an increase of 1,400 cases of venereal disease, which the civil administration's department of health tried to control. Einsatzgruppe C report, 7 Aug. 1941, NA, RG 242, T-175/R 233/p. 10. See Zhytomyr Department of Health memo on the city bordello and western European women, 28 Jan. 1943, and 18 Mar. 1943, ZSA, P1151-1-4.

37 Report of SA Oberführer Paul Theurer, RMfdbO Vertreter sent from Berlin to Zhytomyr to meet Klemm; he also described the Commissars' club and entertainment by ethnic German girls. See report of 16–17 Apr. 1942, CSA, Kiev, 3206-6-5, microfilm at USHMM 31.002M, reel 6.

38 As told by Hrihorii Denisenko, chief archivist, Zhytomyr State Archive, and WWII veteran, who, during a walking tour of the city, pointed out the street corner where her body was thrown from the car. Interview by author, 11 Aug. 1993, Zhytomyr, Ukraine. Also see Abschlussbericht, Becker Case, BAL, 204 AR-Z 129/67, 1023.

39 See SSPF Otto Hellwig's "Bandenbekämpfung," 21 Jan. 1943, ZSA, P1151-1-4; mention of Ukrainian women as spies in report (not dated) of Koziatyn SSPF, "Erfahrungen im Bandenkampf," ZSA, P1182-1-37.

40 It is not clear in this report if the major offense was the shooting or his drunkenness; perhaps it was the combination. See General Commissar, "Lagebericht," Mar. 1943, ZSA, P1151-1-45.

41 Memo of the commissar's labor office to the local army command, 13 July 1942, ZSA, P1465-1-6.

42 For SD report, dated 18 Sept. 1942, on illegal communications between Reich Germans, mainly German soldiers bringing letters to Ukrainians in Germany, see NA, RG 242, T-175/R 17/2520312-26.

43 On orphans, see Heinemann, "Rasse, Siedlung, deutsches Blut," 508-36.

44 Bormann ordered Koch to seize Ukrainian prostitutes; see memo of 23 July 1942, NA, RG 242, T-454/R 92/000894-897. Koch authorized the Gebietskommissar to punish women and members of the local community if they tried to prevent abortions; see Koch's instructions to his commissars, 23 Dec. 1942, ZSA, P1151-1-698. Also see entry of 22 July 1942, Hitler's Table Talk, 587-88.

45 For the German restaurant in Zhytomyr, special German shops, the changing of street names, and special German apartment districts, see City Commissar's file, ZSA, P1151-1-32.

46 Ivan Shynal'skii, interview by author, 20 May 1996, ZSA, Ukraine.

47 These were personal letters sent by Reich Germans who worked in Ukraine, which were picked up by Reich censors and analyzed in 1942-43. NA, RG 242, T-454/R 161/ML 465, folder 10001.

48 SSPF Otto Hellwig order, 30 Sept. 1942, ZSA, P1151-1-9.

49 German, Slovakian, and Hungarian troops in the city would trade their cigarettes, beer, and vodka with the locals; the items were seized by the local police and given to the German administration, which then sold the Ukrainian and German goods to the Schutzmannschaften, described in report, ZSA, P1151-1-26. This report refers to the 31 Jan. 1942 Orpo memo about controlling the black market in the city.

50 Höpel's letter and packages to his wife Emmy in Thüringen were intercepted by the Abwehr in Berlin and forwarded to the SD in Berdychiv in Mar.-Apr. 1943. ZSA, P1151-1-1.

51 Wehrmachtsbefehlshaber, RKU situation report of 5 Nov.-16 Dec. 1941, ZSA, P1151-1-21.

52 This order first appeared during the military occupation but was reissued by the commissars; Holos Volyni (Zhytomyr), 30 Oct. 1941, ZSA, Newspaper Collection.

53 Rosenberg's special staff of art plunderers, the Einsatzstab Reichsleiter Rosenberg (ERR), was also active in Zhytomyr. The city commissar of Zhytomyr Magass complained to Rosenberg's ERR that he could not find enough boxes and materials to pack up the art works from the local museum; City Commissar File, 22 May 1942, ZSA, P1151-1-32. In Berdychiv ERR officials found Balzac's private collections in the local library and sent them to Berlin. CSA, Kiev, 3676-1-44, microfilm held at USHMM, RG 31.0002M, reel 7. See Grimsted, "Twice Plundered or 'Twice Saved'?," 191-244.

54 See the files of the city housing office, ZSA, P1152-1-13; General Commissar memo to Party officials regarding the securing of homes for Reich Germans, 30 June 1942,

ZSA, P1151-1-32; and a Gebietskommissar letter about Jewish homes to be given over to police, Illintsi, 16 July 1942, ZSA, P1182-1-1.

55 For example, the chief doctor at the German infirmary wrote to the commission that he would like to purchase Jewish belongings, such as a piano and an armoire. ZSA, P1151-1-18.

56 29 Dec. 1941, ZSA, P1151-1-137.

57 Mark Koval's'kyi case, 9 Dec. 1941, ZSA, P1151-1-3.

58 RMfdbO, "Notes about Occupied Ukraine," 10 Oct. 1942, NA, RG 242, T-454/R 92/0001038.

59 Göllner inventory, 8 Feb. 1944, ZSA, 2375-1-1.

60 On the variations in living conditions among commissars, see General Commissar Leyser memo to district commissars of 20 Oct. 1942, ZSA, P1151-1-42.

61 See RMfdbO, "Notes about Occupied Ukraine," 10 Oct. 1942, NA, RG 242, T-454/R 92/0001038.

62 German officials who traveled in the region criticized the gendarmes about the rough condition of their uniforms and about not properly greeting one another in public with the official Nazi raised arm; numerous memos were circulated about how to do the proper German greeting and the poor condition of German uniforms, which was an ironic concern for appearance and authority when their general conduct and behavior displayed the utmost depravity. See Commander of the Gendarmerie files, ZSA, P1151-1-9. Also in Leyser's Mar.–Apr. 1943 "Lagebericht," ZSA, P1151-1-45.

63 On the Müller case, see ZSA, P1151-1-383.

64 Ukraïns'ke Slovo (Zhytomyr), 11 Sept. 1941, ZSA, Newspaper Collection. The initial army approach was also outlined in "Richtlinien zur Behandlung der Kollektivfrage," Bfh.rückw.H.Geb.Süd., 28 Aug. 1941, NA, RG 242, T-501/R 5/000799–800.

65 "German troops around Vinnytsia live off the land and suppress the attitude of the farmers," 31 Aug. 1941, NA, RG 242, DW files (German Foreign Office) box 24, file no. 20.

66 Wedelstadt to Klemm, 26 Nov. 1941, ZSA, P1151-1-28.

67 ZSA, P1151-1-21. On the announcement of the Landbaugenossenschaft at Zhytomyr, see Deutsche Ukraine-Zeitung (Luts'k), 23 Sept. 1942, p. 3, Library of Congress, newspaper microfilm 3010. On the Koch-Hitler approach to farms, see "Rede von Koch," 26–28 Aug. 1942, NA, RG 242, T-454/R 92/000895–7.

68 On the 1941 harvest, see Wehrmachtsbefehlshaber Kitzinger's monthly report of 17 June 1942, NA, RG 242, T-454/R 92/000653–56.

69 WiStab Ost leader's report, 2 Nov. 1941. NA, RG 242, T-454/R 110/000242.

70 Moshovskii Order, District Bazar, 13 Jan. 1942, ZSA, P1426-1-2.

71 See reports of the SS and police leader of Ruzhyn, in particular reports of 9 Sept. 1942 and 5 Feb. 1943 and a Mar. 1943 "Lagebericht." ZSA, P1182-1-36, P1452-1-2.

72 Mulligan, The Politics of Illusion and Empire, 63; Laskovsky, "Practicing Law in the Occupied Ukraine," 123–37.

73 RMfdbO trip report, "Aufzeichnungen über die Lage in der Ukraine," 15 Oct. 1942: "The Gebietskommissar and the La-Führer are dictators here with the absolute power . . . they rule arbitrarily." NA, RG 242, T-454/R 92/001046. See speech of General Commissar Leyser's deputy chief of agriculture for the Zhytomyr region to Koch and Rosenberg, who visited Vinnytsia on 17 June 1943. NA, RG 242, T-454/R 91/000878–81.

74 The La-Führer were selected by the military. Many were farmers in the Reich or officials from agricultural offices; their credentials varied widely, but most were ill prepared to manage the Ukrainian collectives and farms without having to resort to terror tactics. See Dallin, *German Rule in Russia*, 318–19; and Chiari, *Alltag hinter der Front*, 68–72.

75 SS and police leader of Koziatyn memo to all gendarme posts and agricultural station leaders, 11 Aug. 1943, ZSA, P1182-1-3. The Ukrainian peasant Maria Atamanskaia, who worked in a collective farm in Chudniv, recalled that the Germans took everything from the farm, but the actual seizures were conducted entirely by Ukrainian police. Maria Albinova Atamanskaia (b. 1925), interview by author, 20 May 1996, Zhytomyr, Ukraine.

76 See General Commissar Zhytomyr, "Lagebericht," 3 June 1942, Bundesarchiv Koblenz, R6/310.

77 RMfdbO, "Notes about Occupied Ukraine," 10 Oct. 1942, NA, RG 242, T-454/92/ 0001038–1046/EAP99/457.

78 Rosenberg, "Instruktion für einen Reichskommissar in der Ukraine," 7 May 1941, IMT, NA, RG 238, 1028-PS; Dallin, *German Rule in Russia*, 130–50.

79 For example, see report on Koziatyn youth camp (8–18 years) in Ruzhyn, Aug. 1942, ZSA, P1182-1-6.

80 Thomas order of 15 Aug. 1942, recirculated in Zhytomyr, 5 Nov. 1942, ZSA, P1182-1-6. Behrens report from Koziatyn, 30 Nov. 1942, ZSA, P1182-1-6.

81 In the city of Zhytomyr, Magass received monthly reports from Pintov, director of the Ukrainian Club, which presented theater plays, operas, and choral concerts; ZSA, P1152-1-11.

82 Göring enjoyed these performances of the Ukrainian theater and ballet and praised the Ukrainian cultural productions as entertainment for the troops; trip report of Economic Inspector, RKU Berlin, 10 Sept. 1942, CSA, Kiev, microfilm held at USHMM, RG 31.002M, reel 3.

83 On the joint Ukrainian-German theater productions in Vinnytsia and Haisyn, see General Commissar Leyser, "Lagebericht" for Mar./Apr. 1943, ZSA, P1151-1-45.

84 Case against Franz Razesberger, Abschlussbericht, BAL, 204 AR-Z 8/80, 51.

85 RMfdbO, "Aufzeichnungen über die Lage in der Ukraine," 15 Oct. 1942, NA, RG 242, T-454/R 92/0001038–46.

86 The Ukrainian Autocephalous Church was established in 1920 during the civil war and nationalist revolution. During the Stalinist purges of the Ukrainian Orthodox Church (beginning with Lipovskii in 1929–30), the Ukrainian Autocephalous

Church was effectively banned. The Moscow-centered Autonomous Orthodox Church in Ukraine was systematically repressed through excessive taxation, revoking church building permits, mass arrests of church members, and the infiltration of the congregations by atheists. See Fireside, *Icon and Swastika*, 45.

87 Metropolitan Dionysius and Archbishop Polikarp are identified in the German report, "Aufzeichnungen über die Lage in der Ukraine," 15 Oct. 1942, NA, RG 242, T-454/R 92/001046. Also see Magocsi, *History of Ukraine*, 628, and Fireside, *Icon and Swastika*, 25–41.

88 The friction between the Ukrainian and Russian Orthodox churches became evident, to the Germans at least, in May 1942; the general commissar's office described how both churches vied for popular support through leaflets, declarations, and pastoral letters. See Klemm, "Lagebericht," 3 June 1942, Bundesarchiv Koblenz, R6/310.

89 BdS Thomas order, 2 Feb. 1942, NA, RG 242, T-454/R 154/ MR 334 EAP 99/439. Klemm order on dissolution of the oblast administration, 1 Feb. 1942, ZSA, P1151-1-21. The local SS and police leaders were asked to monitor how politicized Ukrainian religion might become. The SD leader in the Aussenstelle Vinnytsia, Salmanzig, wrote to the SS and police district leader of Koziatyn, Behrens, about mass baptisms and the Catholic Church. Behrens investigated the Roman Catholic community of Koziatyn and the services that were being held at the cemeteries; Salmanzig-Behrens correspondence of 15 Oct. 1942, ZSA, P1182-1-6.

90 Commissars' request to commander of the Order Police, Oelhafen, and his order, 18 Mar. 1942, ZSA, P1151-1-11. General Commissar Klemm, 10 July 1942, ZSA, P1151-1-141.

91 On the scandals and infighting within the Ukrainian churches, largely centered in Zhytomyr and Vinnytsia, see Berkhoff, "Was There a Religious Revival . . . ?"

92 Ibid., 544.

93 Fireside, *Icon and Swastika*, 116–22.

94 Report of RKU Dept. chief IIIg, Economy and Armaments Inspector, 10 Sept. 1942, CSA, Kiev, 3206-2-116, microfilm held at USHMM, RG 31.002M, reel 3.

95 For example, in Berdychiv the Gendarmerie Hauptmannschaft was located in the office of the army commander. The OT leaders of "OT Einsatzstab Russland Süd" were located in the same office as the general commissar in Zhytomyr; ZSA, P1151-1-26. In Zhytomyr the Nazi Party's welfare organization, the NSV, which distributed Jewish belongings to ethnic Germans, was located in the ground floor of the Commissariat office building, and set up there with the intent of furthering cooperation with the commissar. See Party leader Kersten's report of 5 Apr. 1942, CSA, Kiev, 3206-6-256 microfilm held at USHMM, RG 31.002M, reel 6.

96 General Commissar Klemm, "Lagebericht," 3 June 1942, Bundesarchiv R6/310.

97 Joint order from General Commissar's office and SSPF Hellwig, re: "Gefährdung der Ernte," 8 Sept. 1942, ZSA, P1151-1-9.

98 Koch order, 1 Nov. 1941, CSA, Kiev, 3206-6-1 microfilm held at USHMM, RG 31.002M, reel 6.

99 The OT, Action Group Russia South, took over the General Commissar's departments of street construction, canals, and hydro economy as of 18 Nov. 1942. See the RKU memo in ZSA, P1151-1-469.

100 General Commissar, "Lagebericht," 3 June 1942, Bundesarchiv R6/310, pp. 23–24.

101 Gendarmerie Commander's office, Vinnytsia Hauptmannschaftsbefehl, 5/6 June 1942, "Jüdische Arbeitskräfte," ZSA, P1151-1-703. Also see memo from Commissariat Labor office, 28 Aug. 1942, ZSA, P1151-1-31.

102 Erich Koch, "Lagebericht," Dec. 1941, CSA, Kiev, microfilm held at USHMM, RG 31.002M, reel 3.

103 BdS Thomas, Kiev, 19 Dec. 1942, re: forced labor in Ukraine during June 1942, NA, RG 242, T-454/R 156/MR336.

104 The Aug. 1942 article was printed in Ukrainian newspapers throughout the Zhytomyr region; ZSA, P1151-1-147a. Ukrainian newspapers in the region were published in Ruzhyn, Berdychiv, Chudniv, Zhytomyr, Korostyshiv, Novohrad-Volyns'kyi, Olevs'k, Ovruch, Lel'chytsi, Mazyr, Kalynivka, Vinnytsia, Koziatyn, and Haisyn.

105 See SD situation report on Ukraine, specifically about Novohrad-Volyns'kyi (Zviahel) labor transport and rumors concerning the conditions of Ukrainian laborers, 18 Sept. 1942, NA, RG 242, T-175/R 17/2520312–26.

106 Reitlinger, *The House Built on Sand*, 266–77, and Berkhoff, *Harvest of Despair*, 259–74.

107 See "Daily Routine" report of the Koziatyn Camp, 4 Oct. 1942, ZSA, P1182-1-6. All references in this document to Jewish internees and their treatment were crossed out.

108 As of 25 June 1942, the district commissars took over the establishment and management of camps and requested Ukrainian auxiliaries to stand guard at the camps. After Mar. 1943, Ukrainians were not trusted with the task of fulfilling the commissars' demands against other Ukrainians, so German forces were assigned to more camp duties; ZSA, P1151-1-9.

109 See Commissar Steudel order, 5 May 1943, ZSA, P1182-1-6.

110 General Commissar Klemm, "Lagebericht," 3 June 1942, Bundesarchiv Koblenz, R6/310.

111 Thomas order, 15 Aug. 1942, Koziatyn Camp files, ZSA, P1182-1-6; Ruzhyn SSPgebF file, ZSA, P1182-1-36.

112 BdS Thomas report, 15 Aug. 1942, ZSA, P1182-1-6, Koziatyn Camp files. The Himmler order was sent to Gottlob Berger, who was the SS liaison in Rosenberg's ministry, 1 Jan. 1943. NA, RG 242, T-175/R 140/2668067–68.

113 Chiari, *Alltag hinter der Front*, 56. Gerlach, *Kalkulierte Morde*. Also see Birn, *Die Höheren SS und Polizeiführer*, 226.

114 On the construction projects in Zhytomyr proper—for example, the German section, the streetcars, and Klemm's quarters—see ZSA, P1151-1-32; also see meeting notes of Klemm's administrative adviser, Karl Notbohm, about priority building

projects in the district and tabulations of skilled and unskilled labor, 28 Aug. 1942, ZSA, P1151–131.

115 BdS Thomas or BdO Oelhafen may have also been present. Statement of Kurt Klemm, 22 Aug. 1962, BAL, 204 AR-Z 129/67, Band III, 830.

116 Hellwig order, 20 July 1942, ZSA, P1151-1-706.

117 Klemm statement, 22 Aug. 1962, BAL, 204 AR-Z 129/67, Band III, 830. Statement of Franz Razesberger, 19 Jan. 1957, BAL, 204 AR-Z 8/80, Band III, 207, 830. Klemm memo about uniform to Rosenberg, 12 July 1943, NA, RG 242, T-454/R 91/000873.

118 Rosenberg-Himmler memo, Sept. 1942. NA, RG 242, T-175/R 17/2521105.

119 But, as Timothy Mulligan has pointed out, cooperation among the Germans was hardly by itself sufficient: "In January 1943, roughly 25,000 Reich Germans governed 16,910,008 inhabitants scattered throughout the *Reichskommissariat*'s five cities and 443 *raions*. . . . These dimensions alone ensured that the most basic levels of administration depended entirely on Ukrainians." See Mulligan, *The Politics of Illusion and Empire*, 64.

Chapter Six

1 Hilberg, *The Destruction of European Jews* (1985), 263, 266.

2 As Wetzel put it, Himmler's forces were "federführend"—i.e., in charge. See Otto Bräutigam file, "Guidelines for the Treatment of the Jewish Question," NA, RG 242, T-454/R 154/MR 334 EAP 99/447.

3 Imort, "Forestopia."

4 See witness statements from Vinnytsia, Solomon Goliak (Sept. 1969) and Lev Schein (May 1944), as well as that of a former Ukrainian policeman in Vinnytsia's Kripo office, Konstantin Klimanow (Aug. 1969). BAL, 204 AR-Z 122/68, 195–198 and 299–303; BAL, 204 AR-Z 136/67, 180–182.

5 On the July 1942 structure, see the Kommandobefehl distribution list, ZSA, P1151-1-9. See Dean, "The German *Gendarmerie*, the Ukrainian *Schutzmannschaft* and the 'Second Wave' of Jewish Killings in Occupied Ukraine," 176–81.

6 Franz Razesberger was acquitted by a Vienna court, 26 July 1961. LG Wien: 20 Vr 5774/60, Viennese Post-War Trials of Nazi War Crimes, USHMM, RG-17.003M.

7 At first the Schutzmannschaften were permitted to wear Ukrainian national armbands, which also bore their service number and locale assigned by the Germans. The uniforms consisted of Red Army uniforms with the Soviet insignias torn off. The mobile battalions in Zhytomyr were #108 (688 men), #109 (631 men); #110 (500 men) and Lithuanian battalion #11 (454 men); Latvian battalion #25 (422 men). ZSA, P1151-1-383. Hauptmannschaftsbefehl 5/41, ZSA, 1182-1-17; KdG order of 12 Feb. 1942, ZSA, 1182-1-3. An ethnic German mobile killing unit from Latvia was involved in the Kam'ianets'-Podil's'kyi massacres of Aug. 1941. See Pohl, "Schauplatz Ukraine," 140–43.

8 Klemm order of 3 Dec. 1941, ZSA, P1182-1-3; KdG Kommandobefehl Nr. 4/41, ZSA, P1182-1-3.

9 This order referred to a revision of the Jan. 1942 instructions, which have not been found. Gendarme leaders in Vinnytsia reissued the Mar. 1942 order in June 1942. See Hauptmannschaft Winniza "Sonderbefehl," 12 Mar. 1942, ZSA, P1151-1-9.

10 Gendarme post, Ruzhyn, "Lagebericht," Sept. 1942, ZSA, P1182-1-36.

11 The ages of the German police leaders ranged from thirty-two to forty-six. The SS and police leader for Koziatyn was Heinrich Behrens (b. 1898); the district lieutenant of the gendarmerie of Koziatyn was Christian Kirschner (b. 1898); the district senior guard for Samhorodok was Josef Richter, and the master gendarme in Pohrebyshche was Bruno Mayrhofer. The gendarme station and police headquarters were located in Koziatyn's former Communist Party building; the Ukrainian auxiliaries were in the former militia building. ZSA, P1182-1-1.

12 Their training site was also the former prisoner barracks, which had been the district's Jewish camp in 1942. See BdO "Guidelines for Training the Schutzmannschaft" and Himmler order on the training and schooling of Schutzmannschaften in local posts, 19 Aug. 1942, ZSA, 1182-1-17, 128 and 131.

13 About one-third were agricultural workers; the next biggest group were "casual laborers." See report from gendarme leader at Pohrebyshche, 11 Dec. 1943, ZSA, P1182-1-5, and 21 Aug. 1943, ZSA, P1182-1-35. On plundering and court sentences of Ukrainian police, see Koziatyn and Ruzhyn SS and Police district files, 17 July 1941, ZSA, P1151-1-703, P1182-1-6.

14 Nina Borisovna Glozman, interview by Kira Burova, 2 Feb. 1995, Office of Jewish Affairs and Emigration, Zhytomyr Oblast, Ukraine.

15 SS and police district leader, Behrens, Koziatyn, 6 July 1942, ZSA, P1182-1c-2.

16 "Abschlussbericht," Koziatyn Case, BAL, ARZ 204 137/67, Band II, 227–28.

17 Ibid., 229.

18 SS and Police District Leader Behrens memo of 30 Sept. 1942, ZSA, P1182-1-6.

19 See numerous reports of Jan.–July and Oct.–Nov. 1943, SS and police district leaders of Koziatyn and Ruzhyn, ZSA, P1182-1-6 and P1452-1-2.

20 Report of Meister d. Gen u. Postenführer Mayrhofer to Koziatyn SS and police district leader, 13 May 1943, ZSA, P1182-1-6.

21 Hauptmannschaftsbefehl, Berdychiv, order that begins "a special case has made it necessary to advise that it is forbidden to employ Jewish labor in quarters . . . ," 5 June 1942, ZSA, P1151-1-703; Ruzhyn SSPgebF, 1 Mar. 1943, ZSA, P1452-12.

22 SS and Police Leader Heinrich Behrens order of 6 July 1942, ZSA, 1182-1c-1.

23 Pavlo Gorlach, interview by author, 15 May 1996, Zhytomyr, Ukraine. Gorlach was the half brother of Svetlana Borkovsky, born Luba Gerschmann, a Jewish girl who was protected by his mother and brought to the orphanage. The orphanage at Michailovska Street in Zhytomyr concealed eight Jewish children. On the orphanage, see *Zhytomyrshchyna v period*, 47 (document no. 10); and Zhilbovskaia, "The Memory That I Save." Valentina Petrovna Shchenevskaia, a worker at the orphanage who concealed the Jewish children, was honored by Yad Vashem as one of Zhyto-

myr's "Righteous"; interview by author with Shchenevskaia, 22 May 1996, Zhytomyr, Ukraine.

24 Umanskij, *Jüdisches Glück*, 66–67.

25 Kaienburg, "Jüdische Arbeitslager an der 'Strasse der SS,'" 35.

26 Monthly report of SS and police district leader of Koziatyn, Friedrich Baumgärtner,
Nov. 1942, ZSA, P1182-1-32.

27 The average age in July 1942 and on 9 Mar. 1943 was twenty to twenty-five. ZSA,
P1151-1-383.

28 Of these 16,400 Schutzmänner, 7,000 were in the fire brigade; General Commissar, "Lagebericht," 4 May 1943, ZSA, P1151-1-45.

29 The Hitler-OKW policy of rewarding eastern peoples for bravery was introduced
on 17 July 1942. The Richter nomination is dated 31 May 1943; ZSA, P1182-1-38.

30 The SD shooting was at Germanivka; local collective farmers dug the pit. Koziatyn
Case, BAL, 204a AR-Z 137/67, Band II, 233–35.

31 At Radomyshl' as well as nearby Bila Tserkva, it was suggested by German police
and military leaders that the Ukrainians be given the job of executing the children. In another case, the female ethnic German translator for the gendarme post
at Khmil'nyk, Elsa Säler, was accused in eyewitness accounts of identifying and
shooting Jewish children in the ghetto action on 9 Jan. 1942. Koziatyn case, BAL,
Abschlussbericht II 204a ARZ 135/67, 52. Ereignismeldung about Radomyshl', 19
Sept. 1941, NA, RG 242, T-175/R 233/2722427. August Häfner statement about Bila
Tserkva, 10 May 1966, Trial of Kuno Callsen et al., BAL, 207 AR-Z 419/62.

32 Black, "Police Auxiliaries for Operation *Reinhard*."

33 Himmler and other local German commanders were concerned about the psychological repercussions on the German executioners; there were cases of mental
breakdowns and suicide within the Einsatzgruppen. But this concern did not develop into a formal policy of deploying more Ukrainian police as executioners. On
the psychological effects described by former members of SK4a, see statement of
Dr. Arthur Boss, 23 June 1965, and statement of Victor Trill, 8 June 1965, Callsen
Trial, BAL, 207 AR-Z 419/62. Christopher Browning has written that the dramatic
increase in local auxiliaries in 1942 was representative of a "constant tendency to
assign the actual shooting duties to these units, in order to shift the psychological burden from the German police to their collaborators." See Browning, *Ordinary
Men*, 24–25. Richard Breitman demonstrates that Himmler dealt with the psychological effects in other ways, by, for example, "holding social gatherings . . . and by
teaching the men about the political necessity of these measures." See Breitman,
The Architect of Genocide, 173–74, 195–96.

34 The Zhytomyr training school agenda and schedule are among the SS and police
files from Koziatyn, ZSA, P1182-1-35. Also see the Himmler-Rosenberg agreement
defining the anti-Semitic goals of the training, NA, RG 242, T-175/R 146/2673518–
19. Indoctrination of the Schutzmänner as a German policy began in Aug. 1942;

KdO Zhytomyr order on the "Political Instruction of Schutzmannschaften," and report of 18 Sept. 1942, ZSA, P1151-1-147a; also see the SSPF Zhytomyr memo on ideological training, 14 Oct. 1942, ZSA, P1536-1-1.

35 BdO Ukraine, Polizeischulungsleiter, 22 Aug. 1942, ZSA, P1151-1-147a. Similar themes appeared in the training of Sipo-SD elites. See Matthäus, Kwiet, Förster, and Breitman, *Ausbildungsziel Judenmord?*

36 One of the key figures behind the ideological training of the Order Police in Ukraine was Adolf von Bomhard, who assumed the post of commander of the Order Police, Ukraine, on 3 Oct. 1942, and remained in this position until 26 Oct. 1943; see ZSA, P1151-1-10 and P1151-1-11. For Bomhard's wartime and postwar career and defensive strategy (he was mayor of Prien in 1967 and died in 1976), see Martin Hölzl, "Grüner Rock und weisse Weste."

37 This was according to Himmler's order on the "politische Betreuung der Schutzmannschaft," which was issued on 24 June 1942. Some of the educational themes were spelled out first by the Orpo training leader on 22 Aug. 1942, ZSA, P1151-1-147a, and then by the Schupo office in Berdychiv on 8 Oct. 1942, ZSA, P1155-1-5.

38 See the local Order Police commander's order that gendarmes must remain on secured routes during patrols; Befehl 20/42 no.3, ZSA, P1151-1-9. The Zhytomyr training school agenda and schedule are among the SS and police files from Koziatyn, ZSA, P1182-1-35. Also see the Himmler-Rosenberg exchange over the anti-Semitic goals of the training, NA, RG 242, T-175/R 146/2673518–19.

39 A gendarme leader in Berdychiv revealed that Schutzmänner had been deployed as officers without German commanders and had shown themselves to be especially productive; 25 July 1942, RGVA, Moscow 1323-2-228, pp. 14–15. Also see "Hauptmannschaftsbefehl" from Mazyr that Ukrainian Schutzmänner who do not fight partisans during action should be shot on the spot by a fellow Schutzmann, or, if necessary, by a German commander. Aug. (?) 1942, Minsk Archive 658-1-4, microfilm held at USHMM, RG 53.002M, reel 5. The figure of 5,200 men is in an SS-police report of 23 Oct. 1942, ZSA, P1151-1-383.

40 KdG "Kommandobefehl," 6 June 1942, ZSA, P1151-1-9.

41 "Brown File," RGVA, 7021-148-183, pp. 12, 35.

42 See the report of the RKU, Abteilung Ernährung und Landwirtschaft, 20 Feb. 1942, CSA, Kiev, 2306-1-65, microfilm held at USHMM, RG 31.002M, reel 2.

43 On Koziatyn camp and mealtimes, see ZSA, P1182-1-6. Most of the Jews who were held here were killed before Oct. 1942, though a few remained when the camp was closed in May 1943. See correspondence between the SD Berdychiv chief, Knop, and District Commissar Steudel, 5 May 1943, ZSA, P1536-1-2. On the sawdust ration, see testimony of Lev Schein of 4 May 1944, BAL, II 204 AR-Z 122/68, 299.

44 See SS and police district leader of Koziatyn report to SD Berdychiv, 11 Feb. 1943, ZSA, P1182-1-6, pp. 167–68, and gendarme leader of Pohrebyshche to SS and police leader of Koziatyn, 1 Mar. 1943, ZSA, P1182-1-6.

45 Müssig to district commissars, July 1942 and 27 Oct. 1942, ZSA, P1151-1-139.

46 Regierungsrat Göllner order, 27 Nov. 1941, USHMM, ZSA, reel 3, P1188-2-421, microfilm held at USHMM, 1996.A.0269, reel 3. See the "Judenabgabe" lists of Gebietskommissar Dr. Blümel's office, Nov. 1941 to Feb. 1942, ZSA, P1537-1-282, microfilm held at USHMM, 1996.A.0269, reel 3.

47 Klemm to commissariat offices, 12 Dec. 1941, ZSA, P1182-1-6, p. 170.

48 See the several cases regarding the disposition of former Jewish housing on Liubarska Strasse in the city of Zhytomyr. One mentions that an apartment with Jewish furnishings had been occupied by the German sergeant of the field commander's administration; memo of 12 May 1942, ZSA, P1152-1-13.

49 Housing and furniture requests, Herr Plisko's 29 July 1942 revised procedures for handling of Jewish property, ZSA, P1152-1-16.

50 RKU report to Omi Berlin [Rosenberg ministry in Berlin], 21 May 1943, CSA, Kiev, 3676-4-480, microfilm held at USHMM, RG 31.002M, reel 13.

51 See the "Kommandobefehl" of 5 June 1942, ZSA, P1182-1-4. The deliberate medical neglect and killing of persons with physical and mental disabilities occurred in Vinnytsia under City Commissar Margenfeld. See investigation and statement of Fritz Margenfeld (Stadtkommissar Vinnytsia), from 17 Mar. 1971, BAL, Staatsanwaltschaft Stuttgart, 84 Js 3/71, 3–9.

52 In the general commissar's office, Klemm and Leyser's top advisers were Dr. Zagel, Dr. Moyisch, and Dr. Knust; the chief justice was Dr. Gunkel; the chief public prosecutor was Dr. Derks; the chief of staff of the department of economy was Dr. Karl Amend, and his subordinate chief of industry and manufacturing was Dr. Hollnagel; the chief of labor was Dr. Feierabend. The head of food distribution and farming was Dr. Königk. The chief of administration of policy, who oversaw anti-Jewish measures, was Dr. Rauch. See staff charts and telephone listings in ZSA, P1151-1-42. The average age of the commissars and staff heads was thirty-six to forty-five, which means that their doctorates were granted in the period from the late 1920s to the mid-1930s.

53 See the "Verordnung über polizeiliche Strafgewalt der Gebietskommissar," 23 Aug. 41, in the "Brown File," RGVA, 7021-148-183, p. 56.

54 The deputy's name was (Heinrich?) Sundermeier. See the "Abschlussbericht," Litin Case, BAL, II 204a AR-Z 135/6, 561–563.

55 "Abschlussbericht," Koziatyn Case, BAL, 204 ARZ 137/67 Band.II, 20–22.

56 The civil administration in Belorussia played a similar role, according to Chiari, *Alltag hinter der Front*, 59 and chapter 7.

57 One field commander's report revealed the number of army commanders posted in the southern part of the region. Local military administration commanders were in Berdychiv, Haisyn, Brailiv, Nemyriv, Kalynivka, Waldsee, Kordylivka, Brodetske, Chesseliv, Khmil'nyk, Kozhyshiv, Lityn, Popil'nia, Koziatyn, Myropil, Ivanopil', Voronovytsia, Lypovets', and Illintsi. See report of 6 May 1943, ZSA, P1182-1-6.

58 See Case against Franz Razesberger, BAL, II 204 AR-Z 8/80 I, 66–72.

59 "Abschlussbericht," Koziatyn Case, BAL, 204a AR-Z 137/67, Band II, 225.

60 Ibid., 12. The SD killing sweep in Teplyk and Sobolevka is noted in Kruglov, *Unichto-zhenie evreiskogo naseleniia v Vinnitskoi*, 9–10. The cruel treatment of Hungarian Jewish laborers in Ukraine (attached to the Second Hungarian Army) is detailed in Braham, *The Hungarian Labor Service System*, 35–38.

61 Since the early years of the Third Reich, Hitler promoted a policy of exploiting "inferior" elements through hard labor in the first concentration camps, but it was not until Nazi leaders planned for the war in early 1939 that it was decided that Jews who were banned from the Wehrmacht should instead supply the labor for the military's proposed network of roads in the East. This was decided by officials from the army, the Ministry of the Interior, the Gestapo, the Order Police, and the inspector of the Concentration Camps (Theodor Eicke). See Kaienburg, "Jüdische Arbeitslager an der 'Strasse der SS,'" 15. The use of Jews in forced labor projects and the radicalization of this anti-Jewish policy is examined in Aly and Heim, *Vordenker der Vernichtung*, 40, 462. Also see Gruner, *Der geschlossene Arbeitseinsatz deutscher Juden*.

62 The italics are mine. The important distinction here is the German use of the word "verbrauchen," meaning "used up" instead of simply "used." 14 Aug. 1941, NA, RG 242, T-174/R 233/ p. 13.

63 See Ereignismeldung, 25 Sept. 1941, in *The Einsatzgruppen Reports*, ed. Arad, Krakowski, and Spector, 159, and the unedited version of a related Einsatzgruppe C report of 17 Sept. 1941, in NA, RG 242, T-175/R 233/2722383.

64 Ereignismeldung, 20 Aug. 1941, NA, RG 242, T-175/R 233/2721992.

65 See the report "Kriegsgefangenen-Arbeiterkompanien für Strassenunterhaltung," 11 Sept. 1941, Befh.rückw.H.Geb.Süd., NA, RG 242, T-501/R 5/000729–730.

66 In Oct. 1941 Jews had been placed in DG IV camps near L'viv, where the road originated. See Case against Franz Razesberger, BAL, II AR-Z 204 8/80 I, 80. A much larger number of camps and workers were assigned to the L'viv construction of DG IV; see Pohl, *Nationalsozialistische Judenverfolgung in Ostgalizien*.

67 Report of "Kriegsgefangenen-Arbeiterkompanien für Strassenunterhaltung," in war diary of Bfh.rückw.H.Geb.Süd., NA, RG 242, T-501 R 5/000729–730.

68 See Kaienburg, "Jüdische Arbeitslager an der 'Strasse der SS,'" 20–22.

69 Daghani, *The Grave Is in the Cherry Orchard*, 7. The firms were August Dohrmann-Schütte, Feras, Kaspar, Emmerich, Horst Jüssen, Kaiser, Stoer, Teeras, and Ufer. Among the earliest accounts of DG IV operations/camps and the Holocaust, is Hilberg, *The Destruction of the European Jews*, originally published in 1961; see the 3rd ed., 830–31. Also see more detailed research on this by Angrick, "Forced Labor along the Strasse der SS."

70 Statement of Josef Rader, 14 June 1965, and Statement of Friedrich Halle, 23 May 1966, DG IV Case (Friese et al.), BAL, 213 AR-Z 20/63, 253–260, 220–1. Statement of Karl Klenk, 22 Apr. 1965, Landeskriminalamt Baden-Württemberg, Tgb.Nr. SK.

Zst. III/2-35/6. Thanks to Jürgen Matthäus for the Klenk material. Interrogations related to DG IV are found also in Case 213, BAL, AR-Z 86/60, and the investigation of Vinnytsia's SS and police, BAL, 204 AR-Z 188/67.

71 Nor did the commissars always approve of the construction work in their own districts. In Lityn Gebietskommissar Vollkammer (who had been actively involved in anti-Jewish actions in 1942 and had supplied Jewish laborers for the DGIV, which ran about seven kilometers from his office) filed a complaint to the OT station in June 1942 that the excavation of granite in his district had destroyed valuable farmland. ZSA, P1151-1-495. The agricultural leaders had predicted that the DGIV construction would interfere with local farming because of the wide areas around the sites where laborers and guards were stationed. See WistabOst, "Lage der Landwirtschaft in der Ukraine," 17 Apr. 1942, NA, RG 242, T-454/R 92/000670-4.

72 Statement of Josef Rader, 14 June 1965, DG IV Case, BAL, 213 AR-Z 20/63, 253–260; also see Kaienburg, "Jüdische Arbeitslager an der 'Strasse der SS,'" 28–30. See Daghani's exchange with the OT leader regarding Firma Dohrmann's complaint in Daghani, The Grave Is in the Cherry Orchard, 8.

73 "Feldurteil," Gericht der Kdtr. des Bereiches Proskuriv (FK 183), 12 Mar. 1943, in MHI, Prague, various SS records, carton B142. I am grateful to Jürgen Matthäus for this document.

74 See Pohl, Von der "Judenpolitik" zum Judenmord, and Sandkühler, "Endlösung" in Galizien.

75 Goykher, The Tragedy of the Letichev Ghetto, 10.

76 Kaienburg, "Jüdische Arbeitslager an der 'Strasse der SS,'" 34.

77 Ibid., 27–30.

78 A survivor who worked in a quarry run by Firma Horst Jüssen-Steinbrüche in Tul'chyn reported that they were called to work at 4:30 A.M. and at midday received a "meal" of cabbage soup and peas with maggots. See Hilberg, Die Vernichtung der europäischen Juden, 2:834. Daghani, The Grave Is in the Cherry Orchard, 18–19.

79 Daghani, The Grave Is in the Cherry Orchard, 28–29.

80 The OT held contracts with the governments of Hungary, Romania, and Bulgaria regarding construction projects and labor. Hungarian Jews made up some of the larger labor battalions in Ukraine that were controlled by the OT and Wehrmacht. See Braham, The Hungarian Labor Service System, 25–31. For one of the few overviews of the OT, its numerous labor projects in Nazi-occupied Europe, and its relations with private German firms and other government and Party agencies, see the SHAEF study Handbook of the Organization Todt (London: MIRS, Mar. 1945); copies of this study are held at the NA and USHMM.

81 The Bug River was the demarcation line between Romanian-administered Transnistria and German-occupied Ukraine. See request of the German military to the govenor of Transnistria, Odessa Archives, 2264-1-23, microfilm held at USHMM, reel 11. Hilberg, Die Vernichtung der europäischen Juden, 2:834. Jews from Bessarabia and Bukovina who had been deported to Transnistria were given over to the Germans by the Romanians. The Wehrmacht used the Jews in the construction of bridges and

defense fortifications. "Abschlussbericht," Sittig Case, BAL, II 204a AR-Z 141/67, 366–7. Also see exchanges between Romanian Labor offices and prefects in Transnistria with the Wehrmacht in Odessa on the Trihaty bridge project and DG IV work in Nikolaev, Odessa Archives, 2264-1-23, USHMM, RG 31.004M. I am grateful to Viorel Achim for bringing these reports to my attention and translating the Romanian.

82 See Karl Klenk testimony of 19 May 1967, BAL, 213 AR-Z 20/63.

83 See Ernst Johannes Schmidt (b. 1908) testimony of 4 June 1962, BAL, 204 AR-Z 188/67, Band I, 94–98 and 260–285. The figure of 25,000 is from Kaienburg, "Jüdische Arbeitslager an der 'Strasse der SS,'" 38.

84 Khmil'nyk massacres in BAL, II 204 AR-Z 135/67. Kruglov, *Unichtozhenie evreiskogo naseleniia v Vinnitskoi*, 14.

85 See the telegram to RSD (Reich Sicherheitsdienst) leader, SS Standartenführer Rattenhuber, 28 Jan. 1942, regarding security at Eichenhain and skilled labor at the construction site. This stated that Reichsminister "Dr. Todt will place several hundred Jews at the building site." Security officials (Himmler's SD chiefs) opposed this measure. CSA, Kiev, 3676-4-116, microfilm held at USHMM, RG 31.002M, reel 11.

86 A large portion of the Jewish labor used in the northern part of the Zhytomyr region came from Hungary. The presence of Hungarian Jews in the region was further revealed by a report about an incident of 29 Apr. 1943 when the Germans placed 300 Hungarian Jews in a barn of the collective farm in Kupyshche (Korosten') and set the barn on fire. RKU Rivne to Omi Berlin, 21 May 1943, CSA, Kiev, 3676-4-480, microfilm held at USHMM, RG 31.002M, reel 13. Hungarian Minister of Defense Nagy's inquiry and survivor testimonies estimated that 600 Jews died in the massacre of 30 Apr. 1943. The barns had served as a quarantined area for Jews with typhoid who had been left to die, located on the Dorozhishche collective farm. See Braham, *The Hungarian Labor Service System*, 39.

87 See the "Fernschreiben" of 28 Jan. 1942, CSA, Kiev, 3676-4-116, microfilm held at USHMM, RG 31.002M, reel 11.

88 See the Himmler memo of 10 Jan. 1942 regarding the Jewish question in the East, NA, RG 242, T-454/ R 154/MR334.

89 Hitler arrived on 16 July and stayed until 1 Nov. 1941. He returned on 17 Feb. 1943 and remained through 13 Mar. 1943. See the construction and security memos, RGVA, Moscow 1323-2-231, microfilm held at USHMM, RG 11.001M.15, reel 81, and "Abschlussbericht," Schmidt/Danner Case, Sta München, 111Js 24/69. I am grateful to Konrad Kwiet for bringing "Eichenhain" and related sources to my attention.

90 The RSD developed from a special protection service for the Führer, known as the Führerschutzkommando. The SS and police officers who secured the Führer headquarters were placed under the Geheime Feldpolizei Ost (a special military secret field police group in the East). The chief of this group in Vinnytsia was Fried-

rich Schmidt, and his deputy was Karl Danner. See "Abschlussbericht," Schmidt-Danner Case, BAL, case no. 111Js 24/69.

91 Original German document dated 1 Jan. 1942, quoted in the "Abschlussbericht," Schmidt/Danner Case, Sta München, 111 Js 24/69.

92 Pre-Dec. cleansing of the area is mentioned in Schmidt's report to Rattenhuber, 11 Dec. 1941, CSA, Kiev, 3676-4-116, microfilm held at USHMM, RG 31.002M, reel 11. Rattenhuber ordered the Gebietskommissar to carry out the actions (report of 12 Jan. 1942). Later, at the end of Mar., it was decided to clear the area from the airport to the headquarters. CSA, Kiev, 3676-4-116, microfilm held at USHMM, RG 31.002M, reel 11.

93 GPU (Glavnoe Politicheskoe Upravlenie) — that is, Main Political Office — operated in the Soviet Union during the 1920s and became the NKVD in the 1930s. Officials involved in the Strizhavka operation included four Sipo, twenty Feldgendarmerie and Schupo, and other personnel from the Eichenhain office. See Schmidt's "Short Report about the Activities of the Office in the New Security Area," 12 Jan. 1942, CSA, Kiev, 3676-4-116, microfilm held at USHMM, RG 31.002M, reel 11.

94 Generalmajor Reichtmeier to Zhytomyr gendarme stations (17 of them), 28 Jan. 1942, ZSA, P1151-1-39, USHMM, reel 8. For Nazi searches for "fleeing Jews" from Kamenets Podoliia'yi and from Tschenstochau, Poland, possibly headed toward Vinnytsia area in May and June 1942, see ZSA, P1182-1-1.

95 Massacres in early Aug. and on 13 Sept. 1941 took the lives of 1,550 Jews. Israel Weiner, letter about the fate of his family members in Vinnytsia, 1 May 1944, copy at USHMM, RG 22.00301.

96 Bullets were not "wasted" on the smaller children, who were crushed by hand and then thrown into the mass graves. Soviet witness statements, statement of Lev Aleksandrovich Shein, 5 May 1944, Schmidt/Danner Case, BAL, II 204a/AR-Z 122/68, 300–302. Statement of Fritz Margenfeld, 28 July 1971, BAL, Stuttgart Staatsanwaltschaft, 84 Js 3/71, 1. In the first half of Aug. EK5 killed about 600 Jews in Vinnytsia and 229 Jews in Khmil'nyk; in addition 150 were killed at Tomashpil', and 57 at Litin. See Kruglov, *Unichtozhenie evreiskogo naseleniia v Vinnitskoi oblasti*, 6–7.

97 The brick works was located at the edge of town; it normally housed about 250 workers. Ereignismeldung C report, 21 Aug. 1941, NA, RG 242, T-175/R 233/ 2722029. With regard to its being an OT-Eichenhain operation, see the city commissar of Vinnytsia's report on industry in Vinnytsia, 1 Nov. 1942, NA, RG 242, T-454/R 91/000885–888.

98 Communication between the SS-Police Leader Vinnytsia, Major Pomme, and district commissars of Vinnytsia with the chief of Sipo and SD Vinnytsia (Salmanzig) are described in a security report sent to Rattenhuber, Chief RSD, "Judenfrage in Winniza und Umgebung," CSA, Kiev, 3676-4-116, microfilm held at USHMM, RG 31.002M, reel 11.

99 See the survivor witness statement of Solomon Goliak, 11 Sept. 1969, BAL, 204a

AR-Z 122/68, 196–197; and the statement of Johann Bahmann, 15 Oct. 1965, BAL, 204a AR-Z 122/68, 223–5. This massacre is also described in Gutman, ed., *Encyclopedia of the Holocaust*, vol. 4, s.v. "Vinnitsa."

100 See the report to Rattenhuber (illegible date), "Judenfrage in Winniza und Umgebung," CSA, Kiev, 3676-4-116, microfilm held at USHMM, RG 31.002M, reel 11; also see Ereignismeldung of 29 Aug. 1941, and Einsatzgruppe C report of 14 Aug. 1941, in *The Einsatzgruppen Reports*, ed. Arad, Krakowski, and Spector, 87, 119. See Ancel, *Transnistria*.

101 Razesberger order to SD Vinnytsia, 11 July 1942. CSA, Kiev, 3676-4-116, p. 56; thanks to Richard Breitman for this document. According to Shmuel Spector, this order was rescinded by the local SD office in Vinnytsia and Prützmann to the extent that a small number were killed then and the rest were sent to the Jewish labor camps in the area, and died later in 1942 and 1943. See Gutman, ed., *Encyclopedia of the Holocaust*, vol. 4, s.v. "Vinnitsa."

102 Kriegsverdienstkreuz and Werwolf compound measures, RGVA, 1323-2-231, microfilm held at USHMM, RG 11.001M.15, reel 81.

103 The compound contained a swimming pool, a movie theater, a teahouse, an officer's club, a barbershop, and a residence for Martin Bormann (the military's General Staff chief), Hitler's personal aides, and top security personnel. Two local historians in Vinnytsia, Luiza Bilozerova and Faina Vinokurova, have investigated Werwolf and the fate of the POWs. In Feb. 2003 the actual site was for sale, stirring up local conflicts about its economic value as a tourist site versus its noncommercial value as a memorial site. See Myroslava Sokolova, "Werewolf [sic] for Sale: What Should Happen to Hitler's Former Underground Headquarters?," in the newspaper *Den* (Kiev), 4 Feb. 2003.

104 Himmler's Hegewald compound was run by more than 100 SS officers and 1,000 SS men; it was bordered by the Teteriv and Gryva rivers, placed along the road from Zhytomyr to Berdychiv at a former Soviet air base. Underground communications were established between the bunkers, airport and headquarters. Today it is a large cargo airport located in Ozerne; two of the German bunkers remain, but the Himmler headquarters was largely destroyed during the Nazi evacuation.

105 Testimony of Franz Razesberger, 18 July 1961, 158–162, Landesgericht Wien, 20 Vr/5774/60, microfilm held at USHMM, RG 17.003M, #1103 and 1104.

106 Razesberger got his instructions from Thomas in Kiev. Razesberger claims that they delayed killing the Jews for about a month until May, when they feared the arrival of Himmler. Testimony of Franz Razesberger, BAL, III 204 AR-Z 8/80, 326–327.

107 According to Hülsdunker, he had been told when he arrived in May 1942 that an oral Hitler order had been given to shoot every Jew. The SD Berdychiv office consisted of three officers, two Gestapo/Stapo agents, six SS men, thirty-fifty Ukrainian militia, and twenty-five Ukrainian agents (Kripo and V-männer). See Case against Knop et al. in *Justiz und NS-Verbrechen*, 16:345–49.

108 See Borisovich's testimony in Elisavetskii, *Berdichevskaia tragediia*, 81. I am grateful to Asya Vaisman for translating this testimony from Russian into English.

109 Ehrenburg and Grossman, eds., *The Black Book*, 23.

110 City Commissar's Office, Abteilung IIIa, 26 Oct. 1942, NA, RG 242 T454, roll 91/000885/p. 9. On the 300 Jews in the clothing factory, see Professor Grunberg's report of 10 Sept. 1942. CSA, Kiev, 3206-2-116, microfilm held at USHMM, RG 31.002M, reel 3.

111 See the statement of the former truck driver at Stalag 358, Friedrich Buck, 26 Nov. 1969, in "Abschlussbericht," Case against Franz Razesberger, BAL, II 204 AR-Z 8/80 I, 85.

Chapter Seven

1 In June 1941 Himmler chose the code name "Hegewald" for his East Prussian field headquarters fifty kilometers from Hitler's Wolfsschanze. In mid-July 1942 he established his Hegewald headquarters near Zhytomyr and renamed his East Prussian site "Hochwald." The German verb *hegen* means to "preserve," "look after," or "nurse." A *Hegemeister* is a gamekeeper. In the Nazi context, the term *Hegehof* was rumored to mean a "breeding yard" where reliable Nordic girls begot children with SS men under the jurisdiction of the SS Race and Settlement Office. Multiple references to Hegewald are found in Witte et al., eds., *Der Dienstkalender Heinrich Himmlers*.

2 The Hitler-Himmler vision of the Germanized eastern landscape is described in a number of sources, including the somewhat problematic (self-vindicating) memoir by Albert Speer, *Infiltration*, 296. More reliable sources include Hartenstein, *Neue Dorflandschaften*, 25–28; Madajczyk, ed., *Vom Generalplan Ost zum Generalsiedlungsplan*. Also see Harvey, *Women and the Nazi East*.

3 See W. Smith, *The Ideological Origins of Nazi Imperialism*.

4 Alan Steinweis, "Eastern Europe and the Notion of the 'Frontier' in Germany to 1945," in *Germany and Eastern Europe* (Yearbook of European Studies 13), ed. Bullivant, Giles, and Pape, 62.

5 Harvey, *Women and the Nazi East*, 3.

6 White, "Majdanek"; Pohl, *Von der "Judenpolitik" zum Judenmord*.

7 The concept of "settlement pearls" was presented in an Aug. 1942 meeting at Hegewald. See the "Summary Notes" from the conference on Volksdeutsche, NA, RG 238, No-2278; see also in the entry for 10 Aug. 1942 in *Der Dienstkalender Heinrich Himmlers*, ed. Witte et al., 510–11.

8 Few records about Himmler's Hegewald SS compound survived the war, and many may remain classified in former Soviet archives. See the report of SS Oberführer Jungkunz on the evacuation and destruction of Himmler's headquarters, which reveals the facilities on the compound, for example, two airfields, large military training/exercise facilities, more than twenty houses and building, shops, warehouses, and a "Heroes Cemetery"; evacuation "diary" of events from Nov. 1943,

NA, RG 242, T-175/R 72/2589091–95. There is some description of the base in Breitman, *The Architect of Genocide*, 238, drawn largely from the postwar statement of the SD chief in Zhytomyr who visited the site, Franz Razesberger; statement of 19 Jan. 1957, BAL, 204 AR-Z 8/ 80, 204–6.

9 In Aug. 1942 Himmler expanded Hoffmeyer's position as chief of Sonderkommando Russland by creating the "Volksdeutsche Leitstelle," formally combining various SS offices that dealt with ethnic German programs and resettlement, such as the RKFDV, the Rasse- und Siedlungshauptamt (RuSHA), VoMi, and SS Wirtschafts- und Verwaltungshauptamt into a new SS "coordinating" office for ethnic Germans in the East. It was under the direct command of Higher SS and Police Leader Prützmann in Kiev, but the office itself was situated in Zhytomyr near Hegewald. Lumans, *Himmler's Auxiliaries*, 246.

10 In the Soviet territories, there were no independent offices of Heydrich's EWZ (Einwandererzentralstelle, Central Immigration Office) or of Eichmann's UWZ (Umwandererzentralstelle, Central Resettlement Office). The revised GPO (Generalplan Ost, General Plan East) of May 1942 incorporated the former Soviet territories and planned for settlement centers in Ukraine (Rivne, Shepetivka, Berdychiv, Bila Tserkva, Bobruisk, Piatykhatky, Kryvyi Rih, and Nikolaev). Five months later the plans were scaled back to mainly the Black Sea region and Zhytomyr, with centers in Zviahel, Berdychiv, Zhytomyr, Uman', Nikolaev, and Dnipropetrovs'k. Heinemann, *"Rasse, Siedlung, deutsches Blut,"* 451.

11 Himmler's Hegewald speech, 16 Sept. 1942, NA, RG 242, T-175/R 90/2612809, p. 4.

12 See General Commissar Klemm memo to his district commissars about the meeting with SS-VoMi leader Hoffmeyer on 25 May 1942, ZSA, P1151-1-120.

13 The Hegewald settlement was promoted in the *Deutsche Ukraine-Zeitung* (Luts'k), 5 May 1943. For a comparison of facilities in the Ukrainian Volksdeutsche settlements, see the VoMi report dated 3 Aug. 1943, NA, RG 242, T-175/R 72/2589157.

14 On the different experiences of the Volksdeutsche in relation to the Holocaust, see Bergen, "The 'Volksdeutschen' of Eastern Europe, World War II, and the Holocaust"; Valdis O. Lumans, "A Reassessment of Volksdeutsche and Jews in the Volhynia-Galicia-Narew Resettlement," in *The Impact of Nazism*, ed. Rogers and Steinweis, 81–100.

15 See Aly, "Final Solution"; Aly and Heim, *Vordenker der Vernichtung*; R.-D. Müller, *Hitlers Ostkrieg*; and Koehl, *RKFDV*.

16 R.-D. Müller, *Hitlers Ostkrieg*, 8.

17 Doris Bergen argues in her thoughtful analysis of the Volksdeutsche and the Holocaust that the "tenuousness of the notion of 'Volksdeutsche' actually contributed to the intensification of anti-semitism." True, the Nazi mission to "rescue" the Volksdeutsche served as a rationale for some German perpetrators of the Holocaust. Even Himmler told his men at Hegewald to remember that the current sacrifices and hardships they endured in the East were heroic contributions toward Germany's future Lebensraum. In Zhytomyr, the more common rationale "on paper"

for killing Jews was "to secure the Reich"; this Nazi approach provided an immediate, convincing motivation for actions against the Jews whom the Nazis deemed the most threatening. See Bergen, "The Nazi Concept of 'Volksdeutsche,'" 578.

18 In the summer of 1942, when Zhytomyr's SD chief, Franz Razesberger, issued an oral order to kill the remaining Jews in Berdychiv (many of whom had labored at Hegewald), he explained the murder as a "security precaution." On the Razesberger order, see Case against Knop et al., in *Justiz und NS-Verbrechen*, 16:345–49. See also Dieter Pohl, "Schauplatz Ukraine," in *Ausbeutung, Vernichtung, Öffentlichkeit*, ed. Frei.

19 See Koehl, RKFDV, 49–70. The RFSS ordinance on Party and SS jurisdiction regarding ethnic questions (NO-4237) is reprinted in Koehl, 251–52. On the history of VoMi, see Lumans, *Himmler's Auxiliaries*.

20 The German People's List (DVL) consisted of four categories: Group I represented those deemed racially Aryan and willing to be Germanized; Group II, racially pure Germans who lacked a will to be Germanized but were capable of being Germanized; Group III those with mixed but predominantly Aryan blood and capable of being Germanized, and who could apply for temporary Reich citizenship and then live under racial political surveillance for ten years before receiving citizenship; Group IV were those with only some German blood, assimilated to other groups and unwilling to become German citizens or considered unfit for Germanization. Persons in the last category were handed over to the Gestapo and then were sent to camps or liquidated on the spot. Those who fit into categories I and II were immediately eligible for Reich German citizenship. See Fleischhauer and Pinkus, *The Soviet Germans*, 96–97.

21 VoMi activity report for Sept.–Dec. 1941. "Aussenstelle Zhitomir" was led by SS Obersturmführer Müller, who arrived on 23 Sept. 1941, ZSA, P1151-1-120. On Müller's arrival, see KTB SD454, NA, RG 242, T-315/2216/000146.

22 Later, Himmler's commandos counted 76,737 Volksdeutsche in Dnipropetrovs'k and 127,000 Volksdeutsche in Transnistria. Himmler's VoMi worked with the population under Romanian control in Transnistria and planned to resettle these Germans to Crimea, but these plans were cut short in 1943. In Dnipropetrovs'k Nazi leaders concentrated into settlements 5,376 Volksdeutsche who had been spread across that region's 194 villages. See VoMi report of 3 Aug. 1943, NA, RG 242, T-175/R 72/2589163.

23 Stumpp's *Ostwanderung* (1941) was the second volume in the series *Sammlung Georg Leibbrandt, Quellen zur Erforschung des Deutschtums in Osteuropa*. Leibbrandt was Rosenberg's chief of the political department in the Ostministerium from July 1941 to 1943. For a recent analysis of Stumpp's and Leibbrandt's work in Ukraine and their postwar fate, see Schmaltz and Sinner, "The Nazi Ethnographic Research of Georg Leibbrandt and Karl Stumpp." Also see Brown, *A Biography of No Place*, 193–235.

24 Many of his ethnic German investigators were attached to the army's agricultural inspectors. See Stumpp report to Roques regarding his field work in Zhytomyr, 14 Aug. 1941, NA, RG 242, T-501/R 6/001142.

25 On the goals of NSV in the East, see CSA, Kiev, 3206-6-256, microfilm held at USHMM, RG 31.002M, reel 6; for clothing drives in Zhytomyr, see ZSA, P1151-1-11.

26 On shipment of Jewish belongings from the Reich and from France to Zhytomyr, see the correspondence between party leader Degenhard at RMfdbO and NSV, 2 July 1942, CSA, Kiev, 3206-6-258, microfilm held at USHMM, RG 31.002M, reel 6.

27 See the Einsatzgruppe C report of 7 Oct. 1941, in *The Einsatzgruppen Reports*, ed. Arad, Krakowski, and Spector, 174.

28 Hoffmeyer was "attached to the SD office in Kiev, under the command of HSSPF Russland Süd." Lumans finds that the VoMi representatives relied heavily on local SD task forces, but he does not explore whether VoMi personnel were also involved in the anti-Jewish massacres that the SD forces were simultaneously carrying out. Lumans, *Himmler's Auxiliaries*, 244–45.

29 See the report "Hauptamt VoMi, Aussenstelle Shitomir: Arbeit und Aufgaben der Volksdeutschen Mittelstelle," Sept.–Dec. 1941, ZSA, P1151-1-120. Also see the Hoffmeyer report of 12 Oct. 1941, NA, RG 242, T-454/R 100/000661–670.

30 Klemm to all city and district commissars, 5 Feb. 1942, ZSA, P1151-1-120. This order was quickly followed by a circular memo to the commissars from Koch's office clarifying that the Volksdeutsche Mittelstelle under SS Oberführer Hoffmeyer was charged with the task of taking in and training ethnic German men who could support security and administrative measures, and that the Stumpp teams were surveying through questionnaires the ethnic German settlements and individuals. The commissars were instructed to assist in these efforts as well as care for the needy; Volksdeutsche RKU(IIa) memo, 6 Feb. 1942, ZSA, P1151-1-120.

31 See Schmidt, "Lagebericht" (illegible date), with references to spring 1942, ZSA, P1151-1-142.

32 General Commissar Klemm report on Volksdeutsche teachers to Nazi Party headquarters in Berlin, 5 Mar. 1942, in CSA, Kiev, 3206-6-255, microfilm held at USHMM, RG 31.002M, reel 6.

33 A series of articles appeared in July 1942 about the ethnic German celebrations in Zhytomyr surrounding the building of the kindergarten. *Deutsche Ukraine-Zeitung* (Luts'k), 1 July 1942, 2 July 1942, 5 July 1942, and 9 July 1942, Library of Congress, newspaper microfilm 3010.

34 See "Vermerk," 9 June 1942, CSA, Kiev, 3206-6-255 microfilm held at USHMM, RG 31.002M, reel 6, and "Einweisung von 14 Kindergärtnerinnen zur Betreuung Volksdeutscher in der Ukraine," 21 July 1942, CSA, Kiev, 3206-6-255, microfilm held at USHMM, RG 31.002M, reel 6.

35 See NSV, "Lagebericht," 29 Sept. 1942, Zhytomyr, CSA, Kiev, 3206-6-255, microfilm held at USHMM, RG 31.002M, reel 6. On 16 Dec. 1942, commissars announced that schooling was mandatory for ethnic German children. *Deutsche Ukraine-Zeitung* (Luts'k), 16 Dec. 1942, p. 3, Library of Congress, newspaper microfilm 3010.

36 See the NSV report of 11–12 June 1942 and RMfdbO report of 15 June 1942, CSA,

Kiev, 3206-6-255, microfilm held at USHMM, RG 31.002M, reel 6. Irma Wildhagen and her staff of nurses set up infant-mother stations in Cherniakhiv, Novohrad-Volyns'kyi, Andreïv, Goroshki, and Sadki. See the overview of NSV staff dated 11 Aug. 1942, CSA, Kiev, 3206-6-255, microfilm held at USHMM, RG 31.002M, reel 6.

37 This file on educational materials for German youth in the East contains no date, but it is probably from late 1942–early 1943. ZSA, P1151-1-139. See Koch memo to general commissars about educating Volksdeutsche about racial crimes and punishment vis-à-vis the Jews, 13 May 1942, ZSA, P1151-1-120.

38 Hoffmeyer report, 12 Oct. 1941, NA, RG 242, T-454/R 100/000661–670.

39 RKU circular memo to all Reich German youth leaders, kindergarten teachers, and kindergarten aides on goals of work in Ukraine, 1 Sept. 1942, CSA, Kiev, 3206-6-255, microfilm at USHMM, RG 31.002M, reel 6. Commissariat and NSV officials actively promoted a Lutheran church in Zhytomyr where Pastor Lemke preached about obedience to Hitler. See report of 20 Mar. 1942, ZSA, P1151-1-147.

40 For an insightful analysis of Reich women sent to Poland, see Harvey, "Die Deutsche Frau im Osten," 191–214.

41 Stadtkommissar IIa to VoMi Zhytomyr, 20 Feb. 1942, ZSA, P1151-1-120.

42 Behrens to SD Berdychiv regarding Herbert Hafke, 21 Apr. 1943, ZSA, P1182-1-35.

43 The official ration amounts were published in the "Verordnungsblatt," 20 Feb. 1942, CSA, Kiev, 2306-1-65, microfilm held at USHMM, RG 31.002M, reel 2.

44 See Wedelstadt order of 7 Apr. 1942, ZSA, P1151-1-21.

45 See VoMi memo about ration cards and shops from late Dec. 1941 to early 1942, ZSA, P1151-1-138.

46 Stumpp's representative in Zhytomyr, Erdmann, reported on Volksdeutsche activities there, 30 Apr. 1943, CSA, Kiev, microfilm held at USHMM, RG 31.002M, reel 11. Ethnic German perks included a Black Sea resort trip for training in trades and tours of the Reich; NA, RG 242, T-315/R 2216/000272–273.

47 See Himmler Decree, 9 Dec. 1940, NA, RG 242, T-175/R 194/2732996. See VoMi (undated) memo (in a 1940–41 file) about plans for the Soviet Union, which states that "in essence the financing of the resettlement will come from the confiscated property of those foreign peoples being pushed out." NA, RG 242, T-175/R 194/2732977. Commander Karl von Roques ordered the ethnic Germans be given better homes and supplies available from vacated Jewish homes and local "plunder" depots. Order of Commander Occupied Rear Army South, 28 Aug. 1941, NA, RG 242, T-501/R 5/000803. See NSV "tasks" under the district commissars, "IV. Vorläufige Aufgaben," regarding "Judennachlass," CSA, Kiev, 3206-6-254, microfilm held at USHMM, RG 31.002M, reel 6, p. 5.

48 According to Koch's office, the SS-commissar, or SS-Gebietshauptmann, was a Himmler appointee, but was still part of the district commissariat administration, 16 Dec. 1942. ZSA, P1151c-1-17. Himmler named Otto Jungkunz (b. 1892) the Ge-

bietskommissar of Hegewald. Jungkunz joined the Nazi Party in 1933, worked in the mayor's office in Göttingen, and was the station commissioner at Hegewald before being appointed Gebietskommissar in the fall of 1942.

49 After a meeting with Hitler on 25 July, Himmler hosted a dinner at Hegewald; he brought up the topic of the Volksdeutsche, speaking rather sincerely about his plans for them, and then switched suddenly to the issue of the partisan menace. Himmler's discussion after the Hitler meeting described in the statement of Franz Razesberger, 19 Jan. 1957, BAL, 204 AR-Z 8/80, 204–6.

50 See Jochmann, ed., *Die Monologe im Führerhauptquartier*, 335. The notes from this meeting at Werwolf are undated, but on 9 Aug. 1942 Himmler was at Hitler's bunker with most of the individuals named in the conference notes, and the meeting that followed this one at Hegewald on 10 Aug. concerned the implementation of programs that had been decided the previous day at the Werwolf bunker. Participants in the Werwolf conference about Volksdeutsche were Himmler's chief of personal staff, Karl Wolff; the VoMi director, Werner Lorenz; HSSPF Russland-Süd Hans Prützmann; the SS liaison to Omi, Gottlob Berger; the chief of RKF, Ulrich Greifelt; State Secretary in the Interior Ministry and SS Major General Wilhelm Stuckart; Generalplan Ost designer Prof. Dr. Konrad Meyer; and possibly HSSPF Gerret Korsemann. The file notes from the "Besprechung im Führerhauptquartier" are in NA, RG 242, T-175/R 17/2521076–9. In *Der Dienstkalender Heinrich Himmlers*, the Himmler-Hitler meeting of 9 Aug. 1942 is identified on pp. 509–10.

51 Himmler memo to Gottlob Berger about the incompetence of Rosenberg's commissars regarding the ethnic Germans, Aug. 1942, NA, RG 242, T-175/R 66/2582327. Hitler gave the SS control over partisan warfare in the civilian occupied zones with directive #46 on 18 Aug. 1942; NA, RG 238 477-PS. Himmler appointed Erich von dem Bach-Zelewski SS plenipotentiary for antipartisan warfare in the East at the end of Oct. 1942; NA, RG 238 NO-1661. See Dallin, *German Rule in Russia*, 210–11.

52 Conference notes from Hitler headquarters, NA, RG 242, T-175/R 17/2521076–1079. On Hitler's remarks about Germanizing Ukraine, see Dallin, *German Rule in Russia*, 286. Additional material about the formation of Hegewald is in NA, RG 238, NO-2278; CSA, Kiev, 3206-255-6, microfilm held at USHMM, RG 31.002M, reel 6; NA, RG 242, T-175/R 71/2587879, T-175/R 88/2611402.

53 Ioanid, *The Holocaust in Romania*, 187–201, 232–37. See Zentralstelle Dortmund gegen Dr. Siebert und andere, BAL, 45 Js 26/62, and Dalia Ofer, "The Holocaust in Transnistria," in *The Holocaust in the Soviet Union*, ed. Dobroszycki and Gurock, 136–38.

54 See Oelhafen order about the Selbstschutz, 30 July 1942, RGVA, Moscow 1323-2-255, microfilm held at USHMM, RG 11.001M, reel 81. For the Selbstschutz in Ukraine and Transnistria, see meeting notes, NA, RG 242, T-175/R 17/2521076–79. On restricting ethnic German police and translators to settlements in the promo-

55 By comparison, there were sixteen Selbstschutz schools in Transnistria, which trained 7,000 men. See undated report, NA, RG 242, T-175/R 72/2589180.

56 See Himmler letter to Berger, insisting on his control over the ethnic Germans in Russia, Aug. 1942, NA, RG 242, T-175/R 66/2582327.

tion of ethnic German marriages, see Commander of the Order Police for Ukraine Bomhard order of 17 Sept. 1942, ZSA, P1182-1-23.

57 Rosenberg's response to Himmler's order to Koch, 28 Sept. 1942, NA, RG 242, T-175/R 17/2521081, 2521101.

58 On paper Rosenberg won this battle. It seems that Hitler desired a decentralization of ethnic German politics and resettlement actions, and he also may have wanted to further the Party's role by ordering (during a meeting at Vinnytsia with Himmler, Koch, Prützmann, Koch's deputy Paul Dargel, and Hoffmeyer) that "the arrangement of all folk and German questions happen in RKU exclusively through the General and Gebietskommissar." At the same time Hitler ordered that within the major stronghold of ethnic Germans, specifically at Korosten', Hegewald, Vinnytsia, Halbstadt, and Kronau, the SS should appoint the district commissars. On Hitler decisions from the meeting of 23 Oct. 1942, see Dargel's notes dated 24 Oct. 1942, CSA, Kiev, 3206-255-6, microfilm held at USHMM, RG 31.002M, reel 6.

59 Theo Henschel (b. 18 Feb. 1904, Schlesien). He joined the Nazi Party in 1928 and became a district propaganda leader and SA man. In Dec. 1939, after a few years in the Race and Resettlement Office (RuSHA), he was appointed by Himmler to the latter's personal staff of the RKFDV. Prior to his assignment in Zhytomyr, Henschel led one of the three RuSHA task forces in the 1939 invasion of Poland, organized the seizure of industries around Lodz, and was chief of the SS-Bodenamt in Danzig–West Prussia. See Heinemann, "Rasse, Siedlung, Deutsches Blut," 454–455. See Theo Henschel SS Personnel File, NA, RG 242, Berlin Document Center Records, A-3343, SSO-87A-88A. I am grateful to Isabel Heinemann for providing me with a copy of this file.

60 R.-D. Müller, Hitlers Ostkrieg, document appendix, 193–96.

61 Heinemann, "Rasse, Siedlung, Deutsches Blut," 436–37.

62 Dallin, German Rule in Russia, 286. Dallin misdated the resettlement to Hegewald, perhaps confusing it with the Nov. action in Cherniakhiv (Neuborn).

63 See NSV, "Lagebericht for East," with plans for an Ovruch action, 29 Sept. 1942, CSA, Kiev, 3206-6-255, microfilm held at USHMM, RG 31.002M, reel 6.

64 See Standartenführer Henschel report on Hegewald action, given at the resettlement commission meeting with representatives of the general commissar staff, NSV, SSPF, and VoMi on 6 Nov. 1942, ZSA, P1151-1-120.

65 Himmler had sent an earlier memo to Pohl and Lorenz about supplying for Christmas all the major Volksdeutsche settlements (Hegewald, Transnistria, Halbstadt [Dnipropetrovs'k], Korets', Nikolaev, and Lublin) with items from depots in Lublin and Auschwitz. See Himmler order of 6 Oct. 1942, NA, RG 238, NO-5395 and T-175/R 129/2655141. For a subsequent memo of 20 Oct. requesting that the ethnic

Germans in Hegewald receive an immediate shipment of wares, see Witte et al., eds., *Der Dienstkalender Heinrich Himmlers*, 591–92.

66 This was "according to Koch's Oct. decree on the granting of property to ethnic Germans who have been classified in the German People's List under categories one, two, and three." Koch order of 15 Oct. 1942. *Zhytomyrshchyna v period*, document #71, 104.

67 General Commissar Leyser memo of 16 Nov. 1942, *Zhytomyrshchyna v period*, document #72, 104–5. The original is to be found in ZSA, P1151-1-32.

68 On Kiev settlers sent to Hegewald, making "this area fully settled," see Leyser, "Lagebericht," Mar.–Apr. 1943, ZSA, P1151-1-45. Also see Dallin, *German Rule in Russia*, 286. For the increase in the geographic area of Hegewald, see the RKU survey of the "Generalbezirk Shitomir," 1 Jan. 1943, CSA, Kiev, microfilm held at USHMM, RG 31.002M, reel 3.

69 The SS agricultural leaders were drawn from the ranks of the Order Police and RuSHA. Henschel and RuSHA chief Tesseraux met at Hegewald on 13 Sept. 1942 to plan for these police and economic posts. They specified that the SS men posted in Hegewald be older men with experience in agriculture (about thirty or forty men). See meeting notes from 13 Sept. 1942 meeting and a Henschel memo of 1 Oct. 1942 in Theo Henschel SS Personnel File, NA, RG 242, Berlin Document Center Records, A3343 SSO-87A-88A. Also see Heinemann, "*Rasse, Siedlung, Deutsches Blut,*" 457.

70 There was also a teacher training school in Novohrad-Volyns'kyi, June–July 1943; ZSA, P1151-1-185.

71 See instructions for the rally of 24 Mar. 1943, ZSA, P1151-1-146. A smaller festival occurred at the beginning of May. See *Deutsche Ukraine-Zeitung* (Luts'k), 5 May 1943, p. 3, Library of Congress, newspaper microfilm 3010. Paul Dargel was the deputy to Erich Koch and was later assigned to Bormann as a liaison officer with the Vlasov Army. Reitlinger, *The House Built on Sand*, 434.

72 A Nazi Party district leader in Zhytomyr, Maria Cormann, complained that the Volksdeutsche rations were as poor as those allotted to the local prisoners. See the comparison of ethnic German and non-German rations in Cormann report of 29 Oct. 1942, CSA, Kiev, microfilm in USHMM, RG 31.002M, reel 11.

Chapter Eight

1 This development is examined extensively in Jan Gross's *Polish Society under German Occupation*, an early work in this area of research.

2 Leyser tried to formalize religious structures for the entire commissariat under the leadership of three bishops, two in Vinnytsia and one in Zhytomyr; "Lagebericht," Mar.–Apr. 1943, ZSA, P1151-1-26. See General Commissar Leyser order about the registration of priests, 24 Mar. 1943, ZSA, P1182-1-6. See Wehrmachtsbefehlshaber Kitzinger critique of 17 June 1942, NA, RG 242, T-454/R 92/000653–659.

3 Zviahel Gebietskommissariat, payroll list, May 1943. Of the eighty-seven staff

members, only seven (who were mainly Volksdeutsche) were hired during July–Dec. 1941. See ZSA, P1465-1-7, microfilm in USHMM, Acc 1996.A.0269, reel 6.

4 Armstrong, ed., *Soviet Partisans in World War II*; Fyodorov, *The Underground Committee Carries One*; *Stryvozhena pam'iat'*; Poltava, *The Ukrainian Insurgent Army*; Tys-Krokhma- liuk, *UPA Warfare in Ukraine*; Kohn and Roiter, *A Voice from the Forest*.

5 Weiner, *Making Sense of War*, 156.

6 The first Ukrainian nationalist guerrilla group was formed in Polissia under Boro- vets, who had had ties to the Ukrainian National Republic in 1918–20; Armstrong, *Ukrainian Nationalism*, 103–5. At Ushomir, Jews who had escaped the first massa- cres attacked the town from their hideout in the forest. In 1942–43 small pockets of Jewish resistance formed south of Vinnytsia. See Spector, "Jews in the Resis- tance," 136–37.

7 Andrii Mel'nyk's people secured their base at Zhytomyr with two of his top leaders from the Provid, Omelian Senyk and Mykola Stsibors'kyi. On 30 Aug. 1941 Senyk and Stsibors'kyi walked across a street intersection in Zhytomyr's center and were approached from behind by a young man. The man shot Senyk and Stsibors'kyi. Senyk died instantly, and Stsibors'kyi "bled to death a few hours later." See Arm- strong, *Ukrainian Nationalism*, 68. Apparently a Bandera agent (with German help) carried this out.

8 See the OUN-B report of "Wino," about members being arrested by Germans and not returning, 26 Sept. 1941, ZSA, P1151-1-3.

9 EK5 order of 25 Nov. 1941, in Potichnyj, ed., *The UPA in Light of German Documents*, 99; reprinted from IMT, vol. 39, 269–70.

10 See SD Meldungen Ost, weekly report dated 15 May 1942, NA, RG 242, T-175/R 16/2519847, and frames 2529873–4.

11 The discovered Bandera reports were distributed to the other secret police head- quarters and subcommandos of the Einsatzgruppen in L'viv, Rivne, Kiev, Cher- nihiv, Kharkiv, Horlivka, Kremenchuk, and Dnipropetrovs'k. See Thomas report of 23 Mar. 1942, P1151-1-14. According to BdS Ukraine Thomas, nationalists who were arrested were not to be killed on the spot, but kept for questioning in order to gather more names and information. In certain cases they were killed; if they had played a significant leadership role, they were to be sent to RSHA in Berlin. Thomas order of 22 Feb. 1942, ZSA, P1151-1-14. When Razesberger asked Thomas what he should do with these prisoners in Apr. 1942, Thomas replied that for the time being they should be kept in a concentration camp. Thomas to Razesberger, 14 Apr. 1942, ZSA, P1151-1-14.

12 Razesberger to SS-Brigadeführer Dr. Thomas, 1 Apr. 1941, ZSA, P1151-1-14.

13 Taras "Bulba" Borovets was a native of Volyn; he established the first police units in the German administration in Olevs'k; both Borovets and "his men" (auxiliary Ukrainian police) from Olevs'k went underground in Nov. 1941 and later formed one of the first nationalist partisan groups. Potichnyj, ed., *The UPA in Light of Ger- man Documents*, 6, 47.

14 See General Commissar Klemm reports about partisan attacks, 14 Dec. 1941, ZSA, P11511-21, and 18 Dec. 1941, ZSA, P1151-1-4.

15 Before Nov. 1941, they had worked secretly with the Borovets faction and his "Freikorps," which fought against the Soviets in the northeast areas of Ukraine between Zhytomyr and Kiev. On Borovets-German "relations," see the SD report of 15 May 1942, NA, RG 242, T-175/R 16/2529874–5.

16 Roques memo to civilian authorities, 15 Nov. 1941, ZSA, P1151-1-703.

17 Klemm order, 18 Dec. 1941, ZSA, P1151-1-4.

18 In Feb. 1942 Himmler's command staff cabled that the Pripiat' marsh area had to be subdued with all force, using a combination of Waffen-SS and military units. 19 Feb. 1942, MHI, Prague, Var-SS B27. Statement of Hans Leberecht von Bredow, former commander of the gendarmerie for the Zhytomyr region, 21 May 1962, Kohlmorgen Case, BAL, Sta Braunschweig 1 Js 1848/61. Thanks to Konrad Kwiet for these documents.

19 See the "Kommandobefehl" from the gendarme chief of the region about the vulnerability of police during patrols of fields and forests, 25 June 1942, ZSA, P1151-1-9. A reporting section on partisan attacks was introduced in the biweekly and monthly reports at the end of June; see report of 29 June 1942, ZSA, P1151-1-9. For partisan attacks in the spring of 1942, such as the Soviet POWs' sabotage of factory work, see Commissar Klemm's "Lagebericht," 3 June 1942, Bundesarchiv Koblenz, R/6. Additional attacks are described in the Wehrmachtsbefehlshaber report of 17 June 1942, NA, RG 242, T-454/R 92/000653–4.

20 German policy toward captured partisans reflected their defined categories of racial and political enemies. When the SD began its manhunts against nationalist infiltrators, SS-Brigadeführer Max Thomas asked that partisans be searched and questioned before they were killed. But in early June, when the Germans were conducting thorough cleansing actions of the forest to find and kill Jews in hiding, and when Soviet partisans had begun to murder German officials in El'sk and Bragin, Zhytomyr's commander of the gendarmerie ordered in June 1942 that male bandits and "riffraff" in the forests be shot on the spot. See BdS Thomas, Kiev order to SD chief of Zhytomyr, Razesberger, 23 Mar. 1942, ZSA, P1151-1-14; KdG Zhytomyr orders, 6 June 1942, Minsk collection 658-1-2, microfilm held at USHMM, RG 53.0002M, reel 5; KdG Zhytomyr order, 11 July 1942, ZSA, P1182-1-37.

21 Gerlach, *Kalkulierte Morde*, 942.

22 Zhytomyr's German Security Police chief, Franz Razesberger, and his subordinates gained substantial information by interrogating a captured Soviet partisan named Leontii Onagrov. He "confessed" that around Zhytomyr the Soviet partisans were formed into cells and situated at Deveshyn, Chudniv, Myropil, Baranivka, and Romanivka and on the Luts'k-Zhytomyr border at Shepetivka. See the memorandum of SD chief Razesberger's office to the commander of the gendarmerie at Zhytomyr, 16 Apr. 1942, ZSA, P1182-1-2.

23 Razesberger report of 23–31 July 1942, MHI, Prague, Var-SS B 22. I am grateful to

Konrad Kwiet for this document, as well as many others from the Prague archive. For additional attacks, see SD Meldungen Ost, 7 Aug. 1942, 20 Aug. 1942, 28 Aug. 1942, and 11 Sept. 1942, NA, RG 242, T-315/R 17/2520129–30, 2520186–7, 2520214, and 2520277–8. The Soviets established one of the larger and more significant airfields at Lel'chytsi in Mar. 1943. See Kosyk, *The Third Reich and Ukraine*, 387.

24 Franz Razesberger Statement of 19 Jan. 1957, Case against Razesberger, BAL, 204 AR-Z 8/80, Band III, 205. Witte et al., eds., *Der Dienstkalender Heinrich Himmlers*, 498–99.

25 German and Ukrainian police seized three different Soviet leaflets in Vasilevichi. The first one was a military update about how the Germans had been defeated on the northern front; the second was addressed to the "Peoples of the Occupied Territories," and stated that the Red Army was pushing out the fascist bands and that "all the free Soviet peoples watch over you. . . . [A]s the Germans are pushed back they are destroying 200 km stretches of fields; it is your duty to preserve the grain and protect it from German destruction. Take weapons in your hands, go to the partisans, and destroy the enemy in the rear. Do not forget that your fathers, brothers, and men shed their blood for you in battle. Death to the fascists! Your independence lives!" See the Razesberger report of 12 Aug. 1942 to Thomas regarding events of 17 July 1942 at Vasilevichi, MHI, Prague, Var-SS B22. For Himmler order about changing terminology, see "Kommandobefehl" of 15 Aug. 1942, ZSA, P1151-1-9.

26 Gerlach, *Kalkulierte Morde*, 974. Hitler directive #46, 18 Aug. 1942, in Dallin, *German Rule in Russia*, 210.

27 SD Meldungen Ost, 12 Feb. 1943, NA, RG 242, T-175/R 236/2725410, 2725526.

28 On the Prützmann report, see Gerlach, *Kalkulierte Morde*, 1018. On Himmler's approach, see NA, RG 242, T-175/R 140/2667728. For the local escalation resulting in more incidents of civilian deaths, see Hellwig SSPF Zhytomyr report to all gendarme posts in region, 27 Jan. 1943, ZSA, P1465-1-6.

29 *Stryvozhena pam'iat'*, 209–14.

30 Leyser, "Lagebericht," Mar.–Apr. 1943, ZSA, P1151-1-45.

31 Commander of the gendarmerie of Zhytomyr, report of 19 Nov. 1942, ZSA, P1151-1-9.

32 SD report from the East, 22 Jan. 1943, NA, RG 242, T-175/R 236/2725410.

33 SD report from the East, 12 Feb. 1943, NA, RG 242, T-175/R 236/2725529.

34 The Germans were unable to distinguish among the different Soviet commanders and their units in Zhytomyr. Although Kovpak's were the most well known, in Zhytomyr additional Soviet units were commanded by A. H. Saburov, A. F. Fedorov, M. I. Nauma, B. A. Karasev, I. I. Shitov, and A. M. Grabchak. Soviet and Ukrainian sources also describe a Czech and Polish detachment. See *Stryvozhena pam'iat'*, 208.

35 On movements of Kovpak's units around Zhytomyr, Operation Nixe (Mermaid) and Soviet southern forces under Saburov, Mar.–Apr. 1943, see the SD Meldungen Ost from this period, NA, RG 242, T-175/R 236/2725410, 2725529, 2725679, 2725747–8, 2725795. Mel'nichenko was discovered by the Gestapo in Dec. 1942;

see Gestapo chief Müller (Berlin) message to Himmler (Hegewald) on 12 Dec. 1942, NA, RG 242, T-175/R 68/2584189–93. On Müller's memo to Rattenhuber (then promoted to SS-Oberführer) about Soviet agents in the Werwolf compound, dated 22 July 1942, see Z *arkhiviv VuChK-GPU-NKVD-KGB* 1/2 1999, 428–442, in the Vinnytsia Oblast Archive, P1425-1-35, 14, microfilm in USHMM, RG 31.011M, reel 14. After the war, Rattenhuber was interrogated by the KGB and evidently died in Soviet captivity. I am gratetul to Vadim Altskan for providing and translating the Ukrainian text.

36 Germans placed the nationalist (OUN-B) partisans around Vinnytsia, Berdychiv, and smaller towns like Koziatyn. Bandera leaders also tried to organize the movement in Ovruch; SD report, 11 Sept. 1942, NA, RG 242, T-175/R 236/724822–26. An OUN-B supporter with leaflets, a worker named Boris Zhumenii, was arrested in Ruzhyn at the beginning of Sept. 1942. SS and police district event report for Ruzhyn, ZSA, P1182-1-36. An official from the RKU capital, Rivne, who traveled to Vinnytsia learned that two villages outside the city were totally controlled by Banderites; see the report of Professor von Grünberg (IIg), 10 Sept. 1942, CSA, Kiev, 3206-2-116, microfilm at USHMM, RG 31.002M, reel 3.

37 See Weiner, *Making Sense of War*, 244–64. See Snyder, "The Causes of Ukrainian-Polish Ethnic Cleansing."

38 Armstrong, *Ukrainian Nationalism*, 108.

39 For the rise of UPA and a more favorable account of the Bandera faction, see Kosyk, *The Third Reich and Ukraine*. Of the roughly 40,000 fighters in the UPA, fewer than 1,500 were active in Zhytomyr in early 1943.

40 This was representative of a change in OUN-B principles and policies, which moved toward more ethnic tolerance and democratic ideals. See the resolutions of the Second Congress from Feb. 1943 and the Third Extraordinary Congress from Aug. 1943, in Kosyk, *The Third Reich and Ukraine*, 614, 631. As the Germans evacuated the eastern districts of the Zhytomyr region in Nov. 1943, the OUN-UPA held a secret conference "of the oppressed peoples of Eastern Europe and Asia" in Zhytomyr's northwestern forests; see Kosyk, *The Third Reich and Ukraine*, 397.

41 The Germans began to realize how crucial the elders were to the partisan cause when they investigated the partisan movement in the summer of 1942. They found that at the lowest levels, where the Germans were absent, the partisans were able to survive off the land and in the forests with the cooperation of the elders and local population; the Germans also learned that some Ukrainian leaders were sabotaging German policies by deliberately mistranslating German orders. See orders of the commander of the gendarmerie, Zhytomyr, on fighting the partisans, demanding loyalty from auxiliaries, and threatening locals who support the partisans, Belarus State Archive (Minsk), 658-1-2, microfilm held at USHMM, RG 53002M, reel 5. Regarding Ukrainian mistranslation of German orders, see the 26 Aug. 1942 Hauptmannschaftsbefehl Berdichev, RGVA, Moscow 1323-2-228, microfilm held at USHMM, RG 11.001M, reel 81.

42. Soviet order of Commander Sergeev, chief of the Partisan Movement in the Territories Temporarily Occupied by the Germans, 14 Aug. 1942, in *Soviet Partisans in World War II*, ed. Armstrong, 672.

43. Leontii Antonovich Kozaritskii, interview by author, 20 May 1996, Zhytomyr State Archives, Zhytomyr, Ukraine.

44. SS and police district leader of Koziatyn, logs of killed Schutzmänner, Nov. 1943, ZSA, P1182-1-35.

45. Leyser to Rosenberg, 17 June 1943, NA, RG 242, T-454/R 91/000878-881.

46. General Commissar Leyser, "Lagebericht," Mar.–Apr. 1943, ZSA, P1151-1-45.

47. Gerlach, *Kalkulierte Morde*, 1020.

48. See Leyser memo to all commissars and SSPF Zhytomyr about Koch's instructions, 10 Mar. 1943, ZSA, P1151-1-26. For Leyser's critique and Himmler's response, see 16 June 1943, NA, RG 242, T-175/R 140/2667587-593.

49. Leyser, "Lagebericht," Mar.–Apr. 1943, ZSA, P1151-1-45. The commissars were also becoming suspicious of SS economic enterprises that placed more demands on their resources. In Novohrad-Volyns'kyi the district commissar's office initially refused to provide laborers for the SS-acquired porcelain factory at Horodnytsia, until the Higher SS and Police Leader Prützmann pressured General Commissar Leyser. See records of local SS-operated industries — for example, SS porcelain factories in Berdychiv, Korosten', and Olevs'k — ZSA, P1151-1-383 and P1151-1-22.

50 See the Hitler and Keitel decree on awards for "eastern peoples," 14 July 1942, ZSA, P1182-1-35.

51 On premiums to locals who assisted in partisan warfare, see memorandum from Koch's Department of Food and Agriculture, Rivne, 21 Aug. 1942, RGVA, Moscow 1323-2-255, microfilm held at USHMM, RG 11.001M, reel 81. This program was part of Hitler's commissioning Himmler with the task of destroying partisans by the end of the year through the harshest punitive methods and local reward programs. See Rosenberg instructions to RKU and RKO (Reichskommissariat Ostland), 18 Aug. 1942, NA, RG 242, T-454/R 155/ MR 355 99/476, T-175/R 56/2571325.

52 Gendarme Commander of Zhytomyr, "Kommandobefehl," Nr. 35/42, (15?) Oct. 1942, ZSA, P1151-1-9.

53 See General Commissar Leyser to Reichsminister Rosenberg, 12 Feb. 1943, NA, RG 242, T-175/R 140/2667592-3; also in NA, RG 238, NO-2628.

54 Leyser speech on the occasion of Rosenberg's Vinnytsia visit, 17 June 1943, NA, RG 238, reel A213, frame 088693-699.

55 On the nominations by the gendarme leader of Samhorodok, Richter, see the memo dated 31 May 1943, ZSA, P1182-1-38. Lists of Schutzmänner commendations and awards are found in ZSA, P1182-1-162.

56 Statements of Schutzmann Ivan Koval'skii and of La-Führer Martin Lemke, SSPgebF Koziatyn interrogations, 20 Oct. 1942, ZSA, P1182-1-35.

57 En route, she and other laborers were provided with some hay, one kilogram of bread, one sausage, and no water, enough food for two or three days, but the trip

lasted five to nine days. During Atamanskaia's journey, she recalled, the train sometimes came to an abrupt halt, and one could hear shots fired at those who tried to flee. Maria Atamanskaia, interview by author, 21 May 1996, Zhytomyr, Ukraine; Report of SD Chief Kiev to SD Commander Ukraine, June 1942, NA, RG 242, T-454/R 156/MR336. Also see the Ruzhyn SS and police district leader's activity report about a woman and child shot while trying to jump from a forced-labor train, 5 Feb. 1943, ZSA, P1452-1-2.

58 When suspects fled, German investigations began by bringing in the suspects' wives and girlfriends; often a partisan or deserter would go to a girlfriend's house to seek shelter. See Ruzhyn SSPgebF activity reports, particularly 21 Oct. 1943, ZSA, P1182-1-2, and 8 Aug.–26 Dec. 1943, ZSA, P1182-1-32; also in SD Meldungen Ost of 5 Mar. 1943, NA, RG 242, T-175/R 236/2725620.

59 SS-police in Ruzhyn arrested Nastia Semerchuk, the wife of a suspected partisan. After German and Ukrainian police tortured her, she was returned to her cell. Ukrainian guards later found her dead in the cell; she had hanged herself with a piece of clothing. See Ruzhyn SSPgebF, "Lagebericht," Nov. 1942, ZSA, P1452-1-2.

60 See Moshovskii "Announcement" of 15 Aug. 1942, ZSA, P1426-1-2. Any native police auxiliaries who refused to carry out attacks against partisans were also to be shot on the spot by the leader of the unit, a fellow auxiliary, or, if necessary, by a German gendarme official. The gendarme chief in Mazyr wrote that in accordance with Himmler's commission to fight partisans in Ukraine, the Ukrainian police also had to serve in the fight; SSPF Hellwig ordered that if members of a family assisted the bandits, then the entire family was to be killed. See file from Belarus State Archives (Minsk), 658-1-2, microfilm held at USHMM, RG 53.002M, reel 5.

61 From SSPF Koziatyn, Behrens, daily partisan attack reports, 8 Aug. 1943, ZSA, P1182-1-32. Also see activity report from the SS and police chief at Ruzhyn, 5 Feb. 1943, in which he reported that they had captured another woman supplying food to partisans in Pohrebyshche; ZSA, P1452-1-2. See the Sept. 1943 partisan activity report of SSPF Behrens, Koziatyn, ZSA, P1182-1-32.

62 In Aug. 1942 a Soviet partisan battalion swept through the district of Olevs'k killing Schutzmänner and their families, along with village elders and their wives and children; in one village near El'sk, Stalin's agents shot all the inhabitants. SD Meldungen Ost, report of 11 Sept. 1942, NA, RG 242, T-175/R 17/2520242, 2520277–8.

63 SD Meldungen Ost, 5 Mar. 1943, NA, RG 242, T-175/R 236/2725620.

64 Nechama Tec, *Resilience and Courage*, 264–72, 305–6.

65 Koziatyn SS and police district leader files, Kondratenko Case, July–Aug. 1943, ZSA, P1182-1-37.

66 There may have been more persons in this group, perhaps fifty, but in the raid the Germans battled with twelve men. See Ruzhyn partisan warfare log entry of 18 Aug. 1943 and report of 21 Aug. 1943, ZSA, P1182-1-37. Jewish members of the resistance were concentrated around Vinnytsia.

67 The assassination was followed by "Aktion Richter," massive reprisals against addi-

tional "suspects" on 26 Aug. 1943. Behrens, SS and police leader Koziatyn district, daily reports of partisan attacks, ZSA, P1182-1-32.

68 The wartime and postwar fate of Kondratenko remains mysterious; her records are not among the KGB archives files in Zhytomyr. Possible surviving family members from Koziatyn could not be identified through telephone listings and inquiries in 1996.

69 See Commissar Leyser, "Lagebericht" about partisan warfare and peasant women who live in dirt holes, Mar.–Apr. 1943, ZSA, P1151-1-45, 9.

70 See Leyser memorandum, "Bolschewistische Grausamkeiten," 27 Mar. 1943, ZSA, P1151-1-137.

71 Besides the trip to Germany, winners were also given an increased food ration for six months. Leyser Propaganda Plan, 15 Mar. 1943, ZSA, P1151-1-137.

72 Leyser, "Propagandistische Auswertung der Winnizär Morde," 17 July 1943, ZSA, P1151-1-187. Testimony of Iakov Arsent'evich Sheptur, Vinnytsia, 28 Jan. 1970, BAL, 204 AR-Z 122/68, Band III, 78–80. Sheptur presented the Soviet version of the mass graves, stating that the bodies were from Nazi massacres of 1941, but the account of City Commissar for Vinnytsia Margenfeld corresponds with the German records of 1943 and Rosenberg's report. See *Amtliches Material zum Massenmord vom Winniza.*

73 Quoted from Weiner, *Making Sense of War,* 268, who translated it from the 1 July 1943 issue of *Vinnyts'ki visti.* On the politics of the regional religious leaders from the Orthodox, Uniate, and Catholic Churches, see Berkhoff, "Was There a Religious Revival . . . ?" General Commissar Klemm reported on the factious politicking of the churches in his Situation Report of 3 June 1942, Bundesarchiv Koblenz, R6/310.

74 A Nazi Party official who met with the commissars found the persistence of anti-Ukrainian "colonial" rhetoric alongside the fictitious propaganda themes very striking. He also observed that the commissars complained often that one could not give anything to "these Ukrainians because they do not appreciate it" (!); see report from 23 June 1943, NA, RG 242, T-454/R 92/000193–194.

75 Himmler proposed an evacuation plan as early as 13 Feb. 1943, after the Stalingrad defeat and about the time when SS armored units began to evacuate from Kharkiv, which first fell to the Russians on 14 Feb. But major evacuation action plans were not put into effect until late summer. See Lumans, *Himmler's Auxiliaries,* 247.

76 There were also some personnel changes in late 1943. Henschel was replaced with a new SS director of resettlement named Laforce, and a new NSV leader named Butgereit was brought in to assist Karl Kersten, NSV chief in Zhytomyr.

77 R.-D. Müller, *Hitlers Ostkrieg und die deutsche Siedlungspolitik,* 208 (document #37).

78 By Apr. 1943, when the ethnic Germans in Olevs'k, Pulin, Romanov, and other neighboring districts had been classified, almost half of the population fell into the third category; they had partial German blood (from mixed marriages) but were deemed capable of Germanization. About 4,500 ethnic Germans from Pid-luby and Barashi were also rapidly resettled. See Leyser, "Lagebericht," Mar.–Apr. 1943, ZSA, P1151-1-45.

79 During 1943 Cherniakhiv became the largest ethnic German enclave in the region with 9,046 Volksdeutsche, eight kindergartens, and fifty-one schools. General Commissar Leyser declared it an official SS ethnic German settlement (under SS Oberführer Tschimpke). Försterstadt was formed out of the combined ethnic German villages of Zviahel, Pulin, Korosten', and Horoshki; see Leyser order, 23 Sept. 1943, ZSA, P1151-1-42. The ethnic German population of Hegewald was 8,915, according to report of 3 Aug. 1943, NA, RG 242, T-175/R 72/2589170.

80 NSV leaders complained that they could not find enough homes and facilities to house the 574 new orphans. See report of 29 Sept. 1942, CSA, Kiev, 3206-6-255, microfilm held at USHMM, RG 31.002M, reel 6. The figure of 574 orphans is from the VoMi (Zhytomyr) report of 3 Aug. 1943, NA, RG 242, T-175/R 72/2589170; DVL applications were announced over the radio, as was a call for all ethnic German boys between fourteen and twenty-one to join the Hitler Youth; see schedule of announcements, 20 Feb. 1943, ZSA, P1151-1-120.

81 Heinemann, "*Rasse, Siedlung, deutsches Blut*," 422.

82 There were a total of three Volksdeutsche shops in the city of Zhytomyr; they lacked goods, however, and were poorly managed. See Schwager report of 26 June 1943, ZSA, P1151-1-120.

83 See Leyser memo to district commissars and labor commissions, 31 Oct. 1942, ZSA, P1151-1-120.

84 See the accounts of partisan attacks in Jan.–Feb. 1943 in which the ethnic Germans were highlighted as a partisan target in the Ruzhyn SS and police district leader files, ZSA, P1452-1-2. Volksdeutsche were moved to Cherniakhiv in early 1943 from northern areas "under pressure from partisan warfare" according to Leyser's "Lagebericht" of Mar.–Apr. 1943. In a raid on Hegewald on 8 May 1943, thirty partisans robbed the SS shop and stole vehicles; another attack on 12 May 1943 occurred north of Hegewald in Mazyr. See CSA, Kiev, 3676-4-480, microfilm held at USHMM, RG 31.002M, reel 13. Additional reports of partisan attacks against ethnic Germans are in ZSA, P1182-1-5. Three hundred partisans attacked ethnic German villages at Zviahel and killed ten ethnic Germans; NA, RG 242, T-454/R 17/000418–420. Ethnic Germans were also killed in Haisyn, which was an overnight stopover for a trek coming from Halbstadt (Dnipropetrovs'k). The Selbstschutz took revenge on a nearby village; see the HSSPF Prützmann report of 16 Nov. 1943, NA, RG T-175/R 72/2589088-89.

85 See *Z arkhiviv VuChK-GPU-NKVD-KGB* 1/2 1999, 428–442. Jewish refugees did not form their own resistance movement; they lacked the weapons, having no guns, only some knives. In July 1943 many joined the Lenin detachment of the Stalin Brigade, which contained a "Jewish" unit led by David Mudrik. See Vinokurova et al., *Katastrofa (Shoa) i soprotivlenie / pod obshchei redaktsiei*, 124. I am grateful to Vadim Altskan for this reference and assistance with the translation. Thanks to Ms. Vinokurova for confirming additional details in her correspondence.

Chapter Nine

1 Khaim Borisovich testimony in *Berdichevskaia tragediia*, ed. Elisavetskii, 81. I am grateful to Asya Vaisman for translating the Russian text into English.

2 SD Berdychiv, monthly activity report for Sept. 1943, ZSA, P1452-1-2.

3 In Zhytomyr, the ethnic German guards were assigned to SS grenadier training battalion 31. They were placed along the stream called the Hegebach that ran from Himmler's compound to the airport; the compound was destroyed in part by this battalion, which fell under the command of Kampfkommandant Zhytomyr Generalmajor Strack. Other ethnic German members of battalion 31 were placed on Kiev Street, the main road between Zhytomyr and Kiev on which the Red Army was advancing. See report of Jungkunz to Himmler's personal staff about the evacuation of Zhytomyr, 28 Nov. 1943, NA, RG 242, T-175/R 72/2589091–95. In the evacuation of Berdychiv on 26 Dec. 1943, ethnic German factory chiefs were ordered to remain in industries that provided for the army. NA, RG 242, T-454/R 91/000870.

4 The telegram is dated 16 Nov., but it states that the massacre was on 17 Nov. 1943; see Prützmann telegram to Himmler at Wolfsburg, NA, RG 242, T-175/R 72/2589088.

5 See the RKU report of 13 Nov. 1943, CSA, Kiev, microfilm held at USHMM, RG 31.002M, reel 11, folder 99. The ethnic Germans in these treks were largely women and children; in the summer of 1943 Hitler and Himmler waged an aggressive campaign to draft ethnic German men into the army and Waffen-SS. See Hitler decree on the granting of German citizenship to those foreigners of German descent who were serving in the army, Waffen-SS, and Organization Todt. Ethnic Germans in Ukraine who resided there on 22 June 1941 and fell into the first two categories of the German List were also granted German citizenship and were to be drafted. Hitler decree of 19 May 1943 in CSA, Kiev, 3206-1-79, microfilm held at USHMM, RG 31.002M, reel 2. In July 1943 Himmler ordered that ethnic German men in Ukraine be assigned to the Waffen-SS; Himmler asked Prützmann to make sure that the 7,000 trained men in the Selbstschutz be drafted not into the army but rather into the Waffen-SS. NA, RG 242, T-175/R 17/2522910.

6 Report of SS Chief Jungkunz at Hegewald, 7 Nov.–24 Nov. 1943, NA, RG 242, T-175/R 72/2589091–9116. Abschlussbericht, Case against Friedrich Becker (SS and police Berdychiv), BAL, 204 AR-Z 129/67 IV, 1028–9. Also see evacuation measures, memoranda from Nov. 1943 in ZSA, P1151-1-31, P2375-1-1; "Räumungsbericht des Gebietskommissariats Koziatyn," 8 Nov.–28 Dec. 1943, NA, RG 242, T-454/R 91/000857–67; "Räumungsmassnahmen," 4th Panzerarmee, Berdychiv, 26 Dec. 1943, NA, RG 242, T-454/R 91/000870.

7 Doris Bergen, "The Volksdeutsche of Eastern Europe and the Collapse of the Nazi Empire, 1944–1945," in *The Impact of Nazism*, ed. Rogers and Steinweis, 107.

8 It is not known how many among these ethnic Germans originated from Zhyto-

myr. Fleischhauer, "The Ethnic Germans under Nazi Rule," in Fleischhauer and Pinkus, *The Soviet Germans: Past and Present*, 101. For the horrendous conditions of the evacuations, with mention of the Hegewald trek, see Harvey, *Women and the Nazi East*, 284. See also Ther and Siljak, eds., *Redrawing Nations*.

9 Berdychiv was liberated on 5 Jan. 1944, whereas the struggle over Vinnytsia lasted until 20 Mar. 1944. The Soviets' First Ukrainian Front led the Zhytomyr-Berdychiv assault on 24 Dec. and defeated the Germans' Fourth and First Panzer armies. The four Soviet fronts that swept through the region had "twenty-one combined armies, three tank, and four air armies totalling 2,086,000 men, 31,530 guns and mortars, 1,908 tanks and self-propelled gun mounts and about 2,730 combat airplanes." *Great Soviet Encyclopedia*, s.v. "Right Bank Ukraine," 20:573.

10 Ivan Shynal'skii, interview by author, 20 May 1996, Zhytomyr, Ukraine.

11 BdO Ukraine, Polizeischulungsleiter, 22 Aug. 1942, ZSA, P1151-1-147a.

12 *Ukraïns'ke Slovo* (Zhytomyr), 11 Sept. 1941, ZSA, Newspaper Collection.

13 The Zhytomyr Commissariat employed about 9,000 Ukrainian policemen in Dec. 1942 (1,800 in mobile battalions, 1,000 in the cities, and 6,000 in the countryside). ZSA, 1151-1-883.

14 For the death toll in the Zhytomyr Oblast, which was 220,364 persons, see ZSA, P2636-1-5, pp. 1–2. The Vinnytsia figure is from Weiner, *Making Sense of War*, 170.

15 Weiner, *Making Sense of War*, 9–10.

16 Quoted from ibid., 192.

17 Golbert, "Holocaust Sites in Ukraine," 219.

18 For a brief analysis of contemporary Ukraine in light of its colonial and totalitarian history, see Motyl, *Dilemmas of Independence*.

19 Golbert, "Holocaust Sites in Ukraine," 219.

Bibliography

Archives/Libraries

Bundesarchiv Aussenstelle Ludwigsburg
    Records of Postwar German State Investigations of Nazi War Crimes
Bundesarchiv Koblenz
    Records of the Eastern Occupied Territories, R/6
Library of Congress, Washington, D.C.
    Der deutsche Militärarzt
    Deutsche Ukraine-Zeitung (Luts'k)
    OSS/State Department Intelligence and Research Report
        (German civil occupation of Ukraine)
United States Holocaust Memorial Museum Archives, Washington, D.C.
    Accession 1996.A.0269, Selected Records from the Zhytomyr State Oblast' Archive
    Accession 1998.A.0002, Selected Records from the State Archives of the Russian
        Federation (GARF), Moscow
    Accession 2000.1, Einwandererzentralstelle Litzmannstadt (R 69, Bundesarchiv)
    RG 06.025.02, Records of the Former KGB, Kiev
    RG 11.001M, Selected Records from the Former Special (Osobyi) State Archive
        in the Russian State Military Archive (RGVA)
    RG 15.006, Records Relating to Nazi Genocide in Poland, from the Main
        Commission for the Investigation of Nazi Crimes against the Polish Nation
    RG 17.003M, Viennese Post-War Trials of Nazi War Crimes
    RG 22.003, Israel Weiner Letter concerning the Fate of the Weiner Family
        in Vinnitsa
    RG 31.002M, Selected Records from the Central State Archive of Higher
        Government Organizations of Ukraine (formerly Central State Archive
        of the October Revolution), Kiev
    RG 31.004M, Selected Records from the Odessa State Oblast' Archive
    RG 31.011M, Selected Records from the Vinnytsia State Oblast' Archive
    RG 31.017M, Selected Records from the Rivne State Oblast' Archives
    RG 48.004M, Selected Records from the Military Historical Institute Archives,
        Prague
    RG 53.002M, Selected Records of the Belarus Central State Archive
        (Sara Rosjanski Ross Collection), Minsk
United States National Archives and Records Administration, College Park, Md.
    AA3340, Series MFKL and Series PK, Records of the Berlin Document Center,
        Nazi Party Files

AA3343, Series SSO, Records of the Berlin Document Center, SS Officers
    Personnel Files
"German Counterintelligence Activity in Occupied Russia (1941–1944),"
    U.S. Army Report MS No. P-122
Record Group 242, Captured German Records
Record Group 457, Intelligence Files from the Public Records Office, London,
    German Police Radio Intercepts, Box 1386
T-77 Records of the German Armed Forces High Command (OKW)
T-78 Records of the German Army High Command (OKH)
T-120 Records of the German Foreign Office
T-175 Records of the Reich Leader of the SS and Chief of the German Police
T-311 Records of the German Field Commands: Army Groups
T-312 Records of the German Field Commands: Armies
T-313 Records of the German Field Commands: Panzer Armies
T-315 Records of the German Field Commands: Divisions
T-454 Records of the Reich Ministry of the Occupied Eastern Territories
T-501 Records of the German Field Commands, Rear Areas, Occupied Territories
War Crimes, Record Group 238 (NO series, NG series, PS series, NOKW series)
    and Pre-trial Interrogations, Microfilm series M1019
Widener Library, Harvard University, Cambridge, Mass.
    Slavic Collection
    Ukrainian nationalist memoirs and leaflets
Zhytomyr State Archives, Zhytomyr, Ukraine
    Records of the Zhytomyr General Commissariat and District Offices
    Series: P1151, P1169, P1182, P1189, P1233, P1388, P1426, P1465, P1536, P2375
    Newspaper Collection
        Holos Volyni
        Ukraïns'ke Slovo

Published Primary Sources/Documentary Collections

Alsdorf, Ludwig. *Indien*. Berlin: Deutscher Verlag, 1940.
Amtliches Material zum Massenmord von Winniza. Berlin: Zentralverlag der NSDAP, 1944.
Arad, Yitzhak, ed. *Documents of the Holocaust: Selected Sources on the Destruction of the Jews of Germany, Austria, Poland, and the Soviet Union*. New York: Ktav Publishing House, 1982.
Arad, Yitzhak, Shmuel Krakowski, and Shmuel Spector, eds. *The Einsatzgruppen Reports: Selections from the Dispatches of the Nazi Death Squads' Campaign against the Jews in the Occupied Territories of the Soviet Union, July 1941–January 1943*. New York: Holocaust Library, 1989.
Baranauskas, B., and S. Ruksenas. *Documents Accuse*. Vilnius: Gintaras, 1970.
Corni, Gustavo, and Horst Gies. *Blut und Boden: Rassenideologie und Agrarpolitik im Staat Hitlers*. Idstein: Schulz-Kirchner Verlag, 1994.

Darré, R. Walther. *Neuadel aus Blut und Boden*. Munich: J. F. Lehmann, 1930.

Das deutsche Führerlexikon 1934/1935. Berlin: Otto Stollberg, 1934.

Der Krieg gegen die Sowjetunion, 1941–1945: Eine Dokumentation zum 50. Jahrestag des Überfalls auf die Sowjetunion. Berlin: Argon Verlag, 1991.

Documents on German Foreign Policy, 1918–1945: From the Archives of the German Foreign Ministry. London: H.M. Stationery Office, 1949.

Du Prel, Maximilian, Freiherr, ed. *Deutsche Generalgouvernement Polen: Ein Überblick über Gebiet, Gestaltung und Geschichte*. Krakau: BVO, 1940.

Elisavetskii, S. IA. *Berdichevskaia tragediia*. Kiev: UkrNIINTI, 1991.

Epp, Franz Ritter von. *Deutschlands koloniale Forderung*. Stuttgart: DAI, June 1939.

Friedlander, Henry, and Sybil Milton, eds. *Archives of the Holocaust: An International Collection of Selected Documents*. New York: Garland, 1989.

Handbook of the Organisation Todt. London: MIRS (SHAEF), Mar. 1945.

Haushofer, Karl. *Weltpolitik von Heute*. Berlin: Zeitgeschichte Verlag, 1934.

Heiber, Helmut, ed. *Reichsführer! . . . Briefe an und von Himmler*. Stuttgart: Deutsche Verlags-Anstalt, 1968.

History Teaches a Lesson: Captured War Documents Expose the Atrocities of the German-Fascist Invaders and Their Henchmen in Ukraine's Temporarily Occupied Territory during the Great Patriotic War, 1941–1945. Kiev: Politvydav Ukraïny Publishers, 1986.

Hitler, Adolf. *Mein Kampf*. Translated by Ralph Mannheim. Boston: Houghton Mifflin, 1971.

Hitler's Table Talk, 1941–1944: His Private Conversations. Translated by Norman Cameron and R. H. Stevens. London: Phoenix Press, 2000.

Human Resources Research Institute. *Harvard University Refugee Project*. 37 vols. Maxwell Air Force Base, Ala.: Officer Education Research Laboratory, 1952.

Jacobsen, Hans-Adolf, and W. Jochmann, eds. *Ausgewählte Dokumente zur Geschichte des Nationalsozialismus, 1933–1945*. Bielefeld: Verlag Neue Gesellschaft, 1961.

Jochmann, Werner, ed. *Die Monologe im Führer-Hauptquartier 1941–1944 / Adolf Hitler: Die Aufzeichnungen Heinrich Heims*. Hamburg: Albert Knaus, 1980.

Justiz und NS-Verbrechen: Sammlung deutscher Strafurteile wegen nationalsozialistischer Tötungsverbrechen 1945–1966. 22 vols. Amsterdam: University Press Amsterdam, 1968–81.

Labs, Walter. *Die Verwaltung der besetzten Ostgebieten*. Berlin: n.p., 1943.

Lemkin, Raphael. *Axis Rule in Occupied Europe: Laws of Occupation, Analyses of Government, Proposals for Redress*. Washington: Carnegie Endowment for International Peace, 1944.

Madajczyk, Czeslaw, ed. *Vom Generalplan Ost zum Generalsiedlungsplan*. Munich: K. G. Sauer Verlag, 1994.

Müller, Norbert, ed. *Wehrmacht und Okkupation 1941–1944: Zur Rolle der Wehrmacht und ihrer Führungsorgane im Okkupationsregime des faschistischen deutschen Imperialismus auf sowjetischem Territorium*. Berlin: Deutscher Militärverlag, 1971.

————, ed. *Deutsche Besatzungspolitik in der UdSSR*. Cologne: Paul-Rugenstein Verlag, 1980.

————, ed. *Okkupation, Raub, Vernichtung: Dokumente zur Besatzungspolitik der faschistischen Wehrmacht auf sowjetischem Territorium 1941 bis 1944*. Berlin: Militärverlag, 1980.

————, ed. *Die Faschistische Okkupationspolitik in den zeitweilig besetzten Gebieten der Sowjetunion, 1941–1944*. Berlin: Deutscher Verlag der Wissenschaften, 1991.

Nazi Crimes in Ukraine, 1941–1944: Documents and Materials. Kiev: Naukova Dumka Publishers, 1987.

Noakes, J., and G. Pridham, eds. *Nazism: A Documentary Reader, 1919–1945*. 2 vols. Devon: Exeter Press, 1995.

Oelhafen von Schoellenbach, Hans. *Die Besiedlung Deutsch Südwestafrikas bis zum Weltkriege*. Berlin: Reimer und Hosen, 1926.

Potichnyj, Petro J., ed. *The UPA in Light of German Documents*. Vol. 21 of Litopys UPA. Toronto: Litopys, 1983.

Rosenberg, Alfred. *Der Mythus des 20. Jahrhunderts: Eine Wertung der seelisch-geistigen Gestaltenkämpfe unserer Zeit*. Munich: Hoheneichen-Verlag, 1937.

————. *Race and Race History, and Other Essays*. Edited and introduced by Robert Pois. New York: Harper and Row, 1971.

Russian Oppression in Ukraine: Reports and Documents. London: Ukrainian Publishers, 1962.

Schiller, Otto. *Ziele und Ergebnisse der Agrarordnung in den besetzten Ostgebieten*. Berlin: RMfdBO, 1943.

Stumpp, Karl. *Ostwanderung: Akten über die Auswanderung der Württemberger nach Russland 1816–1822*. Leipzig: S. Hirzel, 1941.

Unsere Ehre Heisst Treue: Kriegstagebuch des Kommandostabes Reichsführer SS, Tätigkeitsberichte der 1. und 2. SS-Inf.-Brigade, der 1. SS Kav.-Brigade und von Sonderkommandos der SS. Vienna: Europa Verlag, 1965.

Vinokurova, Faina, et al. *Katastrofa (Shoa) i soprotivlenie / pod obshchei redaktsiei*. Tel Aviv: Izdanie "Beit lokhamei kha-gettaot," 1994.

Witte, Peter, et al., eds. *Der Dienstkalender Heinrich Himmlers 1941/42*. Hamburg: Christians Verlag, 1999.

Zhytomyrshchyna v period tymchasovoi okypatsii nimets'ko-fashysts'kymy zaharbnykamy, 1941–1944. Zhytomyr, 1948.

Memoirs and Diaries

Bräutigam, Otto. *So hat es sich zugetragen*. Würzburg: Holzer Verlag, 1968.

Burdick, Charles, and Hans-Adolf Jacobsen, eds. *The Halder War Diary, 1939–1942*. Novato, Calif.: Presidio Press, 1988.

Daghani, Arnold. *The Grave Is in the Cherry Orchard*. London: Adam International Publishers, 1961.

Gehlen, Reinhard. *The Service: The Memoirs of General Reinhard Gehlen*. New York: World Publishing Co., 1972.

Goykher, Vladimir. *The Tragedy of the Letichev Ghetto*. New York: V. Goykher, 1993.

Kleist, Peter. *Zwischen Hitler und Stalin, 1939–1945*. Bonn: Athenäum, 1950.

Matla, Zynovii. *Pivdenna pokhidna hrupa*. Munich: Nasha Knyhozbirnia, 1952.

Oberlander, Theodor. *Denkschriften aus dem Zweiten Weltkrieg über die Behandlung der Sowjetvölker*. Ingolstadt: Zeitgeschichtliche Forschungsstelle Ingolstadt, 1984.

Speer, Albert. *Inside the Third Reich*. Translated by Richard and Clara Winston. New York: Macmillan, 1970.

———. *Spandau: The Secret Diaries*. Translated by Richard and Clara Winston. New York: Macmillan, 1976.

———. *Infiltration*. Translated by Joachim Neugroschel. New York: Macmillan, 1981.

Strik-Strikfeldt, Winfried. *Against Stalin and Hitler, 1941–1945*. Translated by David Footman. New York: John Day, 1973.

Stryvozhena pam'iat: Spohady veteraniv 1943–1993. Edited by A. E. Iemelianov, O. M. Kot, L. A. Kozyratsky, P. P. Moskvin, and D. S. Fedotov. Zhytomyr: State Editorial-Publishing Enterprise "L'onok," 1993.

Umanskij, Semjon. *Jüdisches Glück: Bericht aus der Ukraine, 1933–1944*. Frankfurt am Main: Fischer, 1998.

Zhilbovskaia, Cherna Aronovna. "The Memory That I Save." *Shalom* (Zhytomyr), 29 Oct. 1995.

Interviews Conducted by Author

Maria Albinova Atamanskaia, 19 May 1996, Zhytomyr, Ukraine.

Hryhorii Denysenko, 11 Aug. 1993, Zhytomyr, Ukraine.

Pavlo Gorlach, 15 May 1996, Zhytomyr, Ukraine.

Petr Ignat'evich Iunitskii, 20 May 1996, Zhytomyr, Ukraine.

Iurii Alekseevitch Kiian, 19 May 1996, Zhytomyr, Ukraine.

Leontii Antonovich Kozaritskii, 20 May 1996, Zhytomyr, Ukraine.

Eugeniia Malik, 17 Aug. 1992, Zhytomyr, Ukraine.

Galina Efimovna Pekerman, 21 May 1996, Zhytomyr, Ukraine.

Myroslav Prokop, 15 Mar. 1995, Shevchenko Society, New York, N.Y.

Vasilii Ivanovich Rekob, 20 May 1996, Zhytomyr, Ukraine.

Valentina Petrovna Shchenevskaia, 22 May 1996, Zhytomyr, Ukraine.

Ivan Shynal'skii, 20 May 1996, Zhytomyr, Ukraine.

Interviews Conducted by Kira Burova, Zhytomyr, Ukraine

Nina Borisovna Glozman, 2 Feb. 1995

Mikhail Alekseevich Rozenberg, 25 Apr. 1996

Secondary Sources: Selected Books

Abshagen, Karl Heinz. *Canaris*. London: Hutchinson, 1956.

Alexeev, Wassilij, and Theofanis G. Stavrou. *The Great Revival: The Russian Church under German Occupation*. Minneapolis: Burgess Publishing, 1976.

Altshuler, Mordechai. *Soviet Jewry on the Eve of the Holocaust: A Social and Demographic Profile*. Jerusalem: Yad Vashem, 1998.

Aly, Götz. *Endlösung: Völkerverschiebung und der Mord an den europäischen Juden*. Frankfurt am Main: Fischer, 1995.

———. *"Final Solution": Nazi Population Policy and the Murder of European Jews*. Translated by Belinda Cooper and Allison Brown. New York: Oxford University Press, 1999.

Aly, Götz, and Susanne Heim. *Vordenker der Vernichtung: Auschwitz und die deutsche Pläne für eine neue europäische Ordnung*. Frankfurt am Main: Fischer, 1993.

Ancel, Jean. *Transnistria, 1941–1942*. 3 vols. Tel Aviv: Tel Aviv University, 2003.

Andreyev, Catherine. *Vlasov and the Russian Liberation Movement: Soviet Reality and Emigré Theories*. Cambridge: Cambridge University Press, 1987.

Angrick, Andrej. *Besatzungspolitik und Massenmord: Die Einsatzgruppe D in der südlichen Sowjetunion, 1941–1943*. Hamburg: Hamburg Institute for Social Research, 2003.

Anisimov, Oleg. *The German Occupation in Northern Russia during World War II: Political and Administrative Aspects*. New York: Research Program on the USSR, Study no. 56, 1954.

Arendt, Hannah. *The Origins of Totalitarianism*. New York: Harcourt Brace Jovanovich, 1951.

Armstrong, John A. *Ukrainian Nationalism*. 3rd ed. Englewood, Colo.: Ukrainian Academic Press, 1993.

———, ed. *Soviet Partisans in World War II*. Madison: University of Wisconsin Press, 1964.

Banac, Ivo, and Frank Sysyn, eds. *Concepts of Nationhood in Early Modern Eastern Europe*. Cambridge, Mass.: Harvard University Press, 1986.

Barber, John, and Mark Harrison. *The Soviet Home Front, 1941–1945: A Social and Economic History of the USSR in World War II*. London: Longman, 1991.

Bartov, Omer. *The Eastern Front, 1941–45: German Troops and the Barbarisation of Warfare*. New York: St. Martin's Press, 1985.

———. *Hitler's Army: Soldiers, Nazis, and War in the Third Reich*. New York: Oxford University Press, 1991.

Benz, Wolfgang, Hans Buchheim, and Hans Mommsen, eds. *Der Nationalsozialismus: Studien zur Ideologie und Herrschaft*. Frankfurt am Main: Fischer Taschenbuch, 1993.

Benz, Wolfgang, and Helene Langenheim. *Mordfelder*. Berlin: Elefanten Press, 1999.

Berkhoff, Karel. *Harvest of Despair: Life and Death in Ukaine, 1941–1944*. Cambridge, Mass.: Harvard University, 2004.

Bilinsky, Yaroslav. *The Second Soviet Republic: The Ukraine after World War II*. New Brunswick, N.J.: Rutgers University Press, 1964.

Birn, Bettina. *Die Höheren SS und Polizeiführer: Himmlers Vertreter im Reich und in den besetzten Gebieten*. Düsseldorf: Droste Verlag, 1986.

Boehmer, Elleke. *Colonial and Postcolonial Literature*. Oxford: Oxford University Press, 1995.

Bohachevsky-Chomiak, Martha. *Feminists despite Themselves: Women in Ukrainian*

Community Life, 1884–1939. Edmonton: Canadian Institute of Ukrainian Studies, 1988.

———. Political Communities and Gendered Ideologies in Contemporary Ukraine. The Petryshyn Memorial Lecture, Harvard University, 26 Apr. 1994. Cambridge: Harvard Ukrainian Research Institute, 1994.

Borys, Jurij. The Sovietization of Ukraine, 1917–1923: The Communist Doctrine and Practice of Self-Determination. Edmonton: Canadian Institute of Ukrainian Studies, 1980.

Boshyk, Yury, ed. Ukraine during World War II: History and Its Aftermath: A Symposium. Edmonton: Canadian Institute of Ukrainian Studies, 1986.

Braham, Randolph. The Hungarian Labor Service System, 1939–1945. New York: Columbia University Press, 1997.

Brandt, Karl, Otto Schiller, and Franz Ahlgrimm. Management of Agriculture and Food in the German-Occupied and Other Areas of Fortress Europe: A Study in Military Government. Stanford: Stanford University, 1954.

Bräutigam, Otto. Überblick über die besetzten Ostgebiete während des 2. Weltkrieges. Tübingen: Institut für Besatzungsfragen, 1954.

Breitman, Richard. The Architect of Genocide: Himmler and the Final Solution. New York: Knopf, 1991.

———. Official Secrets: What the Nazis Planned, What the British and Americans Knew. New York: Hill and Wang, 1998.

Brown, Kathryn. A Biography of No Place: From Ethnic Borderland to Soviet Heartland. Cambridge, Mass.: Harvard University, 2004.

Browning, Christopher. Ordinary Men: Reserve Police Battalion 101 and the Final Solution in Poland. New York: HarperCollins, 1992.

———. The Path to Genocide: Essays on Launching the Final Solution. New York: Cambridge University Press, 1992.

Browning, Christopher, with Jürgen Matthäus. The Origins of the Final Solution: The Evolution of Nazi Jewish Policy, September 1939–March 1942. Lincoln: University of Nebraska Press, 2004.

Buchheim, Hans, Martin Broszat, Hans-Adolf Jacobsen, and Helmut Krausnick, eds. Anatomie des SS-Staates. 2 vols. Munich: Deutscher Taschenbuch Verlag, 1967.

Buchsweiler, Meir. Volksdeutsche in der Ukraine am Vorabend und Beginn des Zweiten Weltkrieges — ein Fall doppelter Loyalität? Tel Aviv: Bleicher Verlag, 1984.

Burleigh, Michael. Germany Turns Eastward: A Study of Ostforschung in the Third Reich. Cambridge: Cambridge University Press, 1988.

Carell, Paul. Hitler Moves East, 1941–44. Boston: Little, Brown, 1964.

———. Scorched Earth: The Russian German War, 1943–44. Boston: Little, Brown, 1970.

Chamberlin, W. H. The Ukraine: A Submerged Nation. New York: Macmillan, 1944.

Cherednichenko, V. Collaborationist. Kiev: Politvydav Ukraïny Publishers, 1975.

Chiari, Bernhard. Alltag hinter der Front: Besatzung, Kollaboration und Widerstand in Weissrussland, 1941–1944. Düsseldorf: Droste, 1998.

Chirovsky, Nicholas. *An Introduction to Ukrainian History*. 3 vols. New York: Philosophical Library, 1981–86.

———. *Ukraine and the Second World War*. New York: Ukrainian Congress Committee, 1985.

Clark, Alan. *Barbarossa: The Russian-German Conflict, 1941–45*. London: Macmillan, 1957.

Conquest, Robert. *The Harvest of Sorrow: Soviet Collectivization and the Terror-Famine*. New York: Oxford University Press, 1986.

Cooper, Matthew. *The Nazi War against Soviet Partisans, 1941–44*. New York: Stein and Day, 1979.

Dallin, Alexander. *The German Occupation of the USSR in World War II: A Bibliography*. New York: Columbia University Press, 1955.

———. *The Kaminsky Brigade, 1941–1944: A Case Study of German Exploitation of Soviet Disaffection*. Cambridge, Mass.: Russian Research Center, Harvard University, 1956.

———. *German Rule in Russia, 1941–1945: A Study of Occupation Policies*. New York: Macmillan, 1957.

Dean, Martin. *Collaboration in the Holocaust: Crimes of the Local Police in Belorussia and Ukraine, 1941–1944*. New York: St. Martin's Press, 2000.

Dmytryshyn, Basil. *Moscow and Ukraine, 1918–1953: A Study of Russian Bolshevik Nationality Policy*. New York: Bookman Publishers, 1956.

Dobroszycki, Lucjan, and Jeffrey Gurock, eds. *The Holocaust in the Soviet Union: Studies and Sources on the Destruction of the Jews in the Nazi-Occupied Territories of the USSR, 1941–1945*. New York: M. E. Sharpe, 1993.

Doroshenko, Dmytro. *Die Ukraine und das Reich, Neun Jahrhunderte deutsche-ukrainischer Beziehungen im Spiegel der deutschen Wissenschaft und Literatur*. Leipzig: Hirzel, 1942.

Dubnow, S. M. *History of the Jews of Russia and Poland: From Earliest Times Until the Present Day*. Philadelphia: Jewish Publication Society, 1916–1920.

Earle, Ed, ed. *Nationalism and Internationalism: Essays Inscribed to Carlton J. Hayes*. New York: Columbia University Press, 1950.

Ehrenburg, Ilya. *The War, 1941–1945*. London: MacGibbon and Kee, 1964.

Ehrenburg, Ilya, and Vasily Grossman, eds. *The Black Book: The Ruthless Murder of Jews by German Fascist Invaders throughout the Temporarily Occupied Regions of the Soviet Union and in the Death Camps of Poland during the War of 1941–1945*. Translated by John Glad and James Levine. New York: Holocaust Library, 1980.

Erickson, John. *The Road to Stalingrad*. London: Weidenfeld and Nicolson, 1975.

Farmer, Kenneth. *Ukrainian Nationalism in the Post-Stalin Era: Myth, Symbols and Ideology in Soviet Nationalities Policy*. Boston: Martinus Nijhoff Publishers, 1980.

Fedyshyn, Oleh. *Germany's Drive to the East and the Ukrainian Revolution, 1917–1918*. New Brunswick: Rutgers University Press, 1971.

Feldman, Gerald, and Wolfgang Seibel, eds. *Networks of Nazi Persecution: Business, Bureaucracy, and the Organization of the Holocaust*. New York: Berghahn, 2004.

Fireside, Harvey. *Icon and Swastika: The Russian Orthodox Church under Nazi and Soviet Control*. Cambridge: Harvard University Press, 1971.

Fisher, George. *Soviet Opposition to Stalin: A Case Study in World War II*. Cambridge, MA: Harvard University Press, 1952.

Fitzpatrick, Sheila. *Stalin's Peasants: Resistance & Survival in the Russian Village after Collectivization*. New York: Oxford University Press, 1994.

———. *Everyday Stalinism: Ordinary Life in Extraordinary Times: Soviet Russia in the 1930s*. New York: Oxford University Press, 1999.

Fleischhauer, Ingeborg. *Das Dritte Reich und die Deutschen in der Sowjetunion*. Stuttgart: Deutsche Verlags-Anstalt, 1983.

Fleischhauer, Ingeborg, and Benjamin Pinkus. *The Soviet Germans: Past and Present*. New York: St. Martin's Press, 1986.

Fleming, Gerald. *Hitler and the Final Solution*. Berkeley: University of California Press, 1984.

Frankel, Jonathan, ed. *The Fate of European Jews, 1939–1945: Continuity or Contingency?* New York: Oxford University Press, 1997.

Frei, Norbert, ed. *Ausbeutung, Vernichtung, Öffentlichkeit: NS-Lager und Vernichtungspolitik*. Munich: Sauer, 2000.

Friedman, Philip. *Road to Extinction: Essays on the Holocaust*. New York: The Jewish Publication Society of America, 1980.

Fyodorov, A. F. *The Underground Committee Carries On*. Moscow: Foreign Languages Publishing House, 1952.

Garrard, John, and Carol Garrard. *The Bones of Berdichev: The Life and Fate of Vasily Grossman*. New York: Free Press, 1996.

Gellately, Robert, and Ben Kiernan, eds. *The Specter of Genocide: Mass Murder in Historical Perspective*. Cambridge: Cambridge University Press, 2003.

Gerlach, Christian. *Kalkulierte Morde: Die deutsche Wirtschafts- und Vernichtungspolitik in Weissrussland 1941–1944*. Hamburg: Hamburger HIS Edition, 1999.

Gitelman, Zvi. *A Century of Ambivalence: The Jews of Russia and the Soviet Union, 1881 to the Present*. New York: YIVO Institute for Jewish Research, 1988.

———, ed. *Bitter Legacy: Confronting the Holocaust in the USSR*. Bloomington: University of Indiana Press, 1998.

Glantz, David M., and Jonathan House. *When Titans Clashed: How the Red Army Stopped Hitler*. Lawrence, Kansas: University Press, Kansas, 1995.

Gleason, Abbott. *Totalitarianism: The Inner History of the Cold War*. New York: Oxford University Press, 1995.

Goda, Norman. *Tomorrow the World: Hitler, Northwest Africa and the Path toward America*. College Station: Texas A&M Press, 1998.

Grabitz, Helge, Klaus Bästlein, and Johannes Tuchel, eds. *Die Normalität des Verbrechens: Bilanz und Perspektiven der Forschung zu den nationalsozialistischen Gewaltverbrechen*. Berlin: Hentrich, 1994.

Great Soviet Encyclopedia. New York: Macmillan, 1979.

Gröning, Gert, and Joachim Wolschke-Bulmahn. *Der Drang nach Osten: Zur Entwicklung* der Landespflege im Nationalsozialismus und während des 2. Weltkrieges in den "eingegliederten Ostgebieten". Munich: Minerva, 1987.

Gross, Jan. *Polish Society under German Occupation: The Generalgouvernement, 1939–1944*. Princeton: Princeton University Press, 1979.

———. *Neighbors: The Destruction of the Jewish Community in Jedwabne Poland*. Princeton: Princeton University Press, 2001.

Grossman, Vasilii. *Forever Flowing*. New York: Harper and Row, 1972.

Gruner, Wolf. *Der geschlossene Arbeitseinsatz deutscher Juden: Zur Zwangsarbeit als Element der Verfolgung, 1938–1943*. Berlin: Metropol, 1997.

Gutman, Israel, ed. *Encyclopedia of the Holocaust*. 4 vols. New York: Macmillan, 1990.

Hamburger Institut für Sozialforschung, ed. *Verbrechen der Wehrmacht: Dimensionen des Vernichtungskrieges, 1941–1944*. Hamburg: Hamburger Edition HIS, 2002.

Hamm, Michael. *Kiev: A Portrait, 1800–1917*. Princeton: Princeton University Press, 1993.

Hartenstein, Michael. *Neue Dorflandschaften: Nationalsozialistische Siedlungsplanung in den "eingegliederten Ostgebieten" 1939 bis 1944*. Berlin: Verlag Dr. Köster, 1998.

Harvey, Elizabeth. *Women and the Nazi East: Agents and Witnesses of Germanization*. New Haven: Yale University Press, 2003.

Headland, Ronald. *Messages of Murder: A Study of the Reports of the Einsatzgruppen of the Security Police and the Security Service, 1941–1943*. Cranbury, NJ: Associated University Presses, 1992.

Heer, Hannes, and Klaus Naumann, eds. *Vernichtungskrieg: Verbrechen der Wehrmacht 1941 bis 1944*. Hamburg: Zweitausendeins, 1995. English edition: *War of Extermination: The German Military in World War II, 1941–1944*. New York: Berghahn, 2000.

Heike, Wolf-Dietrich. *The Ukrainian Division Galicia, 1943–45: A Memoir*. Toronto: Shevchenko Scientific Society, 1988.

Heinemann, Isabel. *"Rasse, Siedlung, deutsches Blut": Das Rasse- und Siedlungshauptamt der SS und die rassenpolitische Neuordnung Europas*. Göttingen: Wallstein, 2003.

Heller, Mikhail, and Alexander Nekrich. *Utopia in Power: The History of the Soviet Union from 1917 to the Present*. New York: Summit Books, 1986.

Herber, Friedrich. *Gerichtsmedizin unterm Hakenkreuz*. Leipzig: Militzke, 2002.

Herbert, Ulrich, ed. *National Socialist Extermination Policies: Contemporary German Perspectives and Controversies*. New York: Berghahn, 2000.

Herlihy, Patricia. *Odessa: A History 1794–1914*. Cambridge: Harvard Ukrainian Research Institute Press, 1986.

Hesse, E. *Der Sowjetrussische Partisanenkrieg, 1941 bis 1944 im Spiegel deutscher Kampfanweisungen und Befehle*. Göttingen: Musterschmidt, 1969.

Heyer, Friedrich. *Die Orthodoxe Kirche in der Ukraine von 1917 bis 1945*. Cologne: Rudolf Müller, 1953.

Hilberg, Raul. *The Destruction of European Jews*. New York: Holmes and Meier, 1985.

———. *Die Vernichtung der europäischen Juden*. 3 vols. Frankfurt am Main: Fischer, 1991.

———. *The Destruction of the European Jews*. 3rd ed. 3 vols. New Haven: Yale University Press, 2003.

Hildebrand, Klaus. *Vom Reich zum Weltreich: Hitler, NSDAP u. kolonial Frage, 1919–1945*. Munich: Fink Verlag, 1969.

Himka, John-Paul. *Galician Villagers and the Ukrainian National Movement in the Nineteenth Century*. New York: St. Martin's Press, 1988.

Hirschfeld, Gerhard, ed. *The Policies of Genocide: Jews and Soviet Prisoners of War in Nazi Germany*. London: Allen and Unwin, 1986.

Hoffmann, Peter. *Hitler's Personal Security*. Cambridge, Mass.: MIT Press, 1979.

Höhne, Heinz. *The Order of the Death's Head: The Story of Hitler's SS*. Translated by Richard Barry. New York: Ballantine, 1969.

Homze, Edward. *Foreign Labor in Nazi Germany*. Princeton: Princeton University Press, 1967.

Horak, Stephen M. *Poland and Her National Minorities, 1919–1939: A Case Study*. New York: Vantage Press, 1961.

———. *The First Treaty of World War I: Ukraine's Treaty with Central Powers of February 9, 1918*. Boulder, Colo.: East European Monographs, 1988.

Horecky, Paul. *Russian, Ukrainian, and Belorussian Newspapers, 1917–1953: A Union List*. Washington, D.C.: Library of Congress, 1953.

Horne, John, and Alan Kramer. *German Atrocities, 1914: A History of Denial*. New Haven: Yale University Press, 2001.

Hosking, Geoffrey, ed. *Church, Nation, and State in Russia and Ukraine*. Edmonton: Canadian Institute of Ukrainian Studies, 1990.

Hrushevsky, M. *A History of Ukraine*. New Haven: Yale University Press, 1941.

Hunczak, Taras. *Symon Petliura and the Jews: A Reappraisal*. Toronto: University of Toronto Press, 1985.

———, ed. *The Ukraine, 1917–1921: A Study in Revolution*. Cambridge, Mass.: Harvard Ukrainian Research Institute Press, 1977.

Ilnytzkyj, Roman. *Deutschland und die Ukraine, 1934–1945: Tatsachen europäischer Ostpolitik*. Vol. 2. Munich: Osteuropa-Institut, 1955.

Ioanid, Radu. *The Holocaust in Romania: The Destruction of Jews and Gypsies under the Antonescu Regime, 1940–1944*. Chicago: Ivan R. Dee, 2000.

Jäckel, Eberhard. *Hitler in History*. Hanover, N.H.: Brandeis University Press, 1984.

Kamenetsky, Ihor. *Hitler's Occupation of the Ukraine: A Study of Totalitarian Imperialism*. Milwaukee: Marquette University Press, 1956.

———. *Secret Nazi Plans for Eastern Europe: A Study of Lebensraum Policies*. New York: Bookman Associates, 1961.

———. *The Tragedy of Vinnytsia: Materials on Stalin's Policy of Extermination in Ukraine during the Great Purge, 1936–1938*. New York: Ukrainian Historical Association, 1989.

Kater, Michael. *Das "Ahnenerbe" der SS, 1935–1945: Ein Beitrag zur Kulturpolitik des Dritten Reiches*. Stuttgart: DVA, 1974.

Kenez, Peter. *Civil War in South Russia, 1918–1920*. 2 vols. Berkeley: University of California Press, 1971–77.

Kershaw, Ian. *The Nazi Dictatorship: Problems and Perspectives of Interpretation*. London: Edward Arnold, 1985.

———. *Hitler, 1889–1936: Hubris*. New York: Norton, 1999.

———. *Hitler, 1936–1945: Nemesis*. New York: Norton, 2000.

Kershaw, Ian, and Moshe Lewin, eds. *Stalinism and Nazism: Dictatorships in Comparison*. Cambridge: Cambridge University Press, 1997.

Khvyliovyi, Mykola. *Cultural Renaissance in Ukraine: Polemical Pamphlets, 1925–26*. Alberta: Canadian Institute of Ukrainian Studies, 1986.

Klee, Ernst, Willi Dressen, and Volker Riess, eds. *"Gott mit Uns": Der deutsche Vernichtungskrieg im Osten, 1939–1945*. Frankfurt am Main: Fischer, 1989.

———, eds. *The Good Old Days: The Holocaust as Seen by Its Perpetrators and Bystanders*. Translated by Deborah Burnstone. New York: Free Press, 1991.

Klein, Peter, ed. *Die Einsatzgruppen in der besetzten Sowjetunion, 1941/1942: Die Tätigkeits- und Lageberichte des Chefs der Sicherheitspolizei und des SD*. Berlin: Hentrich, 1997.

Klier, John, and Shlomo Lambroza. *Pogroms: Anti-Jewish Violence in Modern Russian History*. New York: Cambridge University Press, 1992.

Kochan, Lionel, ed. *The Jews in Soviet Russia since 1917*. London: Oxford University Press, 1972.

Koehl, Robert. *RKFDV: German Resettlement and Population Policy, 1939–1945*. Cambridge, Mass.: Harvard University Press, 1957.

Kohn, Nahum, and Howard Roiter. *A Voice from the Forest: Memoirs of a Jewish Partisan*. New York: Holocaust Library, 1980.

Kopelev, L. *The Education of a True Believer*. New York: Harper and Row, 1978.

Koropeckyj, I. S., ed. *Ukrainian Economic History: Interpretative Essays*. Cambridge, Mass.: Harvard Ukrainian Research Institute Press, 1985.

Kostiuk, Hryhory. *Stalinist Rule in the Ukraine: A Study of the Decade of Mass Terror, 1929–1939*. New York: Praeger, 1960.

Kosyk, Wolodymyr. *The Third Reich and Ukraine*. New York: Peter Lang, 1993.

Krausnick, Helmut, and Hans-Heinrich Wilhelm. *Die Truppe des Weltanschauungskrieges: Die Einsatzgruppen der Sicherheitspolizei und des SD, 1938–1942*. Stuttgart: DVA, 1981.

Krawchenko, Bohdan. *Social Change and National Consciousness in Twentieth-Century Ukraine*. Ontario: University of Toronto Press, 1985.

———, ed. *Ukraine after Shelest*. Edmonton: Canadian Institute of Ukrainian Studies, 1983.

———, ed. *Ukrainian Past, Ukrainian Present*. New York: St. Martin's Press, 1997.

Kruglov, Alexander. *Unichtozhenie evreiskogo naseleniia v Vinnitskoi oblasti v 1941–1944*. Mohyliv-Podil's'kyi, 1997.

Kubijovyc, Volodymyr. *Ukraine: A Concise Encyclopedia*. 2 vols. Toronto: University of Toronto Press, 1963.

————. *Western Ukraine within Poland, 1920–1939*. Chicago: Ukrainian Research and Information Institute, 1963.

Kuzio, Taras, and Andrew Wilson. *Ukraine: From Perestroika to Independence*. New York, 1994.

Kuznetsov, Anatolii. *Babi Yar: A Document in the Form of a Novel*. Translated by David Floyd. Cambridge, Mass.: R. Bently, 1979.

Lapidus, Gail. *Women in Soviet Society: Equality, Development, and Social Change*. Berkeley: University of California Press, 1978.

Lee, Lloyd, ed. *World War II: Crucible of the Contemporary World; Commentary and Readings*. Armonk, N.Y.: M. E. Sharpe, 1991.

Lennox, Sara, Sara Friedrichsmeyer, and Susanne Zantop. *The Imperialist Imagination*. Ann Arbor: University of Michigan Press, 1998.

Lewin, Moshe. *The Making of the Soviet System: Essays in the Social History of Interwar Russia*. New York: New Press, 1985.

Lewytzkyj, Borys. *Politics and Society in Soviet Ukraine, 1953–1980*. Edmonton: Canadian Institute of Ukrainian Studies, 1984.

Liber, George. *Soviet Nationality Policy, Urban Growth, and Identity Change in the Ukrainian SSR, 1923–1934*. Cambridge, Mass.: Cambridge University Press, 1993.

Linz, Susan, ed. *The Impact of World War II on the Soviet Union*. Totowa, N.J.: Rowman and Allanheld, 1985.

Littlejohn, David. *The Patriotic Traitors: A History of Collaborators in German-Occupied Europe, 1940–1945*. Garden City, N.Y.: Doubleday, 1972.

Liulevicius, Vejas Gabriel. *War Land on the Eastern Front: Culture, National Identity and German Occupation in World War I*. Cambridge: Cambridge University Press, 2000.

Lixfield, Hannjost, and James Dow. *Folklore and Fascism: The Reich Institute for German Volkskunde*. Bloomington: Indiana University Press, 1994.

Longerich, Peter. *Politik der Vernichtung: Eine Gesamtdarstellung der nationalsozialistischen Judenverfolgung*. Munich: Piper, 1998.

————. *The Unwritten Order: Hitler's Role in the Final Solution*. Gloucester, Eng.: Tempus Publishing, 2001.

Luciuk, Lubomyr, and Bohdan Kordan, eds. *Anglo-American Perspectives on the Ukrainian Question, 1938–1951: A Documentary Collection*. New York: Limestone Press, 1987.

————, eds. *The Foreign Office and the Famine: British Documents on Ukraine and the Great Famine, 1923–33*. Kingston: Limestone Press, 1988.

Luckyj, G. *Literary Politics in the Soviet Ukraine, 1917–34*. New York: Columbia University Press, 1956.

————. *Between Gogol and Sevcenko: Polarity in Literary Ukraine, 1798–1847*. Munich: Wilhelm Fink Verlag, 1971.

Lumans, Valdis. *Himmler's Auxiliaries: The Volksdeutsche Mittelstelle and the German Minorities of Europe, 1933–1945*. Chapel Hill: University of North Carolina Press, 1993.

Mace, James E. *Communism and the Dilemmas of National Liberation: National Communism in*

Soviet Ukraine, 1918–1933. Cambridge, Mass.: Harvard Ukrainian Research Institute Press, 1983.

Magocsi, Paul. *The Shaping of National Identity: Subcarpathian Rus', 1848–1948*. Cambridge, Mass.: Harvard Ukrainian Research Institute Press, 1978.

———. *Ukraine: A Historical Atlas*. Toronto: University of Toronto Press, 1985.

———. *A History of Ukraine*. Toronto: University of Toronto Press, 1996.

———, ed. *Morality and Reality: The Life and Times of Andrei Sheptyts'kyi*. Edmonton: Canadian Institute of Ukrainian Studies, 1989.

Manning, Clarence. *Ukraine under the Soviets*. New York: Bookman Associates, 1953.

Markovits, Andrei, and Frank Sysyn, eds. *Nationbuilding and the Politics of Nationalism: Essays on Austrian Galicia*. Cambridge, Mass.: Harvard Ukrainian Research Institute Press, 1982.

Markus, Vasyl. *Religion and Nationalism in Soviet Ukraine after 1945*. Cambridge, Mass.: Harvard Ukrainian Studies, 1985.

Marples, David. *Stalinism in Ukraine in the 1940s*. New York: St. Martin's Press, 1992.

Martin, Terry. *The Affirmative Action Empire: Nations and Nationalism in the Soviet Union, 1923–1939*. Ithaca: Cornell University Press, 2001.

Matthäus, Jürgen, Konrad Kwiet, Jürgen Förster, and Richard Breitman. *Ausbildungsziel Judenmord? "Weltanschauliche Erziehung" von SS, Polizei und Waffen-SS im Rahmen der "Endlösung."* Frankfurt am Main: Fischer Taschenbuch, 2003.

Merl, Stephen. *Bauern unter Stalin: Die Formulierung des Kolchossystems 1930–1941*. Berlin: Duncker und Humblot, 1990.

Michael, Robert, and Karin Doerr. *Nazi-Deutsch: An English Lexicon of the Language of the Third Reich*. Westport, Conn.: Greenwood, 2002.

Militärgeschichtliches Forschungsamt, ed. *Germany and the Second World War: The Attack on the Soviet Union*. 5 vols. Oxford: Clarendon Press, 1991–2003.

Möller, Horst, Andreas Wirsching, and Walter Ziegler, eds. *Nationalsozialismus in der Region: Beiträge zur regionalen and lokalen Forschung und zum internationalen Vergleich*. Munich: Oldenbourg, 1996.

Moses, A. Dirk, ed. *Genocide and Settler Society: Frontier Violence and Stolen Indigenous Children in Australian History*. New York: Berghahn, 2002.

Mosse, George. *The Crisis of German Ideology: Intellectual Origins of the Third Reich*. New York: Schocken Books, 1981.

Motyl, Alexander. *The Turn to the Right: The Ideological Origins and Development of Ukrainian Nationalism, 1919–1929*. Boulder, Colo.: East European Monographs, 1980.

———. *Dilemmas of Independence: Ukraine after Totalitarianism*. New York: Council on Foreign Relations Press, 1993.

———, ed. *Thinking Theoretically about Soviet Nationalities: History and Comparison in the Study of the USSR*. New York: Columbia University Press, 1992.

Müller, Rolf-Dieter. *Hitlers Ostkrieg und die deutsche Siedlungspolitik: Die Zusammenarbeit von Wehrmacht, Wirtschaft und SS*. Frankfurt am Main: Fischer, 1991.

Mulligan, Timothy. *The Politics of Illusion and Empire: German Occupation Policy in the Soviet Union, 1942–1943*. New York: Praeger, 1988.

Murphy, David T. *The Heroic Earth: Geopolitical Thought in Weimar Germany, 1918–1933*. Kent, Ohio: Kent State Press, 1997.

Neufeldt, Hans-Joachim, and Georg Tessin, eds. *Zur Geschichte der Ordnungspolizei, 1936–1945*. Koblenz: Schriften des Bundesarchivs, 1957.

Ogorreck, Ralf. *Die Einsatzgruppen und die "Genesis der Endlösung."* Berlin: Metropol, 1996.

Pinkus, Benjamin. *The Jews of the Soviet Union: A History of a National Minority*. Cambridge: Cambridge University Press, 1988.

Pipes, Richard. *The Formation of the Soviet Union: Communism and Nationalism, 1917–1923*. Cambridge: Harvard University Press, 1954.

Pohl, Dieter. *Von der "Judenpolitik" zum Judenmord: Der Distrikt Lublin des Generalgouvernements, 1939–1944*. Frankfurt am Main: Fischer, 1993.

———. *Nationalsozialistische Judenverfolgung in Ostgalizien, 1941–1944: Organisation und Durchführung eines staatlichen Massenverbrechens*. Munich: Oldenbourg, 1996.

Poliakov, Leon. *The Aryan Myth: A History of Racist and Nationalist Ideas in Europe*. New York: New American Library, 1977.

Poltava, Peter. *The Ukrainian Insurgent Army in the Fight for Freedom*. New York: United Committee of the Ukrainian American Organization, 1954.

Potichnyj, Peter J. *Political Thought of the Ukrainian Underground, 1943–1951*. Edmonton: Canadian Institute of Ukrainian Studies, 1986.

———, ed. *Poland and Ukraine: Past and Present*. Edmonton: Canadian Institute of Ukrainian Studies, 1990.

Potichnyj, Peter, and Howard Aster, eds. *Ukrainian-Jewish Relations in Historical Perspective*. Edmonton: Canadian Institute of Ukrainian Studies, 1988.

Raisin, Jacob. *The Haskalah Movement in Russia*. Westport, Conn.: Greenwood, 1972.

Rapoport, Louis. *Stalin's War against the Jews: The Doctor's Plot and the Soviet Solution*. New York: Free Press, 1990.

Reitlinger, Gerald. *The House Built on Sand: The Conflicts of German Policy in Russia, 1939–1945*. London: Macmillan, 1960.

Reshetar, John. *The Ukrainian Revolution, 1917–1920: A Study in Nationalism*. Princeton: Princeton University Press, 1952.

Rich, Norman. *Hitler's War Aims: The Establishment of the New Order*. New York: W. W. Norton, 1974.

Rogers, Daniel, and Alan Steinweis. *The Impact of Nazism: New Perspectives on the Third Reich and Its Legacy*. Lincoln: University of Nebraska Press, 2003.

Rossino, Alexander. *Hitler Strikes Poland: Blitzkrieg, Ideology, and Atrocity*. Lawrence: University Press of Kansas, 2003.

Rössler, Mechthild, Sabine Schleiermacher, and Cordula Tollmien, eds. *Der "Generalplan Ost": Hauptlinien der nationalsozialistischen Planungs- und Vernichtungspolitik*. Berlin: Akademie Verlag, 1993.

Rudnytsky, Ivan. *Rethinking Ukrainian History*. Edmonton: Canadian Institute of Ukrainian Studies, 1981.

———. *Essays in Modern Ukrainian Political History*. Cambridge, Mass.: Harvard University Press, 1987.

Ruhm von Oppen, Beate, ed. *Letters to Freya, 1939–1945*. New York: Knopf, 1990.

Sandkühler, Thomas. *"Endlösung" in Galizien: Der Judenmord in Ostpolen und die Rettungsinitiativen von Berthold Beitz, 1941–1944*. Bonn: Dietz, 1996.

Schmokel, Wolf. *Dream of Empire: German Colonialism, 1919–1945*. New Haven: Yale University Press, 1964.

Schulte, Theo. *The German Army and Nazi Policies in Occupied Russia*. Oxford: Berg, 1989.

Seaton, Albert. *The Russo-German War, 1941–45*. New York: Praeger, 1971.

Serbyn, Roman, and Bohdan Krawchenko, eds. *Famine in Ukraine, 1932–33*. Edmonton: Canadian Institute of Ukrainian Studies, 1986.

Smelser, Ronald, and Enrico Syring, eds. *Die SS: Elite unter dem Totenkopf, 30 Lebensläufe*. Paderborn: F. Schöningh, 2000.

Smith, Woodruff. *The German Colonial Empire*. Chapel Hill: University of North Carolina Press, 1978.

———. *The Ideological Origins of Nazi Imperialism*. New York: Oxford University Press, 1986.

Snyder, Timothy. *The Reconstruction of Nations: Poland, Ukraine, Lithuania, Belarus, 1569–1999*. New Haven: Yale University Press, 2003.

Spector, Shmuel. *The Holocaust of Volhynian Jews, 1941–44*. Jerusalem: Yad Vashem, 1990.

———, ed. *The Encyclopedia of Jewish Life before and during the Holocaust*. Jersualem: Yad Vashem, 2001.

Streim, Alfred. *Die Behandlung sowjetischer Kriegsgefangener im "Fall Barbarossa."* Heidelberg: Müller Juristischer Verlag, 1981.

Streit, Christian. *Keine Kameraden: Die Wehrmacht und die sowjetischen Kriegsgefangenen, 1941–1945*. Stuttgart: Deutsche Verlags-Anstalt, 1978.

Subtelny, Orest. *Ukraine: A History*. 2nd ed. Toronto: University of Toronto Press, 1994.

Sullivant, Robert. *Soviet Politics and the Ukraine, 1917–1957*. New York: Columbia University Press, 1962.

Sword, Keith, ed. *The Soviet Takeover of the Polish Eastern Provinces, 1939–1941*. New York: St. Martin's Press, 1996.

Szporluk, Roman. *Ukraine: A Brief History*. Detroit: Ukrainian Festival Committee, 1979.

Tec, Nechama. *Resilience and Courage: Women, Men, and the Holocaust*. New Haven: Yale University Press, 2003.

Ther, Philipp, and Ana Siljak, eds. *Redrawing Nations: Ethnic Cleansing in East-Central Europe, 1944–1948*. Harvard Cold War Studies. Latham, Md.: Rowman and Littlefield, 2001.

Thorwald, Jürgen. *The Illusion: Soviet Soldiers in Hitler's Armies.* Translated by Richard and Clara Winston. New York: Harcourt Brace Jovanovich, 1975.

Torke, Hans-Joachim, and John-Paul Himka, eds. *German-Ukrainian Relations in Historical Perspective.* Edmonton: Canadian Institute of Ukrainian Studies, 1994.

Troper, Harold, and Morton Weinfeld. *Old Wounds: Jews, Ukrainians, and the Hunt for Nazi War Criminals in Canada.* Chapel Hill: University of North Carolina Press, 1989.

Tys-Krokhmaliuk, Yuriy. *UPA Warfare in Ukraine.* Translated by Walter Dushnyck. New York: Vantage, 1972.

Überschar, Gerd, and Wolfram Wette, eds. *Unternehmen Barbarossa: Der deutsche Überfall auf die Sowjetunion 1941; Berichte, Analysen, Dokumente.* Paderborn: F. Schöningh, 1984.

Velychenko, Stephen. *Shaping Identity in Eastern Europe and Russia: Soviet-Russian and Polish Accounts of Ukrainian History, 1914–1991.* New York: St. Martin's Press, 1993.

Weeks, Theodore. *Nation and State in Late Imperial Russia.* DeKalb: Northern Illinois University Press, 1996.

Weinberg, Gerhard. *Germany and the Soviet Union, 1939–1941.* Leiden: E. J. Brill, 1954.

———. *The Foreign Policy of Hitler's Germany.* 2 vols. Atlantic Highlands, N.J.: Humanities Press, 1993.

———. *A World at Arms: A Global History of World War II.* Cambridge: Cambridge University Press, 1994.

Weiner, Amir. *Making Sense of War: The Second World War and the Fate of the Bolshevik Revolution.* Princeton: Princeton University Press, 2001.

Werth, Alexander. *Russia at War, 1941–1945.* New York: E. P. Dutton, 1964.

Wexler, Paul. *Purism and Language: A Study in Modern Ukrainian and Belorussian Nationalism (1840–1967).* Bloomington: Indiana University Press, 1974.

Wildenthal, Lora. *German Women for Empire, 1884–1945.* Durham, N.C.: Duke University Press, 2001.

Wildt, Michael. *Generation des Unbedingten: Das Führungskorps des Reichssicherheits-hauptamtes.* Hamburg: Hamburger Edition, 2003.

Wippermann, Wolfgang. *Der "deutsche Drang nach Osten": Ideologien und Wirklichkeit eine politischen Schlagwortes.* Darmstadt, 1981.

Wistrich, Robert. *Wer war wer im Dritten Reich: Ein Biographisches Lexikon.* Frankfurt am Main: Fischer, 1989.

Wynar, Bohdan. *Ukraine: A Bibliographic Guide to English-Language Publications.* Englewood, Colo.: Ukrainian Academic Press, 1990.

Zantop, Susanne, and Frederic Jameson. *Colonial Fantasies: Conquest, Family, and Nation in Precolonial Germany, 1770–1870.* Durham, N.C.: Duke University Press, 1997.

Zeman, Z. A. B. *Nazi Propaganda.* London: Oxford University Press, 1964.

Ziemke, Earl. *Stalingrad to Berlin: The German Defeat in the East.* Washington, D.C.: Government Printing Office, 1968.

———. *Moscow to Stalingrad: Decision in the East.* Washington, D.C.: Government Printing Office, 1987.

Zipperstein, Steve. *The Jews of Odessa: A Cultural History, 1794–1871*. Stanford: Stanford University Press, 1986.

Articles and Conference Papers

Angrick, Andrej. "Forced Labor along the Strasse der SS." Symposium presentation, United States Holocaust Memorial Museum, Oct. 24, 2002.

Arad, Yitzhak. "The Holocaust and Soviet Jewry in the Occupied Territories of the Soviet Union." *Yad Vashem Studies* 21 (1991): 1–47.

Armstrong, John. "Collaborationism in World War II: The Integral Nationalist Variant in Eastern Europe." *Journal of Modern History* 40 (1968): 396–410.

Bergen, Doris. "The Nazi Concept of 'Volksdeutsche' and the Exacerbation of Anti-Semitism in Eastern Europe, 1939–1945." *Journal of Contemporary History* 29 (1994): 569–82.

———. "The 'Volksdeutschen' of Eastern Europe, World War II, and the Holocaust: Constructed Ethnicity, Real Genocide." *Yearbook of European Studies* (1999): 70–93.

Berkhoff, Karel. "Ukraine under Nazi Rule (1941–1944): Sources and Finding Aids." *Jahrbücher für Geschichte Osteuropas* 45 (1997): 85–103, 273–309.

———. "Was There a Religious Revival in Soviet Ukraine under the Nazi Regime?" *Slavonic and East European Review* 78, no. 3 (July 2000): 536–67.

———. "The 'Russian' Prisoners of War in Nazi-Ruled Ukraine as Victims of Genocidal Massacre." *Holocaust and Genocide Studies* 15 (Spring 2001): 1–32.

Berkhoff, Karel C., and Marco Carynnyk. "The Organization of Ukrainian Nationalists and Its Attitude toward Germans and Jews: Iaroslav Stets'ko's 1941 *Zhyttiepys*." *Harvard Ukrainian Studies* 23 (1999, published in 2002): 149–84.

Black, Peter. "Askaris in the 'Wild East': The Deployment of Auxiliaries and the Implementation of Nazi Racial Policy in Lublin District." Unpublished paper presented in Lublin, Poland, Apr. 2003.

———. "Police Auxiliaries for Operation *Reinhard*: Shedding Light on the Trawniki Training Camp through Documents from Behind the Iron Curtain." Conference on the Holocaust and Intelligence, City University of New York, 2–4 June 2003.

Breitman, Richard. "Himmler's Police Auxiliaries in the Occupied Soviet Territories." *Simon Wiesenthal Center Annual* 6 (1989): 23–29.

Browning, Christopher. "The Euphoria of Victory and the Final Solution: Summer-Fall 1941." *German Studies Review* 17 (Oct. 1994): 473–81.

Büchler, Yehoshua. "Kommandostab Reichsführer-SS: Himmler's Personal Murder Brigades in 1941." *Holocaust and Genocide Studies* 1 (Jan. 1986): 11–26.

Bullivant, Keith, Geoffrey Giles, and Walter Pape, eds. *Germany and Eastern Europe: Cultural Identities and Cultural Differences. Yearbook of European Studies* 13 (1999).

Dean, Martin. "The German *Gendarmerie*, the Ukrainian *Schutzmannschaft*, and the 'Second Wave' of Jewish Killings in Occupied Ukraine: German Policing at the Local Level in the Zhitomir Region, 1941–1944." *German History* 14 (1996): 168–92.

Dmytryshyn, Basil. "Nazis and the SS Volunteer Division Galicia." *American Slavic and East European Review* 15 (Feb. 1950): 1–10.

Fitzpatrick, Sheila. "Signals from Below: Soviet Letters of Denunciation of the 1930s." In article series "Practices of Denunciations in Modern European History." *Journal of Modern History* 68 (Dec. 1996): 831–66.

Getty, J. Arch, Gabor T. Rittersporn, and Viktor N. Zemskov. "Victims of the Soviet Penal System in the Pre-War Years: A First Approach on the Basis of Archival Evidence." *American Historical Review* 98 (Oct. 1993): 1017–49.

Golbert, Rebecca. "Holocaust Sites in Ukraine: Pechora and the Politics of Memorialization." *Holocaust and Genocide Studies* 18 (Fall 2004): 205–33.

Grabowicz, George. "Ukrainian Studies: Framing the Contexts." *Slavic Review* 54 (Fall 1995): 674–90.

Grill, Johnpeter Horst. "Local and Regional Studies on National Socialism: A Review." *Journal of Contemporary History* (1986): 253–94.

Grill, Johnpeter Horst, and Robert L. Jenkins. "The Nazis and the American South in the 1930s: A Mirror Image?" *Journal of Southern History* 58, no. 4 (1992): 667–94.

Grimsted, Patricia Kennedy. "Twice Plundered or 'Twice Saved'? Identifying Russia's 'Trophy' Archives and the Loot of the Reichssicherheitshauptamt." *Holocaust and Genocide Studies* 15 (Fall 2001): 191–244.

Harvey, Elizabeth. "Die deutsche Frau im Osten: 'Rasse,' Geschlecht und öffentlicher Raum im besetzten Polen, 1940–1944." *Archiv für Sozialgeschichte* 38 (1998): 191–214.

Heiber, Helmut. "Der Generalplan Ost." *Vierteljahrshefte für Zeitgeschichte* 6 (July 1958): 281–325.

Herwig, Holger. "Geopolitik: Haushofer, Hitler and Lebensraum." *Journal of Strategic Studies* 22 (1999): 218–41.

Herzstein, Robert. "Anti-Jewish Propaganda in the Orel Region of Great Russia, 1942–1943: The German Army and its Russian Collaborators." *Simon Wiesenthal Center Annual* 7 (1990): 33–55.

Hölzl, Martin. "Grüner Rock und weisse Weste: Adolf von Bomhard und die Legende von der sauberen Ordnungspolizei." *Zeitschrift für Geschichtswissenschaft* 50, no. 1 (2001): 22–43.

Horak, Stephen, ed. "Ukrainians in World War II: Views and Points." *Nationalities Papers* (Spring 1982): 1–41.

Kagedan, Allen. "Soviet Jewish Territorial Units and Ukrainian-Jewish Relations." *Harvard Ukrainian Studies* 9, 1–2 (June 1985): 118–32.

Kaienburg, Hermann. "Jüdische Arbeitslager an der 'Strasse der SS.'" *1991: Zeitschrift für Sozialgeschichte des 20 und 21 Jahrhunderts* 11, no. 1 (1996): 13–39.

Kappeler, Andreas. "Ukrainian History from a German Perspective." *Slavic Review* 54 (Fall 1995): 691–702.

Krannhals, H. D. "Politik der Vernichtung: Eine Denkschrift zur Besatzungspolitik in Osteuropa." *Deutsche Studien* 4 (Dec. 1966): 493–517.

Laskovsky, Nikolas. "Practicing Law in the Occupied Ukraine." *American Slavic and East European Review* 11 (Apr. 1952): 123–37.

Mace, James E. "Famine and Nationalism in Soviet Ukraine." *Problems of Communism* 33 (May/June 1984): 37–50.

Manning, Clarence. "Total War and the Ukraine." *Ukrainian Quarterly* 5 (Summer 1949): 239–43.

Matthäus, Jürgen. "What about the 'Ordinary Men'?: The German Order Police and the Holocaust in the Occupied Soviet Union." *Holocaust and Genocide Studies* 10 (Fall 1996): 134–50.

Motyl, Alexander. "Ukrainian Nationalist Political Violence in Inter-War Poland, 1921–39." *East European Quarterly* 19, no. 1 (1985): 45–55.

Parrish, Michael. "Soviet Historiography of the Great Patriotic War, 1970–1985: A Review." *Soviet Studies in History* 23 (Winter 1984–85): 1–30.

Penter, Tanja. "Die lokale Gesellschaft im Donbass unter deutscher Okkupation, 1941–1943." In *Kooperation und Verbrechen: Formen der 'Kollaboration' im östlichen Europa, 1939–1945, Beiträge zur Geschichte des Nationalsozialismus*, edited by Christoph Dieckmann, Christian Gerlach, and Wolf Gruner, 183–223. Hamburg: Wallstein, 2003.

Pritsak, Omeljan, and John Reshetar. "The Ukraine and the Dialectics of Nation-Building." *Slavic Review* 22 (June 1963): 224–55.

Prokop, M. "Ukraine in Germany's WWII Plans." *Ukrainian Quarterly* 11 (Spring 1955): 134–44.

Reshetar, John. "Ukrainian Nationalism and the Orthodox Church." *American Slavic and East European Review* 10, no. 1 (1951): 38–49.

Rudnytsky, Ivan. "The Role of Ukraine in Modern History." *Slavic Review* 22 (June 1963): 199–216.

Schmaltz, Eric J., and Samuel Sinner. "The Nazi Ethnographic Research of Georg Leibbrandt and Karl Stumpp in Ukraine and Its North American Legacy." *Holocaust and Genocide Studies* 14 (Spring 2000): 28–64.

Schumacher, Frank. "The American Way of Empire: National Tradition and Transatlantic Adaptation in America's Search for Imperial Identity, 1898–1910." *Bulletin* (German Historical Institute, Washington D.C.), no. 31 (Fall 2002), 35–50.

Seleshko, M. "Vinnytsia—The Katyn of Ukraine." *Ukrainian Quarterly* 5 (Summer 1949): 238–48.

Smith, A. D. "Nationalism and the Historians." *International Journal of Comparative Sociology* 33, nos. 1–2 (1992): 58–80.

Snyder, Timothy. "The Causes of Ukrainian-Polish Ethnic Cleansing, 1943." *Past and Present* 179 (May 2003): 197–234.

Spector, Shmuel. "Jews in the Resistance and Partisan Movements in the Soviet Ukraine." *Yad Vashem Studies* 23 (1993): 127–43.

Steinberg, Jonathan. "The Third Reich Reflected: German Civil Administration in the Occupied Soviet Union, 1941–44." *English Historical Review* 110 (June 1995): 620–51.

Subtelny, Orest. "The Current State of Ukrainian Historiography." *Journal of Ukrainian Studies* 18 (Winter 1993): 33–54.

Sysyn, Frank. "The Reemergence of the Ukrainian Nation and Cossack Mythology." *Social Research* 58 (Winter 1991): 845–64.

Velychenko, Stephen. "The Official Soviet View of Ukrainian Historiography." *Journal of Ukrainian Studies* 19 (Winter 1985): 81–93.

von Hagen, Mark. "Does Ukraine Have a History?" *Slavic Review* 54 (Fall 1995): 658–73.

Westermann, Edward. "'Ordinary Men' or 'Ideological Soldiers'?: Police Battalion 310 in Russia, 1942." *German Studies Review* 21 (Feb. 1998): 41–68.

White, Elizabeth. "Majdenak: Cornerstone of Himmler's SS Empire in the East." *Simon Wiesenthal Center Annual* 7 (1990): 3–21.

Z arkhiviv VuChK-GPU-NKVD-KGB 1/2 (Kiev, 1999).

Zimmerman, Andrew. "The Tuskegee Institute in German Togo and the Construction of Race in the Atlantic World." Paper presented at the BMW Center for German and European Studies Seminar, Georgetown University, Nov. 2001.

Dissertations

Berkhoff, Karel. "Hitler's Clean Slate: Everyday Life in the Reichskommisariat Ukraine, 1941–1944." Ph.D. diss., University of Toronto, 1998.

Furber, David. "Going East: Colonialism and German Life in Nazi-Occupied Poland." Ph.D. diss., State University of New York–Buffalo, June 2003.

Imort, Michael. "Forestopia: The Use of the Forest Landscape in Naturalizing National Socialist Ideologies of Volk, Race, and Lebensraum, 1918–1945." Ph.D. diss., Queen's University, Canada, 2000.

Index

Hilberg, Raul, 1, 129

Himka, John Paul, 90

Himmler, Heinrich: in Zhytomyr (Hegewald), 3, 8, 70, 101, 117, 127, 150, 155; colonialist thinking of, 19, 22, 26; Germanization campaigns of, 40, 162–79, 197; and management of SS-police forces, 50, 53, 72, 75, 90, 99–100, 104, 144; at Werwolf with Hitler, 172; and antipartisan warfare, 185, 188; and evacuation of Hegewald, 200–201

Hitler, Adolph, 3, 13, 16; view of Ukraine and Ukrainians, 18, 23–24, 27, 162; and imperialism, 25–26, 30, 99, 105, 197; warfare policies and directives of, 32, 53, 56, 58, 66, 96, 98, 185, 189; in Vinnytsia (Werwolf), 70, 101, 111–12, 130, 150, 153, 162, 199; assassination attempt against, 186

Hnivan', 150

Hnivan' quarry, 145

Hoffmeyer, Horst, 40, 167–69

Hofmann, Otto, 174–75

Hryhorii, Bishop (Ohiichuk), 119, 195

Huhn, Heinrich, 86

Hull, Isabel, 67

Hülsdünker, Alois, 156–58

Hungarian Jewish labor, 149, 258 (n. 86)

Hungarian troops, 33, 142

Hungerpolitik, 60, 139

Iatseniuk, 186–87

Imperial models, 3, 18–20, 24–26, 28

India, 3, 24–27, 99

Infantry Regiment 375, 57–59

Iunitskii, Petr Ignat'evich, 180

Jeckeln, Friedrich, 45, 56, 72–73, 75–78, 158–59

Jedwabne, 59

Jewish Council, 47, 87

Jews, 11, 206; in prewar era, 14; massacres of, 55, 58–59, 73–74, 79–83, 91–92, 134, 142; rescue of, 77, 92–93, 134, 145, 158, 183; resistance of, 89–90, 193; in hiding, 92; forced labor of, 141, 143–58. See also Plundering; Pogroms

Kam'ianets-Podil's'kyi, 77

Katyn, 194

Keitel, Wilhelm, 52, 98, 189

Kershaw, Ian, 72

Khmil'nyk, 33, 83, 93, 96, 150

Kieper, Wolf, 79–80

Kiev, 1, 35, 38, 63, 70, 73, 183, 207

Kiian, Iurii Alekseevich, 69

Kindergarten, 169

Kitzinger, Karl, 96, 113

Kleist, Ewald von, 33, 35

Klemm, Kurt, 87, 101; establishes administration, 106–8; career of in 1930s, 107; in conflict with SS-police, 126–28; role of in Holocaust, 139, 160; and Volksdeutsche, 169; and reprisal measures, 184

Klenk, Karl, 149–50

Koch, Erich, 66, 84, 99, 151; anti-Jewish policies of, 88–89, 139; presence in Ukraine of, 107; directives to commissars by, 110–12, 119; meets with Klemm, 127

Kogan, Moishe, 79–80

Kommandanturen, 10, 44, 48, 74, 89, 91, 142

Kondratenko, Maria, 192–93

Kordelivka, 133

Körner, Hellmut, 174

Korosten', 37, 174, 184

Kovpak, S., 184, 186

Kozaritskii, Leontii Antonovich, 187–88

United States Holocaust Memorial
Museum, 16
UPA. *See* Ukrainian Insurgent Army
Utopian socialists, 21

Vasilevichi, 49
Vernichtungskrieg. *See* Operation Barbarossa
Village elders. *See Starosty*
Vinnytsia, 14, 24; military invasion of,
34; military administration in, 45–52,
59; Holocaust in, 46–47, 88, 96, 150–
55; camps in, 61, 66; mass graves in,
194
Vlasov, Andrei, 61, 186
Volhynian Germans, 163
Volksdeutsche, 11, 40, 45–49, 165;
Soviet deportations of, 15–16; in German administration, 41, 45, 50–52,
77, 101–6, 138, 181; and Holocaust,
90, 93–94; Nazi indoctrination of,
169; Nazi resettlement of, 175, 195,
197; evacuation of, 202–4; in Selbstschutz (police force), 173, 199, 201.
See also Hegewald

Volksdeutsche Mittelstelle, 164, 168–69,
172
Vollkammer, Traugott, 141
Volodars'k-Volyns'kyi, 58–59

Wagner, Eduard, 60, 78
Wannsee Conference and Protocol, 143,
151
Wedelstädt, Helmuth von, 171
Wehrmacht atrocities, 54–59, 63, 68, 81
Wehrmacht Propaganda Unit 637, 79
Weiner, Amir, 182, 206
Werwolf, 62, 151–55, 172
Wetzel, Erhard, 130

Youth, 117, 125, 170

Zhytomyr: prewar, 2, 13, 234 (n. 15);
military invasion of, 33–37; security measures in, 56–57; camps in,
61; and Holocaust, 73–74, 79–83,
134; Volksdeutsche in, 171, 197–98;
Holocaust memorial in, 207